The
Voluntary
City

Economics, Cognition, and Society

This series provides a forum for theoretical and empirical investigations of social phenomena. It promotes works that focus on the interactions among cognitive processes, individual behavior, and social outcomes. It is especially open to interdisciplinary books that are genuinely integrative.

Titles in the Series

Ulrich Witt, Editor. *Explaining Process and Change: Approaches to Evolutionary Economics*

Young Back Choi. *Paradigms and Conventions: Uncertainty, Decision Making, and Entrepreneurship*

Geoffrey M. Hodgson. *Economics and Evolution: Bringing Life Back into Economics*

Richard W. England, Editor. *Evolutionary Concepts in Contemporary Economics*

W. Brian Arthur. *Increasing Returns and Path Dependence in the Economy*

Janet Tai Landa. *Trust, Ethnicity, and Identity: Beyond the New Institutional Economics of Ethnic Trading Networks, Contract Law, and Gift-Exchange*

Mark Irving Lichbach. *The Rebel's Dilemma*

Karl-Dieter Opp, Peter Voss, and Christiane Gern. *Origins of a Spontaneous Revolution: East Germany, 1989*

Mark Irving Lichbach. *The Cooperator's Dilemma*

Richard A. Easterlin. *Growth Triumphant: The Twenty-first Century in Historical Perspective*

Daniel B. Klein, Editor. *Reputation: Studies in the Voluntary Elicitation of Good Conduct*

Eirik G. Furubotn and Rudolf Richter. *Institutions and Economic Theory: The Contribution of the New Institutional Economics*

Lee J. Alston, Gary D. Libecap, and Bernardo Mueller. *Titles, Conflict, and Land Use: The Development of Property Rights and Land Reform on the Brazilian Amazon Frontier*

Rosemary L. Hopcroft. *Regions, Institutions, and Agrarian Change in European History*

E. L. Jones. *Growth Recurring: Economic Change in World History*

Julian L. Simon. *The Great Breakthrough and Its Cause*

David George. *Preference Pollution: How Markets Create the Desires We Dislike*

Alexander J. Field. *Altruistically Inclined? The Behavioral Sciences, Evolutionary Theory, and the Origins of Reciprocity*

David T. Beito, Peter Gordon, and Alexander Tabarrok, Editors. *The Voluntary City: Choice, Community, and Civil Society*

The
Voluntary
City

Choice, Community,
and Civil Society

Edited by | David T. Beito
Peter Gordon, and
Alexander Tabarrok

Foreword by Paul Johnson

Ann Arbor
**The University of
Michigan Press**

The INDEPENDENT
INSTITUTE

Copyright © by the Independent Institute 2002
All rights reserved
Published in the United States of America by
The University of Michigan Press
Manufactured in the United States of America
⊗ Printed on acid-free paper

2005   2004   2003   2002   4   3   2   1

A CIP catalog record for this book is available from the British Library.

Library of Congress Cataloging-in-Publication Data

The voluntary city : choice, community, and civil society / edited by
    David Beito, Peter Gordon, and Alexander Tabarrok.
        p.   cm. — (Economics, cognition, and society)
    Includes bibliographical references.
    ISBN 0-472-11240-6 (cloth : alk. paper) — ISBN 0-472-08837-8
(pbk. : alk. paper)
    1. Municipal government.   2. Voluntarism—United States—History.
3. Voluntarism—Great Britain—History.   4. Volunteer workers in
community development.   5. Public-private sector cooperation—United
States.   6. Public-private sector cooperation—Great Britain.   7.
Civil society.   8. Social service.   I. Beito, David T., 1956–   II.
Gordon, Peter, 1943–   III. Tabarrok, Alexander.   IV. Series.
JS78.V6   2002
307.76—dc21   2001006444

Cover image: Evening cityscape © Copyright Bill Ross/CORBIS

Contents

Foreword

Paul Johnson

What should government do? What should it leave to others? This debate, though not always articulated, is as old as settled societies, but it has been reinvigorated by the collapse of socialism and by the privatization of state sectors. It is likely to rage throughout the twenty-first century, producing a contraction of the state, just as the first three-quarters of the twentieth century saw the state's expansion. An overview of history shows that this waxing and waning of the state is a recurrent pattern.

It ought to be possible to define the state's role in absolute terms, applicable anywhere at any time. The argument, as I used to present it to Margaret Thatcher when she was prime minister, runs as follows. The state is and always will be inefficient at doing things. Hence, its activities ought to be confined to those activities that must be done but that cannot be done by the people themselves. As many of the chapters in this book illustrate the people can often do for themselves more than is thought they can do, yet history teaches that, on the whole, the role of the state has not been defined by any sensible account of what it ought to do but rather by its capacity. If the state *can,* it nearly always *does.*

The ancient theocratic states, in which divine as well as secular powers were embodied in the monarch, did more or less everything of importance. The pharaohs of Egypt, for instance, ran trading expeditions to forward their immense public works programs. And the Old Testament shows King Solomon, who did not claim divinity but was a powerful ruler by the standards of his time and place, taking charge of the importation of scarce materials and the recruitment of skilled workmen. In due course, however, nontheocratic societies emerged in self-governing towns on the eastern Mediterranean littoral and in Greece that were characterized by a large private sector, by a limited central authority, and often by rudimentary democracy. In ancient Greece, the city authorities, landowners, and merchants worked together to establish overseas colonies, which in turn flourished and became independent self-governing cities. Prosperity was usually linked with a limited state and oligarchic democracy.

When the Roman Empire in the West disintegrated, the ensuing Dark Ages saw state functions assumed by powerful private individuals or defensible cities. Hundreds of local mints, for instance, issued their own coinages, which rose or fell according to their integrity and inter-estingly were often run by archbishops or bishops (presumably to con-fer some credibility to the implicit promise of the mints not to debase the currency). The so-called feudal system, often used as a synonym for backwardness, was in fact a series of ingenious devices to fill the power vacuum left by the fall of Rome. The king, who lacked the means to govern wide territories effectively, divided them among his tenants in chief, who provided units for his army and certain cash dues in return for the right to administer justice, control local government, and super-vise towns. Such towns paid to run their own markets and, if big enough, were incorporated as cities and had a charter from the king listing their privileges.

The corporation is one of the most important inventions in history. A small-scale alternative to the state for many purposes, it has some of the legal characteristics of the individual but is also perpetual, protean, and ubiquitous—evident by the fact that it is still in universal use today after a millennium and a half of service. The English developed it, both in legal theory and in practice, as a means to get things done. They also practiced the principle of delegation. In Norman times, the king dele-gated immense powers to the bishop of Durham in the North, the earls of Chester in the Northwest, and the Marcher lords on the Welsh fron-tier. These potentates had their own miniature governments or councils to strive to ensure law and order, to raise taxes, and to build public works, as well as to defend their inhabitants. In the more settled parts of the country, landowners and responsible clerics were appointed justices of the peace (JPs), who met quarterly—or more often if required—to try cases, order public works, and deal with any business that arose. The system, which historians have termed "self-government by the king's command," was on the whole efficient and certainly cheap, for JPs were never paid. Until the third quarter of the nineteenth century, quarter sessions were still the main instrument of local government in England and Wales, and they cost the taxpayer virtually nothing.

As the first signs of capitalism emerged and it became possible to raise comparatively large sums for investment in major projects, bold men—the term used was *merchant adventurers*—pooled their resources to buy ships and hire men for overseas ventures. In England in particular (and to a lesser extent in France and the Netherlands), the private sector thus played what was often a predominant part in foreign and colonial policy. In exploring and exploiting the New World, Spain and Portugal, which had no middle class or capital market, employed all the resources of the state to penetrate Latin America. In England, the state played only a minor role. The process began in Ireland, where entrepreneurs known as "undertakers" were allotted the lands of the "wild Irish" and undertook to settle them with former soldiers turned farmers. That was how Ulster was colonized by Protestants. A typical adventurer was Sir Walter Raleigh, who made a good deal of money from his settlements in Ireland and then invested it in the first transatlantic colony at Roanoke in what is now North Carolina. The venture failed, but valuable lessons were learned. A more profitable expedition was Sir Francis Drake's voyage around the world, in which Queen Elizabeth was a minority shareholder, investing one ship and stores. This voyage was one of the great financial coups of history. Partners received forty-seven pounds sterling for every pound invested. The queen's share was enough to pay off England's entire foreign debt and still leave forty-two thousand pounds for investing in the Levant Company. This company was one of a number of semiprivate trading enterprises that laid the foundations of the future British Empire, which at one time covered a quarter of the surface of the globe. I call them *semiprivate* because they operated under royal charters that gave them legal privileges and in some cases monopolies. As they became more important and actually administered foreign territory, they worked in conjunction with the state. The largest was the East India Company, which ran English territories in India for 250 years. It had its own system of government, its own administrative service, and its own army. Lord Clive, victor of the famous Battle of Plassey in 1759, was not a servant of the state but of the company. It was only in the 1870s that the company was taken over by the state and Disraeli made Queen Victoria empress of India.

More important because more durable was the creation of the thirteen colonies of North America. The state had very little to do with this process, which was to change world history, beyond giving charters to the various companies. The Jamestown settlement of 1610 was run by the Virginia Company, under Lord De La Ware (or "Delaware," as they wrote it). Ten years later the company granted eighty thousand acres and fishing rights to the Pilgrims of the *Mayflower*. All the early settlements were conducted by private enterprise under distant and irregular state supervision; this was another case of "self-government by the king's command." John Winthrop had been a justice of the peace in England, so he understood the system well. The colonies drew up their own constitutions, using the English practice as a rough model, and created their own elected assemblies. The first contested election in the New World was held as early as 1637, without any reference to the English government. Toward the end of the seventeenth century, the English state, growing stronger, began to realize the potential wealth of the American colonies and tried to assert its authority over them, but by then it was too late. The colonies already had their own ways of doing things and their own democracies, even if the king still appointed governors. When the test finally came during the American War of Independence, the Americans could already look back on 150 years of devising their own institutions.

If we peer into the origins of English institutions, which in many cases became the exemplars for those in America, we find that success was the result of a partnership between the private sector and the Crown, often in the form of self-perpetuating, nonprofit institutions. This arrangement worked particularly well for schools and university colleges. Eton College, for instance, was founded by Henry VI in the fifteenth century but was thereafter run by a corporate body under a provost, himself appointed by the Crown. Many Oxford and Cambridge colleges operated a similar system, a partnership between the fellows and the Crown, with the fellows making virtually all the decisions but with the Crown sometimes retaining powers of appointment to college headships (e.g., the dean of Christ Church, Oxford, and the provost of King's College, Cambridge). The American university system evolved in a similar manner, though the role of the Crown was necessarily smaller and eventually vanished.

This system of private ownership or management of institutions forming the basic infrastructure of the country, sometimes in partnership with the state, reached its maturity in the eighteenth century. The power of the state was minute, or, rather, much of it was delegated to a variety of institutions and individuals. In a famous essay pointing out the pretensions of economists who argued that the private provision of lighthouses was impossible, Ronald Coase showed that private provision had long been the norm in Britain under the auspices of Trinity House (see Alexander Tabarrok's epilogue [chap. 15] for more on the pretensions of economists). Trinity House was just one example of how the public creation of private institutions operated to improve society. Schools, colleges, town corporations, hospitals, workhouses, owners of private army regiments, the Royal Exchange (which ran the capital market), and owner-builders of roads and canals (the king also owned a number of roads in his private capacity) provide many other examples of a similar beneficial process. Private acts of Parliament were an important part of this history. As Stephen Davies discusses in chapter 2, private acts of Parliament authorized, for instance, the building of turnpikes, canals, urban developments, and later railways in a way that allowed progress without unduly restricting rights to property (see also Daniel Klein's chap. 4 on the provision of turnpikes in the United States). The Industrial Revolution of the period 1760–80, which saw the world's first acceleration into self-sustaining economic growth, was entirely the work of private enterprise. The state had nothing to do with it. Lord North, prime minister during the crucial period, went to his grave without realizing that he had presided over one of the most important developments in history. This "mixed economy" system of doing things—in which individuals and corporations played the major role—was adopted, improved, and made more efficient in the United States.

However, what the state can do, it usually will do—unless firmly resisted by powerful interests. The state began to expand, at first hesitantly and then with increasing confidence as communications improved; national wealth and the state's share of it increased; and democratic public opinions, spurred by a free press, emerged to make demands for human betterment that could not be supplied by the private sector. The nineteenth century saw the state in Britain and the United States running, for the first time, schools, hospitals, and road systems, as well as regulating factories and other places of work. These changes laid the foundations of the Leviathan state of the twentieth century. Great wars speeded the process. The Napoleonic Wars brought, for Britain, the first income tax, which belatedly came to the United States a century later. The income tax proved the greatest engine of state activity the world had ever seen. The American Civil War effectively created an expanding, omnicompetent federal government and abolished much of the delegated authority of states' rights. World War I saw the state involve itself deeply in the economy, taking over and building factories and infrastructure and assuming powers that were later to be exercised in peacetime, permanently. World War II pushed the process further and promoted what were to become welfare states, protecting or oppressing the individual from the cradle to the grave. The assumption now subtly changed. Whatever the state *could* do it *should* do. In the democracies, advocates of the expanding state were impelled not so much by the lust for power as by a quasi-religious faith in the virtues of the state. The state was morally superior to private enterprise because it was not motivated by the desire for profits, and it was a source of greater wisdom because it could mobilize all the resources of the intelligentsia. In the 1950s, the leading proponent of the state in Britain, Professor Richard Titmuss of the London School of Economics, argued that the state had a positive duty to enter all areas of life the instant it was in a position to do so. He gave an example: "As soon as we can control the weather, the government must have a weather policy."

The contraction of the state during the last quarter of the twentieth century came about almost entirely on an empirical basis. One factor was the abysmal failure of the state in its most expanded form—the command economy of the Soviet Union (and of its many imitations in Eastern Europe, Africa, Asia, and Latin America). Other factors were the rising cost and increasing inefficiency of the public sector in Western democracies and the realization that the state was performing badly even in its core duties. In the West, the big metropolitan city was seen as the arena where the state had failed most conspicuously: poor schools, bad but expensive housing, congested traffic, inadequate public services, rising crime, race riots, high cost of living, unemployment, and shortages in skilled labor—all combining to make life in the big city uncomfortable, expensive, and dangerous.

The privatization programs of the 1980s, which still continue, served to open a wide-ranging debate on the role and limits of the state and the extent to which cooperative or private enterprise could take over activities where the state was manifestly performing badly. This volume of essays by distinguished scholars is an important contribution to this debate, and I commend it to everyone who takes a serious interest in trying to make life better for the average citizen. What I particularly like about the contributions is the absence of ideology. There is, for instance, no assumption that profit making or individual enrichment is essential to efficiency in providing services. Quite the contrary, indeed. Nonprofit organizations, driven by altruism and the noble desire to serve the public, have an important role in replacing the state, as in the past. Likewise, there is a case for examining opportunities for the private sector and the state to cooperate in projects or, alternatively, to compete with each other to give the public the best possible deal. What is particularly valuable in the present debate is its freedom: nothing is ruled out on principle, all propositions are seen as worth exploring, and experiment is at the forefront of all activity.

We learned many lessons the hard way in the twentieth century. I suspect that the twenty-first is going to be an exciting period in which our increased wisdom will be applied in novel and surprising ways, improving the quality of our lives and offering matchless opportunities for able men and women to serve humanity. We must put aside all the old prejudices about the state, on the one hand, and about capitalism, on the other. Let us forget about the ideologies of the twentieth century. But that does not mean we must discourage ideas. Now is a time for imagination and fresh thinking. Every concept is worth exploring. The only tests must be: Does it work? Can it be made to work? I am confident—and I envy those who will live to see the change—that in fifty years' time we will be running things, not least our cities, towns, and communities, in radically different ways, which will respond much more closely to human needs than do our present methods. That world will not be Utopia, but it will be, to use the favorite term of the Victorians, an "improvement." This book is its signpost.

1

Toward a Rebirth
of Civil Society

David T. Beito, Peter Gordon, and Alexander Tabarrok

If the most remarkable political events of the twentieth century were the fall of the Berlin Wall and the demise of socialism, then its most auspicious intellectual realignment has been the widespread rediscovery of the virtues of free markets. Today the left and the right have reached a consensus that markets and supporting institutions, such as secure property rights, a sound currency, and a free capital market, are necessary for the material progress of both developed and developing nations.[1] Debate has not ended, however; it has only shifted to higher ground. Markets may be necessary for material progress, but are they sufficient? And what exactly do we mean by progress? Growth in average income is not the only desirable aspect of an economy. Can a market economy protect workers from economic downturns? Can it provide for the downtrodden and unfortunate? And, rising to yet higher ground, what about nonmaterial progress? Can markets be equitable? Can a market society develop community?

The authors of this volume join the debate on the higher ground. They argue that the scope for markets is wider than is now recognized and present exciting evidence that voluntary and contractual arrangements can also develop communities and deliver social services. In part, their evidence comes from a rediscovery of the history of voluntarism in the social services. For example, David T. Beito (chapter 8) and David G. Green (chapter 9) recount the remarkable history of fraternal orders and friendly societies in nineteenth-century America and Great Britain. Fraternal orders and friendly societies provided their members with medical care, unemployment insurance, sickness insurance, and many other social services before the welfare state. Nor were these institutions marginal to their times. Green notes, for example, that "[w]hen the British government introduced compulsory social insurance for twelve million persons under the 1911 National Insurance Act, registered and unregistered voluntary insurance associations—chiefly the friendly societies—already covered at least nine million individuals."

The example of fraternal orders and friendly societies is an important one because it illustrates that the authors do not have a blinkered view of either markets or human nature. With respect to markets, too often the vital role of the nonprofit sector has been ignored. Proponents of markets, especially neoclassical economists, tend to argue as if the profit-maximizing firm were always and everywhere an ideal and as if any attenuation of profit incentives, whether in a nonprofit firm or in a government bureaucracy, were always an unwelcome divergence from this ideal. Proponents of government, while more supportive of the idea/ideal of nonprofits, tend to see the nonprofit sector in capitalist societies as weak, frail, and entirely marginal to the dominant ethos. Yet in contrast to both views, the nonprofit sector in the United States today accounts for some 10 percent of the gross domestic product (GDP) and nearly 15 percent of total employment (Sokolowski and Salamon 1999).[2] Moreover, the nonprofit sector is a major player in such important industries as health, education, and high culture (and was a major player in these industries long before receiving any tax breaks or other regulatory advantages).

The authors of this volume manifestly include nonprofits in the market sector. The inclusion is important because by focusing on for-profit firms, proponents of markets may have overstated the case for markets narrowly conceived. Yet by ignoring the role of nonprofits, opponents of markets may have *understated* the case for markets *broadly* conceived. Alternatively put, what conventional economics refers to as "market failure" may actually be a limited set of problems associated with for-profit firms and markets. If the term "market" is broadened to include nonprofit firms and other voluntary but not-for-profit organizations, the scope of such failure may be diminished.[3] Thus, rather than saying that the authors of this volume argue for a larger role for markets, it is more revealing to say that they argue for a larger role for *civil society*.[4]

One virtue of the term "civil society" is that it is not wrapped up in the same baggage as the term "markets"; in particular, to favor civil society is not necessarily to regard self-interest as the sole or even the most important motivator of human action. Unfortunately, the markets/government debate has often proceeded as if it were a debate between self-interest and other-regardingness. Yet there is growing support for the view that our ancestors learned to forge connections and developed a social nature for the practical reason that such connections enhanced survival, just as their capacity for self-interest did (Ridley 1996; Wright 2000). Humans are neither purely self-interested nor purely other-regarding; humans are individuals who join groups, and they possess all the skills appropriate to such a classification. It should come as no surprise, then, that other-regardingness is not absent from markets and self-interest is not absent from government.

The issue, therefore, is not human nature but rather how different institutions channel human nature. Adam Smith argued that markets channel self-interest into socially beneficial directions—this is the meaning of his famous statement, "It is not from the benevolence of the butcher, the brewer, or the baker, that we expect our dinner, but from their regard to their own interest."[5] The public-choice school of political economy argues that government institutions often channel self-interest in socially undesirable directions (e.g., Gwartney and Wagner 1988). But as of yet, *there is no well-developed theory of how other-regardingness is channeled by civil society or by government.* Although such a theory is not developed here, the authors provide some case studies of the former process that we think will help motivate the formulation of such a theory as well as stimulate more historical study.

The authors argue that the voluntary arrangements that were used in the past (and that in some cases are returning today) have much to offer. An overview of these episodes is presented in the introductions to each part of the book. (Alexander Tabarrok's epilogue [chapter 15] also offers an overview of the essays included in this volume from the perspective of economics and market-failure theory.) The point we wish to emphasize here is that the welfare state did not so much create new institutions as crowd out the civic associations that people had spontaneously fashioned to provide "public goods," "safety nets," and even law and order. Were the spontaneously created institutions of the civil society better than the government institutions that replaced them?[6] The essays in this volume cannot definitively answer this question, but it is remarkable enough that they show that *the question is real.*

The question comes at a propitious moment because for the first time in decades, increasingly severe failures in the governmental sector have led officials to ponder long-neglected arguments for private provision. At this writing, privatized education, social security, highways, prisons, weather forecasts, municipal services, and medical savings accounts are either being implemented or are making their way into "mainstream" political discourse in the United States and abroad. Reform is occurring in fits and starts, but it is occurring.

To be sure, there is a renascent demand for government in the form of the command-and-control environmentalism that has steadily gained force throughout the developed world (Lal 1999).[7] Yet even this new regulation is tempered by growing attention to more flexible, market-compatible ways to limit emissions, dispose of wastes, and protect valuable wildlife stocks and endangered species. Emission bubbles, tradable pollution permits, riparian property rights, privatized elephant herds and fisheries—all of these approaches, once considered radical, are becoming commonplace not only in the United States but around the world.[8] Moreover, support for these sorts of policies is coming not just from proponents of markets but, perhaps more importantly, from environmentalists who are more interested in success than in ideology.

The international trend toward political divestiture and privatization marks a recognition by politicians in nonsocialist as well as formerly socialist states that state planning has stifled cost cutting and innovation (Shleifer 1998). Privatization and competition restore efficiency and result in greater innovation. In the United States, the deregulation of communications, financial services, railroads, energy, and passenger airlines offers examples of this (Winston 1998; Poole and Butler 1999; Morrison and Winston 2000).

Moving farther afield, various school-voucher experiments have raised the possibility of a flowering and vital market in private education. And remarkably, the 1996 U.S. welfare reform bill includes a charitable choice clause that, although now used only to fund a few hundred groups, allows for the privatization of federal welfare through religious charities (Glenn 2000; Geoly 1996).

These current efforts have prominent historical precursors that provide some useful lessons for today. A case in point is the centuries-old record of the private provision of social infrastructure. The work of Beito (chapter 8) and Green (chapter 9) on the history of social insurance in the United States and Great Britain has already been mentioned. In chapter 10, James Tooley examines the record of private education in the United States and Britain in the nineteenth century. Private education is not limited to the past or to developed nations, however; Tooley also examines the remarkable blossoming of private schools for the poorest of the poor in modern-day India. Bruce L. Benson (chapter 6) documents how law merchants met the demand for commercial rule making and adjudication as extended trade networks developed in medieval and early modern Europe; he also discusses modern examples of private civil and criminal arbitration. Stephen Davies (chapter 7) describes how law and order were created in nineteenth-century Britain before the introduction of public police. Private prosecution associations—a not entirely unfamiliar combination of legal insurance, private security guards, and private investigators— were quite successful at controlling crime. Why then the shift to public policing? One clue lies in the fact—amazing to us today—that the English public opposed public policing and jeered the newly created bobbies! Davies explains why. (Also see Tabarrok [chapter 15] for an attempt to draw some general lessons from this history.)

Regarding physical infrastructure, Davies (chapter 2) shows how land markets and private covenants met the challenge of the first wave of English urbanization; Beito (chapter 3) recounts the rise of private places and self-governing enclaves in St. Louis; Daniel Klein (chapter 4) examines the history of private turnpikes in the United States in the early nineteenth century; and Robert C. Arne (chapter 5) describes the first U.S. industrial park as an example of large-scale nonresidential development.

As noted earlier, educational vouchers, privatized welfare, and arbitration all mark a limited return to the production of social infrastructure within the bounds of civil society. In the case of physical infrastructure, however, the return is much more extensive. As a result of the migration of homeowners into developer-created and -managed suburbs, modern-day American communities look increasingly like the private developments of nineteenth-century Great Britain and St. Louis.[9] Across the United States, there are now approximately 205,000 such common interest developments (CIDs) housing more than forty-two million people (Treese 1999). This represents nearly 15 percent of the nation's housing stock, up from 3 percent in 1975 and 1.1 percent in 1970. The return to private communities is a "quiet revolution," little noticed by elites. Yet Robert H. Nelson (chapter 13) argues that the return to private communities "represents the most comprehensive privatization occurring . . . in the United States today" and "may yet prove to have as much social significance as the spread of the corporate form of collective ownership of private business property in the second half of the nineteenth century."[10] Urban planners may tout state planning as the way to develop "livable communities," but when given a choice, prospective homeowners are choosing privately planned, not state-planned, communities.

Profit-seeking developers, not technocrats or visionaries, are the heroes of the CID episode. Just as Nobel-prize winner Friedrich Hayek and fellow Austrian economist Ludwig von Mises demonstrated the folly of top-down economic planning, Jane Jacobs explained the folly of top-down city planning (Jacobs 1961, 1969). In both cases, planners are fatally hobbled by their inability to tap local knowledge, the sheer magnitude of which would overwhelm them. In a competitive market, in contrast, local knowledge reappears, lessening the dependence on politics and increasing flexibility; "public" goods (and spaces) in CIDs are provided more optimally at levels of spatial aggregation that do not coincide with municipalities; benefits capitalization more efficiently finances public-goods provision; and optimal constitutional rules are developed. The fact that the actions of private developers now supply what had been thought to be "public" goods is thus beneficial. Fred E. Foldvary (chapter 11) and Robert H. Nelson (chapter 13) describe in greater detail the theory and practice of private communities, with Nelson offering a way to bring the advantages of such communities to more traditionally governed neighborhoods.

In chapter 12, Donald J. Boudreaux and Randall G. Holcombe make the fascinating point that private communities also come equipped with privately created political structures. Every developer of a private community is also the "founding father" of a polis. Boudreaux and Holcombe argue that the choices of these founding fathers tell us something important about the best constitutions.

In contrast to some of the other authors, Spencer Heath MacCallum (chapter 14) is in substantial agreement with critics of CIDs such as Evan McKenzie (1994). But unlike such critics MacCallum does not favor a return to traditional governance but rather a moving forward to an even more private form of community, built on the hotel model.

Deregulation and privatization in the United States have been proceeding since the late 1970s, even though the twenty-five-year trend presents a decidedly mixed picture. The rise of Superfund and environmental regulation at all levels proceeded concurrently with varying degrees of air, rail, truck, telephone, and banking deregulation. CIDs are a shift away from some local governance, but they must still grapple with top-down control from higher levels. In just the last few years, voters around the United States approved 72 percent of 240 state and local "growth-control" measures. The new laws have substantially weakened the property rights of individual owners, replacing them with a bewildering array of stakeholders and what is in effect a property-rights commons. The tragedy of the commons invariably ensues (Epstein

1985). Ironically, these laws, often supported by self-described followers of Jane Jacobs, have revived the kind of top-down urban planning that Jacobs herself so effectively challenged in the 1950s and 1960s. It is still an open question whether the movement toward CIDs will not be frustrated by a movement toward political control from a higher level of government.

Unfortunately, as governance moves to higher levels, the collective-choice problem of democracy—the incentive individuals face to demand services when they think that others will pay—becomes ever stronger. Yet the mobility of factors (long thought to induce governments to respect property) has recently increased. In part, this is driven by technological developments and is likely to accelerate. Increased mobility of people and capital forces governments to compete as never before, placing a serious check on Leviathan (McKenzie and Lee 1991). CIDs are part of this phenomenon, one more institution that has developed in Hayekian fashion to compete with faltering state institutions.

A traditional attack on property rights centers on the premise of a conflict between self-serving behavior in the marketplace and impulses toward civility and civic association (Schumpeter 1943; Bell 1976). In a justly influential book, *Bowling Alone,* Robert D. Putnam (2000) argues that community and social capital have been in steady decline in the United States since at least the 1950s and 1960s. Putnam has assembled a remarkable amount of data to document the decline and has summarized well a large body of work that shows that a deficit of social capital is associated with a host of negative social consequences such as increased crime, poor economic performance, and political disillusionment. It would be a mistake, however, to correlate this decline with "capitalism," as it coincides more closely with the rise of the welfare state. The rise of the welfare state and the diminution of property rights crowded out the private provision of many collective goods and social services that had shown considerable merit. Moreover, the critics may be wrong in more ways than one, as it has been argued that the virtues necessary for civility, civic association, *and* success in the marketplace are sapped by the welfare state (Murray 1984, 1988).

Putnam himself does not propose any grand unifying theory of social capital and its decline. Refreshingly, he is hesitant when pointing to causes of the decline and even more hesitant about proposing solutions. Yet Putnam does wrongly lump all CIDs with the much-maligned gated communities. In fact, less than 20 percent of U.S. CIDs are gated communities. Those that are gated are in response to government's inability to control crime, as are community-creating neighborhood crime-watch groups (Etzioni 1992). Nevertheless, Putnam's error is exemplary; CIDs are much more of a "solution" than a problem. They help to secure property rights and augment efficiency, providing and managing communal spaces and facilities.

Rather than undermining community, civil society may take root in the communal spaces, facilities, and institutions now taking shape in response to market demands. A possible example of this is enhanced political participation by property owners in the direct governance of their major financial assets, their homes. The primacy of local politics is well known, and CID politics are as local as governance becomes. We do not yet know much about the links between CIDs and civil society, but the pairing appears to be a more promising solution to the crisis in civic engagement than the spatial determinism of the New Urbanists, which banks on mandated porches and bay windows to do the job.

If Americans are experiencing another Great Awakening, as Robert W. Fogel (2000) argues, then what some deride as an escape from community life could in fact become an escape *to* community life. At its most promising, civic engagement could revive voluntary groups that supercede many of the welfare, environmentalist, and regulatory agencies of the modern state.

Just a few years before the fall of the Berlin Wall, Nobel-prize winner James M. Buchanan (1990) worried that unless a constraining constitutional structure were resurrected, the overreaching state would continue to grow. Yet there is no longer simply a one-way street; powerful forces are at work expanding both liberty and prosperity. The episodes documented in this collection show that we are rediscovering a rich array of voluntary institutions and arrangements that were crowded and regulated out of existence by the twentieth-century fling with socialism and progressivism. Many of these voluntary institutions are making a return.

After a century of debate there is now widespread agreement that markets enhance material welfare and reduce conflict. *The Voluntary City* shows that the scope for markets broadly conceived—in other words, the scope for civil society—is even larger than the current consensus recognizes. The voluntary arrangements of civil society are capable of producing a host of so-called public goods such as aesthetic and functional zoning, roads, planning, and other aspects of physical urban infrastructure. Civil society can also produce social infrastructure, including education, conflict resolution, crime control, and many of the social services currently monopolized by the welfare state. Having done all this, can voluntarism foster civic resources in the modern age? Can it restore a "civic voice"? Communitarian theorists Michael J. Sandel (1996) and Robert D. Putnam (2000) fear a crisis for modern democracies unless the "civic strand of freedom" is strengthened. Can voluntary institutions do all this in a bottom-up fashion? If they can, then the events accompanying the fall of the Berlin Wall are much more auspicious than even the most daring have yet suggested. The payoffs from reduced state influence include expanded liberty and prosperity—and perhaps much more.

NOTES

The editors would like to thank Timur Kuran for comments and Carl Close for painstaking editorial assistance throughout this volume.

1. For evidence of the consensus at a popular level see Robert Heilbroner's (1990) admiring discussion of Friedrich A. Hayek and Ludwig von Mises and Cassidy's (1999) discussion of "the Hayek century." Excellent examples of the consensus at work can be found in the field of development economics; see especially Nobel-prize winner Amartya Sen's (1999) *Development as Freedom,* R. Klitgaard's (1991) *Adjusting to Reality,* and D. Lal's (1999) *Unintended Consequences.*

2. The nonprofit sector has been growing over time. The figures quoted in the text are from 1995. Despite the history of voluntarism in the United States, the nonprofit sector is even larger in some European countries. For a survey of global civil society see Salamon et al. 1999.

3. Space precludes an extensive discussion of this point, but an illustration is in order. A standard example of market failure is said to occur when buyers have difficulty measuring quality. Since buyers do not value what they cannot evaluate, sellers can increase profits by reducing quality, thereby cutting costs. Health care and education are sometimes said to fit this example (Barr 1998). It is naïve to think that government provision can solve this problem by fiat; an adequate argument must explain why the incentives to produce quality are greater under government provision than under private provision. Hart, Shleifer, and Vishny 1997 gives one possible reason for this—because there is no residual claimant, government agencies have fewer incentives to maximize profits than for-profit firms. Since cost cutting is driven by the desire for larger profits, government agencies have fewer incentives to cut costs and *may* therefore invest more in quality. The argument is not beyond question, but regardless, it applies equally well to nonprofit firms as it does to governments. As a second example, Blank 2000 argues that government provision may result in higher quality because governments can attract workers who are motivated by "public service" rather than by purely pecuniary concerns and that such workers are more likely to invest in nonobservable quality. Again, although not beyond question, this argument also applies to workers in nonprofit firms, many of whom are motivated by the "missions" of their institutions. (Many for-profit firms also try to instill such values in their employees, perhaps less successfully.) See on these issues more generally Hansmann 1996.

4. The term "civil society," as used here, includes markets as well as churches, clubs, associations, organizations, the family, and other kinship groups—in toto, what may be called the voluntary sector.

5. *The Wealth of Nations,* B.I., chapter 2, Of the Principle which gives Occasion to the Division of Labour, paragraph I.2.2.

6. For those who would argue that the fact that government institutions replaced those of the civil society indicates that the former are superior to the latter we would only note that in many areas the latter are now re-replacing the former!

7. Hopkins (1998) has estimated annualized regulatory costs in the United States over the period from 1977 to 1995: "[e]nvironmental and risk protection" costs rose 179 percent (in constant 1995 dollars) while all other regulatory costs rose by just 2 percent.

8. See Portney and Stavins 2000; Anderson and Leal 1991.

9. Private communities are also prominent in Japan and some European countries; see Kajiura 1994 and van Weesep 1994.

10. The "quiet revolution" quote is from Barton and Silverman, as cited in Nelson (this volume).

REFERENCES

Anderson, T. L., and D. R. Leal. 1991. *Free Market Environmentalism.* San Francisco: Pacific Research Institute.

Barr, N. 1998. *The Economics of the Welfare State.* 3d ed. Stanford: Stanford University Press.

Bell, D. 1976. *The Cultural Contradictions of Capitalism.* London: Heinemann.

Blank, R. M. 2000. When Can Public Policy Makers Rely On Private Markets? The Effective Provision of Social Services. *The Economic Journal* 110 (March): C34–39.

Buchanan, J. M. 1990. Socialism is Dead; Leviathan Lives. *Wall Street Journal,* July 18, A8.

Cassidy, J. 2000. The Price Prophet. *New Yorker,* February 7, 44–51.

Ellickson, R. C. 1991. *Order without Law: How Neighbors Settle Disputes.* Cambridge: Harvard University Press.

Epstein, R. A. 1985. *Takings: Private Property and the Power of Eminent Domain.* Cambridge: Harvard University Press.

———. 1998. *Principles for a Free Society: Reconciling Individual Liberty with the Common Good.* Reading, Mass.: Perseus Books.

Etzioni, A. 1992. Do Fence Me In. *Wall Street Journal,* December 1, A16.

Fogel, R. W. 1999. Catching Up with the Economy. *American Economic Review* 89 (1): 1–21.

———. 2000. *The Fourth Great Awakening.* Chicago: University of Chicago Press.

Geoly, J. C. 1996. Charity Replaces Bureaucracy. *Wall Street Journal,* September 26, A12.

Glenn, C. L. 2000. *The Ambiguous Embrace: Government and Faith-Based Schools and Agencies.* Princeton: Princeton University Press.

Graham, M. 2000. Regulation by Shaming. *Atlantic* (April): 36, 38–40.

Gwartney, J. D., and R. E. Wagner. 1988. Public Choice and the Conduct of Representative Government. In *Public Choice and Constitutional Economics,* ed. J. D. Gwartney and R. E. Wagner. Greenwich, Conn.: JAI Press.

Hansmann, H. 1996. *The Ownership of Enterprise.* Cambridge: Harvard University Press.

Hart, O., A. Shleifer, and R. W. Vishny. 1997. The Proper Scope of Government: Theory and an Application to Prisons. *Quarterly Journal of Economics* 451 (November): 1127–62.

Heilbroner, R. 1990. After Communism. *New Yorker* (September 10): 91–100.

Higgs, R. 1987. *Crisis and Leviathan: Critical Episodes in the Growth of American Government.* New York: Oxford University Press.

Hopkins, T. D. 1998. Regulatory Costs in Profile. *Policy Sciences* 31:301–20.

Jacobs, J. 1961. *The Death and Life of Great American Cities.* New York: Random House.

———. 1969. *The Economy of Cities.* New York: Vintage.

Kajiura, T. 1994. Condominium Management in Japan. In *Common Interest Communities: Private Governments and the Public Interest,* ed. S. E. Barton and C. J. Silverman. Berkeley: Institute of Governmental Studies Press.

Klitgaard, R. 1991. *Adjusting to Reality.* San Francisco: ICS Press.

Lal, D. 1999. *Unintended Consequences: The Impact of Factor Endowments on Long-Run Economic Performance.* Cambridge: MIT Press.

McKenzie, E. 1994. *Privatopia.* New Haven: Yale University Press.

McKenzie, R. B., and D. R. Lee. 1991. *Quicksilver Capital: How the Rapid Movement of Wealth Has Changed the World.* New York: Free Press.

Morrison, S. A., and C. Winston. 2000. A $20 Billion Misunderstanding: The Government's View of Airline Deregulation. *Milken Institute Review,* 3d quarter, 20–29.

Murray, C. 1984. *Losing Ground.* New York: Basic Books.

———. 1988. *In Pursuit of Happiness and Good Government.* New York: Simon and Schuster.

North, D. C. 1981. *Structure and Change in Economic History.* New York: W. W. Norton and Company.

Poole, R. W., Jr., and V. Butler. 1999. *Airline Deregulation: The Unfinished Revolution.* Los Angeles: Reason Public Policy Institute. Policy Study No. 255.

Portney, P. R., and R. N. Stavins, eds. 2000. *Public Policies for Environmental Protection.* 2d ed. Washington, D.C.: Resources for the Future.

Putnam, R. D. 2000. *Bowling Alone: The Collapse and Revival of American Community.* New York: Simon and Schuster.

Ridley, M. 1996. *The Origins of Virtue: Human Instincts and the Evolution of Cooperation.* New York: Penguin Books.

Salamon, L. M., H. K. Anheier, R. List, S. Toepler, S. W. Sokolowski, and Associates, eds. 1999. *Global Civil Society: Dimensions of the Nonprofit Sector.* Baltimore: Johns Hopkins Center for Civil Society Studies.

Sandel, M. J. 1996. *Democracy's Discontent: America in Search of a Public Philosophy.* Cambridge: Harvard University Press.

Schumpeter, J. A. 1943. *Capitalism, Socialism, and Democracy.* London: Allen and Unwin.

Scott, J. C. 1998. *Seeing Like a State: How Certain Schemes to Improve the Human Condition Have Failed.* New Haven: Yale University Press.

Sen, A. 1999. *Development As Freedom.* New York: Alfred A. Knopf.

Shleifer, A. 1998. State versus Private Ownership. *Journal of Economic Perspectives* 12 (4): 133–50.

Sokolowski, S. W., and L. M. Salamon. 1999. United States. In *Global Civil Society: Dimensions of the Nonprofit Sector,* ed. L. M. Salamon, H. K. Anheier, R. List, S. Toepler, S. W. Sokolowski, and Associates. Baltimore: Johns Hopkins Center for Civil Society Studies.

Taylor, M. 1982. *Community, Anarchy and Liberty.* Cambridge: Cambridge University Press.

Treese, C. J. 1999. *Community Associations Factbook.* Alexandria, Va.: Community Associations Institute.

Van Weesep, J. 1994. Condominium Regulation and Urban Renewal in Dutch Cities. In *Common Interest Communities: Private Governments and the Public Interest,* ed. S. E. Barton and C. J. Silverman. Berkeley: Institute of Governmental Studies Press.

Winston, C. 1998. U.S. Industry Adjustment to Economic Deregulation. *Journal of Economic Perspectives* 12 (3): 89–100.

Wright, R. 2000. *Nonzero: The Logic of Human Destiny.* New York: Pantheon Books.

1

Building the Voluntary City

Introduction to
Part 1

Building the Voluntary City

The Voluntary City begins (and ends) with the places in which we live. Some historians have alleged that the "unplanned," pell-mell, laissez-faire urban growth of Britain in the eighteenth and nineteenth centuries created housing of low quality and community structures with little rhyme or reason. Yet oddly, many of the homes and communities built in Britain during this period remain functional, while government housing of the post–World War II era has already crumbled. British historian Stephen Davies (chapter 2) reexamines the evidence and shows that English cities fared remarkably well during the industrial revolution despite or rather because of a lack of city planning. "The urban growth of the earlier period," Davies notes, "was voluntarist and owed nothing to state plans or regulations. It was driven by private initiative and speculation, directed by property rights and private contracts, and shaped and determined by market forces. The outcome was a process of urbanization that was orderly but unplanned."

In the United States, individuals showed the same resourcefulness in discovering market-based and voluntary methods of coping with massive urban growth. David T. Beito (chapter 3) explores the history of the private self-governing enclaves (or private places) of St. Louis. The developers of the private places provided streets and other infrastructure, including sewers and electricity, as well as political governance structures. (The private creation of political constitutions is discussed by Donald J. Boudreaux and Randall G. Holcombe in chapter 12.) Residential developers of this period anticipated many of the tech-

15

niques of modern urban planners. There was a crucial difference, however. The incentives and constraints of consumer and market demand spurred private-place planners both to innovate and to avoid the traps of wastefulness and hubris that so often beset their modern counterparts.

Historians sometimes suggest that government stepped in to provide goods and services, such as urban planning and unemployment insurance, when the market failed to provide these goods and services. Yet in the history of private places we see the opposite process. The entrepreneurs who founded the private places included in their developments thoroughfares and other conduits because inadequate city services left them little choice. Government failure created a market for developers to deliver a full package of residential services and gave buyers incentives to secure these services from the most efficient provider. Private streets did not owe their decline to competition from an efficient state but rather to ever-increasing political controls, including taxes and mandates, which led to the transfer of their capital to the public sector through an incremental process.

During the early nineteenth century, private enterprise in both the United States and Britain also produced the infrastructure for long-distance transportation: highways. Daniel Klein (chapter 4) traces the efforts of the turnpike companies of early America to replace the earlier governmental system of long-distance roads, which had fallen into decay by the late eighteenth century. Despite legislation that limited the ability of companies to prevent free riding and restricted their right to raise tolls, Klein finds that "turnpike success was striking."

By the late twentieth century, this private and largely self-sustaining method of maintaining long-distance roads had given way to a multibillion-dollar federal highway trust fund. Nevertheless, as highway improvements lag, public officials have permitted new construction and operation by private companies that charge tolls. No one is yet predicting a return to private highways in the United States. But the U.S. experience may be important for developing nations. Many such nations have exceedingly poor infrastructure and cash-strapped governments that appear unable or unwilling to build or maintain much-needed roads and highways (Harral 1988). Others have invested large amounts of capital in roads and other public projects, often with help from foreign institutions such as the World Bank, but with little regard for cost, return, or optimal location (Harral 1988; Heggie 1995; Isham and Kaufmann 1999). Given the importance that highway construction has had for U.S. economic growth, further research on the potential for private roads in developing countries and the impediments to such construction is warranted (Fernald 1999; Roth 1996).

Laissez-faire is often contrasted with "planning." Yet all entrepreneurs are planners. The developers of the various elements of the built environment, including large-scale unified projects, have an interest in providing efficient infrastructure and vital services and do so unless prevented by an expanding state-planning function. Davies and Beito (and the chapters in part 3) make this point in the context of housing. Robert C. Arne's (chapter 5) description of Chicago's Central Manufacturing District (CMD), highlighting its range of included services, shows that the same point applies to industrial communities and industrial consumers. Arne explains, for example, how Chicago's CMD—the first such district in the United States—included docks, rail transport, local transportation, electricity, and many business services. In modern times the private builder's job stops mostly at the home door or not that far beyond. The evidence indicates, however, that such a stopping point is governed by politics and is not inherent in the capacities of private enterprise.

REFERENCES

Fernald, J. G. 1999. Roads to Prosperity? Assessing the Link Between Public Capital and Productivity. *American Economic Review* 89 (3): 619–38.

Harral, C. G. 1988. *Road Deterioration in Developing Countries: Causes and Remedies.* World Bank, World Bank Policy Study.

Heggie, I. G. 1995. *Management and Financing of Roads: An Agenda for Reform.* Sub-Saharan Africa Transport Policy Program, World Bank, Working Paper No. 8.

Isham, J., and D. Kaufmann. 1999. The Forgotten Rationale for Policy Reform. *Quarterly Journal of Economics* 456 (1): 149–84.

Roth, G.. 1996. *Roads in a Market Economy.* Aldershot, U.K.: Avebury Technical.

2

Laissez-Faire Urban Planning

Stephen Davies

Between 1740 and 1850 Great Britain experienced a demographic transformation the likes of which had never been seen before. Beginning in about 1740 the population of England and Wales began to increase steadily, with Scotland showing less dramatic but still impressive growth. The rate of increase accelerated after the early 1780s and then became even more dramatic in the first half of the nineteenth century. In 1741 the population of England and Wales stood at about 5.96 million, that of Scotland at 1.2 million. By 1801 the figures stood at 9.37 million and 1.6 million respectively, growth rates of 57 and 33 percent. By 1851 the total population of Great Britain had reached 20.81 million, having doubled in the previous fifty years. (It was to almost double again by 1911.) There had been episodes of population growth before in British history, but never anything so prolonged or so rapid.[1]

Nor was the change simply one of numbers. Even more dramatic than the simple rise in population was the change in its distribution. In those 110 years Britain became not only more populous but far more urbanized, to the point at which by 1851 it could truly claim to be the world's first urbanized society. The second half of the eighteenth century saw large growth in the size of both London and major provincial towns, while after 1780 places such as Manchester and Birmingham suddenly rose from obscurity to the rank of major provincial centers. In 1801 just under 10 percent of the population lived in London, with 7.2 percent inhabiting towns with a population of between 20 and 100 thousand. No town outside London had a population of more than 100,000. By 1841 Manchester and Liverpool both had populations in excess of 250,000 while Birmingham, Leeds, and Bristol had all passed the 100,000 mark. By 1861, 38.2 percent of the total population were living in urban areas with a population of over 20,000.[2]

The years between 1740 and 1850 therefore saw an unprecedented amount of urban growth. Cities and towns of all kinds and sizes grew more rapidly and on a greater scale than ever before in history. The rapidly increasing population was drawn into the towns in ever larger numbers with the rise of industry, creating an enormous demand for housing and the urban fabric in general. This was the kind of situation that, when its like happens today, is regularly described in terms of "crisis" or even "catastrophe." And yet the challenge was largely met.

Housing and other facilities were built and provided. The towns of Britain grew to meet the new demands of a growing population and a transformed economy. There were no great shantytowns around growing cities such as Manchester and Birmingham. Instead a tidal wave of brick and stone swept over fields, turning them into new urban areas. Moreover, the period also saw the creation of great architectural achievements of lasting value in both the great cities and the new towns such as the spas and seaside resorts. The elegance of Bath and Cheltenham, the West End of London and Bloomsbury, the New Town in Edinburgh, and the centers of Glasgow and Newcastle-upon-Tyne—all were built in this period. As this was the first instance of such widespread urbanization our understanding of its nature is crucial for our thinking about the process of urbanization in general, whether historically or today. In particular this instance raises the question of how urbanization can happen in the absence of an apparatus of planning and controls, by voluntary means, and what the results of this may be.

For none of this was the creation of the state or of public authority, local or national. All of this happened in a society with no apparatus of planning laws and regulatory bodies, no public building regulations, no zoning or land-use laws, no direct public action to supply housing or urban services. Until at least the 1830s the tendency was in the opposite direction as old regulations and controls, exercised by municipal corporations and county authorities, were disregarded or abolished. Only in the second half of the nineteenth century was there a move toward greater state control, a move that led to the passage of the Housing and Town Planning Act in 1909 and culminated in the Town and Country Planning Act of 1947. The urban growth of the earlier period was voluntarist and owed nothing to state plans or regulations. It was driven by private initiative and speculation, directed by property rights and private contracts, and shaped and determined by market forces. The outcome was a process of urbanization that was orderly but unplanned. The key was the sophisticated use of property rights, which produced a decentralized and market-responsive form of development and growth. All of this seems very strange and paradoxical to modern commentators, who find the very notion of an unplanned order contradictory.

The result is a historiography that until very recently was dominated by a particular historical narrative. The story presented was that of rapid, "uncontrolled," "chaotic" urban growth that produced a whole range of problems from overcrowding to inadequate housing to an ugly and costly urban environment. This then led to a response that centered on the rise of town planning, initially as an intellectual movement but latterly as an organized profession, and on the reform of the law to impose order through a planning process. The definitive version of this kind of account can be found in William Ashworth's pioneering monograph of 1954, but it can also be found in many other, more recent works.[3] This is a variant of the classic "Whig" historical narrative, which sees the past as defined by a progressive movement from a state of darkness to one of enlightenment, or from a primitive less-developed condition to a more modern and developed one. Some of the more recent works, such as those of Anthony Sutcliffe, offer a more nuanced approach, but the broad thrust is the same.[4]

The elements of this account are these. First, that a market-led system of urban development, while producing good results for the middle and upper classes, was unable to produce an adequate supply of housing for the artisan and working classes. Not enough housing was produced for this section of the community (whereas by contrast there was an oversupply of middle-class housing) because of a straightforward "market failure." According to Sutcliffe, labor, being the weakest bidder in the market, did badly. Second, that the housing that was built was often of poor quality, overcrowded, and unsafe. Third, that the market process, while able to supply housing, was unable to produce essential infrastructure and services such as mains drainage as these were "public goods." These essentially quantitative criticisms are accompanied by qualitative ones. In particular it is argued that the market process did not lead to a "proper geographical division of functions"—or, in plain English, that housing, leisure, work, and shopping were all mixed together instead of being geographically separated. Moreover, there was no overall plan for the town or neighborhood as a whole, resulting in a lack of coordination and harmony. Where "enlightened" landlords did plan the development of their estates, their effectiveness was limited by lack of statutory powers.[5]

Several points can be made about this kind of account. In the first place a large part of it, the qualitative element, rests upon an argument that is ultimately tautological. The thesis that market-directed urban growth produced a disorderly outcome rests upon a particular definition of order that makes it synonymous with conscious intentional planning by an individual or organization. This definition is then made part of the major premise, so producing a circular, tautological argument. There is no consideration of the alternative, Hayekian concept of spontaneous order, according to which an orderly outcome can result from the interaction of many separate individual purposes and actions. Moreover, in this kind of literature the term "plan" is used to conflate or equate two quite distinct phenomena: on the one hand the use of state power to direct the employment of land, labor, and capital; and on the other the use of property rights in a market driven by consumer demand.[6] As one standard reference work puts it: "The comprehensive legislation of the twentieth century has led historians and other commentators to confuse the physical and social planning of towns in earlier times. There is indeed at present a belief that any place in which the disposition of the buildings suggests forethought is a product of the social legislator's art."[7]

There are other more specific objections to be made to this analysis that will be expanded later. Market-led urbanization is criticized from positions that are mutually contradictory. Some of the criticisms are simply untrue, as their own authors grudgingly admit. Finally, much of this criticism is driven by what economists call the "nirvana fallacy," in other words, the criticism of the actual from the standpoint of the ideal, where a real-life situation is attacked for failing to reach not another alternative real-life situation but a hypothetical and unrealizable ideal state.[8]

So, how did urban development actually take place in the years before local government began to take an increasingly active role—that is, before about 1850? The process was essentially simple but involved the use of a number of sophisticated legal institutions. There were two forces driving urbanization in Great Britain after 1750. The first was population growth, which was a precursor of urbanization rather than a consequence. The rapid population growth of the later eighteenth century was matched by a sharp growth in both production and trade, initially in agriculture but increasingly in other sectors as well, particularly manufacturing. The increased productivity of agriculture from the 1690s onward meant that the economy could support a larger urban population than before, while capital accumulation led to larger and more congregated manufacturing units as production moved into towns or created new towns out of villages. All this created a steadily rising demand for housing, leisure and service facilities, workshops, and manufacturing (the last still mainly small units as the move to large-scale factories did not affect the majority of British industry until after 1850). The marked growth in prosperity after 1750, and particularly after 1770, meant that this was an effective demand.[9]

The second driving force was the improvement in transportation brought about after 1750 by the turnpike trusts and canal companies. The trusts in particular wrought a near revolution in transport, transforming the quality of roads, drastically reducing the cost and duration of travel, and bringing about an explosive growth in road transport. This made possible phenomena such as the building and growth of suburbs and satellite towns around major urban centers, these having previously been precluded by the time taken to travel even relatively short distances in winter. Turnpikes also had a great influence on the overall pattern of urban growth as they opened up areas to building, initially producing "ribbon" development along radial routes, followed by secondary "infill" development between the routes. Turnpikes led in practice to two forms of urbanization. In the first an old urban "core" would expand outward along radial routes, producing a starfish-shaped pattern; this can be seen in Manchester, Leeds, and Liverpool. The second saw several nearby small towns and villages all expand and produce a dense interconnecting network of roads, leading to the emergence of a large, multicentered urban area. This can be seen in Birmingham, the Black Country, and the Staffordshire Potteries. In some areas, such as Southeast Lancashire, the two patterns combined to produce a large central town with radial growth surrounded by a necklace of satellite towns.[10] The canals had less influence on the growth of existing towns but played a great part in creating a national market and did lead to the appearance of new canal ports, in some cases built and developed from scratch by the canal companies.[11]

The combination of increased prosperity and leisure with improved transportation also led to a very specific kind of urban development: the building of specialized resort towns. The earliest were spas such as Bath, Harrogate, Leamington Spa, and Buxton, but these were soon followed, after about 1800, by the seaside resorts—such as Brighton, Scarborough, Skegness, and Southport—that were to be such a major feature of the life of Victorian Britain. Sometimes these were developments of existing centers, as at Bath and Brighton, but very often, as in the cases of Skegness and Southport, an entire town was built de novo.[12]

The main immediate effect of the improvement in transportation and rising demand was an increase in land values. In some parts of the country, such as East Anglia, this led mainly to increased agricultural rents and both fueled and was fed by the process of enclosure. Elsewhere, particularly around London and in those parts of the country where the combination of farming and manufacturing (commonly though misleadingly termed "protoindustrialization") was prevalent, the rise in land values created a strong incentive for landlords to develop and build on their land. Simply put, if the agricultural productivity of land was high and/or there was no other strong demand for its use, then the most profitable course for the landlord was to rent it out to tenant farmers. If, however, the demand for land for building was sufficiently strong, then the most lucrative action was to build to get either cash return or ground rents. It was the pattern of demand that determined which form of land use would yield the highest return. This often led to entrepreneurial opportunities that were taken advantage of by enterprising landlords, particularly in the case of resort development. The point is that market incentives, transmitted through the price mechanism, led to both differentiation of land use between agriculture and industry and to a regular supply of land to the building market.

So the first key figure was the landlord. Contrary to the common stereotype, British landlords in this period were often highly entrepreneurial, actively seeking any way to increase their income and maximize the value of their estate.[13] This often took the form of involvement in trade, manufacturing, or mining, but for many the most ready route to greater wealth was to supply land for building. This could be done in a number of ways. Sometimes an entire estate could be disposed of in one piece. More often the land would be broken up into parcels or plots that could be of varying or standardized size. The land could either be leased out or sold at auction. Most landlords preferred to lease or sell the land in plots. The two forms of disposal generated different kinds of income and represented different kinds of investment. With a lease the landlord could expect a regular income from ground rent for the term of the lease, which the leasee would recover from rental or sale of property erected on the land. The shorter the term of the lease, the higher the rent. Because most leases were for fixed sums, the landlord had to assume stable prices over each lease's term. There was also the problem that as the term of the lease neared its end the land and the property erected on it would become increasingly unattractive and so reduce the land's value. This was particularly true in places such as London, where the normal pattern of land disposal was via short-term leases of ninety-nine years. (Elsewhere a common formula was for a lease of 999 years.) The alternative, of freehold sale, meant that the landlord sacrificed a stable guaranteed income from the land in return for a cash sum that could then be invested, although there was still often a residual income in the form of a "chief" rent. Some towns were predominantly freehold, others primarily leasehold. The former included Nottingham, Hull, and Brighton, the latter London, Bath, Manchester, and Liverpool.[14]

The landlords could be either individuals or corporate bodies, the latter category including the Crown. Individuals ranged from great aristocratic families, such as the Devonshires and the Bedfords, to established gentry to urban professionals. Corporate landlords could be urban corporations, charities, colleges of the ancient universities, private companies, or the Church. The common feature of all, however, was that they looked upon land as an investment: buying and selling land was a commercial activity intended to make a profit or generate income. There was not, contrary to a persistent belief, an idea that land was a distinct and peculiar form of property. In some places, such as London or the south side of Birmingham, the pattern was for a few large and coherent estates. Elsewhere—as in, for example, Leeds and Hull—there were many small and more fragmentary estates. There has been a persistent argument that this produced different patterns of development, but as we shall see, recent research does not support this.[15]

Sometimes landlords would develop their estates themselves, but this was unusual. Much more common was the use of a middleman, a speculative developer. These were usually individuals such as Thomas Cubitt, responsible for the development of several large London estates, or the two Woods, who created the Georgian resort of Bath. Sometimes the developer was a private company, as in the case of the Victoria Park company in Manchester or the Cliff Bridge company in Scarborough. Developers would buy or lease land from the landlord and then either build on it themselves or sublet it or resell it to small-scale developers and builders who would develop individual plots. In cases in which landlords wished neither to develop the land themselves nor to pass it on to developers, the remaining option was to sell or lease it directly to the third key party in the process, the small builder.[16]

The actual work of constructing the houses and other buildings erected on the land was normally done by a huge number of small builders. These could be actual building firms, tradespeople and artisans of all kinds, or even private individuals building for their own use.[17] One important phenomenon was the role of freehold land societies and building societies. These were voluntary associations of working people and artisans, each member of the society paying a regular weekly or monthly subscription. The subscribed funds would be used to build houses for the members and, in the former case, to purchase the freehold of any land used for building. Typically, building societies before 1850 were of the terminating variety, whereby each member in turn would build a house as funds allowed and once all had been provided for the society would be disbanded. Voluntary societies of this kind provided an important means for those on lower incomes to accumulate the funds needed for house building and purchase, although the subscriptions meant that the main participants were artisans and skilled laborers.[18]

So the actual building up of the urban fabric was done by a large number of completely distinct and independent builders, each looking to build as quickly as possible for further sale or rent to the ultimate consumer. Two obvious questions arise. First, how was infrastructure provided, given that these small operators would not be able to provide paving or easements for both practical and financial reasons and would be unlikely to provide such services as lighting because of the severe "free-rider" problem associated with such goods? The answer is that infrastructure was provided not by the actual builders but by the developer or, more often, the original landlord. The typical practice for a landlord or developer, following the division of the land into plots, was to lay out streets with pavements, to lay down drains, and sometimes to provide street lighting.[19] (This last was often provided for by a covenant in the lease or sale, as will be discussed later.) This was very much in the interest of the landlord or developer as it made the land more likely to be taken up and meant that a higher rent or price could be charged. Ultimately consumers were less likely to rent or buy property when such services had not been provided, and so the small speculative builders would have little interest in estates where this had not been done. The main exception to this rule was in the case of dense in-fill developments on small areas of land in or near to the older urban areas. Here the demand was so great and the cost of land so high that the developer would typically construct densely packed "court" dwellings without providing any services. The best example of this was in Nottingham, where land in the center of the city was artificially scarce because of the existence of large urban commons, which the unreformed corporation refused to enclose.[20]

The laying out of streets was of course not done at random. In the larger estates and developments it often followed a gridiron plan or a layout designed to enhance the natural advantages of the site. Luxury developments such as the Park in Nottingham or Victoria Park in Manchester were laid out with gently curved roads so that each plot would be private and self-contained.[21] A very common practice was to follow the lines of earlier enclosures or—in the case of land not previously enclosed—the lines of long, strip fields. This was so much the case that in many instances the skilled eye can to this day trace the outline of the eighteenth-century agricultural landscape beneath the modern streets.[22]

A more serious question, however, is this: given that landlords and developers were disposing of even large and coherent estates in a multitude of small packets, why did this not result in a crazy patchwork quilt of individual development? That this did not happen is immediately obvious to anyone who looks even at working-class housing from this period, much less at the uniform terraces of Bath or Bloomsbury. The answer goes to the heart of the matter in making clear for us how a spontaneous, unplanned process could yet produce a great degree of order and even uniformity.

Building and urban development in this period, and indeed thereafter, were regulated by two institutions that both derived from the great play of property rights in law at this time. The first was the Private Act of Parliament. Essentially Parliament can make law in two ways. A Public Act, whether initiated by the government or an individual member, changes the part of the law to which it applies in general, for all of the citizens of the kingdom. A Private Act leaves the general law unchanged but changes it for specific persons. To put it another way, a Private Act gives powers to or alters the legal position of specific named individuals. Today Private Acts are seldom used, one of their surviving uses being to enable individuals to marry when they would otherwise be unable to because of the standard law of marriage. In the eighteenth and nineteenth centuries, however, Private Acts made up a large part of legislation. Whenever a person or group of persons wished to undertake an action that would impinge upon the traditional rights and properties of others they would have to gain the power to do this through a Private Act, in effect asking the sovereign power of the Crown in Parliament to override or amend the existing legal situation in a specific case.[23] Examples of this kind of legislation are enclosure acts, which converted common land into private, and turnpike acts, which converted sections of highway from free public rights-of-way into toll roads run by turnpike trusts. A great deal of urban development depended upon Private Acts—sometimes because it involved the enclosure of commons, sometimes because existing properties or rights-of-way would be infringed, sometimes because it involved the imposition of charges or the erection of tolls. The most common reason was that many estates were either entailed or else held in trust, both of which arrangements precluded piecemeal alienation. A Private Act had to be obtained for the land to be leased out, particularly if this involved a change in use (as of course was the case with development). Among the many large estates requiring such acts were the Grosvenor and Burlington estates in London, the Colmore and Gooch estates in Birmingham, and the Pulteney in Bath.[24]

The point is that unlike the contemporary situation, where such matters—and much else besides—are covered by permanent planning legislation giving statutory powers to various bodies, in this period each landlord or developer who needed to had to apply for an individual, particular Private Act. This was neither a simple nor a cheap process, given the labyrinthine ways of Parliamentary procedure. The first step was to present a petition to Parliament giving full details of the proposed measure. The petition had to contain the entire text of the bill; this could only be done by an experienced (and hence expensive) solicitor. The bill had to comply with the standing rules of both Houses of Parliament, which differed from each other. Each House would hear the petition and then send it to a committee, which would discuss and if necessary amend the bill. Most importantly the committee would hear objections to the bill, whether in the form of an objection lodged before it or through a formal counterpetition. The cost of even a simple act that was not objected to could run to hundreds of pounds, given the need to employ a Parliamentary agent and to gain the full cooperation of Parliament's officials. If an objection were lodged the ensuing hearings and the associated costs (for example, of hiring a barrister) could easily run into thousands of pounds—in pre-1850 funds! This made it essential for all prospective developers, whether landlords or middlemen, to ensure that there were no objections. This was done by extensive informal consultation of all affected parties before the petition was sent to Parliament. Any possible objection had to be either bought off or conciliated by amendments to the proposed developments. Objections could be to the layout or alignment of proposed buildings, to the activities to be carried on within them, to the line of proposed streets or roads, or to the interference with existing rights such as right-of-way or "ancient lights." Estate papers contain correspondence showing how this consultation procedure worked.[25] The first step was usually a public announcement, via the press, of the terms of the proposed bill. The names of the bill's sponsors would be listed, and objectors would be able to write to them before the petition was lodged. The result was an informal but highly effective arrangement by which public concerns were accounted for—an arrangement that was far more effective than the present system of public inquiries. So the need to use Private Acts led to an informal ordering of developments, particularly the larger ones. Again, this ordering was market driven. The greater the demand, the easier it was for developers to buy off objectors. Conversely, in a marginal case, the threat of objection could lead to a proposed development being abandoned.

Far more significant, however, was the use of covenants: this lay at the heart of the "unplanned planning" of urban growth. Unlike Private Acts, covenants were used in almost all urban development of this period and for a long time thereafter. Whenever a piece of land or the power to use that land was transferred from one party to another ("conveyed," in the lawyers' jargon), the transfer, whether a lease or a sale, would normally contain a number of specific stipulations, or covenants. Covenants (literally, treaties) were legally binding agreements between the parties that were part of the contract of sale or lease, so that failure to observe them could render the sale or lease invalid. They controlled or limited the use that could be made of the land or of any fixed property erected upon it. They could apply for a fixed term of years or for the term of the lease but were often "perpetual"—in other words, indefinite. The buyer or lessee was of course aware of them when purchasing or leasing either the land or the property, so that the price of the land or buildings reflected the existence and impact of the covenants.

There was an enormous variety and range of covenants—almost as many, in fact, as there were sales or leases. From the later eighteenth century onward they became the normal way of regulating development. The most common was the building clause, first widely used in London in the later eighteenth century as part of the so-called building lease. This was a lease for a fixed term, commonly for ninety-nine years, by which the leases was bound to erect a building or buildings on the site within a given period of years. The building became the property of the original landlord at the expiry of the lease, although in most cases the lease could be renewed upon payment of a fine. The principle of a covenant stipulating that building should take place within a given time was soon adopted in freehold conveyances and perpetual leases as well. This had the valuable effect of preventing the hoarding of land during periods of high demand and prevented pure land speculation. It also protected the landlord or developer from bankruptcy on the part of the builder. Failure to insert such a time clause into leases could cause disaster: the failure of a development as builders left land vacant or put up temporary or smaller dwellings than the developer had intended.[26]

Almost all conveyances also contained covenants that laid down either the minimum amount of money to be spent on any building or else the minimum rateable value of any property erected. These were to ensure a minimum standard of quality and to prevent adjoining plots and buildings from having their value reduced. A common figure was a cost of one hundred pounds or a rateable value of twenty-five pounds. Following a number of chancery decisions in the first decade of the nineteenth century that declared that simply stipulating that a building be erected was too vague a term to be binding, it also became common to insert covenants specifying the type of building to be erected, so that leases or sales would specifically state, for example, that a dwelling house was to be built.[27]

Also used very frequently from the later eighteenth century onward were covenants that controlled the use made of any buildings. The most common were ones that prohibited certain trades or activities from being carried on. These are still in force in many households in Britain today, so that bemused house buyers learn that they are forbidden by covenants from, for example, keeping pigs, making soap, or keeping a house of ill repute. Many trades were particularly prohibited through such covenants, the slaughtering or keeping of animals and what were often described as "noxious and offensive trades" (in other words, activities such as tanning, soap making, or metalworking, which produced effluent and/or noise) being those most commonly barred. However such "nuisance" covenants frequently went further than this. The letting out of cellars was very commonly forbidden, as was the letting of houses to more than a maximum number of tenants. Some covenants prohibited all kinds of trade, but this was unusual. Many, particularly in the later part of the period, forbade the retailing of alcoholic drink. By this negative rule covenants could, within broad categories, define what the accepted range of uses of a developed estate would be. Where commercial or factory development took place, they could be used to control the kinds of trade carried on and the size and nature of the factory.[28]

All of the kinds of covenants described so far were fairly general and appear frequently in the records. There were also, however, a whole range of far more specific and prescriptive ones, which were found most commonly, but not exclusively, in the more expensive developments. One type laid down the type and quality of the materials to be used in the building, specifying particular kinds of brick or stone or insisting on stone rather than wood for sills and windows. Also common were stipulations regarding the thickness of walls, the nature and quality of the roofing, and the size and placement of windows. Another very common variety of covenant laid down strict guidelines for the height of buildings so that all of the houses erected on a particular street would be the same height and have a common roofline, even if no two houses were built by the same builder.[29]

This kind of covenant could be even more specific and often was. One type, employed widely in London and the major provincial centers, prescribed very precisely the layout and appearance of the facades of all buildings, often down to the most minute details of decoration and architectural style, even to the shape of chimneypots. In extreme cases they would even lay down that the builder must use a design supplied by the estate or developer's office. What went on behind the facade was commonly left to the builder's discretion, but even here strict covenants such as the ones used by the Woods in Bath could include the details of what was permissible in terms of layout, number of rooms, and depth of the property from the frontage.[30]

As well as defining the kinds of buildings and their quality and appearance, covenants were also used to regulate the public spaces and lands between houses. Such covenants tended to be used in the conveyances of land from the original landlord. A very frequent occurrence was a covenant prescribing that the developer must pave the streets and provide sidewalks and street lighting. The developer would then often insert a further covenant putting responsibility for maintaining the pavements and lights on the purchasers or leasees of the property. The usual formula was for house owners to be bound to pave the sidewalk outside their property and the section of the street easement up to the halfway line of the road.[31] The original conveyance would often also use covenants to prescribe the layout and width of streets and passages, as well as to bind developers to install and maintain drainage and sewerage. Some of the covenants used for later suburban and luxury developments, such as those of the Calthorpe estate in Birmingham, insisted on a general duty to keep the environment clean and reputable.[32]

So how were covenants enforced? As Christopher Chalklin says, "It is easy to underestimate the effectiveness of restrictive covenants in this period."[33] One problem of methodology is that to the extent that covenants were effective there will be no written records of their enforcement; the greater their effectiveness, the less need to take noncomplying tenants or builders to court. This leaves the historian trying to demonstrate their effectiveness in the impossible position of trying to prove a negative, in other words, trying to prove that the lack of enforcement is actually a sign of there having been no need for it.

There are cases, however, in which developers or landlords went to court to enforce covenants, usually with success. Chalklin cites the example of a small-scale developer in Liverpool taken to court by the landlord (in this case the municipal corporation) to enforce a covenant requiring him to pave the streets and sidewalks.[34] Moreover, in the later part of the period the courts were increasingly willing to recognize that neighbors had an interest in seeing that covenants of the "type of use and nuisance prohibition" variety were enforced because of the effect on the value of their own property and so allowed neighbors to bring actions for enforcement, even though they were not directly party to the original agreement.

The enforcement of covenants was most successful in the regulation of building aberrance and the layout of developments. As Chalklin, again, observes, "Yet, where compliance was essential to the completion of a scheme as originally planned, as in the case of covenants regarding the facade of houses, a real degree of success was achieved."[35] This success could be achieved by inspection by the estate or developer, in extreme cases such as the Bedford estate in London, or by the provision of detailed instructions and plans by the estate backed up by intensive supervision of the building process.[36] More common were limited inspection and reliance on the law or the threat of revoking or not granting a full lease or sale.

The effectiveness of these and other kinds of covenants can also be gauged by the physical record of the buildings and the urban landscape—a much more satisfactory source for the historian than the written record. Here the evidence is indisputable. The surviving terraces of Bath and Cheltenham and the squares of the great London estates bear witness to this day of the effectiveness of covenants in creating a harmonious and uniform environment. With artisan and working-class housing the physical evidence has often been destroyed, either by war or by later redevelopment, but we do have the evidence of photographs that show that even in poorer housing developments, minimum standards of height, size, and appearance were enforced. It was only in the very cheapest housing, and particularly in secondary in-fill buildings in town centers, that no control was exercised.

There were of course enormous variations in the extent and specificity of covenants and also in the rigor and methods of enforcement. At one extreme were cases such as the Stamford estate in Ashton-under-Lyne in Lancashire or the Bedford, Portland, and Westminster estates in London.[37] Here the covenants were extensive, detailed, and specific, laying down the finest details of use and design. In these instances the estate office or the landlord's officers would play a very active role, supervising the building process to ensure that covenants were complied with and maintaining oversight of the estate after development was completed to ensure that owners and tenants adhered to the conditions of use and maintenance. At the other extreme were cases such as the Norfolk estate in Sheffield, where only the minimum covenants were imposed, requiring that buildings be erected with limited stipulations as to quality and appearance.[38] There was also a whole range of intermediate cases.

A number of explanations for this variety have been proposed, but on examination these do not stand up. The policy of the landlord or family is not a sufficient explanation because of the variation in policy among different estates held by the same landlord. Thus, the Duke of Norfolk, while imposing only minimal covenants in Sheffield, imposed very strict ones in the nearby smaller manufacturing town of Glossop. Again, there is no straightforward correlation of covenants with quality or type of housing. While as a rough rule of thumb it is true that the more expensive and exclusive the development the more strict the covenants, there are many exceptions to this. Ashton-under-Lyne, for example, was not a luxury suburb but a manufacturing mill town. In Hull and in parts of London and Brighton there are both cheaper developments with stricter covenants and more expensive ones with lighter.[39]

Another possible explanation relates detail of covenant to the number of landlords and the size of estates. The argument is that in towns where there was only one landlord or a small number of large estates, it was possible for the landlords or developers to impose strict covenants. This implies as a corollary that small towns would be more likely to see this pattern than large ones. In his work on the development of Southport by the Heskeths and Scarisbricks, John Liddle explicitly argues that the advantage enjoyed by a single large landowner, such as the Devonshire family in Eastbourne, was that a local monopoly position as the supplier of land enabled such a landowner to resist market pressures and choose more careful development over a higher return in the short term.[40] However, the work of David Cannadine and of Donald Olsen contradicts this. Cannadine has shown that there is no clear pattern of sole landlords generating more controlled development, while Olsen's research on Sheffield concentrates on a single very large estate (the Norfolk estate) that controlled most of the available housing land and yet did not employ strict covenants.[41]

Some light may be cast by the history of covenants. Initially their use was rare except in highly exclusive resorts such as Bath. From the 1770s onward, however, their use became much more widespread, to the point that in the early nineteenth century covenants of at least a minimal kind were standard. At the same time they developed in terms of detail and variety: increasingly complex and specific covenants appear in the records, along with local variations. From the 1820s onward there is evidence, particularly in large manufacturing towns such as Sheffield and Birmingham, of resistance on the part of developers and builders to the use of strict (as opposed to general) covenants; this led to the failure of a large development on the Norfolk estate at Allsop Fields.[42] By 1850 a pattern of sorts had emerged with the continuing use of strict covenants in many areas. Examples are found in Southport, parts of Manchester and Salford, and the large Calthorpe estate in Birmingham, while in other areas such as Sheffield only the minimal type was being used. In between, as stated earlier, were all sorts of intermediate forms. What had happened was that a social innovation, the restrictive/prescriptive covenant, had been introduced in the eighteenth century, widely adopted in the later eighteenth and early nineteenth century, and later adapted to a variety of local contexts.

This is commonly taken as evidence of the "failure" of covenants as a mechanism. This, however, is both to miss the point and to fundamentally misunderstand the nature of the institution. The assumption behind all of the arguments set out earlier is that covenants were an antimarket institution, designed to control or check market forces. According to this perspective, covenants were a form of planning by landlords, similar to that employed by the state but with the crucial difference that the state is a monopoly backed by the ultimate power of force. To the extent that they enjoyed a local monopoly position, landlords and developers were able to play the role of the state in their own neck of the woods. However, the example of the Norfolk estate in Sheffield shows, according to this view, that landlords were unable in the last analysis to resist the pressure of market forces that were pushing in the direction of cheaper, uncontrolled (i.e., unregulated by covenants) urbanization. (Why the market should create pressure in this direction is never spelled out.)

As implied earlier, there is a sharp contradiction in much of this.

The argument is that covenants, by imposing extra costs on builders and users, pushed up the price of housing. This is broadly true. However, on the one hand covenants are criticized for keeping up the cost of housing to the point at which it was beyond the reach of much of the population, while on the other hand they are criticized as ineffective because too much working-class housing was being produced with only limited covenants being used. There is an unspoken assumption that the state has a magical power to escape the trade-off between quality and quantity and to provide a mass supply of high-quality housing. The evidence of public housing in the twentieth century in both Britain and the United States should be enough to persuade anyone that this is simply not true.

In fact covenants were not in any sense antimarket, nor were planning and regulatory institutions imposing some kind of order on an unruly system of supply and demand. Covenants were themselves market institutions, part of the market process that brought landlord, developer, builder, and consumer together. They were a market mechanism that enabled landlords and developers to sell "planning," or control of the environment, as part of their overall package. They were in effect a service that enabled the landlord or developer to sell to the ultimate consumer not only land and buildings but also quality, appearance, environment, and services such as lighting and paving. Their status as legal institutions meant that the consumer would know that the regulations by which they were individually bound would also be enforced on their neighbors.

In fact covenants were a sophisticated method for circumventing two apparently severe collective-action problems. First, there was a "prisoners' dilemma" type of problem. While it was in the interests of all inhabitants of an area or all builders on lots to maintain property or to build property of a common, high standard, there was an incentive for individual builders or owners to allow property to decay or erect cheaper buildings. Each actor had to work on the assumption that this is what their neighbors were doing because to assume otherwise would have been to run the risk of a severe loss. So the "rational" course of action would have been to not keep to any standard. Covenants circumvented this problem by imposing a common, enforceable duty on all the builders or inhabitants. This is one of the things the purchaser or leases of lands or buildings was paying for.

Second, covenants were a way around a classic "public goods" problem. The services that were sold and provided via the insertion of covenants—such as environmental quality, lighting, paving, street easements, and the like—are all "public" goods. That is, they have the quality of nonexcludability, so that once they have been provided everyone benefits from them regardless of whether they have paid or not. This creates, in economic theory, the "free-rider" problem, where every individual has an incentive to not pay for or provide a good but to instead rely upon others. The consequence is that the good is under-provided or not provided at all. Covenants were a means whereby developers and landlords could provide such public goods and sell them to the ultimate consumer by "bundling" the public goods with the private good of land use.[43]

However, all goods come with costs. It is true that land encumbered with covenants, precisely because it was more valuable to consumers, would tend to cost slightly more. At the final stage housing built in accordance with prescriptive covenants would often be more expensive (or smaller—one trade-off being between quality and size, whereby covenants decreeing high quality could be combined with smaller property and denser building to produce housing that was still lower priced). The point again is that covenants, being market institutions, were affected by market demand. Consumers would engage in a complicated set of trade-offs among environment, quality, cost to rent or purchase, size, location, and services. The costs of rent or purchase would incorporate the cost of providing the services or quality that covenants decreed. If this was too high for local conditions the property would not sell.

The result was that the system of covenants was flexible and market driven, hence the emergence of local variations in strictness and extent. In some areas, where there was demand for mass-built cheap housing, covenants would be light and loosely enforced, while in other areas there would be a demand for a high-class environment with highly prescriptive and strictly enforced covenants. Developers were able to tailor the extent of their providing "public goods" via covenant to the nature and scope of local demand, as well as account for other factors such as land and building costs. This is in marked contrast to the rigidity and fixity of state attempts to supply these goods through public planning, zoning laws, and the like. The flexibility also extended to the enforcement of covenants. Landlords and developers would often not enforce the building clause in a lease when demand for land was slack, as long as the rent was paid.

So looking at the urbanization process in Britain between 1750 and 1850 we can see a whole range of patterns and types of development, linked to a wide range of covenants as part of the product being provided. This variety is, of course, precisely what we would expect in a situation where market supply of a good is predominant. We can distinguish several broad categories of development. In the first place are large-scale developments with extensive use of covenants. These produced large, uniform developments with a higher proportion of high-cost housing. Examples of this are the New Town in Edinburgh, developed by the corporation but executed through subletting of plots to developers with strict covenants; other Edinburgh estates, such as the Moray estate; and the Bedford, Portland, and Westminster estates in London.[44] We should not assume that such developments were uniformly middle class or professional: the records of the Westminster estate reveal that its population after development included a high proportion of traders and artisans as well.[45] Often, as in Bath, cheaper housing was built behind the uniform facades of crescents and squares. In the second place is the large intermediate class of large- to medium-sized estates with covenants that, while prescriptive, were not as extensive as in the first category. The Cadogan estate in London and the various developments organized by Cubitt, as well as the major estates in Manchester and Birmingham, are examples of this. Here the housing is more mixed, but there is still use of the gridiron plan for street layout as well as prescription of building materials and height. This is not simply a geographical distinction: more than half of London development before 1830 falls into this category. The Clowes estate in Salford and the Park in Nottingham, to give just two examples, had extensive covenants.[46] Third are cases such as Sheffield and Leeds after the 1820s, where the housing was cheap and covenants only laid down minimum standards of uniformity.[47] In addition, there are also special cases, in particular the development of entire towns by single or multiple developers. In some cases, such as Cardiff with the Butes or Ashton-under-Lyne with the Stamfords, the covenants were highly prescriptive, while in cases such as Skegness or Eastbourne in the later part of the nineteenth century the landlord undertook the entire process of creating a custom-made resort.[48] On the other hand are towns such as Huddersfield and St. Helens, where the use of covenants was more limited; in the case of Huddersfield a town was dominated by a single family, the Ramsdens.[49] Towns dominated not so much by a single landlord as by a single industry or employer (e.g., coal in the case of Cardiff) would seem to be the ones most likely to have seen extensive use of covenants. The final special case is of the development of luxury suburbs, with an early example in Victoria Park in Manchester. This kind of development tended to take place more after the mid-Victorian period, with the Calthorpe estate in Birmingham and the various Egerton estates in Manchester being the best examples of this outside London.

The pattern of development described and the use of covenants continued in fact well after 1850; it was only in the years before World War I that this system began to be replaced by a system of national planning. There had been increasing control at a local level by local authorities before then, particularly in the by-then-established urban and industrial areas—this is one reason for the growing contrast between city and suburb that can be observed in the later nineteenth century. This was also the period that saw the rise of the ideology of town planning and the growth of a movement both political and intellectual in its favor.

There were a number of reasons for this. In one sense it was simply a part of the "spirit of the age," of the general movement in favor of planning and control that can be discerned in the years before 1914. A major cause of this movement was the discovery of the slum and of the associated problem of the "residuum" of undeserving poor, which led to calls for a whole range of strategies for dealing with this problem (some, such as forced land settlement and eugenics, now thankfully forgotten), of which urban reconstruction was one. There was also in this, as in other areas, the impact of what Harold Perkin calls the "rise of professional society," that is, the rise to prominence and power in modern societies of a class of professionals, many of whom stood to gain from the enlargement of state activity and state welfare.[50]

In the specific case of Britain there was the great impact from the 1870s onward of the Continental example, above all that of Germany, which became the "pattern nation" that the progressive intelligentsia wished to emulate. The example of Paris and Haussman was also influential. More influential in the long run, however, was the home-grown British product—the Garden City movement of Sir Ebenezer Howard and Sir Frederick Osborn. For many people the argument for town planning was not only or even primarily that it was needed to address specific urban problems such as the continuing existence of slums. They argued rather that industrial society was confronted by a whole series of social problems and that redesigning the urban environment was a way of resolving these problems. One particular argument concerned the need to remove the historic division between town and country by creating an environment that combined both—the Garden City. Such arguments played a major role in the movement to the planning apparatus set up after World War II.[51]

So, to return to our starting point, what of the nature and quality of urban growth in Britain during this crucial period of 1750 to 1850? The argument that this was a disorderly or chaotic process rests upon a particular definition of order and misinterprets the nature of the actual process. This was an orderly process, but orderly in the sense of spontaneous order, institutions such as property rights and markets leading individual actors to produce an unintended but orderly outcome. Also wrongheaded is the argument that instruments such as covenants were a form of planning that produced the order and uniformity of Bath or Cheltenham.

However, some historians, such as Sutcliffe or Ron Neale, would not deny this. Sutcliffe in particular is quite explicitly aware of the nature of the process. His argument is rather, as we have observed, that a market-driven process produced unsatisfactory results. It is an argument, in other words, about market failure. So was there market failure? If there was, was it any worse than the real-world alternative we have experienced in Britain since the Town and Country Planning Act?

There are some points about the record that even the most hostile observers admit. In the first place, the market did ensure a sufficient supply of building land. This is reflected in the relatively low proportion of total building costs attributable to land charges—about 10 to 20 percent.[52] Cases such as Nottingham, where there was a local shortage of land, were exceptional. Second, as all authors admit, there was enough housing built to meet the exploding demand. There was not the kind of housing shortage experienced at times in the post—World War II period. As Olsen puts it, "It [the unregulated market system] provided more middle class housing than the middle class could absorb and a supply of working class housing that, if of minimal standards of amenity, was in most cases adequate for the needs of the people, *at a price that the great majority of the working classes could afford.*" The official history of Sheffield makes the same point as does Maurice Beresford in connection with Leeds.[53]

The key point, however, is the one emphasized in the quote. The unregulated system not only provided housing, but it did so at an affordable price for almost all the population. The market-based nature of the "regulatory mechanism" (i.e., covenants) meant that the cost of housing was not raised by regulatory costs to a point at which it was beyond the reach of the majority—something that happened repeatedly in the twentieth century due to rent controls, zoning laws, and building regulations, leaving the state to meet the deficit through high-cost and low-quality public housing. Much has been made of the poor quality of artisan and working-class housing in this period, but several points must be made. First, had the quality been higher, the housing would have been too expensive for the majority. Nor was there an alternative of better-quality housing provided at the same price, whether by the market or the state. In the real world the alternatives were cheap housing or no housing—we can see the results of this choice in many parts of the world today. Second, as Marian Bowley points out in her standard history, the relationship between quality and price was a fair one.[54] Finally, a point well worth making is that the quality of artisan and working-class housing was better than many allow. This was housing that lasted in many cases for well over a hundred years, until it was swept away by post–World War II reconstruction. The housing that replaced it has often not lasted even thirty years and has had to be demolished with loans and charges still outstanding. As one wag put it, "We have knocked down slums that had lasted for a hundred years and replaced them with slums that have lasted for twenty-five years." As Sutcliffe points out in his comparison of Britain and Germany, the quality of British artisan and working-class housing was much higher than that found on the Continent, "despite less intervention."[55]

Where there was market failure was in the provision of housing for the very poorest, and this was a problem as much of the countryside as the towns. The bottom 10 percent were unable to find anything but unsanitary and overcrowded accommodation. These were immigrants, above all the Irish, and people employed in the casualized and sweated sections of the labor market. However, it is a serious mistake to believe that this status was inevitably a permanent one; for many it was only temporary. Much of the historiography takes the exceptional conditions of the slum areas near the center of the urban areas, such as the East End of London or Angel Meadow and Little Ireland in Manchester, and presents these as being typical. This is often due to an uncritical reliance on a small number of polemical contemporary works and especially on Engels's *Condition of the Working Class,* despite its demolition as a reliable source by William Chaloner.[56]

Moreover, we should ask again what the alternative was. The work of people such as James Buchanan on "government failure" should make us skeptical of the argument that there is a ready and easy alternative to "market failure." The choice is not between a flawed solution and a perfect one but between two unsatisfactory ones, and the judgement to be made is which is the least unsatisfactory. To believe otherwise is to fall into the "nirvana fallacy" mentioned earlier. When comparing unregulated urban growth with the private supply of housing and covenants providing public goods on the one hand with regulated and planned development and the partly public supply of housing on the other we should judge between the two real historical records. It is not clear, to say the least, that public housing in Britain or the United States today is any better than the private slum housing of a hundred years ago.

What of the other specific criticisms made by Sutcliffe and others? One is that a voluntarist approach to growth did not produce a satisfactory spatial division of functions. In fact the combination of market supply of land and covenants did produce a broad division between residential areas and suburbs on the one hand and mixed residential and manufacturing areas on the other. The classic form this took was the division between a residential West End and a mixed East End, found not only in London but also in Glasgow and Leeds. It also led to some functions, especially retailing and warehousing, being concentrated in particular areas, in the case of retailing on main arterial routes and after 1850 in central shopping areas such as London's West End.

It is true that in the "mixed" areas manufacturing and housing were located much closer together than modern town planning would allow. This partly reflected limitations of technology, especially transport. To locate even noxious trades away from the workforce was simply not feasible before the advent of the streetcar and the safety bicycle. Once these appeared, in the later nineteenth century, private entrepreneurs rapidly moved to provide out-of-town industrial estates, one of the first and best examples being the Trafford Park industrial estate outside Manchester, set up in the 1890s. Even before then many major manufacturing works had been sited outside towns on greenfield sites with railway access.

Moreover, this is an instance in which we should perhaps be skeptical about the very basis of the criticism. Is it such a bad thing to have work and residence in close proximity? There is a strong case to be made that the segregation of these functions by modern town planning has actually contributed substantially to many social problems such as unemployment and community breakdown.

Another frequent complaint about voluntarist development is that it led to a progressive segregation of social classes. The evidence shows that at least initially this was simply not true, with a wide social mix in many late-eighteenth-century developments. Also, the "decline of socially mixed neighborhoods" is a phenomenon that historians and commentators keep on discovering. It has been located in the 1980s, 1930s, 1890s, 1840s, 1820s, 1790s, and doubtless even further back!

Like the equally mythical "rise of the middle classes," this phenomenon appears to be happening all the time, which should make us skeptical about the supposed existence of a time when rich and poor lived together cheek and jowl. In any event, while the case against voluntarist growth is arguable, there is little room for doubt about the way zoning laws in the United States and the Town and Country Planning Act in Britain have worked to stop the building of cheap housing in the suburbs and countryside and to preserve these as middle-class enclaves while confining the poor to the inner city or overspill estates.

For almost a hundred years a powerful body of opinion has argued that the growth and building of cities cannot be left to voluntary action and cooperation. The conventional historical account of the first phase of urbanization, between 1750 and 1850, plays a key part in this argument. Investigation reveals, however, that voluntarist arrangements were able to generate institutions and practices that provided the goods and benefits associated with planning but in a more flexible and responsive fashion.

NOTES

1. Holmes and Szechi 1993; Wrigley and Schofield 1983.

2. Ashworth 1954, 7–8.

3. Ashworth 1954, 17–80; Choay 1970; Stewart 1952; Benevolo 1967.

4. See Sutcliffe 1981a, 2–15. See also Sutcliffe 1980a, 1–2. For another example of this later type of work, see Olsen 1982.

5. Sutcliffe 1981a, 3. See also Sutcliffe 1980a, 1–2. Olsen 1982 is a particularly good example of the final kind of argument, regarding the "failure of private planning" due to lack of statutory powers.

6. For a classic example of this kind of conflation see Stewart 1952, 139–42. An extreme example of the definition of order as necessarily the result of conscious design is Hart 1965, 173–85, and especially 174, where the argument is made that because the town is harmonious in design it must have been planned according to a common purpose. What the author is actually describing is the unintended outcome of a common interest on the part of many independent developers—the desire to attract wealthy visitors to the spa. For an example of a distinguished work that does not take this line, see Summerson 1970, 18: "For a town, like a plant or an ant-hill, is a product of a collective unconscious will and only to a very small extent of formulated intention." For Hayek's exposition of this concept, see Hayek 1967a, 96–106.

7. Martin and Mcintyre 1972, 1:214.

8. The term "nirvana fallacy" was invented by Harold Demsetz. I owe this reference to George Selgin.

9. Deane and Cole 1967.

10. For a discussion of the impact of turnpikes on the pattern of urban growth, see Summerson 1970, 269–84.

11. Porteous 1977. See also Porteous 1969, especially 26–45.

12. Granville 1841; Liddle 1982; Bailey 1951; Haddon 1973, 101–88; Neale 1974, 1981; Gurnham 1972.

13. For the landlords' role, see Cannadine 1980. See also Reed 1983.

14. Chalklin 1974, 60–61.

15. Summerson 1970, 40, 98–113. See also Banfield 1890; Olsen 1982. For Leeds, see Beresford 1980, 1988. Also see Jackson 1972.

16. Hobhouse 1971; Spiers 1976; Davies 1982. Chalklin 1974, 74–80, describes the role of the Woods. Also see Wilkes and Dodd 1964; Dyos 1968.

17. Chalklin 1974, 111–14.

18. For building societies in general, see Gosden 1973. See also Chapman and Bartlett 1971. For a skeptical view, see Beresford 1988, 196–202.

19. See for example, Davies 1982; Reed 1983, 111–20. Cannadine 1980, 229–390, discusses the creation of Eastbourne by the Devonshire estate, which involved the large-scale provision of infrastructure.

20. Church 1966. See also Reed 1983, 118.

21. See, for example, Chalklin 1974, 89–98. See also Chalkin 1968; Reed 1983, 120; and Hyde 1943–47, 153–59. For Victoria Park, see Spiers 1976, 13–20.

22. Tindall 1977.

23. Clifford 1885–87.

24. Summerson 1970, 40–45; Reed 1983, 117.

25. Chalklin 1974, 71. For an example of the process, see Clowes Papers (Broughton Park Estate), Local Collection, Manchester Central Reference Library.

26. Chalklin 1974, 110–11, gives details of the failure to develop the Sefton estate in Liverpool because of the omission of a time clause from the building leases granted.

27. Chalklin 1974, 65–66.

28. Chalklin 1974, 104, 137–40.

29. For Bath, see Chalklin 1974, 77–78. For examples from Manchester, see Chalklin 1974, 89–98. For an account of the Bedford estate's use of such covenants, see Olsen 1982.

30. Olsen 1982 gives details of the supervision of developments by the Bedford estate office. For Bath, see Neale 1981.

31. Chalklin 1974, 104–5. As the example cited (from Liverpool) shows, the real problem was not the laying down of paving and easements, as this could be enforced by making it a condition of the lease, but rather the maintenance of paving once the lease had been granted and the original pavement put down, as this was much harder to enforce.

32. For a highly detailed account of the development of the massive Calthorpe estate and its use of covenants, see Cannadine 1980, 81–228.

33. Chalklin 1974, 137.

34. Chalklin 1974, 105, gives the case of James Gill in Liverpool. For a general discussion of the effectiveness of covenants, see Chalklin 1974, 137–40.

35. Chalklin 1974, 139.

36. Olsen 1982.
37. For the Stamford estate, which built almost the entire town of Ashton, see *Royal Commission on the State of Large Towns and Populous Districts,* 1844–45, 2d report. App. Part II.
38. Binfield et al. 1993, 2:18.
39. Summerson 1970, 269–84. For Hull, see Jackson 1972, 110.
40. Liddle 1982, 134.
41. Cannadine 1980, 401–6; Olsen 1973, vol. 1, 333–57.
42. Olsen 1973, vol. 1, 341–43; Binfield et al. 1993, 2:18.
43. For discussion of this and related issues, see the essays in Cowen 1988.
44. Summerson 1970, 102–5, 163–76. For Edinburgh, see Youngson 1966.
45. Reed 1983, 113–17.
46. Kellett 1961, 1061; Butt 1971, 57; Summerson 1970, 190–98; Dyos 1968, 641–90; Chalklin 1974, 81–112.
47. Olsen 1973, vol. 1; Beresford 1988, 57–160.
48. For the case of Cardiff, see Davies 1982, 29–30. For Eastbourne, see Cannadine, 1980, 229–390.
49. Brook 1968; Barker and Harris 1959, 290–304.
50. Perkin 1990.
51. Ashworth 1954, 63–80. For the Garden City movement, see Howard 1902 and Darley 1975.
52. Chalklin 1974, 57.
53. Olsen 1973, vol. 1, 334 (emphasis added); Beresford and Jones 1967, 186–97.
54. Bowley 1966, 360.
55. Sutcliffe 1980c, 48–50.
56. Henderson and Chaloner 1971. The introduction by Chaloner is a systematic critique of Engels's sources and his misuse of them.

REFERENCES

Ashworth, W. 1954. *The Genesis of Modern British Town Planning.* London: Routledge and Kegan Paul.
Bailey, F. A. 1951. The Origin and Growth of Southport. *Town Planning Review* 21 (4):299–317.
Banfield, F. 1890. *The Great Landlords of London.* London: S. Blackett.
Barker, T. C., and J. R. Harris. 1959. *A Merseyside Town in the Industrial Revolution: St. Helens, 1750–1900.* London: F. Cass.
Benevolo, L. 1967. *The Origins of Modern Town Planning.* London: Routledge and Kegan Paul.
Beresford, M. 1980. The Face of Leeds, 1780–1914. In *A History of Modern Leeds,* ed. D. Fraser. Manchester: Manchester University Press.
———. 1988. *East End, West End: The Face of Leeds During Urbanization, 1684–1842.* 2 vols. Leeds: Thoresby Society.

Beresford, M., and G. R. J. Jones, eds. 1967. *Leeds and Its Region.* Leeds: British Association for the Advancement of Science.

Binfield, C., R. Childs, R. Harper, D. Hey, D. Martin, and G. Tweedale, eds. 1993. *The History of The City of Sheffield, 1843–1993.* Vol. 2. Sheffield: Sheffield Academic Press.

Bowley, M. 1966. *The British Building Industry.* Cambridge: Cambridge University Press.

Brook, R. 1968. *The Story of Huddersfield.* London: MacGibbon and Kee.

Butt, J. 1971. Working Class Housing in Glasgow, 1851–1914. In *The History of Working Class Housing,* ed. S. D. Chapman. Newton Abbot: David and Charles.

Cannadine, D. 1980. *Lords and Landlords: The Aristocracy and the Towns, 1774–1967.* Leicester: Leicester University Press.

———, ed. 1982. *Patricians, Power and Politics in Nineteenth Century Towns.* New York: St. Martin's Press.

Chalklin. C. W. 1968. Urban Housing Estates in the Eighteenth Century. *Urban Studies* 5.

———. 1974. *The Provincial Towns of Georgian England: A Study of The Building Process, 1740–1820.* London: Edward Arnold.

Chapman, S. D., and J. N. Bartlett. 1971. The Contribution of Building Clubs and Freehold Land Societies to Working Class Housing in Birmingham. In *The History of Working Class Housing,* ed. S. D. Chapman. Newton Abbot: David and Charles.

Choay, F. 1970. *The Modern City: Planning in the Nineteenth Century.* Trans. M. Hugo and G. R. Collins. New York: G. Braziller.

Church, R. A. 1966. *Economic and Social Change in a Midland Town: Victorian Nottingham 1815–1900.* Leicester: Victorian Nottingham.

Clifford, F. 1885–87. *A History of Private Bill Legislation.* 2 vols. London: Butterworths.

Clowes Papers (Broughton Park Estate). Local Collection, Manchester Central Reference Library.

Cowen, T., ed. 1988. *The Theory of Market Failure: A Critical Examination.* Fairfax, Va.: George Mason University Press.

Darley, G. 1975. *Villages of Vision.* London: Architectural Press.

Davies, J. 1982. Aristocratic Town Makers and the Coal Metropolis: The Marquesses of Bute and Cardiff, 1776 to 1947. In *Patricians, Power and Politics in Nineteenth Century Towns,* ed. D. Cannadine. New York: St. Martin's Press.

Deane, P., and W. A. Cole. 1967. *British Economic Growth 1688–1959: Trends and Structure.* 2d ed. London: University of Cambridge Department of Applied Economics.

Dyos, H. J. 1968. The Speculative Builders and Developers of Victorian London. *Victorian Studies* 11:641–91.

Gosden, P. H. J. H. 1973. *Self-Help: Voluntary Associations in the Nineteenth Century.* London: Batsford.

Granville, A. B. 1841. *The Spas of England.* 3 vols. London: H. Colburn.

Gurnham, R. 1972. The Creation of Skegness as a Resort Town by the Ninth Earl of Scarborough. *Lincolnshire History and Archaeology* 7.

Haddon, J. 1973. *Bath.* London: Batsford.

Hart, G. 1965. *A History of Cheltenham.* Leicester: Leicester University Press.

Hayek, F. A. 1967a. The Results of Human Action but Not of Human Design. In *Studies in Philosophy, Politics and Economics.* London: Routledge and Kegan Paul.

———. 1967b. *Studies in Philosophy, Politics and Economics.* London: Routledge and Kegan Paul.

Henderson, W. O., and W. H. Chaloner, eds. 1971. *The Condition of the Working Class in England,* by F. Engels. London: B. Blackwell.

Hobhouse, H. 1971. *Thomas Cubitt, Master Builder.* London: Macmillan.

Holmes, G., and D. Szechi. 1993. *The Age of Oligarchy: Pre-Industrial Britain, 1722–1783.* London: Longman.

Howard, E. 1902. *Garden Cities of Tomorrow.* London: S. Sonnenschein and Co., Ltd.

Hyde, F. E. 1943–47. Utilitarian Town Planning, 1825–1845. *Town Planning Review* 19:153–59.

Jackson, G. 1972. *Hull in the Eighteenth Century.* Oxford: Oxford University Press.

Kellett, J. R. 1961. Property Speculators and the Building of Glasgow, 1780–1830. *Scottish Journal of Political Economy* 8:211–32.

Liddle, J. 1982. Estate Management and Land Reform Politics: The Hesketh and Scarisbrick Families and the Making of Southport, 1842–1914. In *Patricians, Power and Politics in Nineteenth Century Towns,* ed. D. Cannadine. New York: St. Martin's Press.

Martin, G. H., and S. McIntyre. 1972. *A Bibliography of British and Irish Municipal History.* Vol. 1, *General Works.* Leicester: Leicester University Press.

Neale, R. S. 1974. Society, Belief and the Building of Bath, 1700–1793. In *Rural Change and Urban Growth, 1500–1800,* ed. C. W. Chalklin and M. A. Havinden. Leicester: Longman.

———. 1981. *Bath: A Social History, 1680–1850.* London, Routledge and Kegan Paul.

Olsen, D. J. 1973. House upon House: Estate Development in London and Sheffield. In *The Victorian City: Images and Reality,* 2 vols., ed. H. J. Dyos and M. Wolff. London: Routledge and Kegan Paul.

———. 1982. *Town Planning in London: The Eighteenth and Nineteenth Centuries.* New Haven: Yale University Press.

Perkin, H. J. 1990. *The Rise of Professional Society: England Since 1880.* London: Routledge.

Porteous, J. D. 1969. *The Company Town of Goole: An Essay in Urban Genesis.* Hull: University of Hull.

———. 1977. *Canal Ports: The Urban Achievement of the Canal Age.* New York: Academic Press.

Reed, M. 1983. *The Georgian Triumph, 1700–1830.* London: Routledge and Kegan Paul.

Spiers, M. 1976. *Victoria Park Manchester: A Nineteenth Century Suburb in its*

Social and Administrative Setting. Manchester: Manchester University Press for the Chetham Society.

Stewart, C. 1952. *A Prospect of Cities: Studies Towards a History of Town Planning.* London: Longman.

Summerson, J. 1970. *Georgian London: An Architectural Study.* New York: Allen Lane.

Sutcliffe, A. 1980a. The Debate on Nineteenth Century Planning. In *The Rise of Modern Urban Planning: 1800–1914,* ed. A. Sutcliffe. London: Mansell.

———. 1980b. *The Rise of Modern Urban Planning: 1800–1914.* London: Mansell.

———. 1980c. *Towards the Planned City: Germany, Britain, the United States and France, 1780–1914.* New York: St. Martin's Press.

———. 1980c. The Debate on Nineteenth Century Planning. In *The Rise of Modern Urban Planning: 1800–1914,* ed. A. Sutcliffe. London: Mansell.

———. 1981a. British Town Planning and the Historian. In *British Town Planning: The Formative Years,* ed. A. Sutcliffe. New York: St. Martin's Press.

———, ed. 1981b. *British Town Planning: The Formative Years.* New York: St. Martin's Press.

Tindall, G. 1977. *The Fields Beneath.* London: Temple Smith.

Wilkes. L., and C. Dodd. 1964. *Tyneside Classical: The Newcastle of Grainger, Dobson and Clayton.* Newcastle: J. Murray.

Wrigley, E. A., and R. S. Schofield. 1983. *The Population History of England, 1541–1871: A Reconstruction.* London: Edward Arnold.

Youngson, A. J. 1966. *The Making of Classical Edinburgh, 1750–1840.* Edinburgh: Edinburgh University Press.

3

The Private Places
of St. Louis

Urban Infrastructure through Private Planning

David T. Beito

In the last two decades, the development of urban infrastructure has become a hot topic among historians. The spotlight has been on the late nineteenth and early twentieth centuries. Clay McShane, Joel Tarr, Stanley Schultz, and many others have explored how, faced with rapid growth and upheaval, urban planners, politicians, and civic engineers responded to the challenge of sewering America's cities and paving its streets. Although this literature has added immeasurably to our understanding, much still needs to be written about the long history of privately provided urban infrastructure, in particular streets and sewers.[1]

Since the middle of the nineteenth century, St. Louis and its suburbs have contained an extensive system of privately owned and maintained residential streets. These self-governing enclaves represent case studies in the creation, through voluntary cooperation, of close-knit communities. St. Louis's experience foreshadowed and in certain respects surpassed the twentieth-century pattern of "private innovation preceding public action" described by Marc Weiss:

> The classification and design of major and minor streets, the superblock and cul-de-sac, planting strips and rolling topography, arrangement of the house on the lot, lot size and shape, set-back lines and lot coverage restrictions, planned separation and relation of multiple uses, design and placement of parks and recreational

amenities, ornamentation, easements, underground utilities, and numerous other physical features were first introduced by private developers and later adopted as rules and principles by public planning agencies.[2]

Many of St. Louis's private streets were the brainchild of architect, urban surveyor, and real-estate developer Julius Pitzman. It has been speculated (without much evidence) that Pitzman borrowed from precedents such as the English private square. Between 1867 and 1905, his firm designed an estimated forty-seven private streets or "places." Instead of turning them over to the municipal government (as was standard practice for developers during the period), Pitzman and his fellow investors deeded the streets to the abutting homeowners.[3]

Private Place Development: Initial Stages

The private place evolved slowly as an institution borrowing selectively from earlier experiments. Though not a private street, Lucas Place, laid out in 1851, provided important lessons for later developers. Wealthy banker and railroad executive James H. Lucas planned the street as an exclusive residential enclave for the city's business elite. Lucas recognized the need to erect a buffer to fortify the street's residential status. He donated land on its western edge to the city for a public park, thus effectively limiting through traffic. Lucas also pioneered in the use of deed restrictions. Each deed stipulated a setback line prohibiting placement of buildings within twenty-five feet of the street. Businesses were banned, but churches and schools were permitted. The restrictions could be amended only by consent of those owning the 1,030 feet of land abutting the street.[4]

Shortly after the end of the Civil War, the area around Lafayette Park—like Lucas Place in the city's West End—challenged Lucas Place as the most fashionable neighborhood in St. Louis. The city owned the park, but neighboring landowners voluntarily underwrote most of the early improvements. Private donations of nearly ten thousand dollars paid for an iron fence around the park and virtually all the tree planting. The subscribers discovered, however, much to their consternation, that private subsidy did not translate into private control. In 1867, the city disturbed their seclusion by erecting a bandstand. Although the crowds dampened the peace and quiet, the Lafayette Park area remained a highly desirable residential section.[5]

In 1867, property on Benton Place, the first private street in St. Louis, went on the market. The street had been subdivided a year earlier by Montgomery Blair, who had been Postmaster General under Abraham Lincoln. Blair entrusted design of the street to Julius Pitzman. By the 1870s, at least four other private streets ringed Lafayette Park. Pitzman laid a park median on the street, a feature emulated by later private places. Every lot extended to the center of the median. Following the pattern of Lucas Place, each deed carried restrictions, including a setback from the street of twenty-five feet. Business use and multifamily housing were not prohibited, however. The restrictions provided for the annual election of three commissioners by the lot owners. The commissioners had authority to maintain the street, street lighting, the park median, sewers, and the alley by levying an annual assessment of fifty cents per front foot on each property. Armed with private-street ownership, Benton Place's residents enjoyed a range of powers not possessed by their counterparts in Lucas Place. The commissioners, exercising their proprietary rights, erected a gate at one end of the street and a retaining wall at the other. They could deny access to the alley or park median to residents delinquent in their assessments to the street association. As a last resort, the commissioners could sue in a court of equity to compel payment.[6]

Vandeventer Place, the most ambitious of the early private places, lay outside Lafayette Park's orbit. When it was laid out in 1870, it was located just beyond the western city limits. Pitzman, fresh from his Benton Place commission, supervised the surveying work. At its height, Vandeventer Place boasted the cream of St. Louis society. One mansion cost over eight hundred thousand dollars to build in the 1870s (an amount equal to thirteen million dollars in 2001). The size of Vandeventer Place—two complete city blocks comprising eighty-six residences—dwarfed all previous private places. A line of carriage houses facing the neighboring streets was erected as a sturdy buffer to encroachments. A park median, a feature borrowed from Benton Place, ran the length of the street. Instead of repeating the restrictions in each separate deed, the developers instituted a single "indenture," or restrictive covenant, for the subdivision. Unlike Lucas or Benton Place, the indenture prohibited all but single-family homes. It also set a minimum price for houses of ten thousand dollars, a high sum for its day.[7]

On Benton Place, each resident had title to a separate slice of the street to the center of the park median. On Vandeventer Place, the developers transferred ownership of these areas to three trustees who served for life terms and were required to reside on the street. The consolidation of management and ownership of the street and park under one legal entity was an important innovation. It clearly separated the property entitlements of trustee and lot owner, thus reducing the chance of conflict over responsibility for taxation and upkeep.[8]

From the outset, Benton Place's restrictions had given the lot owners full governing authority. Vandeventer Place's indenture narrowly limited the power of the lot owners. At best, they were junior partners to the trustees. The lot owners could adopt regulations for the subdivision by a two-thirds vote, but these had to be consistent with the original restrictions. With the death or resignation of the last trustee, the indenture allowed the lot owners, by majority vote, to take over authority for enforcement. Although these provisions successfully "democratized" Vandeventer Place, the indenture had an Achilles heel. Any revision of the 1870 restrictions required unanimous consent from all eighty-six lot owners. As soon became apparent, the mustering of 100 percent support for any proposal was almost impossible. The authors of the indenture had a clear intent: they sought to maintain forever more the pristine affluence of Vandeventer Place.[9]

As historian Alexander Scott McConachie puts it, "Vandeventer Place was too pretentiously exclusive for its own good." The restrictions would not have been so crippling had it not been for the virtual preclusion of amending the indenture. By the 1890s, the first signs of decline appeared. The designers had placed Vandeventer Place directly in the path of commercial development. Their mistake, according to the *St. Louis Republic* in 1895, had been to underestimate the rapid "growth of the city. Vandeventer place is now very largely hemmed in by street railroads and business houses, and in the course of a few years this is liable to prove quite a detriment."[10]

The rattle of the streetcars encouraged the wealthy, who had first sought out Vandeventer Place to escape the bustle of the city, to move away. Intended as a buffer, the line of rear carriage houses only brought down the property values of the neighboring streets that it faced. As property values fell, the upkeep of the ostentatious homes became an impossible burden for many owners. When, during the 1920s and 1930s, some members tried to amend the rule prohibiting multifamily housing, they were frustrated by the unanimous-consent requirement. In 1925, the dissidents, alleging that the transformed character of the surrounding neighborhood rendered the restrictions invalid, took their case to the Missouri Supreme Court. Following precedent, the court upheld the indenture because the restricted area itself had not undergone great changes.[11]

The decline of Vandeventer Place accelerated rapidly during the 1930s. Taxes, association assessments, mounting maintenance costs, and sagging property values took their toll. Several of the houses fell into disrepair and had to be condemned. Despite all these adversities, Vandeventer Place survived, albeit in a frayed state. In 1935, journalist Helen Clanton, after attending a meeting of the property owners, noted "the strong feeling that Vandeventer place must and always will be just as it is." The mortal blow came from an unexpected source. In 1947, the Veterans Administration demolished the eastern block of Vandeventer Place to build a hospital. The residents had won every previous legal battle but were helpless when confronted with the government's power of eminent domain.[12]

The forty years after the founding of Vandeventer Place in 1870 represented the golden age of the private place. Local maps during these years listed about ninety private-street subdivisions within the city limits. For the first time, the private-place lifestyle came within reach of home buyers of more modest means.[13]

More than one future private place promoted itself as the next Vandeventer Place. Developers of the Forest Park Addition, which included Portland and Westmoreland Places, set out to make their streets "far superior to Vandeventer place." Even the covenant writers took note. According to West Cabanne Place's indenture, improvements would be made "in a manner similar to Vandeventer Place." The borrowing was selective, however. Authors of a brochure for Bell Place (now Kingsbury Place, Kingsbury Terrace, and Washington Terrace) may have had Vandeventer Place in mind when they characterized their restrictions as the result of "most careful study. The past history of such places in this and other cities makes this a most important consideration." Taking a leaf from Vandeventer Place's book, developers avoided those areas threatened by rapid commercial encroachment and placed a high premium on locations with ready-made buffers, such as parks. Some of the most successful private places in St. Louis surrounded Forest Park. The street layout itself became a shield of protection. Pitzman, in an early departure from the grid system, designed circular streets for Clifton Heights in 1885. Developers were beginning to discover that business users usually stayed clear of curving streets, finding them inefficient for purposes of commerce and transportation.[14]

Vandeventer Place's failure discouraged future covenant framers from imposing the unanimity restriction. Nevertheless, consent requirements for making amendments generally remained high. Over time, indentures became characterized by increasingly voluminous restrictions tempered by ever-broader grants of discretion to the trustees or the lot association. Portland Place's indenture of 1890 borrowed Vandeventer Place's requirement of minimum house prices but added two important modifications. It stipulated a much lower price, six thousand dollars, and permitted the trustees to make exceptions. The trustees were also empowered to dedicate the water and sewer mains (all of which were under private ownership) to the city. Frequently, however, sewers and water mains stayed under private ownership.[15]

Why St. Louis?

Lack of reliable sources makes it difficult to compare the private provision of urban sewers and streets in St. Louis and other cities. Few large municipalities bothered to produce maps or lists of privately owned streets. Those that exist (even in St. Louis) are notoriously incomplete. Nevertheless, impressionistic evidence, including conversations with specialists in the history of urban infrastructure, indicates that private streets were more common in St. Louis than in other large cities.[16]

Various explanations have been offered for the wave of private-place building in St. Louis during the late nineteenth and early twentieth centuries. These include the aggressive work of powerful and enthusiastic sponsors (such as Julius Pitzman); a need for land-use controls in the face of rapid population and economic growth; and the existence of stringent limitations on taxes, spending, and debt, which encouraged developers to finance and operate their own infrastructure. Taken in combination, these factors contributed to the popularity of the private-place model in St. Louis. None alone, however, can provide a catch-all explanation.

Charles Savage has argued that the private place arose to cope with rapid growth and a lack of zoning. This explanation leaves many questions unanswered. Zoning did not exist in any large American city during the nineteenth century. Other cities of similar or greater size, such as Chicago, underwent faster population growth than St. Louis. Only in St. Louis, however, did the combination of covenants and private-street ownership become so widespread.[17]

Certainly, a desire for land-use restrictions accounts for part of the story. Private-place advertisers constantly touted the superiority of their indentures. An ad for Hammett Place was typical. "The restricting deeds," it assured prospective customers, "prevent the erection of inferior buildings, saloons, tenements or objectionable buildings, which is an absolute guarantee to the purchasers of lots in this place that they will be protected and every building erected will enhance the value of the property." Restrictions of this sort, however, were commonly used by developers in other cities. The crucial question still needs to be addressed. Why did the added feature of private-street ownership take hold only in St. Louis?[18]

One possible explanation has often been overlooked by historians: St. Louis was notorious for its inferior urban infrastructure. Necessity demanded a heavy reliance on private enterprise to fill the gap. The city's "home rule" charter of 1876 (the framing of which was authorized by a special amendment to the Missouri Constitution) fortified and tightened already stringent restrictions on taxes and spending. It mandated a top tax limit of 1 percent on every dollar of assessed valuation, imposed stringent restrictions on debt, and required a three-fourths approval for charter amendments.[19]

Although the constitutional amendment allowed St. Louis to annex vast tracts of farmland in the west, thus more than tripling the city's area, it did little to open up new sources of taxation. As a concession to antiannexation sentiment, the city imposed a lower tax rate in the "new limits." It pegged the tax rate at forty cents for every hundred dollars of assessed valuation in the new limits, compared to one dollar in the "old limits." The differential between the areas did not narrow until 1890. Most significantly, the constitutional amendment hemmed in the tax base by making no provision for future annexation. The borders have remained effectively frozen since 1876.[20]

Theoretically, the city paid for street grading and repairs, but more often than not, tax and debt limits left no money available. Financing for paving, curbing, and guttering came out of a ponderous system of special taxes on the abutting land that did not allow installment payments. The charter limitations held spending to low levels throughout the rest of the century. Comparisons with other American cities are revealing. Of the ten largest cities in the country, St. Louis ranked eighth in per-capita expenditures in 1880. In 1890, it ranked ninth.[21]

The revenue system had few defenders and many critics. "Something cannot be made of nothing," concluded the *Missouri Republican* in 1881. "The fault of bad and filthy roadways in the city of St. Louis is not within the power of any administration to alter or change without some plan to provide increased revenue." Still more of a dead letter was a requirement that general revenue pay for all special tax work in excess of 25 percent of assessed valuation. Invariably, property owners funded the balance through private contributions, if at all.[22]

In 1869, "A Sufferer" complained to the *Missouri Republican* that Grand Avenue, a major north/south thoroughfare, was "almost impassable." "The grading was let some eighteen months ago," he complained, "and the money appropriated from the 'new limit' fund of the western wards to do the work, but the money was expended for something else, and there stands Grand avenue in its mud." Twenty years later the avenue, by then the border between the old and new city limits, remained in dismal shape. Finally, unable to obtain help from the city, businessmen in the area pledged twenty-two thousand dollars to pay for paving. This was not an exceptional case. In 1890, St. Louis ranked ninth among the ten largest cities in the percentage of its public-street miles that were unimproved. Fifty-six percent of the public-street mileage in St. Louis had not been graded, curbed, or paved, compared to 57 percent in Cleveland, which was last on the list. As Clay McShane points out, this was a period when a gravel street was considered "paved."[23]

Chaotic and ill-conceived excavations kept even paved streets in a shabby condition. Willy-nilly, the city government and franchised utilities ripped up pavement to lay down track, pipes, and wire. Endless stories of franchise corruption, spotty service, and the padding of street and sewer construction contracts filled the newspapers. In 1900, the *Mirror*, a local muckraking journal, painted a dark but reasonably accurate picture:

> The job in legislation and the trick in the Board of Public Improvements which resulted in the streets of the city being unlighted over seven-tenths of its area.
>
> The streets impassable, unswept, unsprinkled, while the pay roll of the street department has not been decreased with the stoppage of work.
>
> The sewers choked at their mouths, shaky and crumbling throughout their length and all under great strain after every rain.
>
> The foul alleys lined up with unremoved, putrefying garbage.
>
> The depletion of the city treasury by the maintenance on the pay rolls of hordes of tax-eaters in the departments of public work, while practically no public work is being done.[24]

Spending levels were low, but corruption took a toll on the funds that were raised. Lincoln Steffens exaggerated when he nominated St. Louis in his "Shame of the Cities" exposé. Even so, there was much truth in his accusations that "combines" of local officials routinely sold utility franchises in exchange for bribes. Tax and debt limitations did not prevent corruption. They did, however, check its more extravagant expression. As the *Mirror* succinctly put it, "We [the city government] may have been bad, but we were never bold."[25]

The problem of poor and inadequate city services was most apparent in the new limits, or those areas incorporated in 1876. Tax and debt limits and political corruption prevented extension of public sewers (theoretically paid for out of general revenue) beyond the 1876 borders until 1889, long after settlement had become substantial. Taxes, on the other hand, were kept low due to the city's annexation concessions. Poor infrastructure and low taxes combined to give developers in the West End in particular ample incentives and ability to install their own infrastructure.[26]

The transaction costs of using government agencies to build sewers were quite high. The only political alternative open to property owners was to create, by petition, a sewer district in their area and pay for construction by a special tax on all lots of ground in the district. The law did not allow installment payments and required that repairs be paid out of (nearly nonexistent) general revenue. Invariably, developers in the West End opted to bypass these requirements and build by the private-sewer method. The St. Louis City Charter defined "private" sewers as financed, owned, and repaired by private individuals, businesses, or associations. With permission of the city, these could be connected to public sewers.[27]

Private entrepreneurs also underwrote most road improvements on existing public streets in the West End. In the 1880s, property owners formed an association to extend, grade, and pave Forest Park Boulevard, one of the major thoroughfares in the West End. They raised eighty thousand dollars. By the same methods, property owners paved Kingsbury Boulevard, another major street in the West End, and purchased land to add thirty feet to its width. Why did so many developers decide to go further and retain private ownership? Common sense would seem to dictate otherwise. Private-street ownership entailed a litany of added investment costs for the developer. Responsibility for street upkeep continued until the last lot was sold. It was also necessary to create a trust to administer the street. Moreover, local authorities made it difficult if not impossible for residents and developers to selectively dedicate sewer and water mains and still retain ownership of the street.[28]

Closer inspection, however, shows the dubiousness of many of these apparent comparative defects of private-street ownership. In theory, general revenue paid for street repairs and cleaning, but as we have seen, the money was invariably not available. Public-street residents (through the special tax) and private-place owners (through their lot-association assessments) paid directly for sprinkling and initial paving. Private-place associations, however, enjoyed the prerogatives of ownership and control. If a street needed repairing or sprinkling, residents (through their association) could shop around for the cheapest and most reliable contractor. As a writer in the *St. Louis Republic* commented, "in Bell place itself the question has always been asked since the first grading gang commenced work, not 'which is the cheapest?' but 'what is the best?' The roadway is paved better than any downtown or residence street."[29]

This writer waxed eloquent about the sidewalks in Bell Place being as "smooth as billiard tables" and noted that "the sprinkling arrangements for the driveways keep those thoroughfares in perfect condition, mud as well as dust being guarded against." Private-place residents could defend their seclusion and reduce the wear and tear of street pavement through a ban on business hauling. Public-street residents could not. "This is a private street," an advertisement for West Cabanne Place exclaimed; "heavy teaming excluded and dust avoided."[30]

Constant refrains in the press about inadequate and unreliable public infrastructure left their mark. Witness these typical complaints from the *St. Louis Republic*'s real-estate column in 1896: "Real estate agents acknowledge that their business has been seriously retarded . . . on account of the unsatisfactory condition of affairs relating to street reconstruction in the West End. Prospective purchasers after finding residence sites which suit them in every way except that they are located on streets not made, abandon their intended purchase when they are told in plain truth that these streets may not be reconstructed for two years or more. There are hundreds of instances of this kind and agents have grown sick at heart."[31]

Private-place advertisers, on the other hand, could promote their subdivisions as superior and ready-made bundles of infrastructure. According to advertisements for Hammett Place, "sidewalks are made of stone flagging, sewer and water pipes laid over the entire place: magnificent shade trees planted on the streets." The developer of Wagoner Place promised "full improvements—without cost to purchaser—including streets, granitoid walks, sewers, water and gas." Advertisements for the Forest Park Addition touted the subdivision's up-to-date, private, and separate sanitary and storm sewers. It pointed out that water tanks had been placed on each lot to enable periodic flushing of the sanitary mains.[32]

The buyer of a home on a private place was in effect purchasing a "package deal" that included "tied" infrastructure such as streets, sewers, water mains, and security. The use of the tied sale took a variety of forms. In the 1880s, developers subsidized extension of a cable line into Hammett Place and Cora Place to increase saleability. The Lindenwood subdivision, which does not seem to have been a private place per se, boasted its own developer-constructed railroad station and spring-fed waterworks.[33]

Anthropologist Spencer Heath MacCallum's comparison of the hotel and the town invites parallels to the provision of tied services by the private place:

> The hotel has its public and private areas, corridors for streets, and a lobby for its town square. In the lobby is the municipal park with its sculpture, fountains, and plantings. . . . Its public transit system, as it happens, operates vertically instead of horizontally. Utilities, including power and water service and sewerage, are all available. Police and fire protection come under the supervision of the house officer and security staff.

A similar description could also fit tied sales through the shopping center and the condominium.[34]

Government provision of local public goods often crowded out private provision. Even the possibility of government provision could crowd out private provision as developers gambled that expenditures on infrastructure could eventually be unloaded onto the taxpayer. When, as in St. Louis, government appeared unable or unwilling to provide the necessary infrastructure, private provision proved highly effective. Historians have in fact documented frequent examples of infrastructure provided through the tied sale. Ann Durkin Keating, for example, has described how developers in suburban Chicago formed light, water, and gas companies as part of "service combinations" to attract settlement to their subdivisions. (On Chicago, see Robert C. Arne's chapter in this volume.) It is fascinating to speculate how urban infrastructure would have developed if the governmental alternative had not existed.[35]

In making such speculations, the example of the private place offers an excellent starting point. Well after completion of the developmental process, the private place continued to be marketed as a planned, self-contained world where the homeowner could live in a cosmopolitan setting yet be free of the corruption and inefficiencies of the political sphere. Bitter experience with the political process encour-

aged developers and prospective residents alike to regard private ownership as the best available means to ensure the autonomy of the private place.

Coping with Free Riders

An illustration of the private place's exercise of this autonomy was how
it adapted to the pervasive local problem of smoke pollution. By the
1890s, industrial pollution had reached crisis proportions in major
urban areas. In a study of the smoke-pollution problem in St. Louis
and other cities, historian R. Dale Grinder found that by the late nineteenth century, judges had increasingly loosened common-law standards that treated pollution as a nuisance. Stymied in the courts,
aggrieved citizens promoted legislation to limit or ban certain pollu-
tants. This task usually proved time consuming and brought meager
rewards. Of particular import was the widespread burning of soft
(bituminous) coal. For nearly forty years, a coalition of business,
reform, and women's organizations in St. Louis struggled for enactment of controls on soft-coal burning. Not until the late 1930s did they
succeed.[36]

By contrast, as early as the 1890s several of the private places—
including Westmoreland, Portland, and Parkview—had enacted regulations prohibiting residents from burning bituminous coal. The
covenant armed the private place with the ultimate sanction against
violators—a lien on property. The trustees of Washington Terrace
made the most creative use of this authority when they required property owners connecting with the subdivision's private sewers to sign a
contract agreeing not to burn soft coal. In case of a violation, the sewer
connection could be severed. Again, while the sewers and water supply
of private places usually hooked into the city system, private discretion
over street mains provided an important implement of control that
public-street residents lacked.[37]

The key to the private place's enforcement power was its approach
to what economists have called the "free-rider" problem. A free rider in
this case was someone who burned cheaper but pollutant-producing
bituminous coal and thus took a "free ride" off the lungs of others.
Until enough political pressure finally forced the city to pass a law,
harmed parties were left essentially helpless. Private-place residents, on
the other hand, had their own institutions in place and did not have to
depend on the vagaries of the political process. Through the indenture

they could, as economists James M. Buchanan and Roger L. Faith put it, achieve "internalization of externalities." The experience of the private place turns conventional economic theory about the free rider on its head.[38]

Purchasers of homes agreed, under the conditions of the indenture, to pay for infrastructure through the assessments levied by the association. Any free rider who refused to pay yet used the services could be brought to terms through the legal devices contained in the restrictions. Moreover, residents had a direct economic stake in insuring effective assessment collection. When these services were provided by governments, their costs and benefits were widely spread or socialized on a grand scale. The free rider on the private place was a real person known to all concerned. The free rider on government-provided services was usually a faceless abstraction to neighbors.

In addition to smoke, one of the worst free-rider problems in the city was street litter. As the Commercial Club discovered in 1896, ordinances against dumping rubbish on the public streets were "more honored in the breach than the observance." Of the fifty littering cases brought to court in 1895, only three resulted in the full penalty of fines. Political and business leaders tried to cope by organizing (in the long term ineffective) street- and alley-cleaning "moral suasion" campaigns. During one "street cleaning fever," over a thousand people, including schoolchildren, joined in "scraping and brushing up the accumulation of years." In the private place, by contrast, the strictures of the indenture rendered such unwieldy campaigns unnecessary. A local journalist's observations of Portland and Westmoreland Places fit few, if any, public streets in the city. "Within these gates," he wrote, "he who ventures through them finds perfect order and neatness." McConachie sums up vital differences between public streets and private places during the late nineteenth century:

> The development of customs and taboos as a means of keeping up
> the tone of a neighborhood, such as the famous front porch scrub-
> bing of South St. Louis, seems not to have been a facet of the pri-
> vate place style. There was no need for the vigilance and the subtle
> pressures toward conformity which were the price of maintaining
> quality on unregulated middle class blocks.[39]

Several government policies—such as poor enforcement of ordinances requiring that street excavators restore pavement after laying pipe, conduits, or streetcar track—served to encourage free-riding on city services. The average excavator, an editorial in the *St. Louis Republic* charged, was so oblivious to "the spirit of the law" that "he almost seems to think that streets should not be paved, because the improvement gives him inconvenience and extra expense." Socialization of cost and benefit by the city government, by diffusing responsibility, left openings for tremendous waste and duplication of infrastructure. In the private place, the price of miscalculation was borne entirely by the developer or the homeowner—by consenting parties who viewed the service as an economic asset.[40]

Private-place developers came to realize that to attract customers they could not afford to make these kinds of costly mistakes. As a selling point to potential home buyers, developers of Bell Place advertised that "house connections for water and gas are laid to the inside of curb lines, thereby avoiding the necessity of disturbing the street when seeking such connections." In Lewis, Westmoreland, Kingsbury, and other private places, Pitzman caused sewer and water mains to be laid under the park median. This avoided costly pavement excavations to effect repairs. Private-place indentures often limited electric and telephone lines to the alleys or to "easement strips" (owned by the association) along the side of the street.[41]

The Private Place as a Community

Urban designer Oscar Newman has likened private places to "small, independent cities." This comparison has considerable merit. Private places carried on functions that everywhere else have been considered essential government services, including security forces, basic utilities, sewer systems, building codes, parks, and even—to a limited degree— legal systems. Moreover, covenants seem comparable in many ways to constitutions and associations to town meetings. Like local governments, the private place had a revenue system based in the last resort on a lien against the property of noncooperators. The sense of boundary, quite strong among private-place residents, also invites analogies to government.[42]

In other respects, the comparison does not hold up. First, private places did not necessarily enjoy a perpetual existence. Vandeventer Place, among many others, bowed to overwhelming economic pressures. Governments, of course, can also disappear. The incidences of their demise, however, are much rarer, as are the reasons—usually revolution, consolidation, or conquest. As economists Donald J. Boudreaux and Randall G. Holcombe put it, the private-place association is a type of "contractual government" and as such "the closest thing to a real-world social contract as can be found because people must make the explicit choice of moving into the contractual government's jurisdiction, and the government is at no time imposed on anyone."[43]

Another difference is that the private-place association could inspire a degree of mobilization and solidarity unrivaled by even the most tenacious of town meetings. The unanimity or near-unanimity requirement contributed to high attendance at association meetings. At its most potent, the private place represented a prototype of what might be called, in the terminology of historian Lawrence Goodwyn, "workable small-unit democracy."[44]

The strength of private places as communities is well illustrated by their organization in times of crisis. In 1907, residents of several private places foresaw an imminent threat to their survival. The Wabash Railroad owned a right-of-way not far from the southern and western borders of Westmoreland, Portland, and Kingsbury Places. The residents feared that as economic development spread, industries were bound to locate along the railroad sidings. These industrial encroachments would sound a death knell to the integrity of the private places, at least for single-family use. If these had been public streets, the residents might have had no choice but to stand by helplessly and watch their neighborhoods be swallowed by a sea of commerce. Indeed, bereft of covenant-based representation, residents of a public street probably would not been able to foresee that a threat existed in the first place.[45]

These private-place residents chose a pragmatic but highly effective strategy of organizing a subscription campaign to purchase the nearby Rock Island yards. As extra insurance, they financed the construction of luxury apartments on the site to serve as buffers. Finally, they negotiated an agreement with the railroad executives. W. K. Bixby, a resident of Portland Place who had once been the receiver of the Wabash, volunteered to plead the case of his fellow private-place homeowners.[46]

The final agreement is still in force. It includes guarantees that industrial development and switch tracks be excluded from sidings in the area. Most significant of all, the Wabash Railroad promises to install a depressed roadbed for that portion of track closest to the private places. "The results of this foresight," writes McConachie, "can be seen today. North of Delmar Boulevard an industrial complex has grown up along the railroad line. South of Delmar in the neighborhood of the private places the railroad is barely noticeable." These private-place residents learned to use the tools of the market to preserve their existence. In light of Vandeventer Place's experience, they realized the virtues of flexibility and the futility of trying to ignore or suppress the change around them. Effective organization was useless without the ability to adapt to changing economic circumstances.[47]

The Private Places and Land-Use Regulation

Restrictive covenants (including those of private places) have often been depicted as precursors to zoning laws. The Civic League of St. Louis even praised the achievements of private places in its campaign to promote zoning. In 1907 it lamented that "building lines have not been observed; business blocks and livery stables have been permitted to encroach upon purely residential streets; flats have been jammed in between beautiful homes; the choicest paved streets have become main thoroughfares for heavy hauling; and only the 'Places' are protected from the encroachment of street cars, switch tracks, and objectionable buildings."[48]

The comparisons should not be carried too far. City planner Harland Bartholomew, the "father" of zoning in St. Louis, excoriated covenants. Bartholomew condemned such agreements as "wholly ineffectual since they are often violated and are almost invariably completely abandoned upon their expiration." In particular, he disliked private restrictions because they did not fit into the conception of the city as an "organic" planning unit. Bartholomew complained that covenants protected only "specific properties and are not conceived with the idea of protecting the general welfare of the entire city."[49]

In later years, Bartholomew modified his critique of covenants, at least as applied to private places. He even became a trustee of a private place. Nevertheless, his initial disdain of covenants bespoke fundamental tensions in outlook between city planners and private-place developers and residents. Covenant framing was part of a spontaneous process that represented the countless economic transactions of small, particularized economic units on the street and neighborhood levels. To apply Michael Polanyi's terminology, the covenant was a polycentric rather than a monocentric planning method. The process of framing and revision, which was controlled by developers and homeowners, left little role for the city-planning office. Covenant writing exemplified, in the words of economist Don Lavoie, a myriad of "complicated plans, all struggling with and adapting to one another in an unending flux of changing productive relationships." By contrast, as historian

Barbara J. Flint has found, zoning regulation in St. Louis and other cities often ignored both the economic character and the preferences of neighborhoods.[50]

Covenants were not specific to either private places or to St. Louis. By the turn of the century, they had become all the rage among real-estate developers throughout the country. Closer study reveals telling contrasts between private-place and public-street covenants. Public-street covenants generally suffered from the lack of an effective enforcement mechanism. Every property on a particular street would be covered by the restrictions (usually instituted before initial sale by the developer), but enforcement would be completely in the hands of individual lot owners. Left to their own initiative, individuals were often lax in bringing litigation to stop violations. The courts generally ruled restrictions invalid if left unenforced over long periods of time. J. C. Nichols, the developer of Kansas City's Country Club District, described an ordinary chain of events:

> One owner, seeing that another owner has somewhat violated his restriction, goes a little further in the violation. Then some adjoining owner, realizing that the restriction had not been properly regarded by his neighbors, either in disregard or desperation, seriously violates the restriction and suddenly the neighborhood awakens to the fact that the abandonment has become very general and the restrictions of little force.[51]

Historians of covenants have echoed Nichols's observations about the problem of enforcement. "Where enforcement rested on individual or voluntary action," Andrew J. King concludes in his history of covenants in Chicago, "the cost of enforcement and the difficulty of coercing participation generated a desire for public solutions. Though some owners successfully organized to enforce restrictions, their efforts consumed both money and time." Enforcement may have been difficult under the average covenant, but revision was a near impossibility.[52]

The indenture framers for private places tried to overcome this drawback by delegating enforcement power to a lot association or a group of trustees. The average private-street association was an ongoing legal entity, armed with enforcement power and thus alert to preventing violations from getting out of hand. The Kingsbury Place indenture was typical in granting the trustees authority to "employ counsel and institute and prosecute such suits as they may deem necessary or advisable." The private-place association's strength lay in its

ownership of the street and other common areas. As a group with ownership rights, the private-street association had a permanent interest in
protecting the investments of its members. Public-street associations,
on the other hand, too often had to depend on individual vigilance and
the fickle fortunes of "neighborhood spirit."[53]

The Private Place during the Twentieth Century

The first two decades of the twentieth century brought a culmination of
development. Gradually, the private-place model took hold in the suburbs of the city. Parkview, which was founded in 1905, represented the
most significant departure from past practice. Divided between St.
Louis and University City, its 250 homes made it the largest private
place up to that time. The indenture of Parkview abandoned the old
norm of a subdivision-wide assessment for street and alley repairs by
instituting special charges based on the value of front footage of every
lot on a block being improved. The unanimity requirement of Vandeventer Place went by the boards. Under Parkview's rules, only a majority of the lot owners had to agree to approve any revisions. As an extra
safeguard, however, this provision could not go into effect until the
death or resignation of the last trustee.[54]

While Parkview, like previous private places, stipulated minimum
house prices, there were also some innovations. In place of a uniform
rule, it stipulated a separate minimum house price for each block, ranging from four thousand to six thousand dollars, although in the manner of the Forest Park Addition, trustees could make exceptions. Never
before had private-place developers made such sustained appeals to
home buyers of moderate income.[55]

The trustees recognized the tremendous planning implications of
retaining proprietary control of the infrastructure. For example, they
discovered new ways to circumvent free riders. Because the trustees
purchased water from outside sources and then resold it to the residents, they found that they could sever the connection if water bills
were not paid. They even put forward a novel plan to build a "neighborhood heating and hot water plant." It provided that steam heat and
hot water be pumped and then recirculated to each house through two
pipes laid under the street, thus eliminating coal-burning "furnaces,
fuel bills, ash bins and the like." Though the plant was never built (the
reasons why are unclear), the very consideration of such plans indicates
a growing awareness that private ownership of the street easement
offered some revolutionary possibilities.[56]

Along with these trends, however, prospective private-place investors and homeowners had to overcome a lengthening list of disincentives. Most importantly, they were increasingly forced to compete with the increasing levels of governmental spending on infrastructure. Court rulings and new laws lifted legal limitations on special taxes and allowed the assessment of nonabutters to pay for construction and reconstruction costs. Gradually, tax and debt limitations were loosened or evaded, thus freeing general-revenue financing for street and sewer repairs. Per-capita government expenditures nearly doubled between 1880 and 1912. Relieved of financial responsibility for long-term maintenance, developers and prospective residents had less incentive to choose long-term private-street ownership.[57]

Tax increases and local laws slowly chipped away at incentives for private building and ownership of streets and sewers. New laws narrowed the discretion of owners. In 1902, a charter amendment gave the city unlimited power to acquire private sewers by condemnation. Previously, it had been questionable whether the city could obtain sewers through any method, even an outright gift. A later change went still further by mandating that "no map or plat embracing a private place shall be approved unless it conveys to the city the right to place, construct and maintain in such private place, sewers, sewer inlets, water mains, gas mains, underground conduits for electric wires, fire plugs, lamp posts and other conveniences." In effect, the city's franchise monopoly over the public streets had been extended to the private places. Private decisions about use of street easements now could be overridden almost at will.[58]

Although the city government sought and obtained maximum discretion, it did not show much evidence of becoming more eager to acquire privately built streets, sewers, and water mains. This apparent paradox has a simple explanation: the private place was a reliable net-revenue producer for the city government. Private-place owners, through their association fees, relieved the city of spending money for certain services, while at the time they paid the same amount in taxes and assessments as all other citizens. The extra expense of subsidizing the tax-financed counterparts to these services—which they used considerably less than public-street residents—pushed homeowners on more than one private place into going public. The twentieth century witnessed a constant struggle between private places' eagerness to shed certain increasingly burdensome services (sewers, water mains, snow removal, and garbage collection) and their desire to still retain private ownership of (and thus control over) the street.[59]

Despite these hurdles, the private places began a slow revival during 1950s. Some new additions were actually made to their ranks. Homeowners on sections of Pershing and Westminster Avenues formed associations and successfully petitioned the city to privatize their streets. They purchased the water mains and streetlights and assumed their new role as proprietors of Pershing and Westminster "Places." The new private places quickly used their control of the right-of-way to erect gates and close off through traffic.[60]

Urban decay, including a mounting crime rate, had become so acute that for many residents, the advantages of privatization outweighed the additional expense of private-street assessments. By this time, most of the private-place neighborhoods had lost their elite status. Many now had a middle- or upper-middle-income character.

Although less integrated than neighboring streets, private places have not remained all-white areas. Lewis Place, for example, which dates from the early 1890s, is 100 percent black, while West Cabanne Place is nearly 90 percent black. The best current estimate puts the number of street-providing subdivisions in St. Louis and St. Louis County at 450. Of these, only about twenty-five are in St. Louis itself.[61]

The private place deserves much greater attention from historians. The explosive growth in homeowner and condominium associations in recent years underlines the need for new research. Studies thus far have focused on the elites who lived in the private places or on the architecture of the homes themselves. Comparatively little attention has been devoted to examining the private place as an institutional arrangement. If urban historians want to better understand how, in the absence of government intervention, voluntary institutions have provided urban services and coped with inner-city decay, the private place is a good place to begin.[62]

NOTES

This chapter first appeared as David T. Beito and Bruce Smith, 1990. The Formation of Urban Infrastructure through Nongovernmental Planning: The Private Places of St. Louis, 1869–1920. *Journal of Urban History* 16 (3):263–303. Reprinted by permission of Sage Publications.

   1. Schultz and McShane 1977, 389–411; McShane 1979, 279–307; and Tarr 1979, 308–39. For a survey of recent work on urban infrastructure, see Moehring 1982; McShane 1984, 223–28; and Tarr and Konvitz, 1987, 195–226.
   2. Weiss 1987, 3.
   3. Vickery 1972, 10; Washington University 1979, 5. John Noyes, landscape designer for the Missouri Botanical Garden, argued that Pitzman was influenced

by "Baron Haussmann in Paris, and the resulting attractiveness of the streets where building restrictions have been imposed" (Noyes 1915, 206).

4. The deed restrictions remained in effect until the late 1880s, when property owners representing the necessary 1,030 feet consented to allow commercial use and remove the setback requirements. Lucas Place rapidly became a business street. The city speeded the transition by extending the street through Missouri Park in 1889, thus destroying the only buffer to heavy hauling. See Primm 1981, 360; *Missouri Republican* (April 10, 1888); *Missouri Republican* (May 16, 1888); *St. Louis Republic* (January 9, 1889); and Savage 1987, 16–17.

5. *Missouri Republican* (July 11, 1870); Bryan 1962, 8–12.

6. Bryan 1962, 8, 11; Savage 1987, 18; Hunter 1982, 19; Benton Place Account Book, July 1, 1868, April 28, 1901, October 12, 1881 (Benton Place Archives, in possession of Linda Laffey of Benton Place). Also see Samuel Simmons to Montgomery Blair, July 18, 1868; Benton Place, Warranty Deed from Montgomery Blair and Wife to Edward S. Rowse, 1869 (both Container 48, Legal File: "St. Louis: Real Estate, Benton Place, 1869–1870," Papers of the Blair Family, Library of Congress, Washington, D.C.).

7. Vickery 1972, 12–16; Primm 1981, 366; Vandeventer Place, Indenture, June 18, 1870 (Book 413, Recorder of Deeds, St. Louis, Missouri, 25). To calculate these sums in 2001 dollars, I used the dollar conversion calculator of the *Columbia Journalism Review* at <http://www.cjr.org/resources/inflater.asp>.

8. Primm 1981, 366; Vandeventer Place, Indenture. For more on neighborhood associations in other cities during the same period, see Arnold 1979, 3–30. The private-place association differed from the organizations discussed by Arnold because most of its power derived from the ownership of infrastructure.

9. Vandeventer Place, Indenture; *Thomas M. Pierce, Treasurer of Vandeventer Parks, et al. v. St. Louis Union Trust Company,* 311 Mo. 277 (1925); McConachie 1976, 324, 327; and Vickery 1972, 12–16.

10. McConachie 1976, 327; *St. Louis Republic* (May 5, 1895), section 3, 17.

11. McConachie 1976, 326–27. The court concluded that "notwithstanding the assaults of commercial business upon the surrounding neighborhood, the evidence as a whole rather tends to show that Vandeventer Place itself has successfully withstood the advance of the commercial army and has so far maintained its exclusive character as a single family residential district of the highest class." See *Pierce v. St. Louis Union Trust Co.; Pierce v. Sarah Harper,* 311 Mo. 301 (1925).

12. *St. Louis Globe Democrat* (February 19, 1935); Hagen 1970, 342; and Harry B. Wilson to Dickson Terry, January 6, 1958 (St. Louis Neighborhoods Collection, Missouri Historical Society).

13. The estimates were compiled from "Map of the City of St. Louis" (Division of Streets and Sewers, 1897); "Atlas of the City of St. Louis" (St. Louis Plat and Record Company, 1905); "Map of the City of St. Louis" (Division of Streets and Sewers, 1916); and "Map of the City of St. Louis" (City Planning Commission, 1919). All are at the Missouri Historical Society in St. Louis. Undoubtedly, some of the private street subdivisions listed on these maps never went beyond the initial planning stage.

14. *St. Louis Republic* (May 15, 1890); West Cabanne Place, Agreement,

December 28, 1905 (Book 1896, Recorder of Deeds, St. Louis, Missouri, 192); Hunter 1982, 30; and Savage 1987, 36–37. For a social and class profile of the Forest Park Addition, see Young 1986. The Chicago residential developments of Lake Forest (1856) and Riverside (1869) were even earlier exceptions to the grid system (Stern and Massengale 1981, 23–24).

Forest Park Addition, Indenture, May 6, 1890 (Book 951, Recorder of Deeds, St. Louis, Missouri, 244–47). For an illustrated, largely architectural and anecdotal history of Westmoreland and Portland Places, see Hunter 1988.

15. Those private places retaining the unanimous-consent requirement often proved creative in bending the rules in crisis situations. Originally the restrictions for Washington Terrace had also included properties on Delmar Avenue (an adjoining public street). Gradually, Delmar lost virtually all desirability for single-family residences. In 1917, a real-estate operator began building an apartment complex on the avenue in violation of the indenture, which prohibited multifamily housing. The trustees decided against the alternatives of filing suit to prevent construction or proposing a formal change in the indenture, which would have required unanimous consent. Instead, they advised the property owners that because of "changed conditions existing on Delmar Avenue," such a suit would be "unwise." To prevent nullification of the indenture because of nonenforcement, the trustees adopted a policy of giving their formal "consent to waive" restrictions on Delmar while strictly enforcing them on Washington Terrace. See Washington Terrace Trustees to _____, January 25, 1917; Agreement between Washington Terrace Trustees and the United Hebrew Congregation, February 1921; and Stewart McDonald to M. E. Singleton, May 25, 1922 (all Washington Terrace Archives, in possession of Richard J. Scheffler of Washington Terrace).

16. I questioned several historians of the nine largest cities about the frequency of private streets outside of St. Louis: Joel Tarr (Baltimore, Philadelphia, and other cities); Jon Teaford (Cleveland and other cities); Sam Bass Warner Jr. (Boston, Philadelphia, and other cities); Ann Durkin Keating (the Chicago metropolitan area); Mark Goldman (Buffalo); John Ferguson (New Orleans); George Thomas (Philadelphia); and Gunther Barth (San Francisco). While private streets existed in several of these cities, including New Orleans, Philadelphia, and Boston, the number, according to these historians, was not comparable to St. Louis. Numerous calls to city street departments and historical societies in the ten largest cities (Buffalo, Cleveland, Cincinnati, New York City, Chicago, Philadelphia, Boston, New Orleans, and San Francisco) yielded similar results.

17. Savage 1987, 4.

18. *Missouri Republican* (April 22, 1888), 4.

19. Constitution of 1875, Missouri, Article IX, Sections 15–25; Barclay 1962, 17; *Scheme of Separation* 1888, 93; and *St. Louis Republic* (June 5, 1891), 7. As Teaford 1984, 112–16, points out, the electorate in St. Louis feared a return to the city government's lax fiscal record of the late 1860s and early 1870s and thus was particularly reluctant to approve charter amendments increasing taxes, debt, and spending.

20. *Scheme of Separation* 1888, 93; *City Finances* 1890, 48; Schuchat 1937, 120–31; and United States Census Office, *Receipts and Expenditures of One Hun-*

dred Principal or Representative Cities in the United States, Census Bulletin No. 82, June 22, 1891, 4–5.

21. *Scheme of Separation* 1888, 111–12; *St. Louis Republic* (May 5, 1895), 22–24; and United States Census Office, *Report on Valuation, Taxation, and Public Indebtedness, June 1, 1880,* 1884, 220–39. Historian Marshall S. Snow (1887, 27) described the special tax system as "the only practicable method of paving the streets" because charter limitations "made any general fund which could be used for such purposes an impossibility."

22. *Missouri Republican* (April 4, 1881), 4; *City Finances* 1890, xi. The head of the street department observed that because of small appropriations, "it occurs frequently that property owners, if they are willing to pay for the grading and crosswalks, which otherwise would be paid for by the city, improve a public highway privately" (Stemme 1892).

23. *Missouri Republican* (May 22, 1869); *Missouri Republican* (March 7, 1888), 8; United States Census Office, *Social Statistics of Cities,* Census Bulletin No. 100, July 22, 1891, 15; McShane 1979, 279–80. The low percentage of improved streets in Cleveland may have been the by-product of an aggressive annexation campaign. Many "streets" were nothing more than rural dirt roads. Compared to St. Louis, Cleveland enjoyed much greater autonomy on annexation, tax, debt, and spending questions. See Teaford 1984, 86–92; and Teaford 1979, 26, 42–43, 61–62.

24. *Spectator* (September 21, 1889), 21; Board of Public Improvements, *Annual Report,* 1884, 519; *Realty Record and Builder* 14 (September 1907), 1; and *Mirror* 10 (September 20, 1900), 2.

25. Steffens 1903, 545–60; and *Mirror* 11 (August 29, 1901).

26. Chandler 1917, 157–72; *St. Louis Republic* (May 5, 1895), 22. The *Mirror* pointed out that under the charter there was "no possible way of providing adequate sewage for our Western district, as what are now main sewers must be reconstructed, and, under the existing Charter, this can only be paid for out of the general revenues, and there are no general revenues available" (*Mirror* 11 [May 23, 1901], 1). Also see *St. Louis Republic* (June 9, 1891), 12.

27. *The Scheme* (1902), 111–12; *St. Louis Republic* (July 14, 1888), 9; *St. Louis Republic* (June 5, 1891), 7. Although there were fewer complaints about laggard extension of water mains in the West End, the problem did exist. In 1894, for example, city budget constraints spurred developers to build the water main for Flad Avenue (a public street), which runs in a westerly direction from Grand Avenue. See *State ex rel. Attorney General v. City of St. Louis et al.,* 68 SW 901 (1902).

28. *Missouri Republican* (May 13, 1888), 17; *St. Louis Republic* (August 8, 1889), 12; *St. Louis Republic* (March 9, 1890), 13; *St. Louis Republic* (May 5, 1895), 17, 22; and *St. Louis Republic* (April 9, 1890), 12.

29. *St. Louis Republic* (May 5, 1895)O, 17.

30. *St. Louis Republic* (May 5, 1895), 17; *Missouri Republican* (February 19, 1888), 12.

31. *St. Louis Republic* (April 19, 1896), 40.

32. *Missouri Republican* (April 22, 1888), 14; *St. Louis Republic* (May 24, 1891), 22; *St. Louis Republic* (May 16, 1890), 12.

33. Olson 1965, 133–34; Demsetz 1970, 293–306; *Missouri Republican* (June

12, 1887), 5; *Missouri Republican* (May 13, 1888), 17; *St. Louis Globe Democrat* (April 24, 1892), 20; *St. Louis Globe Democrat* (May 1, 1892), 20.

34. MacCallum 1970, 2.

35. Keating 1985, 23. Also see Fogelson 1967, 39–40, 86–87. Economist Daniel Klein argues that businessmen who invested in turnpikes seem to have been motivated primarily by "indirect benefits" such as improved land values and that awareness of these benefits heightened community solidarity. See Klein's essay in this volume.

36. Grinder 1980, 92, 93; Primm 1981, 358.

37. McConachie 1976, 330; *St. Louis Republic* (May 5, 1895), 17; Washington University 1979, 57; Parkview Association, *Annual Report of President,* May 1, 1922, 12–15 (Parkview Archives, in possession of Judy Little of Parkview); Grinder 1980, 98; and Agreement between the Washington Terrace Trustees and Fred M. Williams, March 1925 (Washington Terrace Archives).

38. Buchanan and Faith 1981, 95. See also Fred E. Foldvary's essay in this volume. In his discussion of water pollution in Baltimore, historian Alan D. Anderson (1977) utilizes the economic theory of "negative externalities." Christine Meisner Rosen (1986, 211–56) also addresses several public-goods and free-rider issues from a historical perspective.

39. *St. Louis Republic* (March 10, 1896), 3; Robert Moore of the Joint Committee on Street Cleaning to the President and Directors of the Merchants Exchange of St. Louis, December 28, 1895 (St. Louis Merchants Exchange Collection, Missouri Historical Society, St. Louis); *Municipal Journal and Engineer* (October 1902), 193; *St. Louis Republic* (May 5, 1895), 17; and McConachie 1976, 335–36. As long as residents obeyed the indenture, there seems to have been ample outlet for eccentricities. Harry B. Wilson, who lived in Vandeventer Place, remembered that the "residents were not only disinterested in what their neighbors were doing; they were also totally indifferent to what their neighbors might be thinking of what they were doing." See Wilson to Terry, January 6, 1958.

40. *St. Louis Republic* (July 12, 1903), 8. Delos F. Wilcox, a leading authority on municipal franchises, expressed a typical view when he blamed franchise holders for the "constant tearing up of the streets for the construction or repair of underground fixtures. It often seems astonishing that business can continue to be done in spite of these long-drawn-out and frequently-recurring interferences with the ordinary uses of the city highways" (1910, 122).

41. Hunter 1988, 33; Vickery 1972, 9. On public streets, the chief practical difficulty with laying utilities outside the curb lines was that the easement had to be directly acquired from each individual abutter. Under such a system, the developer, government official, and homeowner had a mutual incentive to rely on the "free" public-street easement. See Hodgkins 1899, 161–63; Wilcox 1910, 91.

42. Newman 1980, 125.

43. Boudreaux and Holcombe 1989. See also the chapters in this volume. My account of Vandeventer Place's decline and fall deserves a caveat. It is true that the changing character of the neighborhood had by the 1940s put the street in dire straits as a residential enclave. Even so, had the Veterans Administration not taken over the property in the 1940s and 1950s, Vandeventer Place may have had a fighting chance of survival.

44. Goodwyn 1978, xix, 319.

45. McConachie 1976, 332–33.

46. McConachie 1976, 331–32; Primm 1981, 367; and *St. Louis Republic* (May 12, 1907), section 4, 1–2. For a list of subscribers, see *St. Louis Republic* (April 10, 1910), section 3, 14.

47. F. A. Delano to E. C. Simmons, January 4, 1906; E. C. Simmons to Oscar L. Whitelaw, January 14, 1907 (both Commercial Club Papers, Missouri Historical Society, St. Louis). Also see McConachie 1976, 333.

48. Civic League 1907, 11.

49. Bartholomew 1918, 1.

50. Polanyi 1951, 191; Lavoie 1985, 37; and Flint 1977, 163, 215. Bartholomew lived in Parkview. In 1945, he cited Parkview's lot association as an example of the kind of neighborhood organization city planners should encourage. See *Parkview Neighbors,* December 1945 (Parkview Archives).

51. Nichols 1929, 139.

52. King 1976, 51.

53. Kingsbury Terrace, Deed, September 21, 1906 (Book 1991, Recorder of Deeds, St. Louis, Missouri, 5). In 1928, Helen C. Monchow conducted a survey of eighty-four from around the country. Only two depended on lot associations for enforcement. As Monchow put it, the "efficiency of such an [owners'] organization as an enforcing agent depends, of course, upon the organization itself, i.e., whether it is an active or only a perfunctory body, whether it is legally constituted or an informal association." See *Use of Deed Restrictions* 1928, 61–64.

54. *St. Louis Republic* (May 24, 1908), section 4, 1; Parkview, Indenture, November 25, 1905 (Book 1910, Recorder of Deeds, St. Louis, Missouri, 1).

55. Parkview, Indenture; Savage 1987, 76; *St. Louis Republic* (June 19, 1904), section 3, 2; *St. Louis Republic* (April 29, 1906), section 5, 10.

56. Parkview, Indenture.

57. In 1880, per-capita government spending in St. Louis was $16.59, against $30.31 for 1912. See United States Census Office, *Report on Valuation,* 226–27; and Department of Commerce, Bureau of the Census, Bulletin 118, *Financial Statistics of Cities Having a Population of Over 30,000: 1912,* 40–41. To trace the gradual loosening of tax, special assessment, spending, and debt limitations, contrast *Scheme of Separation* 1888 and the *Charter of the City of St. Louis, Missouri,* 1914. Also see Porter 1966, 20.

58. *The Scheme,* 1902, 112; *Scheme of Separation* 1888, 113; and *Revised Code of St. Louis,* 1912 (General Ordinances), 352. During the same year, the Missouri Supreme Court upheld the city's authority to purchase private water mains. See *State ex rel. Attorney General v. City of St. Louis et al.* Missouri court rulings have sustained efforts by local governments to impose traffic regulations on private streets, including the installation of stop signals. See Hughes 1959, 594. In 1948, the Missouri Supreme Court ruled that a private street had become de facto "public" for regulatory purposes because the residents had allowed construction of a public school in the subdivision (Weismantel 1960, 44).

59. The Missouri Supreme Court refused to invalidate special taxes on a lot owner to fund a district sewer although it was physically impossible for the property to connect with (and thus benefit from) the sewer. See *Heman v. Schulte et al.,*

66 SW 165 (1901); *Heman v. Allen et al.,* 156 Mo. 542 (1900). Divided between University City and St. Louis, Parkview's history of conflict with officials about transferring certain services has been particularly eventful. See Annual Report of Parkview Trustees, May 9, 1949 (Parkview Archives).

60. Hagen 1970, 334. These street privatizations were enacted under the provisions of Article XXI, Section 14, of the charter (Rev. Code of St. Louis, 1948), which allows abutters to petition the Board of Public Service to have their street vacated. It is not necessary to obtain unanimous consent. The Board of Aldermen, on the recommendation of the Board of Public Service, has complete discretion to reject or accept the vacation (Hughes 1959, 588). The city's power to vacate streets had been sustained by the courts for decades. See, for example, *Glasgow et al. v. City of St. Louis et al.,* 17 SW 743 (1891).

61. Newman 1980, 152; Oakerson 1988, 4. In 1948, in *Shelley v. Kraemer,* 334 U.S. 1 (1948), the U.S. Supreme Court ruled racial restrictions unconstitutional. For more on racial restrictions, including illuminating information about St. Louis, see Vose 1959.

62. From 1975 to 1985, the number of homeowner and condominium associations skyrocketed from twenty-five thousand to ninety thousand (Fitzgerald 1988, 48).

REFERENCES

Anderson, A. D. 1977. *The Origin and Resolution of an Urban Crisis: Baltimore, 1890–1930.* Baltimore: Johns Hopkins University Press.
Arnold, J. L. 1979. The Neighborhood and City Hall: The Origin of Neighborhood Associations in Baltimore, 1880–1911. *Journal of Urban History* 6 (November): 3–30.
Barclay, T. S. 1962. *The St. Louis Home Rule Charter of 1876: Its Framing and Adoption.* Columbia: University of Missouri Press.
Bartholomew, H. 1918. *Zoning For St. Louis: A Fundamental Part of the City Plan.* St. Louis: Nixon-Jones Printing Co.
Boudreaux, D. J., and R. G. Holcombe. 1989. Government by Contract. *Public Finance Quarterly* 17 (3): 264–80.
Bryan, J. A. 1962. *Lafayette Square: The Most Significant Old Neighborhood in St. Louis.* St. Louis: John Albury Bryan.
Buchanan, J. M., and R. L. Faith. 1981. Entrepreneurship and the Internalization of Externalities. *Journal of Law and Economics* 24 (April): 95–111.
Chandler, A. 1917. History of Missouri Sewer Laws. *St. Louis Law Review* 2:157–72.
City Finances: Report of the Comptroller of the City of St. Louis for Fiscal Year 1889–90. 1890. St. Louis: Daly Printing Company.
Civic League of St. Louis. 1907. *A City Plan for St. Louis.* St. Louis: n.p.
Demsetz, H. 1970. The Private Production of Public Goods. *Journal of Law and Economics* 13 (October): 293–306
Fitzgerald, R. 1988. *When Government Goes Private: The Privatization Revolution.* New York: Universe Books.

Flint, B. J. 1977. Zoning and Residential Segregation: A Social and Physical History, 1910–40. Ph.D. diss., University of Chicago.

Fogelson, R. M. 1967. *The Fragmented Metropolis: Los Angeles, 1850–1930.* Cambridge: Harvard University Press.

Goodwyn, L. 1978. *The Populist Moment: A Short History of the Agrarian Revolt in America.* New York: Oxford University Press.

Grinder, R. D. 1980. The Battle for Clean Air: The Smoke Problem in Post–Civil War America. In *Pollution and Reform in American Cities, 1870–1930,* ed. M. V. Melosi. Austin: University of Texas Press.

Hagen, H. 1970. *This is Our Saint Louis.* St. Louis: Knight Publishing Company.

Hodgkins, H. C. 1899. The Economic Arrangement and Construction of Sub-Structures in Streets. *Report of Proceedings . . . of the American Water Works Association* 19 (May 16–19):161–65.

Hughes, R. L. 1959. The Law and Private Streets. *Saint Louis University Law Journal* 5 (fall).

Hunter, J. K. 1982. *Kingsbury Place: The First Two Hundred Years.* St. Louis: C. V. Mosby Company.

———. 1988. *Westmoreland and Portland Places: The History and Architecture of America's Premier Private Streets, 1888–1988.* Columbia: University of Missouri Press.

Keating, A. D. 1985. From City to Metropolis: Infrastructure and Residential Growth in Chicago. In *Infrastructure and Urban Growth in the Nineteenth Century.* Chicago: Public Works Historical Society.

King, A. J. 1976. Law and Land Use in Chicago: A Prehistory of Modern Zoning. Ph.D. diss., University of Wisconsin, Madison.

Lavoie, D. 1985. *National Economic Planning: What is Left?* Cambridge, Mass.: Ballinger Publishing Company.

MacCallum, S. 1970. *The Art of Community.* Menlo Park, Calif.: Institute for Humane Studies, Inc.

McConachie, A. S. 1976. The "Big Cinch": A Business Elite in the Life of a City, St. Louis, 1895–1915. Ph.D. diss., Washington University.

McShane, C. 1979. Transforming the Use of Urban Space: A Look at the Revolution in Street Pavements, 1880–1924. *Journal of Urban History* 5 (May): 279–307.

———. 1984. Essays in Public Works History. *Journal of Urban History* 10 (February): 223–28.

Moehring, E. P. 1982. *Public Works and Urban History: Recent Trends and New Directions.* Chicago: Public Works Historical Society.

Monchow, H. C. 1928. *The Use of Deed Restrictions in Subdivision Development.* Chicago: Institute for Research in Land Economics and Public Utilities.

Newman, O. 1980. *Community of Interest.* New York: Anchor Press/Doubleday.

Nichols, J. C. 1929. A Developer's View of Deed Restrictions. *Journal of Land and Public Utility Economics* 5 (May): 139.

Noyes, J. 1915. The "Places" of St. Louis: An Effective Development of Residential Streets with Building Restrictions. *American City* 12 (March): 206.

Oakerson, R. J. 1988. Subdivisions as Service Provision Units: The Case of Private Streets in St. Louis County. Paper presented at ACIR Conference on Residential Community Associations, June 13–14.

Olson, M. 1965. *The Logic of Collective Action: Public Goods and the Theory of Groups.* Cambridge: Harvard University Press.

Polanyi, M. 1951. *The Logic of Liberty: Reflections and Rejoinders.* Chicago: University of Chicago Press.

Porter, C. H. 1966. Charter Reform in St. Louis, 1900–1914. Master's thesis, Washington University.

Primm, J. N. 1981. *Lion of the Valley, St. Louis, Missouri.* Boulder, Colo.: Pruett Publishing Company.

Rosen, C. M. 1986. Infrastructural Improvement in Nineteenth-Century Cities: A Conceptual Framework and Cases. *Journal of Urban History* 12 (May): 211–56.

Savage, Charles C. 1987. *Architecture of the Private Streets of St. Louis: The Architects and the Houses They Designed.* Columbia: University of Missouri Press.

Scheme of Separation Between St. Louis and County and Charter of the City of St. Louis, with all Amendments and Modifications to May 1, 1902: and Constitutional Provisions Specially Applicable to the City of St. Louis. 1902. St. Louis: Woodward and Tiernan Printing Co.

Scheme of Separation Between St. Louis City and County and the Charter of the City of St. Louis. 1888. St. Louis: Daly Printing Company.

Schuchat, Stanley R. 1937. *Sinking Fund and Bonded Debt of City of St. Louis.* Master's thesis, Washington University.

Schultz, S. K., and C. McShane. 1977. To Engineer the Metropolis: Sewers, Sanitation, and City Planning in Late-Nineteenth-Century America. *Journal of American History* 65 (September): 389–411.

Snow, M. S. 1887. *The City Government of Saint Louis.* Baltimore: Johns Hopkins University Studies in Historical and Political Science.

Steffens, L. 1903. The Shamelessness of St. Louis. *McClure's Magazine* 20 (March): 545–60.

Stemme, F. L. 1892. *How to Obtain Public Improvements in the City of St. Louis.* N.p.

Stern, R. A. M., and J. M. Massengale. 1981. *The Anglo American Suburb.* London: Architectural Design.

Tarr, J. A. 1979. The Separate vs. Combined Sewer Problem: A Case Study in Urban Technology Design Choice. *Journal of Urban History* 5 (May): 308–39.

Tarr, J. A., and J. W. Konvitz. 1987. Patterns in the Development of the Urban Infrastructure. In *American Urbanism: A Historiographical Review,* ed. H. Gillette Jr. and Z. L. Miller. New York: Greenwood Press.

Teaford, J. C. 1979. *City and Suburb: The Political Fragmentation of Metropolitan America, 1850–1970.* Baltimore: Johns Hopkins University Press.

———. 1984. *The Unheralded Triumph: City Government in America, 1870–1900.* Baltimore: Johns Hopkins University Press.

Use of Deed Restrictions in Subdivision Development. 1928. Chicago: Institute for Research in Land Economics and Public Utilities.

Vickery, R. L., Jr. 1972. *Anthrophysical Form: Two Families and Their Neighborhood Environments.* Charlottesville: University Press of Virginia.

Vose, C. E. 1959. *Caucasians Only: The Supreme Court, the NAACP, and the Restrictive Covenant Cases.* Berkeley: University of California Press.

Washington University Historic Preservation Program. 1979. *Urban Oasis: 75 Years in Parkview a St. Louis Private Place.* St. Louis: Boars' Head Press.

Weismantel, W. L. 1960. Public Power to Close Residential Streets to Through Traffic. *Missouri Law Review* 25.

Weiss, M. A. 1987. *The Rise of the Community Builders: The American Real Estate Industry and Urban Land Planning.* New York: Columbia University Press.

Wilcox, D. F. 1910. *Municipal Franchises: A Description of the Terms and Conditions Upon Which Private Corporations Enjoy Special Privileges in the Streets of American Cities.* New York: Gervaise Press.

Young, D. M. 1986. *Living inside the Gates: Private Place Residence as a Factor in Social Consolidation.* St. Louis: n.p.

4

The Voluntary Provision
of Public Goods?

The Turnpike Companies of Early America

Daniel Klein

The heroic role of the agent called "government" in the simple public-goods model is clear enough, but the relevance of the model is still in dispute. A long list of doubters has challenged the premise that the government has the needed information, acts efficiently, and acts in the public interest. Also, skeptics have contended that the free-rider problem of many public goods is not as ineluctable as others have suggested. Historical studies have shown the potency of voluntary association in such fields as lighthouse provision (Coase 1974), education (Ellig and High 1988), bee pollination (Cheung 1973), law and order (Anderson and Hill 1979; Benson 1998), neighborhood infrastructure (Beito, this volume), and agricultural research (Majewski 1989), among others (Cowen 1988; Wooldridge 1970).

To help assess the relevance of the simple public-goods model, I discuss the American experience with private turnpike roads. Extreme publicness marked the turnpikes, both in jointness of consumption and in nonexcludability.[1] The excludability problem was partly the result of legal restrictions on toll collection. These restrictions help to explain turnpike unprofitability, which was discovered quickly. The turnpikes afforded enormous indirect and external benefits, however, to nearby farms, landholdings, and businesses. Since unprofitability was usually foreseen, stock subscription—necessary to construct the road—was essentially a means of paying for road benefits.

There were two excludability problems: people could use the road without paying a toll, and people could indirectly benefit from the road without buying stock. Though they are related, the latter is the crux of the public-goods problem at hand.

The turnpike companies got started in the 1790s and were in sharp decline by the 1830s, though many turnpikes were operating at the turn of the twentieth century.[2] I treat turnpikes in New England and the Middle Atlantic states (New York, Pennsylvania, New Jersey, and Maryland). Except in Pennsylvania, these turnpikes were almost entirely financed by private subscription to stock, while those in most other states were mixed enterprises.[3] Various facets of toll-road history are being explored by a coresearcher and myself, but here the discussion is confined to the public-goods aspect of the turnpikes.[4]

Turnpike Creation and Operation

At the end of the eighteenth century observers saw a transition in road management. Until then local public systems feebly cared for the roads. As settlement expanded and the large Eastern centers sought improved trade routes, pressure for road improvement brought forth a radical alternative: turnpikes, a pay-as-you-go way of financing. A number of publicly operated turnpikes were organized, patterned after the British turnpike trusts of the day, but even this method of road improvement demanded too much from the existing public administration.[5] States turned to private initiative.[6]

The turnpike companies were legally organized like corporate businesses of the day. The first, connecting Philadelphia and Lancaster, was chartered in 1792, opened in 1794, and proved significant in the competition for trade. Regional rivalries led state legislatures to charter turnpike companies as quickly as private individuals petitioned for them. By 1800, sixty-nine companies had been chartered in the states under investigation.[7]

While legislators readily sanctioned road provision by private association, they wrote extensive regulations into the company charters. Charters usually determined the company's total stock, which merely reflected the company's recommendation and could be changed easily. Powers of eminent domain were stipulated, existing trails or public roadbeds were usually granted to the companies, and monopoly assurance against new parallel routes was sometimes granted. Details for construction were given, and of course, toll rates and toll collection were tightly controlled. In most cases, turnpikes were individually regulated, but on the major points all the states imposed very similar regulations. Inspection and enforcement were assigned to state-appointed commissioners or county officials. While the companies abided strictly by the financial regulations, maintenance often did not live up to stipulations, and the local inspection machinery was known to be lenient.[8]

In theory toll rates could be increased if dividends fell short of the low mark (usually 6, 8, or 10 percent of investment) or decreased if dividends surpassed the high mark (usually 10, 12, or 15 percent) (Durrenberger 1931, 111). In fact, dividends persisted far short of the low mark, but with rare exception, toll rates remained at their initial levels (P. E. Taylor 1934, 152). The legislatures did not renege on their promises.[9] Rather, it was common for a company simply not to apply for toll increases.

There are two possible explanations for the absence of rate increases. The first is that the companies may not have been expecting or even hoping to earn direct profits; the reasons behind this interpretation become apparent in the remainder of this essay.

Second, turnpikes could not have enhanced returns by increasing toll rates because of the many concessions to local travelers. Charters required that toll gates be five or, more often, ten miles apart, permitting much traffic to go toll-free. Another means of free travel was provided by the proliferation of informal routes bypassing the gate, known as shunpikes (Durrenberger 1931, 178; P. E. Taylor, 1934, 200–204).[10] The location of a gate was set by the legislature and could be altered only by separate legislative enactment. Had turnpikes been free to multiply and relocate gates they could have better combated shunpiking. Finally, there were toll exemptions. Typically, those exempted included people traveling "on the common and ordinary business of family concerns"—to or from public worship, a town meeting, a gristmill, a blacksmith's shop, and on military duty—and those "residing within one mile of . . . [the] gate."[11] Gatekeepers found it troublesome to deny exemption and were forced to adopt a lenient attitude (P. E. Taylor 1934, 147). Under such conditions, higher tolls would not have increased revenue because travelers passing for free would not have paid higher tolls and those inclined toward evading tolls would have done so more often. In addition, a small fraction of the through traffic would have opted for public roads or other forms of transportation.

Unprofitability

The first part of our public-goods story concerns the universal and well-documented poverty of the turnpikes.[12] Of the Middle Atlantic states, Joseph Durrenberger (1931, 112) writes, "Considered from the standpoint of dividends, turnpike stocks were exceedingly poor investments." Of the many turnpikes of New England, P. E. Taylor (1934, 266) notes, "[I]t is doubtful whether more than five or six paid their proprietors even reasonably well." Though information from the period is fragmentary, P. E. Taylor (1934, 281) finds that turnpike dividends in New England were far below those of other enterprises:

> [I]t is quite obvious that no possible selection of turnpike companies could compare in earning power. . . . Between the years 1825 and 1855, six of the largest textile factories in Massachusetts produced average yearly dividends ranging from 6.48% to 12.79%. The Massachusetts bank averaged 6.53% annual return on its capital investment from 1785 to 1855, while the Union bank produced an average of 6.91% between 1795 and 1855. Three Boston insurance companies doing fire and marine business produced annual dividends averaging 8.38%, 15.44%, and 20.34% during the period 1818–1855.

In contrast, even the undiscounted total net payment of a turnpike was commonly negative. References to average yearly dividends usually put the figure barely above zero.[13] In Pennsylvania the state held a peak of two million dollars in turnpike stocks, but "annual dividends accruing from that investment invariably totaled less than five thousand dollars" (one-fourth of 1 percent) (Hartz 1948, 92). Once we take into account assessments (occasional company demands on stockholders for additional payments), it is not clear whether yearly "earnings" for many turnpikes were even positive.[14] Moreover, the capital value of the stock was usually completely lost. The little trading that occurred was almost always on terms well below par: "Turnpike stock within a few years usually sold at far below its original cost" (Parks 1967, 19).[15]

Turnpikes usually reverted to public control through abandonment. By that time the stock was usually worthless, and the owners were eager to relieve themselves of the responsibility of maintaining the road. Rarely was any compensation made to road investors. It appears that in all of New England only two turnpike companies recouped their original investments when their turnpikes reverted to the public.[16] In fact, only 5 percent of New England turnpikes received any compensation whatsoever when companies surrendered their franchises.[17] It is safe to say that from beginning to end turnpike stock was an abysmal investment.

"Clear from the Beginning"

[I]t seems to have been generally known long before the rush of construction subsided that turnpike stock was worthless.
—F. J. Wood, *The Turnpikes of New England and Evolution of the Same through England, Virginia, and Maryland*

[T]he turnpikes did not make money. As a whole this was true; as a rule it was clear from the beginning.
—E. C. Kirkland, *Men, Cities and Transportation: A Study in New England History, 1920–1900*

If we wish to show that the turnpikes were public goods and that stock subscription was in essence a voluntary contribution, it is necessary to show not only that turnpike stock was a bad investment but also that investors expected as much. Investor expectations are hard to document, but a combination of factors strongly supports the notion that turnpike investment was not expected to be profitable.

Investors in the very earliest turnpike companies might have thought that the stock would be as remunerative as investments in toll bridges had been. When the first private toll-bridge company, the Charles-River Bridge, opened in 1786, it was called "the greatest effect of private enterprise in the United States."[18] Its investors were rewarded with a return of 10.5 percent annually for the first six years. Joseph Davis says, "Its clear promise of financial success, justified by the dividends of its early years, drew attention to the profits awaiting claimants in similar fields" (1917, 2:189; see also 216). Through 1798, about fifty-nine bridge companies were chartered in the states under consideration, principally in New England. Many of them failed and some were unprofitable, but a considerable number, especially in the Boston area, had proven themselves lucrative by the end of the century. In contrast to the turnpikes, the bridges did not suffer from toll evasion or liberal exemptions, and when profits were low investors commonly obtained toll increases (Davis 1917, 2:229). Investors may not have anticipated the special problems that would plague turnpikes, so perhaps the bridge companies were an encouraging example.

After the first decade of turnpike construction all but the most foolhardy must have realized what turnpikes held in store. As early as 1800 the president of the First Massachusetts Turnpike wrote a letter cautioning other investors not to expect remuneration from turnpike stock (Parks 1966, 73). Similarly, former Federalist Congressmen and turnpike president Fisher Ames wrote in 1802, "Turnpikes with fairest prospect of success have seldom proved profitable" (quoted in Parks 1966, 74). In Connecticut, where, viewed comparatively, turnpike dividends were enviable, a newspaper article of 1805 suggested that turnpikes receive "annually on their capital, little, if any, more than half the common and established interest on money."[19]

The examples of unprofitable companies were plain. The few moderately profitable companies were graced with a combination of advantages: low cost of land acquisition, good condition of the preexisting roadbed, minimal bridge building, and substantial traffic volume.[20] Any alert investor could discover whether a particular town's project had similar advantages. Almost invariably it did not.

Perhaps the best reason for rejecting the claims that turnpike investors were searching primarily for direct remuneration is that an alternative hypothesis presents itself.

The Quest for Indirect Benefits

Although dividends were meager, indirect and external benefits of turnpikes were copious. Improved roads lowered transportation costs, stimulated commerce, and increased land values. Henry Clay did not overstate the point when he said:

> I think it very possible that the capitalist who should invest his money in these objects [turnpikes] might not be reimbursed three percent annually upon it; and yet society in various forms, might actually reap fifteen or twenty per cent. The benefit resulting from a turnpike road made by private association is divided between the capitalist, who received his toll, the land through which it passes and which is augmented in its value, and the commodities whose value is enhanced by the diminished expense of transportation. (Quoted in Durrenberger 1931, 125)

The quest for indirect benefits is abundantly evident in contemporary writings. An essay advocating turnpike roads in New York, appearing in 1795, says that such an improvement "lays open all the unexploited resources of a country to come forth to daylight, and to a market."[21] In 1797 we find a discussion in five installments of roads and turnpikes by "A Philanthropist." He expounds at great length on the social importance of good roads and argues that turnpikes are the best means of achieving them. Benjamin De Witt (1972, 215), writing in 1807 of New York's turnpikes, says that turnpikes "encourage settlements, open new channels for the transportation of produce and merchandise, increase the products of agriculture, and facilitate every species of internal commerce." The 1811 tract by William J. Duane (1811, 5) "Addressed to the People of Pennsylvania" challenged the notion that "you are more benefited by having a paltry interest from the bank, than if your money was invested in stocks for roads and canals. . . . [M]oney invested in bank stock is waste in comparison with its employment in enabling you to carry your produce and manufactures to every market; and in raising the value of your woods as well as your cleared lands." Likewise, Fisher Ames in New England said most were turnpikes built "to facilitate country produce on its way to market" (quoted in Parks 1966, 71).[22]

Less explicit evidence for the "indirect-benefits" interpretation is ample. Foremost is that "[s]hares in the various companies were almost invariably owned locally, that is, in the towns through which the road passes" (P. E. Taylor 1934, 165; also see Durrenberger 1931, 102). Naturally, the people in the vicinity of the turnpike would reap the most benefits from it. In the few cases where a sizeable portion of the stock was owned by outsiders, the quest for indirect benefits is still evident. Businessmen in larger commercial centers supported routes that would bring trade. For instance, "Merchants and traders in New York sponsored pikes leading across New Jersey in order to tap the Delaware Valley trade which would otherwise have gone entirely to Philadelphia" (Lane 1939, 156). It might be argued that local ownership was simply a consequence of marketing the shares locally, but the indirect-benefits interpretation seems undeniable when we consider a second factor: those who contributed to a project were generally those who most stood to gain from it: "With but few exceptions, the vast majority of the stockholders in turnpike were either farmers, land speculators, merchants or individuals and firms interested in commerce" (Durrenberger 1931, 104).[23]

As F. J. Wood (1919, 63) notes: "The conclusion is forced upon us that the larger part of the turnpikes of New England were built in hopes of benefiting the towns and local business conducted in them, counting more upon collateral results than upon the direct returns in the matter of tolls." Similarly, Durrenberger (1931, 104) says of the Middle Atlantic states:

[S]ubscribers were usually more interested in the possible benefits the new lines of communication would bring than in the profitableness of the investment. In other words subscriptions were frequently looked upon as contributions to effect some public improvement that would pay its chief return in an indirect manner rather than in dividends.[24]

A Public-Goods Problem?

To what extent can we expect private initiative to have been successful in providing roads? Despite the large social benefits of the roads, it seems that the individual could find no advantage in supporting them. Since citizens knew that turnpike stock was a poor investment, purchasing stock was much like paying for the road. Once stock subscriptions were sufficient to construct the road, there would be no way to withhold the benefits of the road from those who did not contribute. The input of a single individual would not make the difference, or so it would seem. For an arbitrary sample of fifty-four turnpike towns, the 1810 average population was 2,153, 38 percent of which had reached twenty-seven years of age.[25] If, say, half of these people stood to gain significantly from a turnpike and a turnpike engendered benefits for two towns, then 818 people were prospective beneficiaries of a turnpike (which typically had a construction cost of seven hundred to three thousand dollars per mile and a length of fifteen to forty miles).[26] This is hardly a small-group situation. On the basis of narrow self-interest it would have been foolish for any one person to make a voluntary sacrifice. Turnpike stock subscription appears to have been a free-rider problem par excellence; we would expect to find the lamentable results of the simple public-goods model.

Turnpike Provision

In view of the apparent free-rider problem, turnpike success was striking. The movement built new roads at rates previously unknown in America. Over $11 million was invested in turnpikes in New York, some $6.5 million in New England, and over $4.5 million (excluding state investment) in Pennsylvania (Durrenberger 1931, 61, 102; P. E.

Taylor 1934, 211). Wood (1919, 63) informs us that based on the population of 1830, per-capita turnpike investment was approximately $3.90 in Massachusetts. Between 1794 and 1840, 238 private New England turnpikes built and operated about 3,750 miles of road.[27] New York led all other states in turnpike mileage with over 4,000 miles as of 1821. Pennsylvania was second, reaching a peak of about 2,400 miles in 1832. New Jersey's companies operated 550 miles by 1821; Maryland's operated 300 miles of private road in 1830 (Durrenberger 1931, 61, 56, 74, 70). Turnpikes also represented a great improvement in road quality (P. E. Taylor 1934, 334; Parks 1967, 23, 27).

The local turnpike was supported by an area's more prominent citizens, but it is not as though a handful of affluent landowners paid for any particular project. Stock subscription was broad based. In most cases upward of fifty people contributed, usually over one hundred for a larger turnpike, with no one holding more than 15 percent of the stock.[28]

After the most traveled routes had been converted to turnpikes, it became more difficult to raise money for their construction.[29] Nonetheless, turnpikes continued to be built, even though by 1805 hope of direct remuneration had disappeared. Yet between 1805 and 1838 over five hundred turnpikes were chartered and built, each one representing a separate instance of public-good provision.[30] I make no claim that private association overcame the free-rider problem in every case or that turnpike construction satisfied blackboard Paretian conditions. Rather, I claim that even though the turnpikes offered enormous nonexcludable benefits, far outweighing the costs of the projects, a straight application of the simple public-goods model would lead us to doubt that many turnpikes were ever built or that a single one was built after 1805. Why does this model not apply?

The literature on turnpikes is old and primarily narrative. It is not surprising that while they emphasize the inducement of indirect benefits in supporting turnpike construction, turnpike historians have failed to point out, much less address, the free-rider problem involved. In taking up the matter, we must rely on more than narrow turnpike history.

Towns, Independent and Vigorous

Towns of the early nineteenth century were independent and strong, characteristics that have since perished. Through the colonial period the town had become the organizing principle of society. In the first three decades of the republic, the township held almost all of the administrative power of government. The states had uncontested law-making powers, and economies of scale dictated that the counties attend to a few services (courts, prisons, and road commissioners), but the towns governed their own affairs and executed the directives of the state. Alexis de Tocqueville, in his masterful *Democracy in America*, says the towns "are independent in all that concerns themselves alone; and among the inhabitants of New England I believe that not a man is to be found who would acknowledge that the state has any right to interfere in their town affairs." When carrying out state laws, "[s]trict as this obligation is, the government of the state imposes it in principle only, and in its performance the township resumes all its independent rights" (1945, 1:68). The participatory nature of town government in early America has been well noted. This feature often makes it pointless to draw lines separating private and public works.[31]

The unity and effectiveness of towns in part arose from their commercial and social isolation. Until the nineteenth century, people traveled rarely and traded little with those from other towns (P. E. Taylor 1934, 31–32). Self-sufficiency nurtured multitudinous social ties among the townspeople.

Certain historical currents may also have contributed to the spirit of participation. In Revolutionary times religious indoctrination in the individual and religious organization in the community usually ran deep. After the Revolution religious fervor intensified in the movement known as the Second Great Awakening, which was probably helped along by the passage of general incorporation laws for religious congregations (such as New York's in 1784). Whether they were "New Light" denominations or those of longer tradition, religious congregations often showed a penchant for making themselves busy in various improvement endeavors, such as schools, libraries, and poor relief. By generating the requisite social relations, or "social capital" (Coleman 1988), as well as human capital (Seavoy 1978, 60), the religious and benevolent activities not only incited but empowered the application of voluntary efforts to community goals (Matthews 1969; Brown 1973, 68). A related thesis (Elkins and McKitrick 1954a, 1954b) associates local activism with the pervasiveness of leadership roles in a young community.

The Cooperative Citizenry

The strong cooperative spirit of Americans especially fascinated Tocqueville.[32] Writing in the 1830s, he said: "In no country in the world do the citizens make such exertions for the common weal. I know of no people who have established schools so numerous, places of public worship better suited to the wants of the inhabitants, or roads kept in better repair" (1945, 1:95). The citizens' cooperation with government efforts is noteworthy, but more significant is their willingness to forge public improvements by voluntary association:

> Americans . . . constantly form associations. They have not only commercial and manufacturing companies, in which all take part, but associations of a thousand other kinds, religious, moral, serious, futile, general or restricted, enormous or diminutive. The Americans make associations to give entertainments, to found seminaries, to build inns, to construct churches, to diffuse books, to send missionaries to the antipodes; in this manner they found hospitals, prisons, and schools. If it is proposed to inculcate some truth or to foster some feeling by the encouragement of a great example, they form a society. (Tocqueville 1945, 2:114)

Tocqueville also speaks of another often-cited public good: crime prevention. Although no state police existed and local public forces were minimal, "in no country does crime more rarely elude punishment. The reason is that everyone conceives himself to be interested in furnishing evidence of the crime and in seizing the delinquent. . . . I witnessed the spontaneous formation of committees in a county for the pursuit and prosecution of a man who had committed a great crime" (1945, 1:99). Similar private, nonprofit institutions for fire fighting or education in early American society have been studied by economists (McChesney 1986; Ellig and High 1988).[33]

The cooperative spirit expressed itself in enterprises much like the turnpikes. In his comprehensive study of American business incorporations up to 1800, Davis (1917, 2:284–85) points out that many enterprises were undertaken to make improvements and debates whether to count these as business corporations. He readily excludes the marine and agricultural societies, but then come corporations for land improvement, lumber cultivation, and inland navigation. For example, a "case near the line" is that of the River Machine Company, incorporated in 1790 to dredge the Providence River. Davis notes that "[t]he merchants of Providence had agreed to raise $1,000 in forty 'equal shares'" for the project. The company was to collect tolls from certain vessels, but any surplus was to be used at the end of twenty years for other improvements. "Thus no dividends were contemplated," Davis says.

In financing, many turnpikes closely resembled this dredging company: numerous people contributed liberally to the large fixed costs, and then just enough revenue was collected to sustain operations. Before it became standard practice to name a turnpike company according to the towns it connected, the first private turnpike company chartered in New England (1794) was entitled "The Society for Establishing and Supporting a Turnpike Road from Cepatchit Bridge, in Gloucester, to Connecticut Line" (P. E. Taylor 1934, 125). Even after they were given standard business-sounding titles, we occasionally find a turnpike company calling itself a "society."[34]

Selective Incentives (Social Pressure, etc.)

In *The Logic of Collective Action* Mancur Olson (1971, 35) develops the idea of selective incentives:

> [A] *"selective"* incentive will stimulate a rational individual in a latent group to act in a group-oriented way. In such circumstances group action can be obtained only through an incentive that operates, not indiscriminately, like the collective good, upon the group as a whole, but rather *selectively* toward the individuals in that group. The incentive must be "selective" so that those who do not joint the organization working for the group's interest, or in other ways contribute to the attainment of the group's interest, can be treated differently from those who do.[35]

We are especially interested in negative selective incentives, which are punishments for failing to bear an appropriate share of the collective effort.[36] Selective incentives are particularly effective in closed, homogenous groups. The failure of some to cooperate will attract attention: "Their friends might use 'social pressure' to encourage them to do their part . . . and such steps might be effective, for . . . most people value the fellowship of their friends and associates, and value social status, personal prestige, and self-esteem" (Olson 1971, 60).[37] Such was the case for the turnpike communities of one or five thousand people. For the average turnpike stockholder, "those in control [of the turnpike] were his neighbors and personally known to him" (P. E. Taylor 1934, 168). Of voluntary associations in Massachusetts in the turnpike age, Richard Brown (1973, 68) says, "The feelings of personal recognition, self-improvement, and mutual reinforcement that members derived from participation were sometimes as important as the more explicit purposes of the organization."

A number of social-pressure tactics were employed in the case of turnpikes. Foremost were the community gatherings called to make up a plan and sell stock in the company. The town meeting was a central institution in which all important residents were expected to participate. John Sly (1930, 107) reports that in the early 1800s "[t]he town meeting was . . . at the highest point of development." The turnpike meetings were well attended, and stock pledges were made publicly. For example, Wood (1919, 69) says that the Fifth Massachusetts Turnpike "was formally organized at a meeting held in the inn of Oliver Chapin, probably early in 1799, and sixteen hundred shares were issued with a par value of $100 each." Meetings with fifty and one hundred people attending have been recorded.[38] Through introspection if nothing else we can recognize the susceptibility to rousing speeches, the pointed inquiries, and the sidelong glances operating at such fund-raisers.

Turnpike promoters relied on the most basic form of selective incentive: person-to-person solicitation. In an 1808 letter regarding the formation of the York and Conewago Canal Turnpike, the writer tells of those who "have with so liberal a hand contributed to the Turnpike feeling a considerable responsibility, having used every exertion with the people of this place to promote it."[39]

Bearing out Tocqueville's claim that Americans formed committees no matter how "diminutive," we find cases of turnpike companies organizing solicitation forces. For the Hingham and Quincy Turnpike, "[s]everal committees were appointed to solicit subscriptions to the stock of the corporation, and one committee was intrusted with the single duty of so presenting the advantages of the enterprise to Reverend Henry Coleman of Hingham as to give his aid and influence to the undertaking" (Wood 1919, 178). [40] Similarly, we find the following in the minutes book of the Minisink and Montgomery Turnpike Company: "Resolved, That James Finch Jun. and David Mason be a Committee to apply to the People living west of the Shawangunk Mountain for subscriptions. . . ."[41]

Adam G. Mappa, president and chief organizer of the Utica Turnpike, needed no warrant to solicit his fellow townspeople. To win the support of prominent locals, he "set forth in forcible language and at great length the advantages that would accrue to Utica by completion of the road" (Durant 1878, 177). Some details of the campaign are provided in the following extract of an 1808 letter from Mappa to a Mr. Walton:

I have begged with all my power & might pro bono publico. you [*sic*] my dear sir I hope will follow my example . . . [with] our friends Miller and Van Rensselear as soon [as] these gentlemen . . . return and can be taken hold of. Mr. Hogan informed me that he did not know the Turnpike Road was laid over his lands. How can it be possible that you, my dear Walton, did neglect to inform Mr. H. of this advantage and request (as you promised me) his assistance in subscribing generously towards our wants. O my friend, if you forget us, if you abandon the T.P. [turnpike] interest, all is over, we shall sink in the mud & that very dirty too. Retrieve therefore the opportunity lost on the return of friend Hogan, and do not forget any of all those whom you can reach. . . . (Quoted in Jackson 1959, 22)

Mappa's letters are prime examples of what Tocqueville (1945, 2:114) called "the extreme skill with which the inhabitants of the United States succeeded in proposing a common object for the exertions of a great many men and inducing them voluntarily to pursue it." Mappa's letters also show that generating selective incentives is itself a costly public good but that some people will eagerly take it upon themselves to provide them.[42] The Utica Turnpike never paid its stockholders well, but it lasted until 1848, when it was transformed into a plank-road company.[43]

The struggle to gather support is shown in a letter to John Rutherfurd, a subscriber in several turnpikes, about a newly incorporated turnpike through Trenton: "We open the books on Thursday next—and shall try every means to get the company organized—you know how little spirit prevails with the citizens of this place for any public improvement—but intend pushing them hard." Further, the writer expresses his hope that Rutherford "may think so favourable of [the project]—as to give orders to some friend here to subscribe largely—."[44]

Tocqueville and Olson both discuss another mode of selective incentives used by turnpike communities. Tocqueville (1945, 2:119) writes, "nothing but a newspaper can drop the same thought into a thousand minds at the same moment," and comments that by means of a newspaper "you can persuade every man whose help you require that his private interest obliges him voluntarily to unite his exertions to the exertions of all the others." Similarly, Olson (1971, 63) notes that through media propaganda "about the worthiness of the attempt to satisfy the common interest in question," members of a latent group may "develop social pressure not entirely unlike those that can be generated in a face-to-face group."[45]

Newspapers proliferated in America, and people took a keen interest in reports on local affairs (Tocqueville 1945, 2:114–22; Gunn 1988, 52). To spur feelings of duty, announcements of the formation of a turnpike company often spoke of the public worthiness of the road. Within a five-month period the *Courier of New Hampshire* (Concord) carried communications of three different turnpike companies, saying that their project "would be beneficial to the public in general," "would be of great public utility," and "would open extensive communication from West to East through the middle of New Hampshire . . . and would tend to increase the commerce of our own Metropolis."[46] In other announcements the element of moral suasion is more pronounced. After announcing that the books of the Great Northern Turnpike were open for subscription, a communication adds: "N.B. the object of the contemplated road is so obviously important to the public and to individuals, (as it will facilitate a direct intercourse between the cities of Montreal and Albany, without a single ferry, and generally over a level country,) that great hopes are entertained of its speedy execution."[47] A 1798 communication of the Hartford and New Haven Turnpike says, "And it being an object of great public utility, it is hoped the citizens of this state will manifest their public spirit on the occasion, and feel themselves disposed to promote it by an advance of the necessary sums of money, and will without hesitation fill up the subscription."[48]

Between Schenectady and Albany the champion promoter Elkanah Watson went to work.[49] Using the names "A Friend to Turnpikes," "A.Z.," "A Republican," and "The Public Good," Watson appealed to public spirit, patriotism, and commercial interest in his campaigns for turnpikes. Rarely did he appeal to direct remuneration from the stock. In 1801, in one of his many pieces promoting the Albany and Schenectady Turnpike, Watson (1758–1842, 40) declaims:

> [A]s its importance is admitted on all hands, the adventurers are entitled from the public the most decisive and liberal encouragement to complete the road. . . .
>
> As respects the citizens of Albany, especially the mercantile interest, they must be asleep indeed if they can suffer another year to pass over without exerting all their efforts to bring about this important enterprise.

In a later article Watson (1758–1842, 40) reports on the success of a preliminary meeting to found the turnpike and adds: "As our Citizens appear to be universally impressed with the importance of a Turnpike Road connecting the two cities of Albany and Schenectady, and as the same patriotic spirit prevails in the City of Schenectady, a doubt can no longer exist, but the SHARES will be all taken up in a few hours after the Books are opened. . . ." And indeed, beside copies of these articles in his heavily annotated scrapbook, Watson scribbled, "the happy Moment was here—the foregoing publications paved the way + never anything more spiritedly received—"

Watson labored hard for other turnpikes, including one connecting New York and Albany. In an article from 1800 (1758–1842, 36), he writes, "The object is so truly important, so desirable, and so popular, that little doubt can be entertained, but that the legislature will grant a charter, and that the 3000 shares . . . will be immediately taken up." Notice how Watson, by pretending confidence in imminent support, tries to mitigate the assurance problem in securing support and to incite the vigilant do-gooder to take up the call. In his scrapbook Watson penned, "unsuccessful attempts have been made to obtain a charter. . . . It must eventually succeed." Later he added, "1808—the Road from N.Y. to Albany—has been executed this present year—who began it?" Besides testifying to Watson's self-satisfaction, these annotations testify to the social leverage of newspapers.

Social pressure seems to have also found its way into the assessment and payment of land damages. Right-of-way was commonly paid for in stock rather than money (P. E. Taylor 1934, 165). "A Philanthropist" (1797) says that those giving up land to a turnpike "will receive an equivalent to their damages, in the appreciate value of their farms and situations, and from other accommodations." Such benefits probably gave promoters of the turnpike a moral bargaining chip when coming to an agreement, as indicated in the 1798 announcement of the Hartford and New Haven Turnpike mentioned earlier: "It is hoped that those persons through whose land said road is laid, will become subscribers to the amount at least of the sum assessed to them in damages."

We could speculate on other forms of social pressure. In the few cases of turnpike-run lotteries it is easy to imagine a role for social pressure in the sale of tickets (Wood 1919, 293; Lane 1939, 161). The list of turnpike stock holders was public information and may have been circulated to spur contributions.[50]

Even if selective incentives had been prevalent we could not expect them to have been well recorded. Yet some tangible signs of such incentives can be found. Our understanding supplemented by an understanding of the turnpikes and of the ethos of the day, it is fair to conclude that social pressures played a conspicuous role in the provision of hundreds of turnpikes.

Conclusion

> Local freedom, . . . which leads a great number of citizens to value the
> affection of their neighbors and of their kindred, perpetually brings
> men together and forces them to help one another in spite of the
> propensities that sever them.
> —Alexis de Tocqueville, *Democracy in America*

Early American communities overcame an apparent free-rider problem
in financing hundreds of turnpike companies. For companies organized after 1805, the hope of a small return surely oiled the magnamin-
ity of the turnpike contributor, but the central explanation for investment in these companies lies elsewhere. Community isolation, citizen
familiarity, and a weak, decentralized government bred close social ties
and a strong participatory ethic.

But does the quaint story of townspeople working together to
build a highway have much bearing on modern problems? Hackensack
has changed a lot since 1810. Neighbors are often strangers, so how can
we expect social pressure and the like to curtail free riding? Two observations follow.

First, despite the growing interest among economists in nonegois-
tic behavior, voluntary public-goods provision still seems to be one of
those areas in which the representative economist suffers from a trained
incapacity. It has been shown experimentally that economists are comparatively insensitive to free riding (Marwell and Ames 1981); often
they seem blind to its avoidance as well. Whether it be a street association or the American Cancer Society, suasion tactics often yield results,
as reported regularly in the *Nonprofit and Voluntary Sector Quarterly.*
Such tactics, I am told, are operating for toll-road projects underway in
Virginia, California, and the Midwest, where groups of developers are
donating land and volunteering to build some of the necessary secondary facilities (Poole 1988, 511).

Second, if our voluntary impulses are deemed ineffective to the
provision of public goods, that in itself is a policy issue. The ability of
voluntary association to provide infrastructure, education, security,
and poor relief depends on the exercise and spontaneous development
of certain institutions, activities, and sentiments. Since governmental
bodies dominate these services it is no surprise that our faculties of
association remain degenerate. When a problem arises, government is
expected to deal with it. Participation does not become a personal
responsibility, and organizing leadership does not become a source of
social esteem. Thus there is a lesson in the broader circumstances of

early America, which bred effective voluntary forces, as well as in the specific ways those forces established turnpikes.

NOTES

For constructive feedback, I thank Cristopher Baer, Thomas Borcherding, Tyler Cowen, Walter Grinder, Bob Higgs, Jack High, Randy Kroszner, Timur Kuran, Don Lavoie, John Majewski, Janusz Ordover, Sheldon Richman, Ronald Seavoy, Jeremy Shearmur, David St. Clair, and Lawrence H. White. I also wish to thank those at historical societies, libraries, and archives who have helped me with this research. For financial assistance I thank the Institute for Humane Studies at George Mason University and the C. V. Starr Center for Applied Economic Research at New York University.

This chapter first appeared in *Economic Inquiry* 28, no. 4 (1990): 718–812. Reprinted by permission of Oxford University Press.

1. These two factors combined with an omniscient, omnipotent, and Paretian government and no further complications constitute "the simple public-goods model." The classic presentations of the model are Samuelson 1954 and Samuelson 1955.

2. This was especially the case in New Jersey, Maryland, and Pennsylvania. In later days turnpikes were numerous but shorter.

3. In 1806 the Pennsylvania state government began subsidizing turnpikes by purchasing stock. In 1822 it held about 30 percent of the collective stock of the turnpike companies (Durrenberger 1931, 55, 102).

In the other states under consideration here, turnpikes were almost entirely privately funded. There were four minor instances of state aid in the states of New Jersey, New York, and Maryland, which combined amounted to $42,500—a minuscule sum (a small fraction of 1 percent) relative to private investment (Durrenberger 1931, 98). The city of Albany subscribed to one hundred shares of the (First) Great Western Turnpike Road, which accounted for 9 percent of the company stock as of the middle of 1802; see Book I of Subscribers (BV Sec. Great Western), New York Historical Society. Parks 1966, 72–73, mentions a "few instances" of town aid in New England.

In other states, funding for turnpikes was mixed. G. R. Taylor 1951, 23–26, gives summary information on the turnpikes of Virginia, South Carolina, Ohio, Kentucky, and the lower South. The turnpike literature on the states outside New England, the Middle states, Maryland, and Virginia is minimal. Delaware seems to have had a few turnpikes that may well have been entirely privately financed. The best work on Virginia's substantial system of mixed enterprise is Hunter 1957.

4. For an analysis of the political decisions concerning the turnpikes, see Klein and Majewski 1988b.

5. Like the American system, the British system of turnpike trusts was decentralized. However, the trusts were public bodies, borrowed to construct their roads, and performed better financially (Pawson 1977).

6. On road management prior to the turnpikes and the beginning of the

turnpike era, see the two most important works on the turnpikes: Durrenberger 1931 (esp. 9–26); and P. E. Taylor 1934 (esp. 1–135). See also Ringwalt 1966, 22–27. On the attempt at public turnpikes see Durrenberger 1931, 97; G. R. Taylor 1951, 122–25; and Hollifield 1978, 2–3.

7. See Klein and Majewski 1988b for a table of turnpike chartering in the states under consideration from 1792 to 1845.

8. On lax inspection see Durrenberger 1931, 94; P. E. Taylor 1934, 112. For greater detail on the regulation of the turnpikes, see Klein and Majewski 1988b.

9. New England states did not always set explicit profit margins, but the states were willing to change tolls for companies in financial distress. The Massachusetts General Turnpike Law, 1805, chapter 79, for example, makes no mention of legal profit margins. For an example of margins explicitly set in New England, see Wood 1919, 218. On the legislature not reneging see Durrenberger 1931, 155; P. E. Taylor 1934, 140, 152; Handlin and Handlin 1947, 120.

10. Turnpike president Fisher Ames reported that his company's revenues would be about 60 percent greater if not for shunpikes (Parks 1966, 154).

11. The first quote comes from "General Powers of Turnpike Corporations," Law of Massachusetts, 1805, chapter 79, 649; the second is from New York's general law, 1807, chapter 38, 56.

12. A small number of turnpikes managed to consistently pay dividends above 3 percent (P. E. Taylor 1934, 277; Durrenberger 1931, 113–15; Hollifield 1978, 4; Parks 1966, 127–32). Due to low initial expenditures, Connecticut turnpikes did much better than those elsewhere (P. E. Taylor 1934, 190; Parks 1966, 91–99).

13. Tufts (1834, 867), a Massachusetts correspondent of Albert Gallatin (U.S. Secretary of the Treasury, 1801–13) said in 1807 that aside from two turnpikes, "all the other turnpikes in the State will not, upon an average, yield more than 3 per cent per annum, net income." In 1828, a report on Pennsylvania turnpikes said, "[n]one have yielded dividends sufficient to remunerate the proprietors. Most of them have yielded little more than expenditures for repairs" (quoted in Durrenberger 1931, 113–14). Bloodgood (1838, 97) remarks of the turnpikes of New York: "Generally they have never remunerated their proprietors, nor paid much more than the expense of actual repairs."

The fragmentary statistics in P. E. Taylor 1934 for fifteen companies show dividends for a combined 427 years of operation (270–71, 277). (All the companies are from Massachusetts, Connecticut, and Rhode Island; the figure for the Hingham and Quincy corporation is excluded because it operated a lucrative toll bridge in connection with a short piece of road [P. E. Taylor 1934, 276].) I calculated the average annual dividend to be 2.9 percent; Taylor evidently felt it was meaningless to calculate a summary figure, the reason surely being that the sample is undoubtedly biased. It is much more likely that records would have been preserved in a case where dividends were paid than where they were not. A strong indication of the bias is that for nine other companies in the tables no dividend figures are recorded, but in a separate column each one reports such comments as "$9660.35 net loss"; "income . . . ceased to pay expenses"; "have never been able to make but one dividend, and that at the rate of two percent"; and "of but Little Profit to your Petitioners."

Thus the fragmentary evidence and, more importantly, the impressions of contemporary observers suggest that throughout the states under consideration turnpikes on average paid no more than 2 percent per year, *not counting the loss of capital value.*

14. On assessments, see P. E. Taylor 1934, 159–60. Many companies simply issued no-par stock and demanded assessments as required. If assessment payments were delinquent, eventually the shares would be revoked and auctioned off. Long lists of delinquent shares can be found in the *Courier of New Hampshire* (Concord) (June 11, 1804; October 23, 1808).

15. P. E. Taylor 1934, 273, and Parks 1966, 119–20, detail rapidly falling stock prices. The great Pennsylvania auction of state-owned assets in 1843 gives a clear picture of the capital value of turnpike stock at that time. Shares in scores of turnpike companies—48,956 shares in total—were put up for auction, and 32,224 of them were not sold because they could not command a price of one dollar. The 16,732 shares that were sold commanded an average price of $3.40. Or $25, he state had paid of 50 percent, or $100 for them ($100 was most common) (Hartz 1948, 104, 232–38).

16. There is ambiguity on this point in that Wood (1919, 181) refers to a company that was fully compensated that P. E. Taylor (1934, 324) does not list. Since Taylor uses Wood, perhaps he found an error in Wood's report, leaving only one company that recouped its investment.

17. The calculation is based on P. E. Taylor's figures (1934, 324), using the figure of 238 for total operating turnpikes, as explained in note 27.

18. *Massachusetts Centinel* (May 13, 1786), quoted in Davis 1917, 2:188.

19. *Connecticut Courant* (Hartford) (June 19, 1805), 3.

20. Compared to the others, the Derby Turnpike, running between Derby and New Haven, was outstanding in financial performance, averaging dividends of 5.1 percent annually from 1801 to 1896 and recouping its capital investment when reverting to the public in 1897. (Note that in comparison to other businesses this performance is mediocre at best; see the section on unprofitability in this chapter, especially the quote from P. E. Taylor [1934, 281].) According to P. E. Taylor (1934, 279), "A combination of factors—monopolistic situation in a productive area, no land damages, and therefore low capital investment, existence of a gate almost within the limits of a large city, careful control by a close corporation—combined to make this a profitable enterprise."

21. "Turnpike Roads," by A Friend to Turnpikes [Elkanah Watson], *Albany Gazette* (December 27, 1795); reprinted *Albany Register* (June 13, 1796), 2.

22. See also Reed 1964, 59–61, 125, 135–37.

23. See also Ringwalt 1966, 31; Lane 1939, 168.

24. Legal historian James Hurst (1982, 103) agrees: "[T]hese highways . . . principally served the need of local economies for low-return, overhead capital beneficial much more to other activities dependent on the facilities than to the immediate gain of the providers."

25. For no particular reason, I listed proper nouns that appeared in the names of Massachusetts turnpike companies chartered from 1800 to 1810 that looked like the names of townships. I then searched for their populations in the 1810 census; those I did not find presumably are not towns or are towns in other states. I

excluded Boston (population 33,250) from the list; the largest in the list was Salem (population 12,613).

26. There is great variance in construction costs. A key factor was whether the turnpike took over a preexisting roadbed so that construction would be reduced and land damages minimal. Also important was the extent to which bridges were necessary. P. E. Taylor 1934, 210, estimates the average cost per mile to have been $4,500 in Massachusetts; $1,065 in New Hampshire; $1,000 in Vermont; $700 in Rhode Island; and $640 in Connecticut. See also P. E. Taylor 1934, 185–90, 348–40; Durrenberger 1931, 84–95.

27. P. E. Taylor 1934, 208. Note that Connecticut's two public turnpikes chartered in 1792, one of which was taken over by a private company, are excluded (P. E. Taylor 1934, 122–25; Wood 1919, 334–36) and that P. E. Taylor made arithmetic errors (see note 29 for details).

28. There were a few cases of concentrated holdings, particularly in New England. Unconcentrated stockholding was fostered in part by installment purchase with a very small down payment and, particularly in the Middle Atlantic states, restrictions on stock purchase and voting rights (Durrenberger 1931, 103–7; P. E. Taylor 1934, 101–2, 156, 158–65). Glazer (1972, 164, 166) finds that a relatively successful "minority of interested citizens dominated most voluntary associations" in Cincinnati in 1840 and concludes that such associations were as "pervasive and important, but probably not as popular, as Tocqueville observed." A disproportionate number of the activists in Glazer's sample, however, were settlers from New England, the focus of Tocqueville's observations.

29. Of the 385 private New England turnpike companies chartered through 1842, 147—or 38 percent—failed to build roads. These numbers come from P. E. Taylor 1934, 208, 237–46, and Reed 1964, 75. Some errors in P. E. Taylor 1934 to account for: the sum of the incorporations listed on p. 208 is 241, not 230; and table VII, on p. 208, disagrees with the individual listings (337–44) for 1796, 1800, 1801, 1804, and 1834. For incorporation of successful roads, I have used 3 for 1796, 13 for 1800, 10 for 1801, 17 for 1804, and 5 for 1834. P. E. Taylor 1934, appendix III, on p. 346, lists 1 for Vermont for 1804; I have used zero. These alterations are all based on Taylor's own individual listings, which are corroborated by Wood 1919. For total incorporation in Connecticut I have used Reed's figures, which differ from Taylor's for 1797, 1805, 1806, and 1818. I am assuming that the additional incorporations from Reed 1964 failed to build their roads.

The stillbirth figures for Massachusetts, Rhode Island, and Connecticut (P. E. Taylor 1934, 164, 337–41, 346) show the following: of the companies chartered between 1794 and 1800, 3 of 35 (9 percent) failed to build roadways; between 1801 and 1807, 29 of 103 (28 percent) failed (the 1801 incorporation entry, on p. 164, should be 12); between 1808 and 1814, 13 of 35 (37 percent) failed; between 1815 and 1842, 31 of 85 (36 percent) failed. Of the Middle states and Maryland, Durrenberger (1931, 107) says, "it is safe to say that at least one-third of the turnpike corporations chartered never built a mile of road, due chiefly to their inability to raise necessary capital."

30. Adding up individual listings in P. E. Taylor 1934, 337–44, we find 129 successful New England companies chartered between 1805 and 1838. For those years New York chartered 383 turnpike companies, Pennsylvania 271, New Jersey

44, and Maryland 65, but we do not know how many of these successfully built roads. Even if we suppose a 50 percent mortality rate for these incorporations—surely an overestimate—they would represent 381 turnpikes built after turnpike unprofitability was obvious.

31. Pisani (1987, 751) writes, "Recent scholarship suggests that the line between public and private corporations has been overdrawn: that distinction was not as clear in the eighteenth and early nineteenth centuries as it became once the business corporation reached maturity. Virtually all corporations combined elements of both." See Kammen 1975 and Seavoy 1978 on the overlap of the public and private sectors.

32. Tocqueville's analytic contributions are nicely summarized in Wade 1985.

33. "Federalism's tendency to disperse power to the local level reinforced the dependence of Americans on quasi-governmental associations, such as commercial federations, civic organizations, and booster clubs, that often served as better forums of collective action than did formal institutions of government" (Pisani 1987, 744).

34. Two examples are found in the *Connecticut Courant* (July 17, 1801), 2, 3.

35. See also Olson 1982, 20–23, 32–39, 85–87.

36. Using a standard of welfare, Olson views negative selective incentives as "coercive." I speak of "coercion" and "voluntarism" using a standard of property rights, with the social pressures presently discussed as *damnum absque injuria.* For a somewhat sanguine treatment of formal positive selective incentives, which Olson calls "tie-ins," see Klein 1987.

37. In *The Rise and Decline of Nations,* Olson (1982, 24) adds to his discussion of selective incentives the notion that selective incentives are more effective the more homogenous the group members are in taste, attitudes, and lifestyles. Turnpike communities would certainly be considered homogenous by today's standards. Landa 1981 discusses the importance of homogeneity in trading groups.

Regarding Olson's emphasis on face-to-face interaction, see Frank 1988 on how true feelings and intentions are reflected in physiological impulses. For an extended discussion of selective incentives and how traditional sociological questions can be addressed using the individualistic reasoning typical of economics, see Hechter 1987. On the study of community and cooperation, Higgs 1987 alerts economists to the achievements of sociologists and psychologists. For a brief survey touching on how communitarian factors in classroom experiments influence public-good contributions, see Dawes and Thaler 1988, 193–95; and Isaac and Walker 1988. For evidence and discussion of honest-preference revelation, see Bohm 1972 and Brubaker 1975.

38. Kirk 1912, 22; *Connecticut Courant* (March 19, 1798), 3.

39. Henry Miller to Thomas Willing Francis, January 17, 1808 (Conewago Canal Collection, New York Public Library, Manuscripts). The turnpike was chartered and constructed in 1809.

40. That so much energy was expended in securing the "aid and influence" of a clergyman suggests other forms of selective incentives.

41. Minisink and Montgomery Turnpike Company Minute Book (BV. Sec.), July 8, 1811 (New York Historical Society).

42. See Kahneman, Knetsch, and Thaler 1986 for experimental evidence of people's demand that wrongdoers be punished.

43. Plank roads are turnpikes with plank surfacing. They came in an enormous wave in the late 1840s and 1850s. They constitute a separate chapter in private road management; see Klein and Majewski 1988a.

44. Peter Gordon to John Rutherfurd, April 8, 1806 (New York Historical Society, Rutherfurd Papers). Another letter to Rutherfurd regarding a different turnpike indicates that Rutherfurd promised to buy eight or ten shares provided that a certain route was settled on. Thus the writer concludes the letter: "The object is so important, that it makes us very solicitous to obtain funds, especially from those who have been so liberal as to offer their aid" (John Doughty to John Rutherfurd, June 28, 1810 [New York Historical Society, Rutherfurd papers]).

I have found other bits of evidence of conditional subscription—conditioned on the route of the road. I am confident that conditional subscription does not pose a challenge to the claim that participatory norms and social pressure account principally for turnpike financing. First, route selection was hardly an issue for most turnpikes, as most were constructed on preexisting roadbeds. Second, directness usually was an explicit requirement in turnpike laws; in fact, many turnpikes made a fetish of rectilinearity (P. E. Taylor 1934, 285; Durrenberger 1931, 85). Finally, it must be recognized that by any sensible geometry a turnpike route could be skewed in only a few places and that each possible skew would offer benefits to a sizeable group that would then face a free-rider problem in bidding against other groups for their preferred route. But this is not to deny that conditional subscription may have played an occasional role in determining where a connecting stretch would be laid or how a corner would be cut.

45. A classic study of social pressures exerted through the media is Merton 1946, which is entirely devoted to a marathon war-bond broadcast by Kate Smith.

46. April 11, 1804; August 1, 1804; March 14, 1804.

47. *Albany Gazette* (June 6, 1805), 2.

48. *Connecticut Courant* (November 19, 1798), 2.

49. Watson was prominent in New York internal and agricultural improvements and was an early exponent of a great canal through New York. He was a champion promoter in his day, but in later years, at least on the score of the ridiculous, plank-road messiahs surpassed him mightily (Klein and Majewski, 1988a).

50. Consider the fraternity magazines and neighborhood March of Dimes drives that reveal the names and contributions of donors.

REFERENCES

Anderson, T., and P. J. Hill. 1979. An American Experiment in Anarcho-Capitalism: The *Not* so Wild, Wild West. *Journal of Libertarian Studies* 3(1):9–29.

Benson, B. 1998. *To Serve and Protect: Privatization and Community in Criminal Justice.* New York: New York University Press.

Bloodgood, S. D. W. 1838. *A Treatise on Roads, Their History, Character and Utility.* Albany: Oliver Steele.

Bohm, Peter. 1972. Estimating Demand for Public Goods: An Experiment. *European Economic Review* 3(2):111–30.

Brown, R. D. 1973. The Emergence of Voluntary Associations in Massachusetts, 1760–1830. *Journal of Voluntary Action Research* (spring): 64–73.

Brubaker, E. R. 1975. Free Ride, Free Revelation, or Golden Rule? *Journal of Law and Economics* 18(1):147–61.

Cheung, S. N. S. 1973. The Fable of the Bees: An Economic Investigation. *Journal of Law and Economics* 16(1): 11–34.

Coase, R. H. 1974. The Lighthouse in Economics. *Journal of Law and Economics* 17(2): 357–76.

Coleman, J. S. 1988. Social Capital in the Creation of Human Capital. *American Journal of Sociology* (supplement): S95–S120.

Cowen, T., ed. 1988. *The Theory of Market Failure: A Critical Examination.* Fairfax, Va.: George Mason University Press.

Davis, J. S. 1917. *Essays in the Earlier History of American Corporations.* 2 vols. Cambridge: Harvard University Press.

Dawes, R. M., and R. H. Thaler. 1988. Anomalies: Cooperation. *Journal of Economic Perspectives* 2(3): 187–97.

DeWitt, B. [1807] 1972. A Sketch of the Turnpike Roads in the State of New York. In *The New American State Papers,* vol. 1. Wilmington, Del.: Scholarly Resources, Inc.

Duane, W. J. 1811. *Letters Addressed to the People of Pennsylvania Respecting the Internal Improvements of the Commonwealth by Means of Roads and Canals.* Philadelphia: Jane Aitken.

Durant, S. W. 1878. *History of Oneida County, New York.* Philadelphia: Everts and Ensign.

Durrenberger, J. A. 1931. *Turnpikes: A Study of the Toll Road Movement in the Middle Atlantic States and Maryland.* Valdosta, Ga.: Southern Stationery and Printing Co.

Elkins, S., and E. McKitrick. 1954a. A Meaning for Turner's Frontier, Part I: Democracy in the Old Northwest. *Political Science Quarterly* 69 (September): 321–53.

———. 1954b. A Meaning for Turner's Frontier, Part II: The Southwest Frontier and New England. *Political Science Quarterly* 69 (December): 565–602.

Ellig, J., and J. High. 1988. The Private Supply of Education: Some Historical Evidence. In *The Theory of Market Failure: A Critical Examination,* ed. Tyler Cowen. Fairfax, Va.: George Mason University Press.

Evans, C. J. 1916. Private Turnpikes and Bridges. *American Law Review* 527–35.

Frank, R. 1988. *Passions Within Reason: Prisoner's Dilemmas and the Strategic Role of the Emotions.* New York: W. W. Norton.

Glazer, W. S. 1972. Participation and Power: Voluntary Associations and the Functional Organization of Cincinnati in 1840. *Historical Methods Newsletter* (September): 151–68.

Gunn, L. R. 1988. *The Decline of Authority: Public Economic Policy and Political Development in New York, 1800–1860.* Ithaca: Cornell University Press.

Handlin, O., and M. F. Handlin. 1947. *Commonwealth: A Study of the Role of Gov-*

ernment in the American Economy: Massachusetts, 1774–1861. New York: New York University Press.

Hartz, L. 1948. *Economic Policy and Democratic Thought: Pennsylvania, 1776–1860.* Cambridge: Harvard University Press.

Hechter, M. 1987. *Principles of Group Solidarity.* Berkeley: University of California Press.

Higgs, R. 1987. Identity and Cooperation: A Comment on Sen's Alternative Program. *Journal of Law, Economics, and Organization* 3(1): 140–42.

Hollifield, W. 1978. *Difficulties Made Easy: History of the Turnpikes of Baltimore City and County.* Cockeysville, Md.: Baltimore County Historical Society.

Hunter, R. F. 1957. The Turnpike Movement in Virginia, 1816–1860. Ph.D. diss., Columbia University.

Hurst, J. W. 1982. *Law and Market in United States History: Different Modes of Bargaining Among Interests.* Madison: University of Wisconsin Press.

Isaac, R. M., and J. M. Walker. 1988. Communication and Free-Riding Behavior: The Voluntary Contribution Mechanism. *Economic Inquiry* 26(4): 585–608.

Jackson, H. F. 1959. The Utica Turnpike. *New York History* (January): 18–32.

Kahneman, D., J. L. Knetsch, and R. H. Thaler. 1986. Fairness and the Assumptions of Economics. *Journal of Business* 59(4): S285–S300.

Kammen, M. 1975. A Different "Fable of the Bees": The Problem of Public and Private Sectors in Colonial America. In *The American Revolution: A Heritage of Change,* ed. J. Parker and C. Urness. Minneapolis: Associates of the James Ford Bell Library.

Kirk, E. R. 1912. Turnpike Road from Buckingham to Newtown. *Bucks County Historical Society* 20–24.

Kirkland, E. C. 1949. *Men, Cities and Transportation: A Study in New England History, 1920–1900.* Cambridge: Harvard University Press.

Klein, D. 1987. Tie-Ins and the Market Provision of Collective Goods. *Harvard Journal of Law and Public Policy* 10(2): 451–74.

Klein, D., and J. Majewski. 1988a. Private Profit, Public Good, and Engineering Failure: The Plank Roads of New York. Institute for Humane Studies, George Mason University, Working Paper 88/3.

———. 1988b. Privatization, Regulation, and Public Repossession: The Turnpike Companies of Early America. Photocopy, University of California, Irvine.

Landa, J. T. 1981. A Theory of the Ethnically Homogeneous Middleman Group: An Institutional Alternative to Contract Law. *Journal of Legal Studies* 10 (June): 349–62.

Lane, W. J. 1939. *From Indian Trail to Iron Horse: Travel and Transportation in New Jersey, 1620–1860.* Princeton: Princeton University Press.

Majewski, J. 1989. Farming and the Public Good: Social Incentives and Agricultural Research in England, 1600–1850. Photocopy, Department of History, University of California, Los Angeles.

Marwell, G., and R. Ames. 1981. Economists Free Ride, Does Anyone Else? *Journal of Public Economics* 13:295–310.

Matthews, D. G. 1969. The Second Great Awakening as an Organizing Process, 1780–1830: An Hypothesis. *American Quarterly* 21 (spring): 23–43.

McChesney, F. C. 1986. Government Prohibitions on Volunteer Fire Fighting in

Nineteenth Century America: A Property Rights Perspective. *Journal of Legal Studies* 15(1): 69–92.

Merton, R. 1946. *Mass Persuasion: The Social Psychology of a War Bond Drive.* New York: Harper and Brothers.

Olson, M. 1971. *The Logic of Collective Action: Public Goods and the Theory of Groups.* Cambridge: Harvard University Press.

———. 1982. *The Rise and Decline of Nations.* New Haven: Yale University Press.

Parks, R. N. 1966. The Roads of New England, 1790–1840. Ph.D. diss., Michigan State University.

———. 1967. *Roads and Travel in New England, 1790–1840.* Sturbridge, Mass.: Old Sturbridge Inc.

Pawson, E. 1977. *Transport and Economy: The Turnpike Roads of Eighteenth Century Britain.* London: Academic Press.

"A Philanthropist." 1797. Roads and Turnpikes. *Connecticut Courant* (Hartford), May 1, 3; May 8, 2; May 22, 1; May 29, 1; June 26, 1.

Pisani, D. J. 1987. Promotion and Regulation: Constitutionalism and the American Economy. *Journal of American History* 74 (December): 740–68.

Poole, R. W., Jr. 1988. Resolving Gridlock in Southern California. *Transportation Quarterly* 42 (October): 499–527.

Reed, N. 1964. The Role of the Connecticut State Government in the Development and Operation of Inland Transportation Facilities from 1784 to 1821. Ph.D. diss., Yale University.

Ringwalt, J. L. [1888] 1966. *Development of Transportation Systems in the United States.* New York: Johnson Reprint Corp.

Samuelson, P. A. 1954. The Pure Theory of Public Expenditure. *Review of Economics and Statistics* 36(4): 387–89.

———. 1955. Diagrammatic Exposition of a Theory of Public Expenditure. *Review of Economics and Statistics* 37 (November): 550–56.

Seavoy, R. E. 1978. The Public Service Origins of the American Business Corporation. *Business History Review* 52 (spring): 30–60.

Sly, J. F. 1967. *Town Government in Massachusetts, 1620–1930.* Harnden, Conn.: Archon Books.

Taylor, G. R. 1951. *The Transportation Revolution, 1815–1860.* New York: Rinehart and Co.

Taylor, P. E. 1934. The Turnpike Era in New England. Ph.D. diss., Yale University.

Tocqueville, A. de. [1835, 1840] 1945. *Democracy in America.* 2 vols. New York: Vintage Books.

Tufts, C. [1807] 1834. Letter on Turnpike Roads of Massachusetts. Appendix to Gallatin's Report on Roads and Canals. In *American State Papers, Miscellaneous*, vol. 1. Washington, D.C.: Gales and Seaton.

Wade, L. L. 1985. Tocqueville and Public Choice. *Public Choice* 47(3): 491–508.

Watson, E. 1758–1842. Commonplace Book. E. Watson Papers, package 1, vol. 12, New York State Library, Albany.

Wood, F. J. 1919. *The Turnpikes of New England and Evolution of the Same through England, Virginia, and Maryland.* Boston: Marshall Jones Co.

Wooldridge, W. C. 1970. *Uncle Sam, the Monopoly Man.* New Rochelle, N.Y.: Arlington House.

5

Entrepreneurial City Planning

Chicago's Central Manufacturing District

Robert C. Arne

The businessman of today is a creator, a builder and an economist. . . .
The only way to make money is to render a service for humanity; to supply something that people want, and to carry things from where they are
plentiful to where they are needed. He who confers the greatest service
at the least expense is the man whom we will crown with honor and
clothe with riches.
—*Advertisement for the Central Manufacturing District*

Historians of architecture and city planning have sometimes maintained that however efficient capitalism was at within-firm planning, it
was incapable of planning large unified land districts (Sutcliffe 1980).
The viability of entrepreneurial planning—planning designed to anticipate the demands of customers and make a profit off of satisfying these
economic demands—is evident, however, in many instances, of which
Chicago's Central Manufacturing District (CMD) is a notable example.

Differences in the nature of public and private planning may be
clarified by a study of planning in the CMD, where private decision-
makers planned the structure of a city district and its internal regulation, including the provision of vital services ordinarily considered to
be outside the scope of private enterprise.

The most common method of city planning in the United States
makes use of elements of both political or governmental planning and

entrepreneurial planning. Governments lay out the streets and lots (or tell contractors to lay them out); entrepreneurs plan the use of the lots. Government regulation and financing of lot usage increased in the twentieth century to the point at which construction of a single building on Times Square took the approval of thirty agencies. By increasing control over property—the essence of ownership—through regulation, taxation, and zoning, the city and the federal government are increasingly assuming a monopoly on city planning. On a smaller scale, mobile-home parks, condominiums, and shopping malls represent an alternative to either public planning or private monopoly: private, centralized ownership of the infrastructure with private, decentralized ownership of units using that infrastructure.[1] Shopping-mall developers build the physical infrastructure of the shopping mall, in the process handling the political difficulties of construction, and then they lease space to individual stores. Developers or their management companies also provide continuing services like security, advertising, and cleaning. Mobile-home parks lease space to individual mobile-home owners and provide security, privacy, and even regulation (e.g., rules against excessive noise) to members who pay for membership in this type of community.

Large-scale entrepreneurial planning has also been used to construct residential communities, including the private places of St. Louis and modern planned communities like Reston, Virginia; Llewelyn Park; and Sea Ranch. (For more on St. Louis and Reston, see David T. Beito's and Fred E. Foldvary's contributions to this volume.) The Sea Ranch Association, a corporate body in Northern California, purchased farmland along the coastline after World War II and developed it for purposes of profit and pleasure. Everyone who purchases beachfront property from the Sea Ranch (ultimately ten thousand residents) becomes a voting and fee-paying member of the association and receives an array of services from the corporation: roads, sewers, electricity, fire protection, security patrols, hiking trails, golf, tennis, swimming—even a private airstrip. One outstanding element of Sea Ranch planning is its insistence upon architectural quality, upon uniformly rich glass-and-redwood houses. To avoid the tacky houses built in local coastal cities planned by governments (e.g., Santa Cruz, Big Sur), the association's architects insist upon approving each house's plan for its beauty as well as its structural integrity.

Aside from the absence of welfare programs, educational facilities, and municipal bureaucracy, Sea Ranch differs from a publicly administered town because entrance into the community and provision for all of its services is by means of voluntary, explicit, contractual agreement. Instead of providing services to a population with diverse interests, Sea Ranch caters to a specific market of consumers: users of recreational and retirement housing. While providing for specific demands well—demands expressed by money—it refuses to provide for social needs not expressed by market demand.

Entrepreneurial Planning in Chicago's Central Manufacturing District

Like Sea Ranch, the CMD is a privately owned district that provides sites for consumers to build upon and communal services normally provided by government. Unlike Sea Ranch, the CMD is an industrial and warehousing district.

Instead of beaches, meadows, and redwood forests, one finds convenient rail transportation and efficient warehousing provided by the managers of the CMD. To understand CMD planning, it is necessary to look first at the services that CMD chose to provide in their historical perspective and then to look briefly at the CMD consumer's reaction to these services.[2]

The CMD owes its existence largely to the foresight of a single entrepreneur: Frederick Henry Prince (1859–1953). Prince, a financier and railroad magnate with business interests around the world, had acquired the Central Junction Railway of south Chicago in 1892. This little railway connected the Union Stockyards with Chicago's major trunk lines to other cities. Seeing that the stockyards would not provide enough business for his railway, Prince began purchasing land north of the railway and stockyards and west of Halstead in 1902. Upon a 250-acre piece of property that was once a cabbage patch and a lumber yard, he erected $20 million worth of streets, sewers, rail facilities, docks, and other improvements (approximately $400 million in 1999 dollars).

As only one industrial estate—Trafford Park in Manchester, England—had ever been built before, Prince clearly anticipated a demand for unusual services. His entrepreneurial success depended largely upon his decision to locate in south Chicago. The CMD was readily served by the rail facilities of the Chicago Junction Railway. The south bend of the Chicago River provided easy water transportation, while roads led to the city center, just fifteen minutes away by car, and to other parts of the city that was then blooming around CMD property. By 1923, 48 percent of Chicago's population would live within four miles of the CMD, offering it a large local market and a large and diverse labor pool. Chicago itself lay at the geographical nexus of the nation's productive activity, at the center of its markets and the hub of its railways.

In November 1905, the CMD opened its first building: a new plant for the United States Leather Company on South Morgan Street. By 1908, the CMD had developed into a full-scale industrial district that would experience rapid construction over the next ten years. A bond issue covered the initial costs of the construction of buildings, docks, streets, and other permanent improvements. Replicating city functions on entrepreneurial terms, the CMD provided vital centralized services in transportation, construction, finance, and diverse other services. By 1909, the Clearing Industrial District, located just west of Chicago, had learned of the CMD's success and was the first to copy it successfully.

Often, the CMD combined cars into trains to save switching charges on freight going outside of Chicago. The Fifteenth Street Union Freight Station distributed goods to teams entering the city or suburbs. The Union Boat House at Twenty-Sixth Street loaded ships for lake passage. Waterways were dredged and canals dug to accommodate shipping.

As rail lines actually went to the door of each factory (each of which also had a dock for teams), every factory had reason to demand excellent rail service. By moving to a district where they could rely upon the railways, firms saved themselves thousands of dollars in drayage costs and delays in congested downtown terminals. The Junction Railway's traffic agent in the CMD coordinated all freight shipments, handled complaints, checked delays, and made sure that empty cars were delivered to factories on time. The whole railway system was cleared of unmoved cars every twenty-four hours at most. The traffic bureau of the associated industries of the CMD was a membership-supported organization formed to demand better service from the railways and to deal with the Interstate Commerce Commission. CMD companies, by virtue of their common management and location, effectively pooled their money to obtain lobbying services that no single firm could provide itself. According to the CMD, shippers received "97% efficiency" in the shipment of dry goods (*Central Manufacturing District* 1915, 26).

The district had its own architectural department and its own engineers to supervise the construction that the district routinely completed for its customers on a daily basis. By buying construction materials in bulk and building rail lines directly to construction sites, the CMD saved construction money. Buildings were erected by means of competitive contracts among responsible contractors. The CMD boasted that it built buildings more cheaply and well than anywhere else in

Chicago (*Central Manufacturing District* 1915, 15). Carl Conduit (1973, 175) an expert on Chicago architecture, states:

> The Central Manufacturing District is so important in the history of the planned industrial district that certain technical features are worth pursuing in detail. Economy resulted not only from the unity of design but equally from the large scale of the project, the concentrated plan, and the rapidity with which individual buildings were erected. . . . [T]he construction of the military warehouses set extraordinary records [one being built in six months]. . . . Feats of this kind were accomplished by a carefully prepared method: the architect provided preliminary plans for the contractor's estimates; excavation began the following day and continued while correctly detailed excavation and foundation plans were prepared, usually in complete form by the fourth day; building plans were completed during the foundation work, sometimes within ten days. . . . [L]ow wages and extensive unskilled work in the building process allowed contractors to hire hundreds of men who would be retained throughout the period of construction.

According to Conduit (1973, 141), who gives a positive overall assessment of CMD development, "All the buildings were designed by the architect S. Scott Joy, who provided standardized structural and planning features and a formal unity that confers harmony without monotony. The trustees of the district demanded the highest architectural standards, to which the various residents agreed upon becoming tenants, and all the evidence indicates that the trustees received what they asked for. . . ." In the first seven years of the CMD's existence, its engineers and architects planned and provided communal services to serve their tenants:

> In laying out the District, great care has been taken to arrange buildings, tracks, streets, and driveways in order to secure maximum efficiency, light and air without sacrificing attractiveness. . . . Many of the streets in the District are private streets which have been improved with cement curbs, cement sidewalks, substantial granite block . . . and, wherever possible, wide grass parkways have been put in. Adequate sewer and water lines with fire hydrants have been installed, ornamental lamp posts have been erected and all District streets are well lighted by electricity. The District has its own street-cleaning department, and maintains a force of gardeners to care for its business boulevards. (*Central Manufacturing District* 1915)

Fire safety was assured by spreading apart the buildings, by wire-glass windows and metal frames, and by the CMD's 250,000-gallon sprinkler tower and underground connecting pipes. Careful attention was paid to preventing fires in the district, as attested by insurance companies like Morris, Case, Loman, and Hubbard. (*Central Manufacturing District* 1915). The Chicago fire department was responsible for the district's fire service. Security patrolled the grounds on motorcycle to supplement the city's police protection, which the district clearly appreciated (*Central Manufacturing District Magazine,* October 1918). The Chicago Junction Railway provided a private police patrol of its tracks, thereby also patrolling the CMD, into which its tracks entered. In 1914, this force made 114 arrests and had an amazing 100 percent conviction rate. By 1914, the CMD had developed an integrated system of management and planning, one that expanded intensively as the CMD expanded extensively.

In 1915, the CMD purchased properties along Pershing Road. There, the CMD developed a district with even better-integrated central services. Its features included centralized power and steam-generation plants; communal warehouses on a grand scale; centralized sprinklers controlled by underground tunnels leading to a water tower; standardized streets, sidewalks, streetlights, and grass parkways; and an excellent six-story Central Union Freight Station for consolidating freight. Lots were standardized "to accommodate the most economical building units, to eliminate waste ground, and to give an ideal arrangement of improvements and facilities with free accessibility" (*Central Manufacturing District Magazine,* July 1955, 12). To accommodate additional shipping of below-carload parcels, the CMD burrowed concrete traffic tunnels sixteen feet wide and eight feet tall between plants and its freight station so that electric tractors could haul goods back and forth.

District improvements were not inevitable developments of an initial plan. The district improved as its methods of planning evolved and as market forces suggested. Central power and steam were provided only when individual production proved inefficient. The second decade of the twentieth century saw the CMD making strides forward in banking, warehousing, communications, contracts, and even pollution control. Moreover, the CMD discovered the profitability of bringing together the leadership of the district into an industrial community united by a common magazine and a gathering place.

During the Great Depression, only one company (out of hundreds) failed in the CMD. The CMD's generous financing policies accounted for this amazing record: the district reduced rental and interest payments, extended credit, and forgave temporary mispayments in the 1930s. District financing for private plants on margins as low as 20 percent had, in fact, been important since the CMD's birth. The CMD Bank opened in 1912 with $200,000 in assets. By 1915, its assets exceeded $1.5 million. By 1935, the CMD and its bank had financed land, buildings, and improvements totaling $100 million. Frederick Prince's $20,000 land purchase and $20 million initial financing had grown into a $175 million investment by 1955, an investment whose replacement value would be three times as much. Industrial finance explained this success almost as much as transportation and community services did. This community had invested in itself, counting on the development of each business to aid the development of all.

The CMD would sometimes build a plant to a particular company's order and then rent it to that company, allowing it the option to purchase the plant with rental payments. The district expected to make up losses in construction and rentals with increased rail business. Consequently, industrial tenants were screened for both character and prospective freight demand. Location contracts included either direct sales of land, whereby the tenant was required to erect a building within a specified time; long-term leases; or contracts of purchase whereby the trustees erected factories or warehouses in return for cash or credit.

Communications were essential to an industrial community; businesspersons needed to speak to each other and to the outside world frequently and sometimes in comfortable circumstances. To get messages out fast, they relied upon express shipments by famous concerns like Wells Fargo and Brinks, working from offices within the district. In 1915—the national phone monopoly made phone competition illegal—two private telephone companies offered services to manufacturers. Even more important for community and communication was the CMD Club, the heart of industrial planning and operations in the district. Its membership consisted of the prominent businesspeople of the district; its activities included everything from district board meetings to informal luncheons for district members and their clients to the organization of the yearly CMD golf tournament. A CMD ideologist of 1911, Elbert Hubbard, explained the advantages of social contact in the concentrated district: "In order to do business nowadays, wise men agree that you have to be where business is being done. In this way you take advantage of the enthusiasm, the hope, the courage, the uplift and the example of many men working together for a mutual benefit. Isolation and segregation are awful handicaps to success" (Hubbard 1911, 8).

The CMD also informed, maintained, and developed its community with publications. Communal pride and industrial advertising were often coequal purposes of company publications. Elbert Hubbard's (1911) pamphlet, *Little Journey to the Central Manufacturing District,* boldly claimed that farmers, businessmen, bankers, and advertising men were the most important men on earth and that the CMD was the place where those great men worked. In 1911 and 1915, the district published two books that consisted of a descriptive and historical article about the district accompanied by over a hundred pages of photographs and laudatory letters written by businesses in the district. These publications, intended to draw more business to the CMD and more shipping to the Junction Railroad, had the effect of pooling and reducing the advertising costs of all the firms in the district.

From 1916 to at least 1964, the district published the monthly *Central Manufacturing District Magazine.* Aside from explicit advertisements, this magazine routinely included articles about the success of its businesses; about general problems of business ("Market Demand for Food"); about general problems that related to CMD businesses ("The Science of Business Location"); and about Chicago politics. Other articles discussed boys' clubs, the evils of communism, artificial stone, recently deceased district businessmen, and the district traffic club. They were replete with pictures of trucks and factories and smiling kids. Naturally, this was an advertising publication that spoke in laudatory tones to attract clients.

While the district did not offer welfare services of its own in the manner of a city, it did boast of offering a certain type of welfare to its workers. Hubbard, who considered business to be the "science of human service," thought the CMD offered "practical co-operation, reciprocity, mutuality, progress, success, health, wealth and happiness" (Hubbard 1911, 21). Business itself, with the jobs and services that accompanied it, was the best form of welfare, according to Hubbard. Indeed, the district did provide jobs and services by the thousands.

Managers, however, wondered who should benefit from these services. A 1917 article in the company publication addressed the need to retain the health and livelihood of steady and honest workers "who have the welfare and interests of their employers at heart" (*Central Manufacturing District Magazine,* August 1917, 16). Articles like this one, more ominously, spoke of the classes of workers that were clearly not welcome in the district: those who really did not want to work or worked unsteadily; those who threatened "order"; and those who did not care for themselves enough to follow their employer's doctor's advice and maintain their health. Companies distributed well-being based upon the moral and economic standards that best serves the marketplace. All distribution was voluntary and contractual.

Given these standards, the CMD did provide many services to its workers and to the nation as a whole: "District policy called for planning, lighting, heating, and safety which would benefit employees as well as employers" (*Central Manufacturing District Magazine,* June 1955, 18). The CMD frequently bragged of good housing "built for workers at cost" that workers sometimes found near its plants, of its own surgeon and ambulance service, and of the workers' lounges and recreational facilities within various plants. According to Ibata (1985), "Prince's Union Stock Yard & Transit Co. even owned and operated an elevated line, the Stockyards-Kenwood line, which ran from the yards east to the lake front." The district proved its patriotism in laudatory articles about companies sacrificing buildings and men sacrificing their time and lives in the world wars. To some extent, the district even provided the public service of pollution control, at least so far as that service affected its own property. In November 1917 the directors voted to fill in the "greasy covered surface of the silent waters" of Bubbly Creek before they completed the Pershing Road development (*Central Manufacturing District Magazine,* November 1917, 10).

In creating a community, the Junction Railway's entrepreneurial planning seemed successful: "The system of co-operation was idealized: the District land, the District Club, District Friends and District Spirit are a part of it" (*Central Manufacturing District Magazine,* October 1918, 19). In creating profits and development, the district's record of expansion speaks for itself. By 1949, the relatively tiny Junction Railway was shunting nineteen thousand cars daily on its 224 miles of tracks, serving 635 industries. (It was leased by the New York Central Railway in 1922.) By 1915, most of the sites in the original districts were filled. The district purchased the Kedzie District in 1919, pioneering the use of one-story construction there. In 1922, the CMD purchased and developed three hundred acres in Los Angeles along familiar lines of management. In 1931, the CMD purchased the four-hundred-acre Crawford District. According to Mary D. Schopp, Crawford introduced *elasticity* to district planning: "In Crawford, private streets, switchtracks, and other improvements are installed as dictated by the settlement of the tract. In other words, aside from the necessary, skeleton groundwork . . . the developing of the tract does not become fixed until the industries have been located according to individual requirements" (*Central Manufacturing District Magazine,* August

1955). Thus, plants did not have to purchase lots larger than were necessary. Furthermore, they were assured priority buying rights of lands adjacent to their present plants—a plus for dreams of expansion. For reasons like these, the CMD did six million dollars worth of construction in 1951. By then, the CMD had acquired over nine hundred acres of property to accommodate its more than three hundred major firms. Besides the original territory, it managed industrial properties at Pershing Road, Forty-Third Street, Kedzie Avenue, Crawford Avenue, and Calumet.

The CMD's customers in the years before 1964 must be discussed before the story of the CMD can be told completely. Why did they like what the CMD offered? Why did they buy its services? The CMD's customers included over three hundred nationally known firms producing either light and medium manufactures or warehousing and mail-order services. Most of these firms moved from crowded places in central cities to larger plants with room for expansion, ready transportation, healthier conditions, and better help.

From the evidence of the fifty-five letters written and reprinted in 1911 and the fifteen letters written and reprinted in 1939, several CMD services were evidently most popular. First in importance were the Junction Railway's superior service and the savings in teaming and labor that direct rail service to factories provided. Following was the CMD's location in Chicago with its markets, general district services, fine construction, prompt rail shipments, capacity for plant expansion, and good and cheap labor.

Satisfaction, however, cannot be entirely quantified. The Lowe Brothers Company (paint and varnish makers) explained their satisfaction with district performance: "Freedom from fire risk . . . attractiveness of surroundings, the promptness of the freight service (both incoming and outgoing), and the excellence of the general arrangement" (Central Manufacturing District 1911, 63). The Luxfer Prism Company said, "Our saving on teaming alone practically pays the interest on our investment, and taking the location, conveniences and faculties together, we could find none better adapted to our business anywhere" (Central Manufacturing District 1911, 83).

Hately Bros. Provisions and Grain appreciated the labor market and the "good order" maintained in the district. Marsh and Bingham Company praised the well-paved and clean streets. Greenpoint Metallic Bed Company claimed that railroad shipments went out within an hour and a half of being called. Other companies appreciated the lawns, street cleaning, snow shoveling, and sprinkling services, which made the manufacturing district as much like a park as possible. Their comments reflect the bucolic aspirations of a business class that was then building parks and moving to the suburbs. Marvin Stone, a producer of corrugated cartons, said that the "lawns and shrubbery . . . [put] employees in a frame of mind that doesn't lend entirely to the commercial aspect of just keeping a job" (*Chicago Manufacturing District Magazine,* 1939, 122). Grass, apparently, was part of what made the CMD a community. Carl Quanz, of the Bridgeport Brass Company commented, "Another consideration was the fact that the District is privately owned and this gave us a considerable degree of protection, which was not possible elsewhere" (*Central Manufacturing District Magazine,* 1939, 100). H. E. Poronto, president of United States Cold Storage Corporation, summed up the value of the district to companies:

> We have operated here for nearly 25 years. . . . It is a pleasure to recommend the Central Manufacturing District for industrial locations. It not only provides unexcelled physical facilities for handling freight, but its fine community spirit, its club, its bank, its traffic bureau and its convenience of location from all parts of Chicago all add to the pleasure, prestige, and profit of doing business in this section, which has come to be the outstanding industrial development of the country. (*Central Manufacturing District Magazine,* 1939, 126)

Since the 1960s, the CMD has suffered unsurmountable difficulties, despite the advantages advertised in 1964—a "complete package of financing, planning, engineering and construction . . . adequate financing, private switch tracks and private streets" (*Central Manufacturing District Magazine,* June 1964). Having sold off many of its original properties, the CMD no longer manages even its remaining Chicago holdings, as it did before 1964. The CMD Club and the magazine no longer exist. Conrail runs the old Junction Railway. The general decline of U.S. manufactures relative to foreign companies and the service sector; the desirability of suburban living and the transportational ease of achieving it; the political unrest and crime of the South Side in the 1960s; and the lack of a reasonable attitude towards industry by Chicago government (which does not necessarily mean low taxes) explain the decline of industry on the South Side, as they explain the decline of big cities relative to suburbs in general. With modern plants demanding room for expansion and single-story operation, south Chicago is now too crowded. The demise of the railroads relative to trucking rendered the CMD's rail transportation less advantageous.

The Central Manufacturing District Company, now called CMD Midwest Corp., survives to this day because of its entrepreneurial flexibility in the conditions of the current economy. It is still a privately held business, the realty arm of F. H. Prince and Co., now run by Frederick Prince's grandsons and cousins. The CMD moved west and to the suburbs with the 350-acre Itasca industrial park, the 675-acre St. Charles Business Park, and an industrial park in Phoenix. Outside of the central city, the original CMD idea of private development and central services (now including wide lanes for trucking and proximity to O'Hare Airport) lives on in projects like the 1957 Centex project in Elk Grove Village: "When substantially completed 14 years later . . . Centex was the world's largest industrial development, with 1,500 companies, 35,000 employees and a $1 billion net worth" (Ibata 1985).

In 1983, CMD Midwest started the Meridian-Business campus, a 617-acre campus in Aurora, Illinois; soon it will start another Meridian campus in North Carolina's high-tech area near Durham. Copying Silicon Valley's success with industrial parks, which the CMD itself once inspired, Meridian used "landscaping and earth mounding to differentiate three distinct zones: Light industry on the south; research and services in the center; and, around the lake network in the eastern third of the park, high end offices" (Ibata 1985). Frederick Prince, interviewed for the *Tribune* in 1975, said: "The business park concept looks like a healthy baby, . . . we've shifted from being a world of steak and potatoes people to one of Perrier and white wine people. . . . We've always felt we should be innovators. The high-amenity business campus fits that image" (Ibata 1985).

Entrepreneurial and City Planning Compared

The CMD's entrepreneurial planners shared more in common with America's public or city planners than might be expected. Both placed economic growth and the interests of businesspersons high on their list of priorities. Even Chicago's great architect Daniel Burnham tried to incorporate business interests into Chicago's master plan. Like Progressive reformers, the CMD sought efficient management without democratic participation by the masses. Both, contrary to the expectations of architectural historians, were capable of planning districts according to some standard or order. Both, surprisingly, provided extensive communal services and developed a sense of community among at least some residents. The example of Sea Ranch shows that private planning and management, like public planning, can take place in residential as well as industrial districts. Why then do the type of managing organization and the method of governing matter?

This question cannot be answered entirely using the evidence presented earlier. Further empirical study of this issue would have to include quantitative comparisons of the effectiveness of entrepreneurial and public planning. Which, for instance, generated more jobs and income? Which planning agency provided more communal services first? Were those services necessary and efficiently procured? How do the daily engineering inspections of the CMD's construction compare to the after-the-fact inspections of city building inspectors? One might also ask which bureaucracy was more efficient, which provided necessary regulation at the lowest administrative cost. One might compare industrial districts founded by the city or federal government with the CMD. Conduit (1973, 141) says that the CMD was the model for the modern industrial parks established under urban-renewal programs. Neither the taxpayer nor the taxpayer's subjective but unquantifiable preferences must be forgotten in any empirical study. The costs of private decision-making (e.g., monopoly, externalities) must be weighed against the costs of public decision-making (e.g., corruption, inefficiency, economic rent-seeking).

In what ways, then, is it possible to compare city planning to entrepreneurial planning? Most importantly, the form of rule differed between the CMD and the American city. The child of an entrepreneur, the CMD existed to maintain the profits of his company. Usually this concern led management to initiate policies that rapidly developed the district, making the most efficient use of physical and economic resources, so that Junction Railway profits would soar. Profits could not be obtained except by conferring benefits (e.g., a well-built factory in a well-planned district) to customers who voluntarily paid for these benefits and who arranged for them on a voluntary, contractual basis. Through the CMD Club, managers were encouraged to participate in the economic and communal life of the CMD. Though the CMD provided workers with thousands of jobs and products, workers benefited from this community only incidently. They generally were not invited to participate in its vital planning functions.

Political entrepreneurship, in contrast to economic entrepreneurship, probably will not provide economically rational—or even democratically justifiable—solutions. Economists like Mancur Olson (1982) and George Stigler (1975) and historians like John Mollenkopf (1983) suggest that the concentrated resources and information of minorities will tend to overwhelm and overtax the resources of unorganized majorities. By choosing votes instead of profits as the standard to be rewarded, the political process almost certainly sacrifices the economic efficiency that the CMD achieved by aiming straight at profits. Contractors in the CMD, for instance, were not chosen because they helped out in campaigning. As the central government assumed more city functions in the twentieth century and as city government itself now provides more regulation and services, city government is gently crowding out private decision-making, making public rule more monopolistic and public debate more centered on the relationship between local and national power. Diverse interests are served by this process, with taxpayers and consumers losing out to rent-seekers who profit from legal privilege.

Unlike cities, the privately owned industrial districts incorporated economic interest directly into planning. Governmental cities surrendered monopoly profits to utilities whose services were often bought by political support and "honest graft." The CMD incorporated transportation interests into planning with seemingly fewer maladies; it was, in fact, the railway that built the CMD and that had the greatest interest in its economic welfare. Competition disciplined economic interests from exercising monopoly powers.

In the Progressive era, some city governments tried to copy business procedures to make government efficient. Even Burnham's 1909 Chicago plan was designed with efficiency high in the architect's mind. Progressive reformers, fearful of ethnic rule through political bosses, sought to make government "merely a business agency" that would be "most successful and efficient" when managed by people selected based on the amount of "special adaptation to work" (Schiesl 1977, 8). They formed commission forms of government in Houston, Des Moines, and 160 other cities. Such efforts were doomed to failure. Government can calculate the costs of services it might provide. It cannot, however, calculate their economic value because that value depends upon the subjective judgments of consumers. Citizens became most dissatisfied with government as a "business agency" when their economic goals diverged from those of the government and their fellow citizens.

When districts (or towns) are run for profit, they acquire a quantitative standard for success. Those activities or services that increase profits should be continued; those that do not should be terminated. Organizations like hospitals or universities, of course, can choose to ignore purely economic standards in their planning schemes if they deem certain services or activities valuable and if they find people willing to subsidize them while they provide such services. Profit and loss calculations, Martin Schiesl (1977, 146) maintains, are inappropriate to city government because the city "presents a problem of government in which the human element, such as the everyday wellbeing, schooling, hygiene, and the general happiness of a vast community of men, women, and children, is ever present."

A crucial difference between city planning and entrepreneurial planning is related to the use of information. City planning should centralize information and direct its use to the representatives of the people. Without personal knowledge of local circumstances, government planners must decide if a service (e.g., public streetlights) is valuable or not. Usually they establish rules and procedures for such decisions that rule out local exception. Even if special interests (e.g., the representatives of the rich, the bosses, labor, interested businesses) did not capture the political process, as they are likely to do, democratic governments are often unable to make as efficient use of information as would those whose livelihood depends upon intimate contact with that information.[3] To some extent, cities have recognized the advantages of decentralized planning by refusing to plan the uses of individual lots. There, the consumer and the producer of the property agree upon its usage, subject to some regulation.

Where planning is private, thousands of individuals make use of their specialized knowledge of their own needs and resources, coordinating their activities through a price system that no central power could replicate. Only high demand for the CMD's array of services can explain its growth; only low demand can explain its decline as a manufacturing center. No centralized planner can process as much knowledge as the marketplace can when it calibrates supply with demand. The CMD acknowledged this fact by rebelling against the centralized dominion of the city of Chicago over its public streets. It built and maintained its own _ streets so that it could control the right-of-way, thereby giving local freight traffic precedence over car and wagon traffic.

Only entrepreneurial trial and error can determine whether a central steam plant is _economically_ efficient (as opposed to technologically efficient) in certain economic circumstances. This method of trial and error can sometimes achieve goals that could not have been conceived by any centralized plan itself (Hayek 1972). Recognizing this fact, the CMD left the planning of its Kedzie District streets to the uncoordinated plans of its consumers as they asked for particular parcels of land. City planners can, however, direct economic resources to goals that the public deems valuable (by evidence of its votes) but that it is unable—or unwilling—to pay for voluntarily.

Entrepreneurial planning also differs from city planning in its attitude toward economic failure. The market discourages failure; the city often subsidizes it. When entrepreneurs tried to rent homes to the middle class, they ended up paying for the undesired result: unrented homes. When cities provided unprofitable housing projects, we all ended up paying for them. Mollenkopf (1983, 298), calling for national intervention, wants to restrain competition among cities (and probably among industrial districts) because he considers it harmful to local political reform and to human values not purchased in the marketplace (like a sense of community).

The level of individual participation is another distinguishing feature of entrepreneurial communities, as compared to public communities. In a democracy, individuals are encouraged to participate in democratic planning. After all, they are forced to submit to democratic will. (Generally, they submit readily, *as if* they were engaging in voluntary, contractual behavior.) Entrepreneurial communities may have varying levels of participation, according to factors of supply and demand. Condominium associations, demonstrating the profitability of participation, often have democratic voting procedures. Participation may depend upon shares of stock. Entrepreneurial communities recognize that participatory planning of central services is bothersome to many. Enjoying legal and personal protection under the law and retaining the option to secede from association, companies at the CMD ceded planning, regulation, and voting rights to Prince and the CMD trustees. "In the Central Manufacturing District, all the legal battles—smoke, noise, light, heat, sewage, pavements, water sidewalks, taxes—all have been fought. You know just what you have and what you can do, and you know what you will have to pay" (*Efficiency and the Central Manufacturing District* 1923).

Because the members of a voluntary community already share common interests, consensus can be achieved more easily in entrepreneurial communities than in city government. Turn-of-the-century business leaders wanted small government because they did not trust government; in particular, they did not trust the working-class majority that might have dominated government. By insisting on small government and failing to recognize the entrepreneurial opportunities of planning, they ended up insisting upon underprovisioned communal services—services that they willingly paid for in the CMD.

Parks, for instance, were communal services routinely provided by donor-supported park commissions. There was no effective way of collecting user fees for parks. Yet the grass lawns of the CMD performed the function of a park—on a scale appropriate to the industrial nature of the district. Sea Ranch is a park; its commissioners merely put the roads and trails in to let people enjoy nature's wonders. These entrepreneur-mandated improvements, coupled with extensive rules of preservation, took the place of city park commissions and charitable donors.

Conclusion

Chicago's Central Manufacturing District, a for-profit entrepreneurial community, is important because it initiated the industrial-park movement in America. CMD history destroys the myth that only government can create large-scale, unified district planning. Planning and central service were not lacking in the CMD; they were the very reasons for its existence and success. If private planning fails to meet the needs of consumers in a changing technological environment, as the CMD's eventually did, then private communities themselves should fail, as the CMD did, and be replaced by other managerial enterprises. Tax-subsidized cities may temporarily maintain outdated economies and methods of production, but such conservatism is not productive of the general welfare.

A city's decision to provide government—to provide justice through its monopoly on legitimized violence—need not be connected to its managerial decisions to provide streets, lights, snow removal, transportation, or even fire services. Private city managers may provide businesses and residents with the most efficient economic services—without the expense and uncertainty of city government. They may manage information better in the interests of everyone. Unlike politicians, motivated by factions of constituencies, they will have a clear economic stake in the long-term development of cities. They will not produce one type of city but as many types as there are people to attract. We may see environmentalist cities that ban cars, Christian temperance cities that ban liquor, and capitalist cities that maximize growth. Each will, in its own way, compete to provide services most efficiently.

NOTES

1. See Spencer Heath MacCallum's contribution to this volume and MacCallum 1970 for further discussion of the planning of shopping centers, hotels, and mobile-home parks.

2. For a general history of the district, one that shows its important role in national affairs, see the articles by Schopp (1955) and Ibata (1985).

3. Mancur Olson's *The Rise and Decline of Nations* (1982) argues cogently that special interests representing minority factions will probably take over the political process. Olson shows that small groups are more capable of acquiring information about their interests and membership, that they are better able to coordinate political activities in their interests, and that they are capable of receiving rewards (subsidies or monopoly profits) that more than pay for their political activities. In American city government, his theories have been illustrated by the high profits of monopolized public utilities (e.g., streetcars, power generators) and, in a noneconomic context, by the power of white racist minorities in Chicago's ethnic neighborhoods. In both cases, small groups out-politicked public sentiment.

REFERENCES

Central Manufacturing District: A Book of Descriptive Text, Photographs and Testimonial Letters about Chicago Junction Railway Service and the Central Manufacturing District—The Center of Chicago "The Great Central Market." 1915. Chicago: Central Manufacturing District.
Conduit, C. 1973. *Chicago, 1910–1929: Building, Planning, and Urban Technology.* Chicago: University of Chicago Press.
Efficiency and the Central Manufacturing District. 1923. Pamphlet. Chicago: Central Manufacturing District.
Hayek, F. A. [1944] 1972. *The Road to Serfdom.* Chicago: University of Chicago Press.
Hubbard, E. 1911. *A Little Journey to the Central Manufacturing District of Chicago.* East Aurora, N.Y.: Roycrofters.
Ibata, D. 1985. Chicago Claims Credit for First Industrial Park. *Chicago Tribune,* February 17, 16.
MacCallum, S. H. 1970. *The Art of Community.* Menlo Park, Calif.: Institute for Humane Studies.
Mollenkopf, J. 1983. *The Contested City.* Princeton: Princeton University Press.
Olson, M. 1982. *The Rise and Decline of Nations.* New Haven: Yale University Press.
Schiesl, M. J. 1977. *The Politics of Efficiency.* Berkeley: University of California Press.
Schopp, M. D. 1955. Fifty Golden Years. *CMD Magazine* (June–October).
Stigler, G. 1975. *The Citizen and the State: Essays on Regulation.* Chicago: University of Chicago Press.
Sutcliffe, A. 1980. *Towards the Planned City: Germany, Britain, the United States and France, 1780–1914.* New York: St. Martin's Press.

2

Law and Social Services in the Voluntary City

Introduction to
Part 2

Law and Social Services
in the Voluntary City

Is law possible without the state? Surprisingly, the answer appears to be yes. The most famous, and durable, example of market-based law and order is the "law merchant," the voluntarily evolved and enforced law that governs trade among international merchants. Bruce L. Benson (chapter 6) investigates the ancient and modern law merchant in both Europe and the United States. In the centuries after the collapse of the Roman Empire the peoples of medieval Western Europe faced a bewildering absence of central authority. Despite severe limits on information and communication, medieval and early modern Europeans saw the value of institutions and procedures that facilitated trade. Through a process of trial and error they discovered that the forces of reputation and social sanction were strong enough to enforce law *if that law was created in a process that all of the participants regarded as fair.* The code of the law merchant was respected because it was fair, and it was fair because it had to be respected if it was to be obeyed. The substantive rules that made up the law merchant were therefore intimately bound up with the voluntary nature of the process. When overarching authority does exist, so that voluntarism is no longer necessary for law, we may have fewer grounds for thinking that the process of law-making will evolve toward substantively fair rules.

Benson argues that law merchants fell into disuse as a means of solving local disputes not because of market failure but because judges in criminal and common-law courts, who were often paid out of litigation fees, found it in their financial interest to take jurisdiction over commercial cases. The law merchant remained important in international law, however, and in the late twentieth century arose again in local disputes in the form of private arbitration. Ironically, the same criminal and common-law courts that had once been so antagonistic encouraged this revival as a means to relieve congestion. Today, arbitration and the conflict-resolution business have become growth industries. These and other methods of private adjudication offer a variety of efficiencies over state systems and have even spread to environmental mediation and community disputes (Benson 1998).

Although many people now take for granted the public-sector responsibility for criminal justice, it was not always so. Rather, as Stephen Davies (chapter 7) reveals, centralized provision is a recent phenomenon. In the nineteenth century, criminal justice was primarily the domain of communities and private prosecution associations. Prosecution associations created an array of crime-fighting methods. One of the most effective was publicizing their membership lists to put thieves on notice that the long arm of the prosecution association would come after them if their members were victimized. The old system was eventually overwhelmed, but not by crime. Instead, the private system could not be bent to meet the state's expanding interest in controlling morality and economics. Even today vestiges of the old system remain in the form of bounty hunters, without whom the bail system would break down completely (Chamberlin 1998). As a further indication of the importance of private crime-control efforts consider that private security guards in the United States today outnumber public police and that every year millions of crimes are averted by armed citizens (Benson 1998; Kleck 1997). The failure of the public sector to control crime and the current revival of private policing suggest that exclusive reliance on the public sector is not only impractical but potentially dangerous.

The law-merchant courts were not the only institutions spontaneously providing what many now call "public services." As our modern public-sector institutions continue to be stressed, we can learn much from the rich history of private and voluntary provision of such services as welfare, medical care, and education.

David T. Beito's second contribution to this volume (chapter 8) discusses the fraternal societies that arose during the nineteenth century to look after the indigent prior to the establishment of the welfare state. Many of these voluntary associations functioned as sickness- and life-insurance orders; membership in these organizations was in the tens of millions. Yet by the twentieth century private groups increasingly became constrained by regulations. Much of the mutual-aid function today has become the purview of the welfare state. Could a return to the fraternal orders of the nineteenth century be possible or even desirable? Perhaps not, on both scores. The lesson to be learned from these historical investigations, however, is not that we should return to the institutions of the past. Twenty-first-century institutions are unlikely to duplicate nineteenth-century institutions. As Friedrich Hayek (1967, 35) points out, in the social sciences we are "confined to describing kinds of patterns that will appear if certain general conditions are satisfied, but can rarely if ever derive from this knowledge any predictions of specific phenomena." But knowing, as we do now, that voluntary institutions evolved in the nineteenth century to meet the needs of participants at the time should give us more courage to experiment with voluntary institutions in the twenty-first century.

David G. Green (chapter 9) discusses the "friendly societies" of Britain and Australia, which were similar to America's fraternal orders. Amazingly, Green notes that "[w]hen the British government introduced compulsory social insurance for twelve million persons under the 1911 National Insurance Act, registered and unregistered voluntary insurance associations—chiefly the friendly societies—already covered at least nine million individuals." Voluntary insurance was preferred to the poorhouse because voluntary institutions were better able than government handouts to maintain the individual's sense of self-respect. Contrary to much of what is written about the poor and working classes before the welfare state, these citizens were not "passive victims of events" but rather proactive and creative. They formed societies that called forth the best in themselves.

In the case of education, James Tooley (chapter 10) shows that in the nineteenth century, prior to any major state involvement in education, literacy and school attendance rates in England, Wales, and the United States were already at 90 percent and rising. Moreover, in many developing countries today a substantial private-education industry exists to alleviate the failure of government-run schools. In the United States, the weaknesses of the government schools have spurred a search for alternatives such as charter schools, private schools, and home schooling. Though their numbers are still small, these arrangements have a potentially large effect because of the competition they offer to nearby government schools.

REFERENCES

Benson, B. 1998. *To Serve and Protect.* New York: New York University Press.
Chamberlin, J. A. 1998. Bounty Hunters: Can the Criminal Justice System Live Without Them? *University of Illinois Law Review* 1998:1175–1205.
Hayek, F. A. 1967. The Theory of Complex Phenomena. In *Studies in Philosophy, Politics and Economics.* Chicago: University of Chicago Press.
Kleck, G. 1997. *Targeting Guns.* Hawthorne, N.Y.: Aldine de Gruyter.

6

Justice without Government

The Merchant Courts of Medieval Europe and Their Modern Counterparts

Bruce L. Benson

Virtually all legal scholars subscribe to the theory that for a law to be recognized, it must be backed by some sort of absolute authority.[1] As a consequence, they also generally assume that an effective legal system and coercive state power must inevitably go hand in hand. This view, however, is inconsistent with historical experience. Anthropologists and historians long ago documented the existence of stateless legal systems among groups ranging from the preconquest Irish clans to North American Indian tribes. By comparison, scholars have paid comparatively little attention to a more modern example of law without government—mercantile law, or the "law merchant." In one form or another, the law merchant has operated continuously for at least a thousand years.

The Medieval Law Merchant

The rise of the law merchant in Europe can be traced at least as far back as the tenth and eleventh centuries.[2] Rapid expansion in agricultural productivity during this period meant that fewer laborers were required to produce sufficient food and clothing to sustain the population. This agricultural boom stimulated higher levels of trade, thus providing new opportunities for a larger segment of the population to earn a livelihood in the emerging towns and cities. One consequence of and impetus for this increased economic productivity and urban population growth was the emergence of professional merchants to facilitate the trade of both agricultural commodities and the products of the new urban centers.

These merchants wanted to expand international trade, but highly localized legal systems stood in their way. To get around this problem, an international system of commercial law—the medieval law merchant—began to develop and evolve. As Harold Berman has noted, commercial law emerged during this period "as an integrated, developing system, a *body* of law," one that regulated virtually every aspect of commercial transactions in *all of Europe* (and frequently outside Europe) after the eleventh century.[3]

Unlike many modern legal systems, the law merchant "governed" without the coercive power of a state. It was *voluntarily produced, voluntarily adjudicated, and voluntarily enforced.* Indeed, it had to be.[4] The law merchant's legitimacy rested on a complex network of reciprocal and voluntary relationships supported by reputations. Merchants formed their own courts in each urban center, market, and trade fair to adjudicate disputes in accordance with their own evolving laws. Merchant justice was a participatory process. Judges were always merchants chosen from the relevant merchant community. They were experts in commercial matters who had the respect of the community at large. The basic foundations of commercial law as we see it today were laid during this period.

How could thousands of merchants from such diverse backgrounds (both culturally and geographically) produce law? What was the source of recognition of this law? The best way to answer these questions is to realize the parallels between the development of commercial law and the development of markets. In any free market, traders enter into voluntary exchanges. Often the only "bond" is the reputation of the traders. The market determines the value of disparate goods so that "equal" exchanges are possible. Indeed, without market-determined prices, the concept of equality in value has little substance. Furthermore, merchants frequently change roles as buyers and sellers so that the duties that arise out of exchange are reversible.

When the merchant class began to develop in various urban centers, localized business practices (customs) also developed. International trade required that major conflicts among local customs be eliminated. As merchants began to transact business across political, cultural, and geographical boundaries, they transported trade practices to foreign markets. Those previously localized customs that they discovered to be common to many localities became part of the international law merchant. Furthermore, where conflicts arose, those practices that proved to be the most efficient at facilitating commercial interaction supplanted those that were less efficient.[5] As international trade expanded, the benefits from uniform rules *and* uniform application of those rules superseded the benefits of discriminatory rules and rulings that might favor a few local individuals. As Berman points out, by the twelfth century, commercial law had evolved to a level where alien merchants had substantial protection in disputes with local merchants and "against the vagaries of local laws and customs."[6]

The laws that came to dominate the international law merchant were those that reinforced rather than superceded business practice. In effect, they commanded merchants to do what they had already promised to do.[7] Because individuals had to *voluntarily* adopt a certain practice (enter into a contract) before it could become common usage, the law merchant had to be objective and impartial. Reciprocity, in the sense of mutual benefits and costs, is the very essence of trade. Both parties enter into an exchange because each expects to obtain something more valuable than what is given up. The legal principle of reciprocity of rights, however—developed in the late eleventh and early twelfth centuries and still understood today—involves more than mutual exchange. It involves an element of fairness of exchange. Thus, commercial law required that exchanges had to be entered into "fairly."[8] Fairness was a required feature of the law merchant, of course, precisely because its "authority" arose voluntarily from recognition of reciprocal benefits. Individuals would not *voluntarily* recognize a legal system that they did not expect to treat them fairly. The best evidence for the objectivity and impartiality of the law merchant, reflecting this emphasis on fairness, was its universal recognition. Commercial law was further strengthened by its participatory nature.

Merchants formed their own courts to adjudicate disputes in accordance with their own laws. Winners and losers alike accepted these courts' decisions because they recognized the reciprocal benefits of doing so. There was also another motive for compliance: the threat of ostracism by the merchant community at large. A merchant who refused to accept a court ruling would not be in business for long because fellow merchants ultimately controlled an individual's reputation and therefore ability to trade. William C. Wooldridge notes that the threat to reputation and the potential boycott of all future trade "proved, if anything more effective than physical coercion."[9] Nevertheless, this sanction, while a real threat, was not often required. The value of a reputation for dealing in "good faith," Leon Trakman explains, "was the essence of the mercantile agreement. Reciprocity and the threat of business sanctions compelled performance. The ordinary undertakings of merchants were binding because they were 'intended' to be binding, not because any law compelled such performance."[10]

Merchants established their own courts for several reasons. For one thing, state law often differed from mercantile law, thus necessitating a separate judicial system. A second reason was that resolutions of commercial disputes often required consideration of highly technical issues. In such cases, the merchant courts used judges who were experts in that particular area of commerce, unlike royal-court judges who often adjudicated disputes about which they knew nothing. Merchant-court judges were merchants chosen from the relevant merchant community (fair or urban market), some of whom ultimately specialized in the provisions of justice.[11]

Perhaps the most widely noted characteristics of the mercantile courts and their advantage over royal courts were their speed and informality.[12] Merchants of the time had to complete their transactions in one urban market or fair and quickly move to the next. A dispute had to be settled swiftly to minimize disruption of business affairs. This speed and informality could not have been equitably achieved without the use of judges who were highly knowledgeable of commercial issues and concerns and whose judgments would be respected by the merchant community at large. Participatory or communal adjudication was, therefore, a necessary characteristic of the law merchant.

In this same light, merchant courts, in contrast to their governmental counterparts, kept rules of evidence and procedures simple and informal. To steer clear of unnecessary litigation, delays, and other disruptions of commerce, appeals were forbidden.[13] Similarly, these courts avoided lengthy testimony under oath; usually did not require notarial attestation as evidence of an agreement; recognized debts as freely transferable through informal "written obligatory," a process developed by merchants themselves to simplify the transfer of debt; considered actions by agents in transactions valid without formal authority; and recognized ownership transfers without physical delivery.[14] Despite the frequent illegality of these procedures in various national courts, the merchant courts did not hesitate to adopt them because they promoted speed and informality in commerce and reduced transaction costs. Although supporters of state-produced law as enforced by royal courts, which was developing during this same period, take pride in its rationality and progressiveness, the fact remains that it never matched the law merchant's rapid adaption to the requirements of an ever-changing commercial system.

Despite the advantages of the law merchant, the common-law and civil-law systems of Western Europe and America eventually absorbed it either in part or in whole. Why? In the next section the process and consequences of that absorption are briefly explored.

The Absorption of the Law Merchant into Royal Law

Around the twelfth century, governments in Europe began to systematically "enact" the customary rules established by the law merchant.[15] England codified the Carta Mercatoria in the fourteenth century. Merchants continued to use their own courts, however, so governments also began to make laws that would move merchants into the royal courts and/or make merchant courts less desirable. In England, for example, the Statute of the Staple of 1353 presumably gave "merchant strangers" protection in the fourteen major trading centers for "staple" products—mainly wool, leather, and lead. Of course, such protection already existed under the law merchant, so this was largely a codification of custom. Similarly, the statute specified that disputes involving these foreign merchants would be settled under the law merchant rather than under royal law or any law of the city that might apply. Significantly, appeals could be taken to the chancellor and the king's council, thus establishing an unprecedented role for the royal courts in enforcement of commercial law. Perhaps more importantly, by creating the possibility of appeal, the statute served to weaken the authority of the merchant courts and the law merchant itself. The potential for appeal made the law merchant appear to be less decisive law. Indeed, common-law institutions became relatively more acceptable because of the increasingly undermined authority of law-merchant institutions.

Several competing court systems existed in England prior to the seventeenth century. Separate royal common-law courts (e.g., Common Pleas, King's Bench, Exchequer), the canon-law courts, royal prerogative courts such as the royal maritime courts, and the merchant courts, among others, competed with one another for various parts of the dispute-resolution business. The common-law courts ultimately triumphed over most of the competition, however. The method of victory was similar in each instance, so the emphasis in the discussion following is on the competition between the common-law and merchant courts. It must be stressed, however, that other courts also actively pursued commercial disputes.

Although merchants courts remained available for commercial disputes until the early seventeenth century, their caseloads gradually shifted into government courts. William M. Landes and Richard A. Posner suggest that the royal courts worked gradually to take more and more cases away from the merchant courts because this was in the financial self-interest of the English judges, who were paid in large part out of litigation fees during this period.[16] This probably added incentives to governmental efforts to absorb the law merchant. Furthermore, because the merchants really remained free to choose between their own courts and the royal courts throughout this period, the fact that merchants chose the royal courts in increasing numbers implies that those courts must have been doing a good job of *applying the law merchant*. The *threat of competition from private merchant courts* always remained (even though their authority was somewhat diminished); if the *royal courts* wanted the merchants' business they *had to enforce law as the merchants saw fit.*[17]

In 1609, the common-law ruling in *Vynior's Case* (4 Eng. Rep. 302 [1969]) substantially altered the competitive relationship between royal and merchant courts, with the advantage going to the royal courts. The dictum pronounced by Lord Edward Coke in reviewing the case, which had been previously judged under private arbitration, was "that though one may be bound to stand to the arbitrament yet he may countermand the arbitrator . . . as a man cannot by his own act make such an authority power or warrant not countermandable which by law and its own proper nature is countermandable."[18] This ruling meant that the decisions of private courts, including the merchant courts, could be reversed by the royal courts because an arbitrator's purpose was, according to Coke, to find a suitable compromise, while a judge's purpose was to rule on the merits of the case. In effect, it withdrew the Statute of the Staple's guarantee that merchant disputes would be settled according to the law merchant rather than royal law. The use of private courts in England for commercial disputes virtually disappeared after the sixteenth century.

The law merchant did not die, but it changed, becoming less universal and more localized under state influence. It began to reflect the policies, interests, and procedures of the kings of various nation-states. The transformation was most striking in England, where the courts rejected many of the underpinnings of the law merchant after Coke's 1609 ruling.[19] Merchants became increasingly constrained under the common-law system as the informal, speedy institutions they had developed disappeared for well over two centuries. Still, the law merchant could not be completely eliminated for a very good reason. Custom prevailed in international trade, and England was a great trading nation. English judges had to compete with other national courts for the attention of international merchants' disputes, and thus they had to recognize commercial custom in cases involving international trade if they hoped to attract such cases.

The Modern Law Merchant

Some legal historians cite Lord Mansfield as the "founder of commercial law" in England, but in fact, as Trakman points out, Mansfield actually reintroduced the international law merchant into English law.[20] Mansfield argued quite forcefully that England's commercial law had to develop as business practice developed and had to recognize business custom and usage. Common-law judges had some incentives to listen to Mansfield's arguments. International competition by national courts for the attention of merchants was apparently getting more intense.[21] As England's relative position in world trade began to decline, common-law courts began to lose international business disputes to other nations' courts. One important reason for this was that the European countries' civil law had been much more receptive to the law merchant than had English common law.[22] This source of competition was one factor that forced common-law courts to once again recognize the law merchant. A second impetus for once again recognizing the merchants' law may have come later, however, when commercial arbitration reemerged and the common-law courts' hold on intranational commercial law once again came under *significant competitive threat.*

The modern resurgence of commercial arbitration can be traced to the U.S. Civil War. The Union's naval blockade of the Confederacy resulted in tremendous court congestion in England due to contract claims regarding the purchase, delivery, and sale of cotton to British markets—claims that would have taken years to untangle.[23] Many ship owners became unwilling to run the blockade, and a lot of those who tried had their vessels sunk. Prices fluctuated unpredictably. Further complications arose due to British neutrality and to contraband-of-war laws. Insurance was either unavailable or carried new and extremely complex provisions developed in light of tremendous uncertainty. These provisions required reinterpretation with each new contingency. Because of all the difficulties and uncertainties associated with the blockade and the resulting public-court backlog, the Liverpool Cotton Association agreed to insert arbitration clauses in their contracts. The majority of disputes involved Liverpool merchants because they handled most of the cotton trade at the time. Arbitration proved so inexpensive and convenient compared to public-court adjudication, as well as less disruptive to business arrangements (the adversarial nature of public-law suits tended to cause many more hard feelings, leading to the termination of profitable business relationships, while the compromising character of arbitration tended to preserve them), that other Liverpool commercial associations quickly adopted the device.[24]

Within a short period, the success of arbitration in Liverpool led to its adoption in London. The large commodity dealers (of corn, oil seed, cotton, and coffee) established arbitration clauses first, followed by stock dealers and produce merchants. Eventually, professional associations of architects, engineers, estate agents, and auctioneers took up the practice, regularly putting clauses in all their contracts guaranteeing that disputes over transactions would go to arbitration rather than to government courts. These groups and individuals quickly recognized the benefits of arbitration *despite* Coke's 1609 ruling. It appears that common-law recognition of the law merchant was inevitable. But more significantly in the context of this presentation, arbitration was back to stay.

The International Law Merchant

The law merchant continued to rule in varying degrees in international commerce even as it was subjugated within national legal systems. Indeed, modern international commercial law is a universal law. Agreements among merchants are the primary source of legal uniformity because agreements among governments may take years or even decades to draft and implement.[25]

Today, many international trade associations have their own conflict-resolution procedures. Other traders rely on the International Chamber of Commerce (ICC), which has established a substantial arbitration institution. ICC arbitrators are experts in international commerce. Arbitrators from a nationality different from those who are parties in the dispute are typically chosen. Much like the procedures of the medieval fair and market courts, the procedures of the ICC and other international arbitration tribunals are speedy and flexible reflections of the reciprocal arrangements of the international community of merchants, who back decisions and agreements that arise from their adjudication processes.[26] The fact is that the international law merchant, free from the dominant influences of governments and localized politics, has developed and grown much more easily and effectively than has intranational commercial law.

The American Law Merchant

Merchants brought their law to colonial America and quickly moved to establish their own systems of rules and dispute resolution even as common law was subjugating the law merchant and its courts in England.[27] Custom and private arbitration institutions dominated commercial law and its enforcement throughout the eighteenth century. Commercial arbitration, for example, was used to settle disputes in and between the New York and Philadelphia business communities as those communities developed in the seventeenth century.[28] As John R. Aiken explains in his examination of the Dutch period in New York, for instance: "Arbitration in New Netherlands in the 17th century . . . was frequent, swift, and relatively simple compared to the English common law."[29] One cannot look to public-court records in order to determine the level of arbitration activity because arbitration decisions were almost never appealed to these courts. Thus, William C. Jones draws upon newspapers, merchant letters, and the records of the New York Chamber of Commerce, as well as legal records, and finds that arbitration was in constant and widespread use throughout both the Dutch colonial period studied by Aiken (1624–64) and the British colonial period in New York (1664–1783).[30] Indeed, one of the first actions taken by the New York Chamber of Commerce at its first meeting, on April 5, 1768, was to make provisions for arbitration, and the chamber's first arbitration committee was appointed on June 7 of that year.[31] There is evidence of "considerable demand" for arbitration services from the chamber, as committees were appointed regularly until 1775, when the chamber temporarily suspended meetings because of the war.[32] But on September 7, 1779, a committee was again appointed, and arbitration meetings continued throughout the Revolutionary period. In fact, during British occupation of New York, the chamber's arbitration committee was the only court for civil cases—civil disputes were referred to the chamber by the British occupation forces.[33]

After the Revolution, the New York Chamber of Commerce continued to provide arbitration to its members.[34] There is also substantial evidence of arbitration in other states.[35] The fact is that government courts of the period did not apply commercial law in what the merchant community considered to be a just and expeditious fashion: "Not only did courts, according to one New York merchant, dispense 'expensive endless law'; they were slow to develop legal doctrine that facilitated commercial development."[36] Although the relevant body of precedent law for the American courts was English common law, including Coke's 1609 common-law ruling subjugating arbitration to the government courts, the use of commercial arbitration continued to develop during the colonial and post-Revolutionary periods. Given this and other precedents, private arbitration clearly did not take its authority from the state, and indeed, according to the relevant state-made law, arbitration decisions had no legal authority.[37] In actuality, however, arbitration decisions were authoritative. Authority arose from reciprocal arrangements developed within the merchant community and individual recognition of potential reputation affects associated with refusing to accept an arbitration decision.

Even as state court systems developed and matured over the period from 1775 to 1835, they remained hostile to arbitration. The courts' attitude toward arbitration during the period might even be described as one of increasing hostility, but "there was no time during the period when arbitration was not known and used by a significant number of people."[38] In fact, new sources of arbitration emerged to replace other arrangements. For example, in New York, as the economy grew and diversified, the Chamber of Commerce gradually became less important as a provider of arbitration services; more narrowly focused, specialized "commercial groups, whether formally organized or not," developed internal arbitration procedures.[39] The New York Stock Exchange, founded in 1792, formally provided for arbitration in its 1817 constitution, for example, and it "has been working successfully ever since," primarily to rectify disputes between New York Stock Exchange members and their customers.[40]

The trend of increasing hostility by common-law courts toward arbitration began to reverse in the 1830s in some states.[41] It must be recognized, however, that arbitration was firmly in place before this reversal in court attitude began; furthermore, arbitration developed in states whose courts were slow to change, such as New York, as well as in states whose courts changed more rapidly. For instance, there is evidence of arbitration for members of the New York Commercial

Exchange at least as early as 1861, and perhaps earlier.[42] As merchants organized into various associations and exchanges, provisions were *always* made for the arbitration of disputes among members. Thus, there is considerable evidence of widespread use of arbitration provisions in contracts and of arbitration performed under the auspices of trade associations and mercantile exchanges. The volume of evidence is particularly heavy for the last four decades of the nineteenth century, well in advance of the passage of modern arbitration statutes.[43]

The declining importance of the New York Chamber of Commerce as a source of arbitration services is important in the context of the following discussion of the political impetus for arbitration statutes. The chamber continued to offer its members arbitration services, "at least in a desultory fashion, throughout the nineteenth century," but use of the chamber's services gradually declined through the first half of the century and ultimately disappeared altogether.[44] As the chamber lost its dominant position in New York commercial arbitration, "it began to seek support from the state in its efforts to provide adjudicatory facilities for its members."[45] Its state charter was amended in 1861 to explicitly provide for an arbitration committee and to provide that awards of the committee could be entered as judgments of courts of record if the parties desired such court enforcement. Despite this court backing, however, the chamber continued to lose ground to other arbitration arrangements. Thus, an 1874 amendment to the charter was obtained that provided for appointment by the state governor of "an arbitrator of the Chamber of Commerce of the State of New York" to be paid by the chamber; in addition, members could be *summoned* to arbitrate their disputes, although they could escape the chamber's jurisdiction by filing an objection with the arbitrator.[46] An 1874 act was added that specified that members of the Chamber of Commerce "could be required by requisition to bring their cases before this [the Chamber's arbitration] court whose judge was to be paid by the state."[47] Why were such statutes sought by the chamber? The chamber's arbitration tribunal had lost sight of some of the factors that make arbitration attractive. It had a permanently sitting judge rather than allowing the parties the ability to choose an arbitrator with particular expertise. The judge was even to be paid by the state, so those businesspersons who preferred to escape the government's influence might have been wary of the chamber's arbitrator. At any rate, even though a judge was appointed, though chamber members were supposedly required by statute to take their disputes to this judge, and though a chamber arbitration ruling could take on the force of a court ruling if the parties agreed, the chamber attracted virtually no arbitration business after this. Instead, individuals turned to their smaller formal and informal groups to arbitrate disputes. Consequently, the chamber's arbitration judge was only paid by the state for the first two years after appointment. As Jones concludes, "It would appear thus that the Chamber constantly tried to provide arbitration facilities for its members, but it never devised a completely satisfactory system."[48]

Some observers have argued that the decline and ultimate disappearance of chamber arbitration reflected a general decline and disappearance of all commercial arbitration during the nineteenth century, with business disputes shifting into the state courts.[49] State courts apparently did increase their commercial dispute—resolution activity during this period, but the fact is that commercial arbitration was in constant use throughout the century under the auspices of informal business groups, formal trade associations, and organized mercantile exchanges. Public judges in America have been somewhat more receptive of the law merchant than their English counterparts.[50] Indeed, the Uniform Commercial Code indicates that *business practices and customs have served as the primary source of substantive business law.* "The positive law of the realm," as Trakman observes, "was forced to conform to the mandate of the merchants, not vice versa."[51] This may reflect the jurisdictional divisions that exist in the United States, which imply that U.S competition for disputes may be much more significant than in England. Furthermore, the potential for arbitration as an alternative to public courts always existed in the United States, *forcing public courts* that sought to adjudicate commercial disputes to *dispense law as the merchant community had developed it.* Nonetheless, arbitration was in constant use throughout the nineteenth century, and the late part of the century saw an even more rapid development of arbitration relative to litigation. Indeed, this apparently created enough arbitration demand for the chamber's efforts to supply arbitration arrangements to reemerge. One factor explaining the rapid increase of arbitration relative to public courts is the growing problem of court congestion and trial delay. In addition, "the growth of the regulatory state unsettled advocates of commercial autonomy who turned to arbitration as a shield against government intrusion."[52] By the end of World War I, arbitration had clearly made "the courts secondary recourse in many areas and completely superfluous in others."[53] Thus, arbitration in North America "did not suddenly come into being . . . [in 1920] because of the passage of a statute making agreements to arbitrate future disputes enforceable. Rather it has existed with and without the benefit of statutes" for several centuries.[54] Merchants avoided government courts because those tribunals did not apply commercial law in what the merchant community considered to be a just and inexpensive fashion.

The practice of commercial arbitration in the United States has continued to grow since its reemergence at the beginning of the twentieth century. By the 1950s, arbitration settled an estimated 75 percent of commercial disputes, and by 1965, the use of commercial arbitration was increasing at the rate of about 10 percent per year.[55] This trend appears to be accelerating, although statistical data on the extent of commercial arbitration are not available. Many industries and most trade associations now insert arbitration clauses into all their contracts.

Nonmerchant Influences on the Evolution of Arbitration

When arbitration reemerged in the United States during the late nineteenth and early twentieth centuries, support came from a surprising source. Influential lawyers proposed that voluntary arbitration *by lawyers* should be used to alleviate court congestion. Public respect for lawyers, the judiciary, and the courts was on the decline during the early twentieth century, and court congestion was becoming a relatively significant problem.[56] Thus, lawyers were on the defensive.[57] They were searching for a means to reduce court congestion and simultaneously increase the standing of judges and lawyers. However, if an alternative forum to the public courts was to be established, lawyers wanted a forum that they might be able to influence and perhaps even dominate. Arbitration was already developing rapidly as an alternative forum, and some lawyers had begun to recognize the competitive threat commercial arbitration posed to the government's adversarial dispute-resolution process. They hoped to dominate arbitration as well. In contrast, businesspersons wanted speedy, inexpensive dispute resolution based on business custom and practice. They wanted the law merchant. Thus, despite merchants' different motives, the Chamber of Commerce supported the New York Bar's strong lobbying effort to obtain state recognition of arbitration's "legality." These efforts led in 1920 to a New York statute designed to overturn Lord Coke's common-law ruling of 1609, which still served as precedent in the United States. This statute made arbitration agreements binding under state law and enforceable in New York's courts. Since then, almost all of the other states have passed similar laws.[58]

Landes and Posner reflect the view of many observers of the legal process when they contend that arbitration clauses in contracts are "effective, in a major part anyway *only* because the public courts enforce such contracts; if they did not, there would often be no effective sanction against the party who simply breaches the contract to arbitrate."[59] In other words, they claim that private arbitration is a viable option to public courts *because* it is backed by those public courts. This claim is demonstrably *false*. For one thing, the historical development of the law merchant indicates that a significant boycott sanction can be produced by the commercial community. Indeed, as noted earlier, the international law merchant survives and flourishes to this day without the backing of a coercive government authority. Beyond that, arbitration caught on and developed in the United States *before* 1920—that is, before an arbitrator's award could be taken into a public court. Indeed arbitration's popularity prior to 1920 indicates that legal coercion is not essential for its success. Moreover, the boycott is still a highly effective sanction.[60] A merchant who refuses to abide by an arbitration ruling finds future access to his or her trade association's arbitration tribunal withdrawn or sees his or her name released to the association membership. These penalties are far more fearsome, Wooldridge notes, "than the cost of the award with which he disagreed. Voluntary and private adjudications [are] voluntarily and privately adhered to if not out of honor, out of self-interest."[61] This does not mean that the New York statute and all those that followed have not had an impact on arbitration. In fact, *arbitration became a less attractive alternative to the public courts than it would have otherwise been in the absence of these laws.*[62]

Lawyers became actively involved in commercial arbitration *because* of these statutes. Businesspersons, for instance, filed an enormous number of court cases after passage of the New York statute to try to determine what characteristics of arbitration would be considered "legal" by the courts.[63] Cases involved such issues as the appropriate way to select arbitrators, whether lawyers had to be present, whether stenographic notes of the proceedings should be taken, and so on. Businesspersons, forced to pay attention to the prospect of judicial review, had to make their arbitration processes compatible with statute and precedent law *including* procedural aspects of common law. One observer of the period following 1920 noted that "[t]here is irony in the fate of one who takes precautions to avoid litigation by submitting to arbitration, and who, as a reward for his pain, finds himself in court fighting not on the merits of his case but on the merits of arbitration"; this "monumental tragicomedy" demonstrates the success of the gov-

ernment legal process at "thwarting legitimate efforts to escape its tor-
tuous procedure."[64]

The use of arbitration is no longer limited to commercial disputes
between merchants. The practice has spread to other areas as well. By
1970, insurance companies were arbitrating over fifty thousand claims.[65]
The National Association of Home Builders has begun a Home Owners' Warranty program, which offers arbitration of buyers' complaints
against the association's builders. The warranty had been applied to
roughly 950,000 homes by 1981, and 1,800 such cases were resolved by
the American Arbitration Association (AAA) alone in 1980.[66]

Consumer disputes are also increasingly being handled through
arbitration. The Council of Better Business Bureaus operates arbitration programs for consumers in many parts of the country. It encourages businesses to precommit to arbitration of customer complaints.
Then, if customers are not able to achieve satisfactory solutions with
the business, they can turn to the local Better Business Bureau (BBB).
Typically the BBB attempts informal conciliation, but if that fails it
gives the customer and business the choice of an arbitrator from a pool
of volunteers to resolve the disagreement. In many cases it holds the
arbitration hearing in the consumer's home so the defective merchandise can be examined. One of the largest areas of consumer arbitration
by the BBB concerns automobiles and auto insurance. Several auto
manufacturers have contracts with the Council of Better Business
Bureaus to arbitrate car owners' complaints about the firms' cars or
service. In addition, the AAA arbitrates over fifteen thousand auto
insurance cases per year.[67]

Arbitration is being used in other consumer disputes as well. For
example, medical-malpractice arbitration, which dates from 1929, is on
the rise as malpractice litigation has become more costly and widespread.
As in commercial arbitration, prior agreement is important in these
cases. Subscribers to the nation's largest prepaid medical care system, the
Kaiser Foundation of Health Plans of California, agree to arbitrate any
claims when they sign up, for instance, and the hospital and medical
associations in California sponsor a two hundred–hospital arbitration
system.[68] The AAA also offers medical-malpractice arbitration.

Although the character of arbitration has been substantially
influenced by the efforts of government to subjugate it, the advantages
obviously remain considerable.[69] The same advantages explain the very
recent phenomenon of private *for-profit* dispute-resolution firms and
"rent-a-judge" systems.

Rent-a-Judge Justice

A statute in California that has been in existence since 1872 states that individuals in a dispute have the right to have a full court hearing before any referee they might choose.[70] In 1980, there was a seventy thousand–case public court backlog in California with a median pretrial delay of over fifty months. Thus, it is not too surprising that two lawyers who wanted a complex business case settled quickly "rediscovered" the statute; they found a retired judge with expertise in the area of dispute, paid him at attorney's fee rates, and saved their clients tremendous time and expense.

No count of the number of rent-a-judge cases tried since 1980 exists, but the civil-court coordinator of the Los Angeles County Superior Court estimates that several hundred disputes had been so settled through the first five years of operation in their county. Most of the private cases involve complex business disputes that litigants "feel the public courts cannot quickly and adequately" try.[71] Private judging is now a growth industry across the country. Indeed, several private for-profit *firms* have entered the justice market in several states during the past few years.[72] Although California's statute and several like it in other states treat all decisions of private judges like arbitrated judgments, there are a couple of subtle differences between this new system and traditional arbitration. First, individuals and firms in several states are now actively selling their services as judges to earn profits; second, arbitration clauses in previously existing contracts play no role in bringing disputes into these private courts.[73] Furthermore, these courts are expanding their scope to consider noncommercial disputes, as are other sources of private dispute resolution.

Private Courts for Noncommercial Disputes

During the last several years, private courts have come into existence to resolve many civil disputes. Private for-profit courts now consider such matters as divorce, for instance, and participatory tribunals mediate or arbitrate consumer complaints, insurance claims, and so on. The private sector has not moved into the area of criminal adjudication to a great extent yet, but there are indications that such a move is possible.

The primary techniques of nonjudicial dispute resolution are mediation and arbitration.[74] Mediation involves impartial third parties who help the two parties in a dispute reach their own agreement. Arbitration corresponds to the public courts and private commercial courts in the sense that impartial persons are given authority to determine the outcome of a dispute. Mediation generally involves compromise, where each party grants concessions, but an arbitrator does not seek a compromise in the same sense—an arbitrator reaches a decision based on the merits of the case presented by the two parties in the dispute. Both nonjudicial mediation and arbitration are widely used in areas of commercial and consumer disputes, labor-management relations, neighborhood and family strife, and even in environmental clashes.

The example of environmental mediation is especially intriguing and casts doubt on the conventional wisdom that the existence of "externalities" requires government intervention because private-sector individuals will be unable to solve such problems. Interestingly enough, environmental disputes are increasingly being solved through private mediation. Numerous examples of successful mediation of environmental disputes now exist, including: (1) an agreement on water levels between a lakeside community in Maine and the hydroelectric dam controlling the levels; (2) agreements needed to convert a large power plant in Massachusetts from burning (imported) oil to (domestic) coal; (3) settlement of a dispute over the siting of a city landfill in Wisconsin; (4) the establishment of a recreation trail along an abandoned rail spur in Missouri; and (5) settlement of a dispute regarding a proposed logging operation in the Francis Marion National Forest in South Carolina, which threatened the nesting grounds and therefore the likely extinction of the rare Backman's warbler. These and other successes have led some observers to conclude that "litigation is just not efficient. There are incredible delays, high costs and even when someone is declared the winner he doesn't feel like a winner."[75] Court rulings may, for instance, be made on the basis of some narrow technical point that leaves the basic issue unresolved, so that the victory is really empty. Furthermore, the adversarial court system does not seek a compromise to which both parties *voluntarily agree;* it *forces* a solution that at least one, and perhaps both, of the parties find unsatisfactory, virtually guaranteeing future confrontations.

Mediators are less bound by formal rulings than are government judges. Mediators may chair meetings between groups involved in the dispute, carry messages between the groups, act as fact finders, make recommendations, and so forth. The basic purpose of all such actions is to help the parties reach a mutually agreed upon compromise by aiding in the negotiation process.[76]

Community Conflict Resolution

The AAA in Philadelphia ran one of the earliest community dispute-resolution projects. The overcrowded courts began diverting minor criminal cases to this private court in 1969. Its success provided the impetus for the movement of minor criminal cases into neighborhood justice centers. During the 1970s and early 1980s, the AAA became increasingly involved in minor criminal and civil disputes such as neighborhood fights and juvenile offenses.[77] The AAA's Community Dispute Division is today its most rapidly growing division as more and more neighborhoods recognize the advantages of arbitration and/or mediation.

T. S. Denenberg and R. V. Denenberg point out that since the 1960s arbitration and mediation have been used in a large number of programs to resolve "conflicts that courts may find too trivial or too elusive: domestic quarrels, squabbles between neighbors and similar animosities among ethnic groups."[78] Community Conflict Programs have been developed in Los Angeles; Philadelphia; Kansas City; Atlanta; San Francisco; Miami; Boston; Garden City; New York; and Cleveland. The programs have been designed to seek compromise solutions to disputes by using volunteers from the neighborhood to serve as mediators (and at times arbitrators). Advocates of community dispute resolution, such as the vice president of the Ford Foundation, which has sponsored a number of the programs, point out that the courts are often not appropriate forums for many of these disputes because the court is an adversarial environment while the disputants are not in fact adversaries but rather spouses, friends, lovers, relatives, neighbors.

These programs recently have been going beyond such disputes, however, to consider criminal incidents. In one example from Los Angeles, an Asian grocer filed a complaint against a black youth who had robbed his store. The store owner did not want to involve the police because he wanted to avoid alienating his black customers.[79] In another case, a teenage burglar agreed to undertake twenty hours of cleanup work as restitution.

Community conflict resolution tends to work well when it is voluntary and truly community based. Unfortunately, "alternative dispute resolution" has come to be seen by lawyers and judges as a solution to the problem of public-court congestion and inefficiency. Consequently, lawyers and judges, aided by the Justice Department, have supported and sponsored such programs as adjuncts to the existing court system. In fact, the Justice Department acknowledged in a 1980 report that several of its projects were basically extensions of the courts with which they were affiliated; very few involved cases generated from within the community itself.[80] Participation is not quite voluntary when it is suggested by a criminal-justice bureaucrat.[81] Many neighborhood dispute-resolution centers are thus accurately perceived to be part of the government justice system. Without government subsidies such imposed systems are likely to wither and die.

Does this mean that private mediation and arbitration are not viable alternatives for community dispute resolution? Definitely not. Community dispute-resolution centers in stable neighborhoods founded on voluntary recognition of reciprocities rather than on government coercion may succeed. Indeed, such mediation systems were widespread well into this century among Jewish and Chinese groups in several U.S. cities.[82]

Conclusions

Individuals must face incentives to obey laws and to accept court rulings when disputes under the law arise. One source of incentives is government coercion, but that is not the only source. Individuals can be persuaded to recognize the authority of law if there are clear personal gains from doing so. An examination of the medieval and modern law merchant reveals that government law and government courts are not necessary to establish an effective legal system. Individuals simply must perceive the reciprocal benefits from participating in a voluntarily produced legal system. Such reciprocity may arise as a consequence of market exchange, as under the law merchant, but it can also arise through kinship or religious affiliation or as a result of other mutual interests (e.g., neighborhood integrity, homeowner associations). Thus, the reasons for the success of the law merchant and the impact of government efforts to influence its evolution provide considerable insights for better understanding the success of some modern alternative dispute-resolution arrangements and the potential failure of others. Where the alternative has been voluntarily chosen because of reciprocal recognition of legal authority, it is likely to be effective and survive on its own merits. On the other hand, if outsiders force individuals to accept the alternative and its authority stems from its affiliation with the government courts, it is likely to survive only with continued coercion and subsidization.

NOTES

1. For important exceptions and for criticisms of this view, see Fuller 1964 and Fuller 1981. Also see Hayek 1967 and Hayek 1973. For detailed theoretical discussions of the source of legal authority in the absence of state backing and references to relevant literature, see Benson 1992 and Benson 1993.

2. See Berman 1983; Trakman 1983; Benson 1989; Greif 1989; and Milgrom, North, and Weingast 1990.

3. Berman 1983, 333. Emphasis original.

4. Trakman 1983, 13.

5. Trakman 1983, 11.

6. Berman 1983, 342. Some differences remained across various localities, but this does not imply that the legal system was inefficient or reflected local discriminatory practices. Indeed, the remaining diversity reflected differential preferences for relatively minor variations in commercial practices and institutions among the merchant groups that tended to frequent the various markets or fairs, thus enhancing the universal recognition of developing commercial law. See Trakman 1983, 20–21.

7. Trakman 1983, 10.

8. Trakman 1983, 12; Mitchell 1904, 16.

9. Wooldridge 1970, 96.

10. Trakman 1983, 10. Also see Greif 1989; and Milgrom, North, and Weingast 1990.

11. Milgrom, North, and Weingast 1990.

12. Berman 1983, 347; Mitchell 1904, 13.

13. Trakman 1983, 16.

14. Trakman 1983, 14.

15. Berman 1983, 341.

16. Landes and Posner 1979, 258.

17. The gradual shift of merchant cases to government courts might suggest that government courts were providing and enforcing a "better" law than the law merchant. Certainly the voluntary shift implies that merchants found it in their own self-interest to use government courts. However, note that not all litigation and enforcement costs were covered by fees; taxpayers were subsidizing some aspects of government law enforcement. The relevant self-interest motive actually appears to be that merchants were able to shift part of the cost of adjudicating and enforcing their law onto others, not that government courts provided better law. See Benson 1990, chapter 3. In addition, of course, the merchant courts' authority was being reduced through the creation of rights to royal-court appeal.

18. Quoted in Lazarus et al. 1965, 18.

19. Trakman 1983, 26–27.

20. Trakman 1983, 27.

21. Trakman 1983, 27.

22. Trakman 1983, 24.

23. Wooldridge 1970, 99.

24. Wooldridge 1970, 99.

25. For more details, see Trakman 1983, Berman and Dasser 1990, and Benson 1992.

26. Trakman 1983, 3.

27. Aiken 1974; Auerbach 1983; Benson 1995; Benson 1999; Jones 1956; Odiorne 1953; Odiorne 1954; and Smith 1961, 180, 188.

28. Aiken 1974; Auerbach 1983; and Jones 1956.

29. Aiken 1974, 160.

30. Jones 1956, 209.

31. Jones 1956, 207.

32. Jones 1956, 207.

33. Jones 1956, 209.

34. Jones 1956, 211.

35. Jones 1956, 219; Auerbach 1983, 180, 188; Odiorne 1953; and Odiorne 1954.

36. Auerbach 1983, 33.

37. See Benson 1995 and Benson 1999. In 1698 Parliament passed the first Arbitration Act, stating that once an arbitration award was made, the common-law courts should not overturn the award, either for an error in law or an error of fact. Thus, the courts were directed to let arbitration awards stand unless they were made under fraudulent or otherwise unfair procedures. The doctrine of revocability was not overturned by the statute, however, and more significantly, the common-law courts of postrevolutionary America were not constrained by this English statute.

38. Jones 1956, 213.

39. Jones 1956, 212.

40. Lazarus et al. 1965, 27.

41. See Levy 1993; Benson 1995; and Benson 1999 for discussions of the evolving position of state courts toward arbitration.

42. Jones 1956, 217.

43. Jones 1956, 214–15.

44. Jones 1956, 215.

45. Jones 1956, 215.

46. Jones 1956, 216.

47. Jones 1956, 216.

48. Jones 1956, 216.

49. For example, see Auerbach 1983.

50. Trakman 1983, 33.

51. Trakman 1983, 34.

52. Auerbach 1983, 101.

53. Wooldridge 1970, 101.

54. Jones 1956, 218.

55. Auerbach 1983, 113; Lazarus et al. 1965, 20.

56. Willoughby 1929, 7–26.

57. Auerbach 1983, 103.

58. For more details on the development of arbitration statutes and lawyers' role in the process, see Benson 1995 and Benson 1999.

59. Landes and Posner 1979, 247. Emphasis added. Also see, for example,

Willoughby 1929, 56; Lazarus et al. 1965, 31, 125; American Arbitration Association 1981, 34; Domke 1984, 27; and Murray, Rau, and Sherman 1989, 435.

60. Benson 1992; Benson 1995; Benson 1999.

61. Wooldridge 1970, 101.

62. See Benson 1995 and Benson 1999 for detailed analyses of state arbitration statutes' passage and of their impact.

63. Sturges 1930.

64. Isaacs 1930.

65. Wooldridge 1970, 101.

66. Denenberg and Denenberg 1981, 5.

67. Denenberg and Denenberg 1981, 8.

68. Denenberg and Denenberg 1981, 10.

69. For more detail on the effect of lawyers on arbitration under the state
arbitration statutes, see Benson 1995 and Benson 1999.

70. Pruitt 1982.

71. Pruitt 1982, 51.

72. Koenig 1984.

73. See Landes and Posner 1979, 237; Willoughby 1929, 56; Lazarus et al.
1965, 31, 125; American Arbitration Association 1981, 34; Domke 1984, 27; and
Murray, Rau, and Sherman 1989, 435. All imply that private adjudication is not a
viable option without previously existing arbitration clauses in contracts. The
emerging judicial market casts doubt on this claim.

74. For a brief discussion, see Denenberg and Denenberg 1981, 2. For more
detail, see Fuller 1981.

75. Denenberg and Denenberg 1981, 21.

76. Denenberg and Denenberg 1981, 21.

77. Poole 1978, 55.

78. Denenberg and Denenberg 1981, 15.

79. Denenberg and Denenberg 1981, 18.

80. Cook, Roehl, Sheppard 1980, 4–6.

81. As Sheppard, Roche, and Cook (1979, 56) put it, the "suggestions" by
prosecutors and other officials in the criminal-justice system to volunteer have been
"very persuasive."

82. Recall that reciprocity was the basis of recognition of the law merchant
and compliance with the merchant courts. Such reciprocity need not be based on
commercial interests. It can be founded on family, ethnic group, religion, or neighborhood ties (as well as on noncommercial contracts, such as neighborhood associations), but it must be voluntary. See, for example, Auerbach 1983, 27; and Benson 1991. Also see Ellickson 1991 for a modern example of nonstate dispute
resolution among neighbors in rural Shasta County, California.

REFERENCES

Aiken, J. R. 1974. New Netherlands Arbitration in the Seventeenth Century. *Arbitration Journal* 29 (June): 145–60.

American Arbitration Association. 1981. *Lawyers' Arbitration Letters, 1970–1979.* New York: Free Press.

Auerbach, J. S. 1983. *Justice Without Law.* New York: Oxford University Press.

Benson, B. L. 1989. The Spontaneous Evolution of Commercial Law. *Southern Economic Journal* 55 (January): 644–61.

———. 1990. *The Enterprise of Law: Justice Without the State.* San Francisco: Pacific Research Institute.

———. 1991. Reciprocal Exchange as the Basis for Recognition of Law: Examples from American History. *Journal of Libertarian Studies* 10 (fall): 53–82.

———. 1992. Customary Law as a Social Contract: International Commercial Law. *Constitutional Political Economy* 2 (winter): 1–27.

———. 1993. The Impetus for Recognizing Private Property and Adopting Ethical Behavior in a Market Economy: Natural Law, Government Law, or Evolving Self-Interest. *Review of Austrian Economics* 6:43–80.

———. 1995. An Exploration of the Impact of Modern Arbitration Statutes on the Development of Arbitration in the United States. *Journal of Law, Economics, and Organization* 11 (October): 479–501.

———. 1999. To Arbitrate or to Litigate: That is the Question. *European Journal of Law and Economics* 8 (2): 91–151.

Berman, H. J. 1983. *Law and Revolution: The Formation of Western Legal Tradition.* Cambridge: Harvard University Press.

Berman, H. J., and F. J. Dasser. 1990. The "New" Law Merchant and the "Old": Sources, Content, and Legitimacy. In *Lex Mercatoria and Arbitration: A Discussion of the New Law Merchant,* ed. T. E. Carbonneau. Dobbs Ferry, N.Y.: Transnational Juris Publications, Inc.

Cook, R. F., J. A. Roehl, and D. I. Sheppard. 1980. *Neighborhood Justice Centers Field Test—Final Evaluation Report.* Washington D.C.: U.S. Department of Justice.

Denenberg, T. S., and R. V. Denenberg. 1981. *Dispute Resolution: Settling Conflicts Without Legal Action.* New York: Public Affairs Committee, Inc. Public Affairs Pamphlet No. 597.

Domke, M. 1984. *Domke on Commercial Arbitration.* Rev. ed. Ed. G. M. Wiker. Willmette, Ill.: Gallaghen and Co.

Ellickson, R. C. 1991. *Order Without Law: How Neighbors Settle Disputes.* Cambridge: Harvard University Press.

Fuller, L.. 1964. *The Morality of Law.* New Haven: Yale University Press.

———. 1981. *The Principles of Social Order.* Durham, N.C.: Duke University Press.

Greif, A. 1989. Reputation and Coalitions in Medieval Trade. *Journal of Economic History* 49:857–82.

Hayek, F. A. 1967. *Studies in Philosophy, Politics and Economics.* Chicago: University of Chicago Press.

———. 1973. *Law, Legislation, and Liberty.* Vol. 1. *Rules and Order.* Chicago: University of Chicago Press.

Isaacs, N. 1930. Review of Wesley Sturges, *Treatise on Commercial Arbitration and Awards. Yale Law Review* 40:149–51.

Jones, W. C. 1956. Three Centuries of Commercial Arbitration in New York: A Brief Survey. *Washington University Law Quarterly* 1956 (February): 193–221.

Koenig, R. 1984. More Firms Turn to Private Courts to Avoid Expensive Legal Fights. *Wall Street Journal,* January 4.

Landes, W. M., and R. A. Posner. 1979. Adjudication as a Private Good. *Journal of Legal Studies* 8 (March): 235–84.

Lazarus, S., J. Bray Jr., L. L. Carter, K. H. Collins, B. A. Giedt, R. V. Holton Jr., P. D. Matthews, and G. C. Willard. 1965. *Resolving Business Disputes: The Potential of Commercial Arbitration.* New York: American Management Association.

Levy, J. T. 1993. The Transformation of Arbitration Law, 1835–1870: The Lessening of Judicial Hostility Towards Private Dispute Resolution. Mimeograph, Brown University.

Milgrom, P. R., D. C. North, and B. R. Weingast. 1990. The Role of Institutions in the Revival of Trade: The Law Merchant, Private Judges, and the Champagne Fairs. *Economics and Politics* 2 (March): 1–23.

Mitchell, W. 1904. *Essay on the Early History of the Law Merchant.* New York: Burt Franklin.

Murray, J. S., A. S. Rau, and E. F. Sherman. 1989. *Processes of Dispute Resolution: The Role of Lawyers.* Westbury, N.Y.: Foundation Press.

Nader, L. 1979. Comment. In *The Pound Conference: Perspectives on Justice in the Future,* ed. A. L. Levin and R. R. Wheeler. St. Paul, Minn.: Pound Conference.

Odiorne, G. S. 1953. Arbitration Under Early New Jersey Law. *Arbitration Journal* 8:117–25.

———. 1954. Arbitration and Mediation Among the Early Quakers. *Arbitration Journal* 9:161–69.

Poole, R. W., Jr. 1978. *Cutting Back City Hall.* New York: Universe Books.

Pruitt, G. 1982. California Rent-a-Judge Justice. *Journal of Contemporary Studies* 5 (spring): 49–57.

Sheppard, D. I., J. A. Roche, and R. A. Cook. 1979. *National Evaluation of the Neighborhood Justice Centers Field Test—Interim Report.* Washington D.C.: U.S. Department of Justice.

Smith, J. H. 1961. *Colonial Justice in Western Massachusetts.* Cambridge: Harvard University Press.

Sturges, W. A. 1930. *A Treatise on Commercial Arbitrations and Awards.* Kansas City: Vernon Law Book Company.

Trakman, L. E. 1983. *The Law Merchant: The Evolution of Commercial Law.* Littleton, Colo.: Fred B. Rotham and Co.

Willoughby, W. F. 1929. *Principles of Judicial Administration.* Washington, D.C.: Brookings Institute.

Wooldridge, W. C. 1970. *Uncle Sam, the Monopoly Man.* New Rochelle, N.Y.: Arlington House.

7

The Private Provision of Police during the Eighteenth and Nineteenth Centuries

Stephen Davies

Ever since they first appeared cities have been associated with crime, delinquency, and public disorder. Consequently, dealing with such matters has had a central place in their administration. A succession of authors has seen the city as the source of moral corruption; as plagued by crime; and as the focus of insurrection, revolt, and political unrest. (The countryside, by contrast, is portrayed as the seat of simple virtues and the peaceful life.) The more intellectual form of this vision is the argument that cities, because of their size and impersonality, are a form of human society that does not produce the stable and intimate personal relations that are found in their antithesis, the village or small town. As a result urban society is said to lack the dense networks of social institutions that sustain a traditional social and moral order and is rather made up of isolated individuals who are both the perpetrators and the victims of delinquency.[1] This vision has had great effects on public policy and continues to shape many interpretations of both the past and the present, but it is almost entirely false.

Nowhere is the vision more false or its effects more widespread than in the history of crime and policing and, by extension, in contemporary debates about law and order in the modern city. Crime and policing are areas of historiography that have seen an explosive growth since the 1960s, with many old beliefs undermined but with some central ones remaining unchallenged until only recently. Most of the historical research concentrates on the period between about 1750 and 1860.[2] The reason for this is straightforward: those years saw a funda-

151

mental change in both the theory and practice of policing and law enforcement, creating the system we still largely have today. Clearly this shift is connected to the contemporaneous move from a predominantly rural to a primarily urban society, but the nature of the connection is much debated.

Like many important changes of practice, this one was preceded by a transformation of thinking and ideas, which centered on the notion of "police." Until the later eighteenth century this term had a wide meaning, referring to the general responsibility of rulers for the maintenance of public order, justice, and law and a safe and salubrious environment. By the mid-eighteenth century, in the writings of the cameralists and others, it had come to include a wider concern of rulers and states with the physical and moral well-being of their subjects. It was used in this original sense by Adam Smith, who defined "police" in 1766 as being "the regulation of the inferior part of government, viz. cleanliness, security, and cheapness or plenty"—or in other words, most of what we would now call the general practice of government. Interestingly, he specifically associated this with cities and urban life.[3]

In the late eighteenth and early nineteenth centuries the term "police" came to be defined much more narrowly, to refer only to the state's ultimate responsibility for the maintenance of public order and the enforcement of law, particularly criminal law. Along with this went an increasing tendency to see this function as one that could *only* be carried out by the state and its agents. This developed into the idea that the state should exercise this responsibility through a particular kind of institutional medium, that of an organized and uniformed body, staffed by professionals and paid for by taxation. It was then a short step to using the terms "police" and "policing" to describe the personnel and their activities. This in turn led to the advocacy by a number of authors of the creation of such a force as the correct response to the new situation created by large-scale urbanization. An important point, made by authors such as Les Johnston and Carolyn Steedman, is that the activity was still often defined by these people in ways that owed much to the older, more wide-ranging use of the term "police."[4] As we shall see, advocates of a police force saw its function as a wide-ranging regulatory one; only gradually did such a force come to be defined in a narrow and specific way.

Today it is simply taken for granted by most people that the primary responsibility for the investigation of crime and the maintenance of public order lies with a paid, full-time, state police force. It is true that in recent years there has been an explosive growth in the private security industry, but such firms typically supply only some of the various goods covered by the term "policing," typically that of guarding property. Other goods, above all those of investigating breaches of the criminal law and maintaining public order, remain the domain of a state monopoly service. The growth, or rather rebirth, of private policing is highly significant, but the public and most opinion-formers are not yet aware of its extent or significance.[5] Above all there is little idea of the way order is maintained within civil society independently of the state by various kinds of voluntary and informal action.[6]

The monopolizing of law-and-order enforcement by the state is a relatively recent development, particularly in the Anglo-Saxon countries, dating back only to the early nineteenth century. In Britain the first state police force of the modern kind was set up in 1829 with the creation of the Metropolitan (i.e., London) Police. Despite the recommendations of the 1839 Royal Commission on Constabulary and the passage of a number of permissive acts, it was not until the passage of the 1856 County and Borough Police Act that it became mandatory for all local authorities to establish a police force paid for out of local taxation. In the United States the move in this direction was also patchy and slow, particularly of course in the West. Although there was a longer history of state policing on the Continent, even there the nineteenth century saw a major extension of the role of the state and a decline of that of civil society.[7]

The old legal order that was replaced in the nineteenth century in Britain had a number of features that distinguish it sharply from the one we have today. The system of civil and criminal courts was a state monopoly (although only a complete one in Scotland from 1747).[8] However, the enforcement of the law was almost entirely in the hands of private individuals and communities. Every parish had an official, the parish constable, whose task it was to arrest malefactors and investigate crimes. Constables, however, only held office for one year at a time and were, like most officials of the period, part-time and unpaid. Their real role was to act as facilitators or assistants to private individuals, for the central feature of the old system was that the main responsibility for investigating and above all prosecuting crimes rested with the injured party. This could be very expensive, especially after lawyers became commonly involved, a phenomenon dating to the early eighteenth century. Even after the introduction of the county allowance in 1752, by which prosecutors had part of their costs reimbursed out of public funds, it remained a major investment of both time and money to bring a criminal prosecution.[9] The point is that absent the initiative of injured parties or their kin, no investigation of crimes would take place. (The exceptions to this rule were particularly atrocious offenses and ones that directly involved the state and its agents, such as smuggling.) As one recent work puts it, "[T]here was little or no attempt at criminal detection. Crime was brought to the courts when victims prosecuted offenders. Officials did not go out to find it."[10]

The other features of the system that attract comment are the central place of the death penalty and the common use of pardons to mitigate the severity of the penal code. By 1800 over two hundred separate crimes had attracted the ultimate sanction, and throughout the eighteenth century Parliament constantly sought to make the penal code more rigorous and severe. At the same time the number of sentences commuted to a lesser penalty or set aside by a pardon increased—all this in the context of a system that so favored the defendant that one is moved to reflect that it was something of a miracle that anyone was ever convicted. This had the paradoxical result that while the number of capital crimes rose steadily between 1600 and 1800, the number of executions actually declined.[11]

This last feature has been the center of a debate over the nature and purpose of the system. In a major article published in 1975, Douglas Hay argues that the system was designed to sustain an ideology that was the true basis of the power of a ruling class and that the apparent inconsistencies and common use of discretionary powers were designed to create opportunities for the rulers to create and maintain habits of deference and subordination on the part of the lower orders. The system was therefore "rational" inasmuch as it was part of an elaborate system of class rule and had the effect of sustaining the ruling class in its position.[12] This view has been criticized in two important articles, by John Langbein and Peter King. King in particular argues that far from being a means of elite control, the system actually placed great discretion and decision-making power in the hands of ordinary people, as it was they who had to make the key decisions, above all that of whether or not to prosecute. In King's view the legal system was a service both used and controlled primarily by the "middling sort" who made up the majority of the population.[13]

This highly insightful point can be extended. In fact, the maintenance of order in preindustrial Britain was due in very large part to informal and private sanctions and was carried out mainly within the structures of civil society. Few crimes ever led to court trials. In very many cases there was a "composition," or private agreement, between two parties, as the primary goal of most victims was the recovery of stolen goods. The law was very much a matter of last, not first, resort. The prosecution and punishment of particular cases were meant both to deal with particularly egregious crimes and to have an exemplary function.[14] This situation was described by reformers as one of disorder, a view taken up by later historians, but as a more recent work points out, this view depends upon a particular definition of order, one that takes it to mean a situation in which the laws made by the state are generally obeyed and all offenses against those laws are prosecuted wherever possible. A common, alternative way of defining order is to see it as a state of affairs in which conflicts between individuals and groups are minimized and people have general security in their persons and property.[15] In general the old system was able to achieve this for most people and for longer than commonly supposed, via the workings of a largely flexible and informal set of arrangements backed up by a formal legal system driven by private initiative.

It is clear, however, that the system was under increasing strain by the end of the eighteenth century. Several of its institutions such as the "hue and cry," a responsibility to search for and pursue malefactors, had fallen into desuetude.[16] More serious was the strain put on its central institutions by a number of developments. From about the 1720s many laws were made that were concerned with moral and economic regulation and with the abolition of traditional economic rights and privileges. These combined to create an enormous amount of new business, which threatened to overwhelm the system and could not easily be dealt with by the old, informal methods. The growing importance of lawyers in the legal process caused a sharp increase in the cost of legal proceedings, which put them beyond the reach of many people. There was also an increasing problem of corruption, particularly at the lower levels of the judicial system. Finally there was the undoubted impact of such developments as improved transportation and growing urbanization. These both made it easier to dispose of stolen goods as they could now be taken away from the scene and sold with less danger of their being traced. In populous areas criminals were increasingly anonymous individuals instead of persons who were well known to their neighbors. In general the growth of population and mobility meant a decline in the kind of detailed private knowledge that drove much of the old system—at least initially.

Certainly, there was a widespread feeling in later-eighteenth-century Britain that crime was increasing at a rapid rate. The state of the records and the inherent problems of interpreting criminal statistics make it impossible to say for certain if this was true or not, though it probably was, at least in London and the southeast.[17] This is beside the point, however. What is important is the existence at that time of an almost universal belief that there *was* indeed a crime wave, as it was this belief that shaped people's opinions and actions. At the same time the

developments described earlier meant that a smaller and more arbitrarily selected number of cases were prosecuted and brought to trial.
This lay behind the huge increase in capital sentences. As Langbein
points out in his critique of Hay, there is a simpler explanation than
Hay's for this feature of the old order, already identified in Leon Radzinowicz's classic study.[18] In all legal systems there is a trade-off between
severity of punishment and likelihood of conviction. The less likely the
latter, the more severe the punishment must be to maintain a fixed level
of deterrence.[19] The British, in Radzinowicz's view, chose to rely upon
severe punishment and low chances of conviction because of their
opposition to the idea of a state police force and prosecutorial system.
The problem was that by the end of the eighteenth century the severity
of (nominal) punishment was actually proving counterproductive
because it led to an increasing unwillingness on the part of victims to
prosecute and juries to convict—which in turn led to yet further extensions of severe penal sanctions.

All this led to a whole range of proposals for reform of criminal-
law enforcement. One of these emerged as successful, that of moving to
the new idea of a state police force. The move to a state police force in
Britain has received a lot of attention from historians. Until recently it
was seen as a process that was both inevitable and benevolent in its
effects. There is some disagreement over the extent to which it was the
product of an ideology, that of Benthamism, rather than simply the
response of practical-minded individuals to difficult problems, but this
is a secondary issue. The general consensus, as found in the works of
authors such as Charles Reith and John Tobias, was that the changes
were the inevitable and only possible response of ruling elites to the
breakdown of an existing system of law enforcement that was in any
case barbarous, backward, and inefficient.[20] The crucial factor in this
account is the process of rapid and large-scale urbanization, which
affected Britain from the 1740s onward. Here the notion of the nature
of urban society alluded to earlier plays a key part. This supposedly led
to the collapse of the old system and made a new one necessary. The
story of how a state police force appeared in Britain is therefore seen as
one of the narratives of the move from a traditional society to moder-
nity, with the modern city both the cause and focus of change. The
British case is seen as a model for the study of the growth of state law
enforcement in other countries. Although this way of thinking no
longer commands simple assent from professional historians, it
remains the dominant account in the popular mind.

However, in both Britain and the United States there was a rival
response to the undoubted changes of the late eighteenth and later nine-

teenth centuries, one that grew out of the old system and reflected a very different concept of the nature of the police function, locating it in civil society rather than in the domain of politics and public choice. This led in terms of institutions to the appearance and development in both countries of voluntarist organizations and systems of law enforcement. This alternative development was "crowded out" by the move to a state police force but remains significant both historically and in its implications for present-day questions. It also leads to a different interpretation of the nature and impact of urbanization in general and, consequently, of the possibilities for voluntary action in cities then and now.

The key to understanding the voluntary response to the problem of law enforcement lies in rejecting or severely amending the picture of urbanization and urban life given earlier. Cities—particularly large, expanding ones—are marked by problems of crime and disorder, but these are typically associated with the first phase of urbanization. To put it another way, they tend to happen among first-generation urbanites, people who have migrated to the city from the countryside. Among such populations traditional social structures and relations have indeed been fractured or even destroyed. However, the central feature of urbanization at a social level is the very rapid appearance of new social institutions and networks to meet the needs of the new urban population. These appear spontaneously, out of voluntary collective action. Many of the typical features of modern urban life, supposedly destructive of community and collective action, actually make this process easier. The larger population means there is a wider range of skills and greater knowledge available to be used and organized. The greater density of population makes it easier to mobilize this knowledge as it becomes easier to meet others and to create and sustain permanent organizations. In economic terms, the greater density of population reduces the cost of collective action for individuals while raising the benefits. These costs are also reduced, and institution-building made easier, by the greater resources—in other words, by the wealth and facilities available in the city. Contrary to popular opinion, personal isolation is much reduced in the city as compared to the village or even the small town. A common element of accounts of life in the rural United States in the period before 1950 is its soul-destroying loneliness and isolation. Greater social contact is historically particularly significant for women, who often become the key figures in community action and organization. Better and cheaper transport again makes it easier to communicate, to disseminate and use information, and to organize. It is true that in contrast to the village or small town, the city creates more privacy and encourages social individualism, but this can actually lead to more rather than less collective action because of the greater number of active individuals and mobilizers it creates.

The original "supplement" to the existing system of law enforcement was the offering of rewards to individuals who either detected a crime or gave evidence that led to a successful prosecution. The intention was to use the incentive of material gain to make the knowledge of crime dispersed among the population more accessible to the victims and the authorities. Such rewards came in two forms: those offered by the state or public authorities, which could themselves be either statutory, in other words, established by law and applying to any instance of a particular crime, or specific, in other words, relating to a particular event; and those offered by private persons, either individually or collectively. The second kind appeared later than the first but were more significant. By the early nineteenth century the use of rewards was so widespread that it may be said to have become an integral part of the system. Closely related was the institution of the "common informer," by which people other than the victim of a crime were allowed to lay charges and then to claim a part of any reward.[21]

More significant, however, was the growing use of newspaper advertisements. Advertisements offering rewards for information leading to the recovery of stolen goods or the prosecution of offenders began to appear in newspapers in large numbers from the 1730s, as the number and circulation of both provincial and metropolitan newspapers grew dramatically. Such advertisements typically contained both details of the stolen goods (very often horses) and details of the crime, as well as an occasional description of the suspected perpetrator. The rise of a provincial press and the increased use of such advertisements reflected both the improvement of communications, brought about by turnpike trusts, and the growth of towns. Crime advertisements were, to quote the outstanding work on the topic, "simply one of a multiplicity of ways in which individual English men and women took advantage of the market in information created by the spread of commercial printing."[22] What they did was not only to disseminate information but also make possible cooperation among people who did not directly know one another and had never even met. The importance of the rewards offered was that they gave individuals a direct interest in what would otherwise have been of no personal concern to them. This shows how urbanization made possible new ways of using and mobilizing social knowledge, in this case knowledge of crimes. Before the advent of the newspaper a stolen horse would be almost impossible to trace and recover once it had been taken out of the neighborhood, and the same was true of other portable stolen goods. With advertisements the area within which investigation and pursuit were practicable was greatly expanded.

Advertisements also made it possible to mobilize civil society in a much more thorough way and over a wider geographical area. The old institution of hue and cry had rested upon a general public responsibility to watch out for possible criminal acts. This became more difficult with greater mobility and anonymity. With the important information made available through newspapers, criminals and potential criminals were subject to a form of general social surveillance by the public. There was also a move to what John Styles calls "impersonal detection," in other words, investigation of crimes by third parties not connected to the original victim. This meant in practice a move away from reliance upon state machinery to a greater role for civil society. As Styles puts it:

> It is striking . . . that the intensified surveillance brought about by the eighteenth century detective advertisement was neither the planned consequence of an official initiative nor was it crucially dependent upon the activities of officials. On the contrary, it depended on public rather than official action; on a form of general access broadcasting of information rather than on the transmission of information through a limited number of closely controlled official channels. Indeed, insofar as the eighteenth century printed crime advertisement replaced the seventeenth century hue and cry, it entailed a shift away from a surveillance based on the official machinery of law enforcement towards a surveillance based on the market in information created by the spread of commercial printing.[23]

The use of advertisements appears, on the evidence, to have been successful. Unfortunately it is effectively impossible to find out about those cases that led to the recovery of stolen goods but not to prosecution, as this outcome did not generate any official record. What we do have are the records of cases brought to court as a result of advertisements. These show that advertisements were highly successful in bringing cases of horse theft and serious property crimes in general to trial. The proportion of advertisements that had a successful outcome was almost certainly low, but two points should be made: the rate still compares favorably with the clear-up rates of modern police forces; and this situation was an improvement on what had gone before.[24] Overall, the success of this mechanism was increasing as time passed and urbanization became more pronounced, particularly with the growth of nationally circulated London-based papers. This increasing success is one reason why reformers such as John and Henry Fielding, Patrick Colquhoun, and Edwin Chadwick—all advocates of a state police force—were so interested in the potential of a national journal devoted to crime advertising and intelligence.[25] Advertising also played a central part in the main voluntary response to the needs of criminal-law enforcement—associations for the prosecution of felons.

Although prosecution associations were a major feature of criminal-law enforcement between about 1750 and 1850, it is only recently that they have received any attention from historians. The initial pioneering work in research was done by Hay and by Adrian Shubert. The latter's thesis was published in article form in 1981, and important essays were later published by David Philips and King.[26] What this research shows is that prosecution associations were widespread and spontaneous and were developing and expanding their range of activities up to the 1840s. The earliest form they took were collective agreements to prosecute, found from the 1690s onward, by which people in a given locality bound themselves to share the cost of prosecutions, thereby diminishing the cost for any one individual and increasing the likelihood of any one individual bringing a prosecution. More formal and permanent organizations began to appear after 1750, and there was a large growth in their number during the 1770s and 1780s. During the 1820s these groups began to take on a wider range of activities and increase in size, and there are signs of connections and links being made among individual associations.

Associations for the prosecution of felons were essentially private associations or clubs. They are just one example of the enormous range of clubs and societies set up in the course of the eighteenth and early nineteenth centuries, which met almost every imaginable human need. The number of prosecution associations will probably never be known, but it was certainly very large. One record lists 189 in existence in the 1830s, while the Constabulary Commission's report in 1839 lists 575, admitting that this is a serious underestimate. The guesses given by Shubert, Philips, and King for the number active between 1750 and 1850 range from 1,000 to 4,000; the evidence of newspapers in particular would tend to support the higher rather than the lower figure.[27] Most were formed in response to a local crime wave or a particularly atrocious crime. They would be formed after an initial meeting that would launch the society and invite subscriptions as well as elect officers and patrons. The essential aims were twofold: to provide mutual assurance for the members by sharing the costs of investigation, detection, and prosecution; and to provide the public good of security from crime by the increased deterrent effect of a higher level of prosecution. They were intensely local institutions and were only starting to grow out of this localism by the end of their effective existence in the 1850s. Their local nature is easily explained: the organizational costs of setting up and running an association over anything other than a small area were so great that it was simply impractical to undertake the task. As areas became more densely populated and communications became easier and cheaper, however, the effective area that could cooperate to sustain an association became larger, both geographically and in terms of population.[28]

From surviving records we can get a clear idea of the makeup and organization of prosecution associations. Although gentry or even peers appeared on subscription lists, they were not active members. The active ones were overwhelmingly drawn from the same groups that made up the bulk of the membership: farmers, tradesmen, and small property owners in general. The only group disproportionately represented among the active members was the clergy. It is significant that these were precisely the people who, on King's evidence, were the main users of the existing legal system and therefore had the greatest incentive to reduce and spread the growing cost of prosecutions.[29] Most associations were small in size, with twenty to sixty being the most common number of members. This is an average figure, for the membership would often fluctuate over time. Some associations managed to establish large memberships, defined as over one hundred, and the evidence suggests that once this kind of level had been reached it could be sustained over a long period. Such large associations were more common after 1820.[30] Associations, like other clubs, were run by an elected management committee, of which the secretary and treasurer were the most important members. The ultimate authority was a general meeting of all the members, usually annual but sometimes more frequent, which would not only conduct business but also be an occasion for a great deal of conviviality and entertainment—an important part of the association's activity as it brought the members together and promoted feelings of solidarity and sociability.

Being voluntary organizations, prosecution associations were dependent upon the subscriptions paid by their members. The simplest and most common system was one in which all members paid the same amount on an annual basis. The usual alternative was to pay one fairly large subscription on joining, followed by additional payments on an ad hoc basis, determined by the association's activities and finances. Some associations, particularly the larger ones, charged different rates according to the means of the member; this was usually determined by the level of poor rate paid or value of land owned. (The poor rate was used as the basis by most urban associations, while land value was more common in rural areas.)[31] As associations took on a wider range of functions there would often be additional subscriptions to pay for these services. The costs of belonging to an association were surprisingly low: the figures quoted by Philips show that over half charged an annual rate of 10s. 6d. or less, which put these associations well within the reach of the overwhelming majority of the population at this time.[32] The expenditures of associations were varied. The administrative costs were low, usually under ten pounds per year, but other costs could be much higher. By far the most expensive activities were the running of independent watches or patrols, which became a more frequent feature of association activity from about 1820 onward. However, for most associations for most of the period, the major expense was the cost of defraying criminal prosecutions. These could be very expensive, involving the outlay of hundreds of pounds in a particularly difficult or drawn-out case, and although some of these costs could be recovered from the county allowance they could still be substantial. The main problem was one of cash flow, inasmuch as prosecution costs came in on an irregular and often unpredictable basis—hence the frequent resort to ad hoc extraordinary subscriptions. However, the very high cost of prosecutions shows why associations were so common: a case costing forty to fifty pounds after the allowance would have been beyond the means of all but the wealthy, so the pooling of costs via an association must have led to many cases being investigated and prosecuted that would otherwise have been left untouched.[33]

Associations provided a number of services to their members. When members reported an offense committed against them the association would investigate the crime and try to apprehend the malefactor and recover any stolen goods. This involved the printing of handbills and the placing of advertisements in local newspapers (or even national papers in the case of stolen horses). The advertisements would normally offer a reward for information, and most associations had a standard scale of rewards for information leading to a prosecution or recovery of goods, graduated according to the severity of the offense. These were made widely known by being broadcast via posters and regular advertisements in the press. In an area with an active association the general public would all know what reward was being offered for any particular offense committed against a member.[34] Associations also offered rewards for the apprehension of offenders and would pay the expenses involved. They took an active role themselves and would pay for the expense of traveling in search of offenders, hiring detectives, and paying constables and other officers. All of this involved an expenditure of both time and money beyond the means of most of the members. The main service, though, was to pay for and organize prosecutions. This involved inter alia hiring a solicitor (associations normally retained one on a permanent basis); preparing the brief; arranging witnesses; covering the cost of lawyers' charges and legal fees; and paying the costs of attending the trial for both prosecutor and witnesses (these costs could be considerable because of the need to travel to the county town where the assizes were held).[35]

In addition, associations increasingly came to take on an insurance role. Their main purpose can be defined as providing insurance against the cost of investigating and prosecuting crime, but latterly many offered recompense to their members if stolen goods were not recovered or no offender was prosecuted, usually in the form of some set proportion of the value of the goods. It is revealing, however, that this was never their primary role; as their name suggests, that role was and remained the prosecuting of offenders. Associations also offered their members benefits that were not explicit services but rather side effects of membership. The most important by far was the deterrent effect of membership on potential thieves. All associations regularly broadcast the names of their members by word of mouth, handbills, and advertisements so that criminals would know that an offense against these people would certainly result in investigation and possibly prosecution, more probably than in the case of a nonmember. Some associations had provisions in their rules allowing for the bringing of prosecutions on behalf of nonmembers, but Philips finds that this was hardly ever done; one case where this was done frequently, that of the West Ham association, saw a severe "free-rider" problem and the near bankrupting of the association.[36] Philips argues that such provisions were included in rules for exceptional use, to enable the association to rid the neighborhood of notorious villains. This would seem the most likely explanation for such provisions since the main goods being provided by associations were essentially private ones that could be exclusively provided to paying members.[37] One exception to this was the widespread practice of associations offering or contributing toward publicly advertised rewards for the arrest and conviction of criminals when an offense against one of their own members was not involved. Even the practice of having a regular offer of rewards for information in cases in which only the association's own members were involved had a public-good aspect. In one case the association involved (the Barnet association) declared that "[t]he Committee were convinced that the system [of contributing to public rewards] is calculated for the safety of the inhabitants at large"—in other words, that it promoted a public good.[38] This does raise the whole issue of how far prosecution associations produced a public good of diminished levels of crime and better observance of the law as a neighborhood effect or positive externality and, secondarily, the question of how far this was a motive for people to set up or join associations. As we shall see this was an important issue in the debate over policing in the 1820s.

By the early nineteenth century the larger and more active associations had come to offer a service that, while directly beneficial to their own members, had an important public-good aspect—the provision of local watches and patrols, or in other words, of something approaching a private police force. For obvious reasons of both need and practicality this was a phenomenon found among urban and suburban associations. In doing this they were building on another aspect of the voluntary development of the legal system: the funding by private subscription of supplementary watches and patrols. One common feature of eighteenth and nineteenth century towns and cities was private watchmen. Individuals would employ private watchmen to guard and protect their own property, whether houses or places of business. Often such watchmen were simply employed as individuals, but increasingly they were hired out by companies that can be seen as forerunners of modern security firms since they provided exactly the same service.[39] Clearly the good being supplied here was strictly private—the protection for a fee of a specific residence or place of work such as a shop or warehouse. However, increasingly groups of people would combine together to fund a watch. Initially these tended to be groups of traders who would collectively pay for protection for all of their properties. The crucial step came when groups of individuals within a parish or other local government unit agreed to collectively subscribe funds for employing a public watch or foot patrol, in other words, one that was not simply protecting the property of specific individuals. Sometimes this was a purely private measure; more often it was done to supplement the functions and activity of the parish constable. Most of the cases we know about are from London and its environs, but this simply reflects the survival of records. A major source is the papers of successive Parliamentary inquiries into the police of the Metropolis in the period before 1829. One report of 1828 identifies privately financed police units in no fewer than forty-five parishes within a ten-mile radius of London. In Islington the home office encouraged a voluntary subscription to pay for regular foot patrols, which attracted ninety-three subscribers. A similar case was that of the Liberty of the Rolls in the city of London itself—this example is discussed in a pamphlet advocating voluntary policing by John Prince Smith, later a leading Liberal politician in Germany.[40] In practice it proved difficult to sustain such privately funded supplementary police, partly because of the cost of unrealizable schemes for "preventative police" (discussed later in the chapter) but mainly because of severe free-rider problems. As the 1828 report put it, "The present system which prevails in many parishes, of defraying the expense of the watch by partial subscriptions, is manifestly unfair. It throws the burden exclusively on those who are willing to subscribe, while the advantage is common to all parties who are interested in the security of property, whether they subscribe or not."[41] However, many areas were able to surmount this problem by use of powers contained in local improvement acts, especially lighting acts, and such subscription-funded forces were widespread right up to 1856. Another important example of a force of this kind was the Thames River police, set up in 1798 as a private venture but then put on a statutory basis in 1800.[42]

Another common solution to this public-goods problem was for supplementary patrols to be mounted by prosecution associations. Given problems of sustaining the organization and funding such a watch in the absence of other organization, such as the powers created by a watching and lighting act, prosecution associations increasingly took on the role of providing this service. Here the task could be met by an existing, formal organization. The key point, however, is that in this case the public good provided by the patrols was tied up with the private good of assurance against the costs of investigation and prosecution.[43] Most of the examples that we know about are from London, but this was probably a phenomenon of large urban areas in general. The most famous case of an association providing such a service was that of the Barnet association in north London, and we know about it largely through the propagandizing efforts of its secretary, Thomas Dimsdale. However, the 1828 report gives details of similar schemes in Tottenham, Acton, Croydon, Deptford, and Kingston upon Thames (the last being supported by 20 percent of the inhabitants via a subscription paid to the association). The 1836 *Report of Commissioners for Inquiring into County Rates* also gives details of such schemes from other parts of the country.[44] Dimsdale's evidence in the inquiries of 1828, 1836, and 1839 gives details of the schemes and services offered by the Barnet association and the effect these had in reducing the level of crime in the area.[45] The number of officers in the patrols increased from two in 1828 to six by 1836. The kinds of services offered by the Barnet association and others clearly fit the description of private policing. Here the public-good free-rider problem was still apparent, as Dimsdale's own evidence to the 1828 inquiry makes clear, but the value of the private benefits together with the public one was enough to ensure that people still joined the association and paid its subscriptions in sufficient numbers for it to continue.[46]

However, there is an important distinction to be made between the kind of policing provided increasingly by prosecution associations and subscription arrangements and that advocated by the reformers. It is clear from the evidence of Dimsdale and others that the policing offered by the associations was responsive—in other words, it concentrated mainly on responding to and investigating reported crime and making use of information provided by the public. The preventative aspect was simply the deterrent effect on potential criminals of the greater chance of being apprehended. This was quite different from the idea of preventative policing advocated by reformers such as Colquhoun and Jeremy Bentham, which had as its central feature the prevention of crime by preemptive action by the authorities, above all the rigorous supervision and control of the poor by regular patrols and surveillance of their neighborhoods. The Members of Parliament (MPs) and officials conducting the various inquiries were well aware of this distinction, and one of the main emphases of their questions to witnesses such as Dimsdale concerned the extent to which associations were or could be involved in such a preventative exercise.[47] The activities of the associations and other private bodies in providing patrols and police officers were aimed not at some form of supervisory preventative policing but at strengthening and making more effective the system based on private prosecution.

All this raises the question of the significance of prosecution associations and other private policing agencies and the motives of those who joined them. Shubert argues that people set up and joined associations because of discontent with the old system and because they wanted something like the new one that ultimately replaced it. So according to this view support for associations entailed support for a public police force. The key point for Shubert is that association members were, by joining, showing that they favored a form of public policing and a system in which all offenders were prosecuted. Tobias also takes this view, arguing that associations were a stopgap response to the inadequacy of the old system prior to the introduction of the state police.[48] The counter perspective of King and Philips is that this is too simplistic, with a wide range of views to be found among associations and their members.[49] The evidence very much supports this counter view. Much of it suggests that while association members sought reform and development of the existing system, they did not agree with anything like the system advocated by Chadwick or, before him, Colquhoun. There is a false dichotomy in some of the older discussions—in other words, the idea that people either wanted to uphold the old system in its entirety or else move to the one that the Benthamites wanted. Surely what many wanted was reform but in a different direction. The association officers from the metropolitan area who gave evidence to the inquiries in the 1820s and 1830s mostly expressed qualified support for some kind of public police. Yet examination of the records shows firstly that this support was not a primary motive for their activities—public policing was not a measure they were actively campaigning for—and secondly that what they favored was the provision on a public basis of the kind of service they already provided, not the one advocated by the reformers.[50]

One important question here, already alluded to, is that of how far prosecution associations and other voluntary action promoted a public good of reduced crime and greater public safety and the extent to which this was a motive behind voluntary action. It is clear firstly that private measures such as rewards, advertisements, and the activities of prosecution associations did deliver these public goods inasmuch as they increased the probability of detection, prosecution, conviction, and often the chance of a severe sentence such as transportation to a penal colony in Australia or the Americas or death. All of this must have had a deterrent effect on potential criminals, to the extent that they were acting as utility-maximizing individuals. The evidence given by association officers and public officials to public inquiries was overwhelmingly of the view that private action had brought about marked local improvement in such things as the level of crime.[51] The second point is that this was clearly a motive behind joining associations, as the recruiting advocacy of people such as Dimsdale makes plain, but it was also linked to the provision of a private good. This derived from a system in which the key decisions in law enforcement, above all the decision to prosecute, remained in private hands.

In this context what prosecution associations did not do is as crucial as what they did. As Shubert puts it, "the associations were distinctive in their almost exclusive concern with crimes against person and property, and especially the latter. With only the rarest of exceptions, crimes against morality, public order and the state did not concern them."[52] As we shall see, this specific focus reflected a particular view of the causes and nature of crime, especially in urban society, and of the role of the state. As Shubert points out, there were many other voluntary organizations that did concern themselves with such matters, notably Associations for the Suppression of Mendicity, Societies for the Reformation of Manners, and Associations for the Defense of Liberty and Property. The prosecution associations were also not political bodies; unlike many other organizations of that time, and later they were not focused on generating political pressure or campaigning for specific changes in the law.

One interesting comparison is between the voluntary prosecution associations in Britain and their closest American counterparts, vigilante movements. The earliest of these date from the 1760s in the Carolinas, and they were a marked feature of the frontier areas throughout the nineteenth century. Many, especially the anti–horse thief societies set up in the Eastern states such as New Jersey from the 1780s onward, were very similar to the British prosecution associations. However, the vigilante movements that figured so prominently in the history of areas such as California and Montana showed one vital difference from the earlier American cases and the British societies.[53] Vigilante movements typically performed the entire function of the law—including trial, sentence, and punishment as well as detection, arrest, and prosecution—whereas prosecution associations confined themselves to the latter set of activities. This suggests something about the relationship between voluntary action and the state in the two cases. In the American case the entire lawmaking function of the state was absent and was provided by private action, while in the British one it was only the enforcement role that was being supplied by an enhanced private provision via the collectivizing of costs.

All of this private initiative in law enforcement came to an end with the introduction of the "new police" in the middle part of the nineteenth century. This is not surprising; it was a classic case of "crowding out"—the process by which the state's entry into a particular area leads to the disappearance of private alternatives. The gradual disappearance of prosecution associations, private auxiliary police, and crime advertisement reflected the way that the new police came to take over not only the investigation of crime but also its prosecution, so that a major area of decision-making and control was transferred from civil society to the state. This change has until recently been presented as a simple case of progress in an inevitable direction. However, knowing what we now do, the following scenario makes more sense. By the period from 1780 to 1840 Britain was experiencing rapid change, particularly large-scale urbanization. Both aspects of and responses to this were changes in the practice of law enforcement and the associated development of a number of ideas about policing and the nature of crime. By the 1820s and 1830s there were a number of possible directions this evolutionary process could have taken. The developments embodied in institutions such as prosecution associations were features of one of the routes that was not taken. This clearly leads to a number of questions.

Firstly, from what the records tell us, in what direction were voluntary forms of action leading by the 1830s? The problem is that this can lead into a fruitless counterfactual, more appropriate for an "alternative world" science-fiction story. However, we can discern the trends of development in the voluntary system of law enforcement up to the 1830s. Over time prosecution associations were becoming larger, longer lasting and better organized. All of the ones that fit this description come from the period after 1800. They were also beginning to form stronger connections and links among themselves. The use of advertising and private information collection and dissemination was becoming more sophisticated and effective. Private bodies were taking on a wider range of functions, above all that of providing what we would now recognize as the core functions of a police force. The kind of police service that private action was providing was defensive and detective/responsive, depending to a large degree upon intelligence gained from the general public and, via rewards, from actual criminals and their associates. The decisions that drove the activities of the system and its officials, whether parish constables, associations, or private police officers, were ultimately personal and local. By contrast voluntary action and bodies of this kind were not influenced or motivated by concerns about public order, the stability of the political system, or personal morality. Finally, the tendency was for private, personal decision-making power to increase rather than diminish because the entire effect was to expand the capacity of individuals to act by reducing financial and informational constraints. So to conclude, in Britain between about 1750 and 1840, the changes associated with urbanization were bringing about a number of developments that were producing a privately funded and organized form of policing that was decentralized and that in its activity was driven by the decisions and interests of private individuals.

The evidence is that at a local level this was leading to an improvement in the effectiveness of the law-enforcement system and was as effective as—and more cost-effective than—the "new police" being introduced in a piecemeal fashion after 1829. In this context we should note the evidence given to the commission that drew up the 1839 constabulary report. While the published report itself, drawn up by Chadwick, set out a sharp indictment of the old system and a call for a radically new kind of police, the Chadwick papers, which contain the actual evidence submitted to the commission, show that the majority of respondents saw no need for a new police force or radical reform of the kind that Chadwick wanted.[54]

So the second question must be, in that case why were some people, above all the political elite, persuaded by the case put forward by advocates such as Colquhoun and Chadwick? It was certainly not because they saw the activities of private organizations such as prosecution associations as in any way illegitimate. As Radzinowicz puts it, "No one had ever questioned the principle that if a man were able and willing to pay, he could ensure greater security for himself or his property by organizing a private police force of his own." "[F]or a long time," Radzinowicz tells us, "various forms of emergency police promoted by private or semi-public initiative were regarded as an essential and healthy development, deserving official support and encouragement."[55] It is true that Chadwick in the 1839 report deprecated "the practice of investing private hands with public powers for their own use," but in this, as in much else, his views were at that time in the minority. On looking at the evidence we can discern a number of reasons.

In the first place there were a number of arguments about the extent to which law enforcement was ultimately a public good. A comment that appears in all of the reports from the 1820s and 1830s concerns the unfairness of people enjoying a benefit that they were not paying for. It is important to stress that this was seen as a problem of unfairness and not one of efficiency.[56] There was also considerable concern that the effect of the local improvement brought about by associations' activities was simply to displace crime and disorder from one area or neighborhood to another. The third concern, which follows from this, was that the provision of enforcement services by private initiative was neither uniform nor universal, and in some people's eyes this violated principles of natural justice and of the proper role of government.[57] However, these concerns by themselves were not enough to push the political elite into the drastic step of setting up a state police force; after all, these points could have been made at any point in the history of the existing system and had not led to action before.

The real reason was that private initiative was not dealing and could not deal with a number of issues and problems that the elite increasingly felt were of central importance in the new urban society. The older generation of historians argues that crime and the breakdown of law and order occasioned by urbanization were their central concern, along with an expanded view of the responsibilities of the state. More recent work by authors such as Allan Silver, Clive Emsley, Robert Storch, and Carolyn Steedman suggests that there were other concerns that carried greater weight, and the evidence of the records, as well as that presented by earlier historians such as Radzinowicz, clearly supports this view.[58] In the first place there were the growing fear and concern about threats to public order and the stability of the political system. Such concerns began to appear with the Gordon riots in 1780 and the controversy over the political career of John Wilkes but received a massive boost with the outbreak of the French Revolution. After 1815 there was continuing fear over the threat posed by plebeian radicalism, while the 1830s and 1840s saw the emergence of Chartism. By the 1830s this kind of concern had come to focus on the supposed threat presented by the appearance of a large, urban working class (largely artisan, in fact), which was easily identified with the class of sansculottes that had played such a dramatic role in France. As the records show, a constant preoccupation of the elite was with the capacity of the existing system of law enforcement to deal with threats to public order such as riots, demonstrations, and strikes.[59] There were attempts to meet these by voluntary action, but these were clearly hopelessly inadequate.[60] This could leave the authorities with no alternative to the calling out of regular troops or the yeomanry. Clearly, from this perspective, there was a need for some kind of permanent constabulary to maintain order without raising the stakes too high, as the use of troops would have done.

Even more significant, to judge by the amount of words spent on it, was the growing alarm, almost panic, over what was perceived to be the morally corrupt and degenerate state of the mass of the population. From the 1780s onward there was an active movement among parts of the elite for what was known as the "reformation of manners." This took the form of attempts to control the poor and their games and entertainments and moves to bring matters such as adultery, fornication, drunkenness, and gambling within the scope of the criminal law.[61] This pressure, which came initially from the Evangelical movement within Anglicanism, was resisted by Tory politicians such as Canning as well as by radicals, but it came to command increasing support.[62]

The crucial event was the emergence of the argument in the works of Colquhoun and others that there was a general condition of moral decay brought about by "luxury" (affluence, in modern terms) and the growth of cities and that this decay was responsible for both political unrest and a huge growth in crime. This diagnosis led Colquhoun to argue "that the object of criminal laws and police should be not only the maintenance of public order and the prevention of crime but also the correction of conduct by imposing restraints on the habits of the lower classes."[63] In this argument no real distinction is made among concerns over moral degeneracy, public order, and crime because they are all seen as intimately interconnected. However, the addition of these two other sets of worries to the simple one of criminality meant that action was required of a kind that could not simply be provided by an improved system of prosecution and detection of crimes and offenses against person and property.

The solution, for people like Colquhoun, was reform of the criminal law to create a simple structure of incentives, together with the creation of a preventative police. This is very close to the old, wider use of the term "police" and means a police force that has a supervisory, inspectoral role, the purpose of which is to control and regulate the lives of the "dangerous classes," in other words, the poor. This invigilatory force would also focus on other groups—two specifically singled out were Jews and Gypsies, the main ethnic minorities in Britain at that time. By the later 1820s the Irish had come to occupy center stage as the main delinquent group.[64] This kind of view was strongly resisted by a wide range of opinion, which is one reason why it took such a long time to be put into effect. Not all opponents of these ideas were uncritical supporters of the existing system. Sir Samuel Romilly was the great advocate of reform of the penal code to reduce the number of capital offenses and create a system in which greater certainty of punishment would go along with milder and more humane sentences. He was also a strong opponent of the idea of a preventative state police on libertarian grounds and argued instead for increasing the active role of the public and for voluntarism in general. (In this connection he argued for a revival in modern and voluntary form of the Saxon system of frankpledge.) Other Whig politicians such as Henry Brougham took a similar view.[65] Radicals such as Francis Place took the line that what was needed was grassroots democracy at the level of the parish, coupled with an expansion of voluntary activity. There were also different opinions as to the extent and origins of criminality. Tory politicians such as William Windham argued that the level of crime was not as high as supposed and that much of the worry about moral decay was what we would now call a "moral panic."[66] The position of many radicals and Whigs derived from that taken by Adam Smith. He argued firstly that there was no correlation between more laws and police and more security; if anything the opposite was true. He also argued that the real cause of crime was dependency and the survival of feudal relations, while the spread of commerce and markets would change social relations and bring about moral improvement.[67] A similar view was taken by Cesare Beccaria and Wilhelm von Humboldt, both of whom argued that an activist police would actually cause crime because of the multiplication of offenses and the criminalization of trivial acts. This position led to an advocacy of voluntarism and of an expanded role for the public and individual decision—precisely the direction that spontaneous developments were taking.[68] In this connection we should note that the detailed proposals put forward by Colquhoun and later Chadwick had many competitors: there was a wide range of reform proposals on offer, many of which built on the existing developments.[69]

However, it was the arguments of the Benthamites for a state police as part of a tutelary state that ultimately carried the day.[70] Gradually more and more of the elite came to support at least some part of this program. One reason for its success was the adept use by politicians such as Sir Robert Peel of gradual and piecemeal but irreversible reform as a way of outmaneuvering and disarming opposition—an early example of what a contemporary author calls "micropolitics."[71] The other main factor was the combination of circumstances in the 1820s and 1830s, including such matters as widespread rural unrest and the emergence of Chartism, which persuaded many that Britain was indeed facing an unprecedented crisis. By the 1850s it was clear that this view was mistaken, but by then changes had been made.

The later history of policing is, however, deeply ironic in view of the kinds of arguments made earlier. As new police forces were set up in one major city after another the original program of an invigilatory force was indeed tried on many occasions. The result was precisely what the critics had predicted—an increase in recorded crime and a breakdown in relations between police and public reflected in, among other things, high levels of attacks on the police and antipolice riots.[72] The result was that the preventative style of policing was rapidly abandoned, particularly as police forces increasingly developed a professional identity and became self-controlled and -directed.[73] There were attempts to revive aggressive preventative policing, especially in the 1860s, but these did not last long, and by the later nineteenth century a clear type of policing had emerged. What was it? It was, in fact, pretty much the kind of policing that private action had been moving toward providing in the earlier part of the century—responsive, detective, and relying upon information from the public. The key difference of course was that a whole range of decisions, particularly ones about prosecution, was now in the hands of the police. It was the cooperation of the public that made this new kind of policing effective. So the reality of what happened, as opposed to the intention, is best seen as a nationalization of a previously private area of decision-making.

All of this is of more than mere historical interest. The kind of issues that divided people in the eighteenth and nineteenth centuries on matters such as the causes of crime, the best way of dealing with it, and the nature and purpose of punishment are still with us. Moreover, recent years have seen a revival of both the idea and practice of private policing in response to the perceived inadequacies of the existing public system.[74] Given that protection against crime and the enforcement of the criminal law are major concerns of most people today and above all of city dwellers, the questions of the origins of criminality and the most effective ways of dealing with it are pressing ones. The evidence of the past is that there are voluntary alternatives to the kind of public policing that appeared in the mid-nineteenth century. The kind of policing we have today is not the only inevitable form for urban, industrialized societies. It is simply the form that was chosen at a particular point of historical time, in preference to others. Given that all admit the vital importance of the role of the general public in the creation of order and the enforcement of criminal law, the boundary between state and civil society in this area should not be taken as fixed and determinate, now or historically.

NOTES

1. Although this view of city life can be traced back to Roman authors such as Juvenal, it had its definitive modern statement in the works of nineteenth-century sociologists such as Toennies and Simmel. See Toennies 1957; Cahnman and Heberle 1971. For a more recent statement that has also become a classic, see Wirth 1938, 1–24.

2. See, for example, Emsley 1983 and Emsley 1987. Also see Steedman 1984; Philips 1980; Philips 1983; Bailey 1981; Beattie 1986; and McLynn 1989.

3. Smith 1978, 485; see also 331.

4. Johnston 1992, 4–6.

5. Johnston 1992, especially 71–136. For a comprehensive overview of pri-

vatization in the field of police services, see Benson 1998. Also valuable are South 1988; Albanese 1986, 86–91; and Cunningham and Taylor 1985.

6. On order without the state, see Benson 1990 and Ellickson 1991.

7. Lenman and Parker 1980 gives an overview of the long and slow movement from community to state. Philips 1980, in the same collection, looks at the British case. The outstanding collection of essays is Hay and Snyder 1989. See also Hart 1955, 416–22; Styles 1987; Philips 1977; Steedman 1984; and Emsley 1987.

8. In Scotland before 1747 there were de facto private courts or "heritable jurisdictions," although these had lost a great deal of their power in a judicial coup in 1709. See Davies 1980.

9. Hay and Snyder 1989, 20–35. For the increase in costs brought about by the involvement of lawyers see Langbein 1978, 263–316.

10. Johnston 1992, 9.

11. Sharpe 1984.

12. Hay 1975.

13. King 1984, 25–58; Langbein 1983, 96–120.

14. For a general discussion, see Lenman and Parker 1980.

15. Wrightson 1980; Brewer 1980, 18–27.

16. The "hue and cry" was an ancient institution dating back to Anglo-Saxon times. By the seventeenth century it had become formalized as a system whereby warrants were passed on from one township or parish to another, giving details of offences and suspects and requiring the inhabitants and above all the constable to watch out for and if possible apprehend the suspect. See Styles 1989, 55–112, especially 82–86.

17. Beattie 1986; McLynn 1989.

18. Langbein 1983; Radzinowicz 1948–68.

19. Jeremy Bentham (1931) argues that "the more deficient in certainty a punishment is, the severer it should be." A modern statement can be found in Becker 1968.

20. Critchley 1967; Tobias 1967; Reith 1938; and Reith 1943. See also Robinson 1979, 35–49.

21. Radzinowicz 1948–68, 2:58–59, 2:83–137, gives details of the rewards offered both by the state and by private individuals, whether acting alone or collectively via subscription. For the "common informer," see Radzinowicz 1948–68, 2:138–47.

22. Styles 1989, 57.

23. Styles 1989, 88.

24. Styles 1989, 75–88.

25. Styles 1989, 88–95.

26. Shubert 1981; Philips 1989; King 1989.

27. *Report of Commissioners for Enquiring into County Rates* 1836, vol. 27, part 1, 46, 189; King 1989, 172–73; Philips 1989, 120–21.

28. For the classic account of the economics of this process, see Buchanan 1988.

29. King 1984; King 1989, 173–77; Philips 1989, 134–36.

30. Philips 1989, 134, 170. Of the fourteen large associations identified by Philips, all but one date from after 1800 and nine from after 1820.

31. Poor rates were a tax paid for the relief of the poor on the value of fixed property such as houses. Given that most taxes were either indirect (e.g., excise taxes) or paid mainly by the wealthy (e.g., land taxes), this was the simplest way of estimating a member's wealth.

32. Philips 1989, 135–37.

33. For the kind of costs a difficult case could impose, see Philips 1989, 115–18, 136. The costs of running a foot patrol were considerable but could still be less than those of a difficult case and had the great advantage of being regular and predictable and hence easier to budget for. In his evidence to the 1828 Inquiry into the Police of the Metropolis, Thomas Dimsdale stated that the cost to the Barnet Association was seventy pounds per annum. See Radzinowicz 1948–68, 2:211–13.

34. For "deterrent" advertisements of this kind, see Styles 1989, 67–68. For an example of a set table of rewards, see the one drawn up by the Barnet Association in 1784, reprinted in Radzinowicz 1948–68, 2:457–58.

35. Philips 1989, 114–18, 138–39.

36. *Report from Select Committee on Police of Metropolis* 1828, vol. 6, 201–2, 204–5.

37. Philips 1989, 140.

38. Radzinowicz 1948–68, 2:458. The text makes clear that while some of the rewards apply to offenses against members (notably highway robbery), others apply whether committed against a member or nonmember. Even the clause against highway robbery includes within its terms "other persons who shall by the Commitee be considered as under their protection."

39. For the later history of this kind of service, see Johnston 1992, 18–20.

40. For the details of these forces, see Radzinowicz 1948–68, 2:205–9, 464–66 (the pamphlet by Prince Smith is cited at 2:207) and *Report from Select Committee on the Police of the Metropolis* 1828, vol. 6, 402–17.

41. *Report from Select Committee on the Police of the Metropolis* 1828, vol. 6, 31.

42. The Thames River police were originally set up by the West India merchants as a private measure to reduce theft and pilfering of cargoes. See Radzinowicz 1948–68, 2:349–78.

43. Philips 1989, 145–59, makes this clear without employing the concept of "bundling up."

44. Radzinowicz 1948–68, 2:207–9; *Report from Select Committee on the Police of the Metropolis* 1828, vol. 6, 201–12, 245–62; *Report of Commissioners for Inquiring into County Rates* 1836, vol. 27, part 1, 189.

45. *Report of the Royal Commission on Constabulary* 1839, vol. 19, 122–3, 129–31, 168–9; *Report from Select Committee on the Police of the Metropolis* 1828, vol. 6, 211–13.

46. *Report from Select Committee on the Police of the Metropolis* 1828, vol. 6, 212, contains the following passage, which the committee chose to highlight in their report: "There will be found persons in our neighbourhood who shelter themselves under the willingness of persons paying the expenses, and they not paying. Mr Byng is a very liberal contributor and great patron, and many other gentlemen, and I am happy to say he has less depredation than anybody; but there are persons in the humbler walks of life who say, 'No, your patrol will pass my door; I won't con-

tribute at all.' 'They take advantage of the benefit of it without contributing to the means of supporting it?' Yes."

47. See, for example, *Report from Select Committee on the Police of the Metropolis* 1828, vol. 6, 192–94, 206–13, 226–43.

48. Shubert 1981, 37–39; Tobias 1979, 126–28.

49. Philips 1989, 148–49; King 1989, 202–5.

50. See, for example, the evidence of George Dacre, Nathaniel Matthew, Thomas Dimsdale, Richard Cooke, Richard George, and William Garland in the 1828 report. All of these individuals stated that they would approve of *a scheme such as the one operated in their own parish* being made general but not any change in the nature of policing or the prosecution system. See *Report from the Select Committee on the Police of the Metropolis* 1828, vol. 6, 201–6, 206–9, 211–13, 243–45, 246–49, 252–56.

51. *Report from the Select Committee on the Police of the Metropolis* 1828, vol. 6; King 1989, 185–200.

52. Shubert 1981, 25.

53. Brown 1976, 79–109; Brown 1975; Brown 1969, 154–226; Little and Sheffield 1983, 796–808. Benson 1998 reviews the evidence on American vigilantism in the context of police privatization.

54. Brundage 1986, 55–64. See also Storch 1989, 211–66.

55. Radzinowicz 1948–68, 2:203.

56. This suggests the truth of the argument made by De Jasay (1989, 205–18)—that it is the inherent unfairness of the relationship between providers and free riders that undermines voluntary arrangements rather than undersupply or inefficiency.

57. See, for example, *Report from Select Committee on the Police of the Metropolis* 1828, vol. 6, 30: "Is it the effect of your police to drive the thieves out of your circuit, and drive them into the adjoining parishes ?–No doubt of it." This is from Dimsdale's evidence, but the same question was raised with every witness.

58. Silver 1967; Storch 1989, 212–17; Storch 1976, 481–509.

59. The various Parliamentary inquiries all spent as much time on riot and civil disturbance as they did on crime. Also a key concern, as Storch (1975; 1976; 1989) and Brundage (1986) make clear, was the fear of *rural* protest, particularly after the "Captain Swing" disturbances.

60. See, for example, the schemes reproduced in Radzinowicz 1948–68, 2:466–70.

61. Radzinowicz 1948–68, 3:141–210. For the specific case of the move to criminalize adultery see 2:193–94; see 2:498–506 for a list all of the laws against "immorality" that were in force in 1804.

62. Radzinowicz 1948–68, 3:198–210.

63. Radzinowicz 1948–68, 3:327. See 3:211–315 for a detailed discussion of Colquhoun's ideas, the proposals they generated, and the resistance to them. See particularly 3:232–36, 3:236–38.

64. On the idea of preventative or invigilatory police see Radzinowicz 1948–68, 3:246–98, especially 3:265–84. For the singling out of Gypsies and Jews, see 3:273.

65. Radzinowicz 1948–68, 3:366–72.

66. Radzinowicz 1948–68, 3:209.
67. Radzinowicz 1948–68, 3:422–23. See also Smith 1978, 332–33, 485–87.
68. Radzinowicz 1948–68, 3:426–31.
69. For some of these, see Storch 1989, 211–21. For the most interesting, which advocated the private provision of a national force via the mechanism of insurance, see Mereweather 1814, 243–63.
70. The account given by Radzinowicz of the Benthamites' arguments is still one of the best. See Radzinowicz 1948–68, 3:431–77. A crucial point was the winning over of the landed county elites to reform ideas. For this, see Storch 1989, 236–52.
71. Pirie 1988.
72. Storch 1975, 61–90; Jones 1982.
73. Davies 1985.
74. Johnston 1992; Benson 1998.

REFERENCES

Albanese, J. S. 1986. The Future of Policing: A Private Concern? *Police Studies* 9:86–91.
Bailey V., ed. 1981. *Policing and Punishment in Nineteenth Century Britain.* London: Rutgers University Press.
Beattie, J. 1986. *Crime and the Courts in England, 1660–1800.* Oxford: Clarendon.
Becker, G. S. 1968. Crime and Punishment: An Economic Approach. *Journal of Political Economy* 76 (March/April): 169–217.
Benson, B. 1990. *The Enterprise of Law.* San Francisco: Pacific Research Institute.
———. 1998. *To Serve and Protect: Privatization and Community in Criminal Justice.* New York: New York University Press.
Bentham, J. [1789] 1931. *Theory of Legislation.* New York: Harcourt Brace Co.
Bordua, D., ed. 1967. *The Police: Six Essays.* New York: Wiley.
Brewer, J. 1980. An Ungovernable People? Law and Disorder in Stuart and Hanoverian England. *History Today* 30 (January): 18–27.
Brown, R. M. 1969. The American Vigilante Tradition. In *The History of Violence in America,* ed. H. D. Graham and T. R. Gurr. New York: Wiley.
———. 1975. *Strain of Violence: Historical Studies of American Violence and Vigilantism.* New York: Oxford University Press.
———. 1976. The History of Vigilantism in America. In *Vigilante Politics,* ed. H. J. Rosenbaum and P. C. Sedeberg. Philadelphia: University of Pennsylvania Press.
Brundage, A. 1986. Ministers, Magistrates and Reformers: The Genesis of the Rural Constabulary Act of 1839. *Parliamentary History* 5:55–64.
Buchanan, J. 1988. An Economic Theory of Clubs. In *The Theory of Market Failure: A Critical Examination,* ed. T. Cowen. Fairfax, Va.: George Mason University Press.
Cahnman, W. J., and R. Heberle, eds. 1971. *Ferdinand Toennies on Sociology.* Chicago: University of Chicago Press.

Cowen, T. 1988. *The Theory of Market Failure: A Critical Examination.* Fairfax, Va.: George Mason University Press.

Critchley, T. A. 1967. *A History of Police in England and Wales, 900–1966.* London: Constable.

Cunningham, W. C., and T. Taylor. 1985. *Private Police and Security in America.* Portland, Ore.: Butterworth-Heinemann.

Davies, S. 1980. The Courts and the Scottish Legal System, 1600–1747: The Case of Stirlingshire. In *Crime and the Law: The Social History of Crime in Western Europe Since 1500,* ed. V. A. C. Gatrell, B. Lenman, and G. Parker. London: Europa Publications.

———. 1985. Classes and Police in Manchester. In *City, Class and Culture,* ed. A. J. Kidd and K. R. Roberts. Manchester: Manchester University Press.

De Jasay, A. 1989. *Social Contract, Free Ride.* Oxford: Clarendon Press.

Ellickson, R. C. 1991. *Order Without Law: How Neighbors Settle Disputes.* Cambridge: Harvard University Press.

Emsley, C. 1983. *Policing and Its Context, 1750–1870.* London: Macmillan.

———. 1987. *Crime and Society in England, 1750–1900.* London: Longman.

Gatrell, V. A. C., B. Lenman, and G. Parker, eds. *Crime and the Law: The Social History of Crime in Western Europe Since 1500.* London: Europa Publications.

Graham, H. D., and T. R. Gurr, eds. 1969. *The History of Violence in America.* New York: F. A. Praeger.

Hart, J. M. 1955. The Reform of the Borough Police, 1835–1856. *English Historical Review* 70:416–22.

Hay, D. 1975. Property, Authority and the Criminal Law. In *Albion's Fatal Tree: Crime and Society in Eighteenth Century England,* ed. D. Hay, P. Linebaugh, and E. P. Thompson. New York: Pantheon Books.

Hay, D., P. Linebaugh, and E. P. Thompson, eds. 1975. *Albion's Fatal Tree: Crime and Society in Eighteenth Century England.* New York: Pantheon Books.

Hay, D., and F. Snyder, eds. 1989. *Policing and Prosecution in Britain, 1750–1850.* Oxford: Clarendon Press.

Johnston, L. 1992. *The Rebirth of Private Policing.* London: Routledge.

Jones, D. 1982. *Crime, Protest, Community, and Police in Nineteenth Century Britain.* London: Routledge and Kegan Paul.

Kidd, A. J., and K. R. Roberts, eds. 1985. *City, Class and Culture.* Manchester: Manchester University Press.

King, P. 1984. Decision-Makers and Decision-Making in the English Criminal Law 1750–1800. *Historical Journal* 27:25–58.

———. 1989. Prosecution Associations and Their Impact in Eighteenth Century Essex. In *Policing and Prosecution in Britain, 1750–1850,* ed. D. Hay and F. Snyder. Oxford: Clarendon Press.

Langbein, J. 1978. The Criminal Trial before the Lawyers. *University of Chicago Law Review* 45 (2): 263–316.

———. 1983. Albion's Fatal Flaws. *Past and Present* 98:96–120.

Lenman, B., and G. Parker. 1980. The State, the Community and the Criminal Law in Early Modern Europe. In *Crime and the Law: The Social History of Crime in Western Europe Since 1500,* ed. V. A. C. Gatrell, B. Lenman, and G. Parker. London: Europa Publications.

Little, C. B., and C. P. Sheffield. 1983. Frontiers and Criminal Justice: English Private Prosecution Societies and American Vigilantism in the Eighteenth and Nineteenth Centuries. *American Sociological Review* 48:796–808.

McLynn, F. 1989. *Crime and Punishment in Eighteenth Century England.* London: Routledge.

Mereweather, H. A. 1814. Insurance Against Robbery; or the Present System of the Police Considered and a New One Proposed. *The Pamphleteer* 3:243–63.

Philips, D. 1977. *Crime and Authority in Victorian England: The Black Country, 1835–1860.* London: Croom Helm.

———. 1980. A New Engine of Authority: The Institutionalisation of Law Enforcement in England, 1780–1830. In *Crime and the Law: The Social History of Crime in Western Europe Since 1500,* ed. V. A. C. Gatrell, B. Lenman, and G. Parker. London: Europa Publications.

———. 1983. A Just Measure of Crime, Authority, Hunters, and Blue Locusts: The Revisionist's Social History of Crime and the Law in Britain, 1780–1850. In *Social Control and the State,* ed. S. Cohen and A. Scull. Oxford: M. Robertson.

———. 1989. Good Men to Associate and Bad Men to Conspire: Associations for the Prosecution of Felons in England, 1760–1860. In *Policing and Prosecution in Britain, 1750–1850,* ed. D. Hay and F. Snyder. Oxford: Oxford University Press.

Pirie, M. 1988. *Micropolitics.* Aldershot, Hants, U.K.: Wildwood House.

Radzinowicz, L. 1948–68. *A History of English Criminal Law and its Administration From 1750.* 4 vols. New York: Macmillan.

Reith, C. 1938. *The Police Idea.* Oxford: Oxford University Press.

———. 1943. *British Police and the Democratic Ideal.* Oxford: Oxford University Press.

Report of Commissioners for Enquiring into County Rates. 1836. Parliamentary Papers.

Report from Select Committee on Police of the Metropolis. 1828. Parliamentary Papers.

Robinson, C. D. 1979. Ideology as History: A Look at the Way Some English Historians Look at the Police. *Police Studies* 2:35–49.

Rosenbaum, H. J., and P. C. Sedeberg, eds. 1976. *Vigilante Politics.* Philadelphia: University of Pennsylvania Press.

Sharpe, J. 1984. *Crime in Early Modern England, 1550–1750.* London: Longman.

Shubert, A. 1981. Private Initiative in Law Enforcement: Associations for the Prosecution of Felons, 1744–1856. In *Policing and Punishment in Nineteenth Century Britain,* ed. V. Bailey. London: Croom Helm.

Silver, A. 1967. The Demand for Order in Civil Society. In *The Police: Six Essays,* ed. D. Bordua. New York: Wiley.

Smith, A. 1978. *Lectures on Jurisprudence.* Edited by R. L. Meek, D. D. Raphael, and P. G. Stein. Indianapolis: Liberty Classics.

South, N. 1988. *Policing For Profit.* London: Sage Publications.

Steedman, C. 1984. *Policing the Victorian Community: The Formation of English Provincial Police Forces, 1856–1880.* London: Routledge and Kegan Paul.

Storch, R. J. 1975. The Plague of Blue Locusts: Police Reform and Popular Resistance in England, 1840–57. *International Review of Social History* 20:61–90.

———. 1976. The Policeman as Domestic Missionary: Urban Discipline and Popular Culture in Northern England, 1850–1880. *Journal of Social History* 4:481–509.

———. 1989. Policing Rural England before the Police. In *Policing and Prosecution in Britain, 1750–1850,* ed. D. Hay and F. Snyder. Oxford: Leicester University Press.

Styles, J. 1987. The Emergence of the Police: Explaining Police Reform in Eighteenth and Nineteenth Century England. *British Journal of Criminology.*

———. 1989. Print and Policing: Crime Advertising in Eighteenth Century Provincial England. In *Policing and Prosecution in Britain, 1750–1850,* ed. D. Hay and F. Snyder. Oxford: Clarendon Press.

Tobias, J. J. 1967. *Crime and Industrial Society in the Nineteenth Century.* London: Batsford.

———. 1979. *Crime and Police in England, 1700–1900.* New York: St. Martin's Press.

Toennies, F. [1887] 1957. *Community and Society.* East Lansing: Michigan State University Press.

Wirth, L. 1938. Urbanism as a Way of Life. *American Journal of Sociology* 44:1–24.

Wrightson, K. 1980. Two Concepts of Order: Justices, Constables and Jurymen in Seventeenth Century England. In *An Ungovernable People: The English and Their Law in the Seventeenth and Eighteenth Centuries,* ed. J. Brewer and J. Styles. London: Hutchinson.

8

"This Enormous Army"

The Mutual-Aid Tradition of American Fraternal Societies before the Twentieth Century

David T. Beito

> The tendency to join fraternal organizations for the purpose of obtaining care and relief in the event of sickness and insurance for the family in case of death is well-nigh universal. To the laboring classes and those of moderate means they offer many advantages not to be had elsewhere.
> —New Hampshire Bureau of Labor, *Report* (1894)

The social-welfare world of the poor has changed considerably since the turn of the twentieth century. It is not difficult to find dramatic evidence of progress. Most obviously, there has been a substantial reduction in the percentage of Americans who are poor. Even in 1929, about 40 percent of the population still lived in poverty. The corresponding figure for 1998 was 12.7 percent. The poor have also enjoyed notable material and physical gains in terms of income, diet, health, and housing conditions.[1]

There are other much less reassuring statistical measures, however. The decline in poverty has coincided with increased rates of dependence on governmental aid. In 1905, only 1 out of every 150 Americans (excluding prisoners) resided in a public or private institution of any kind, including almshouses, asylums, orphanages, and hospitals. The number of Americans who depended on outdoor relief was also small. As late as 1931, only ninety-three thousand families received mothers' pensions, the state-funded antecedents to Aid to Families with Dependent Children (AFDC). In 1995, by contrast, 17 percent of the U.S. population received means-tested assistance.[2]

Paradoxically, this rise in the welfare rolls has occurred despite a substantial decline in poverty rates. This raises an obvious question: how were poor people once able to avoid dependence? Part of the answer is that they could fall back on a wide diversity of self-help and mutual-aid arrangements, most of which no longer exist. Some of the most important of these were fraternal societies such as the Knights of Pythias, the Sons of Italy, the Polish National Alliance, and the Independent Order of Odd Fellows.

Defining characteristics of fraternal societies were (more or less) the following: an autonomous system of lodges, a democratic form of internal government, a ritual, and the provision of mutual aid for members and their families. Members of female organizations that met these criteria generally embraced the term "fraternal" rather than "sororal." In contrast to the hierarchical methods of modern welfare, fraternal aid rested on a principle of reciprocity. Donors and recipients often came from the same, or nearly the same, walks of life; today's recipient could be tomorrow's donor, and vice versa.

By the early nineteenth century, two fraternal types were predominant: secret and insurance orders. The former emphasized ritualism and eschewed uniform payment schedules. The second type devoted somewhat less attention to ritualism and openly solicited recruits with the lure of health- and life-insurance protection. This dichotomy should not be exaggerated. The line between the secret and the insurance order was often a blurred one. Moreover, both fraternal types shared a common emphasis on mutual aid. As a spokesman for the Modern Woodmen of America (which called its members "neighbors" and lodges "camps") wrote in 1934, "[A] few dollars given here, a small sum there to help a stricken member back on his feet or keep his protection in force during a crisis in his financial affairs; a sick Neighbor's wheat harvested, his grain hauled to market, his winter's fuel cut or a home built to replace one destroyed by a midnight fire—thus has fraternity been at work among a million members in 14,000 camps."[3]

Confraternities and Guilds

It is not my purpose here to provide a comprehensive history of fraternal societies in the United States. Instead I will try to sketch some highlights of their development prior to the twentieth century. Any thorough attempt to study this subject must take into account the work of Alexis de Tocqueville. His famous discussion of voluntary associations from the 1830s has become a staple of the literature:

> Americans of all ages, all conditions, and all dispositions constantly form associations. . . . The Americans make associations to give entertainment, to found seminaries, to build inns, to construct churches, to diffuse books. . . . Wherever at the end of some new undertaking you see the government in France, or a man of rank in England, in the United States, you will be sure to find an association.[4]

Contrary to the impression that might be left by this quotation, the American love affair with voluntarism had deep roots in the Old World. Tocqueville's words, with only slight modification, could have been applied to the role of associations in England and Spain during the Middle Ages. The two associational forms that most closely resembled American fraternal orders were confraternities and craft guilds. For this reason, I will discuss their development in some detail.

Like fraternal societies, confraternities were oath-bound, lay-controlled voluntary organizations that did not officially discriminate on the basis of class or occupation. They grew rapidly in Western Europe after the twelfth century. A confraternity usually derived its name from a religious figure, such as a patron saint or the Virgin Mary. Women could and often did join, but both custom and formal rules generally barred them from leadership positions. In theory, and to a great extent reality, confraternities were democratic and egalitarian. The members, garbed in hooded "liveries," marching in procession, with candles in hand, regularly appeared at funerals of other members to pray for their safe journey through purgatory to paradise.[5]

Much like the fraternal societies of a later age, confraternities were leading outlets for sociability and prestige in many communities. They also served as sources of social welfare. Confraternities dispensed cash to relieve sickness and other emergencies, endowed hospitals, paid for funerals, underwrote dowries for poor women, advanced low-interest loans, arbitrated legal disputes, established schools, and built bridges for religious pilgrims. Historian Maureen Flynn characterizes the confraternities of medieval Spain as "collective insurance agencies" and as pioneering "'institutions' of social welfare." She concludes that they anticipated modern actuarial practices (at least in a crude way) by assessing members on the basis of risk and age. For Ronald F. E. Weissman, Italian confraternities were purveyors of "vital forms of social insurance in life and death."[6]

Attempts to draw analogies between the functions of confraternities and those of modern welfare and insurance institutions, while valid to some degree, should not be overdone. As many historians of the subject have cautioned, the spiritual agenda always took precedence over any monetary benefits. Many confraternal budgets in Italy and England, for example, allocated far more to the purchase of candles than to social welfare. The candle was an essential investment because it lighted "the path through the vale of tears" to the bliss of "eternal life." These religious priorities probably made sense to most recipients, who did not join primarily for economic rewards.[7]

Confraternities also anticipated fraternal societies in their ability to win a mass following. There were over 160 confraternities in London alone during the fifteenth century. Zamora, Spain, a city of about eight thousand people, had one confraternity for every fourteen households during the same period. In Italy, confraternities established footholds in almost every sizable village. Historian Christopher Black has estimated that about one out of four Italian adults in the sixteenth century was a member at one time in their lives.[8]

Many features of the craft guilds of the Middle Ages can also be detected in modern fraternal societies. Like confraternities, craft guilds relied on rituals, an elective form of internal government, and the provision of sickness and burial benefits. Taking the analogy still further, they built hospitals, operated joint stock companies, and subsidized the arts. Some founded towns and cities. In contrast to confraternities, which were open to all believers, craft guilds restricted membership to a single occupation.[9]

In other respects, craft guilds more closely resembled arms of governments than they did voluntary associations. An individual joined primarily to gain an entree to political and regulatory privilege. "Freedom of the gild," writes Jack C. Ross, "was never an unlimited right for all people, and it was this selectivity that gave the gilds their place in the stratification system and the ability to provide rewards, financial, social, and religious, to members."[10]

While craft guilds and confraternities eventually declined throughout Europe, the timing and details varied greatly. In Spain and Italy, confraternities were still forces to be reckoned with during the late eighteenth century and even later. They also established footholds in Latin America. German craft guilds in many cases maintained their preeminent status until the middle of the nineteenth century. In Great Britain, on the other hand, craft guilds and confraternities had suffered serious reversals by the sixteenth century. Both types of institutions reeled under accusations of harboring sedition and creating unfair economic privilege. Confraternities were especially suspect because of their Catholic trappings, such as the worship of saints, belief in Purgatory, and prayers for the dead. The Chanceries Act of 1547 dealt a fatal blow. Under its provisions, confraternities became branded as subversive organizations and lost their property holdings.[11]

The Rise of Freemasonry

The demise of confraternities and craft guilds confined mutual aid, as manifested by formal voluntary associations, to the margins of British social life for well over a century. Other sources of welfare assistance, such as the poor law, Protestant churches, and elite-endowed philanthropic organizations, struggled to fill the gap. This era was also one of transition. New institutions of mutual aid slowly emerged. Many of them built upon medieval precedents such as confraternities and craft guilds.[12]

Freemasonry stands out as the most famous example of mutual aid that arose during the seventeenth and eighteenth centuries. Historians have yet to reach a consensus on the origins of this paradigmatic secret society. Much of this confusion can be traced to the early Masonic fascination with secrecy and habit of inventing fantastic tales of antiquity. The overriding goal of the ritual was not historical verity but "instructing" members as they climbed the degree ladder. They learned from the ritual about Freemasonry's illustrious role in the construction of Solomon's temple, the design of the pyramids of Egypt, and the founding of the Knights Templars of the Middle Ages.[13]

Nowadays, even official historians of Freemasonry dismiss these fanciful accounts, and most scholarly studies trace Masonic origins to either England or Scotland in the seventeenth century. Beyond that, there is still a lack of consensus. A common theory holds that Freemasonry emerged in some way out of stone (or operative) masonry. The groundwork may have been laid by the gradual admission of nonoperatives to the lodges or other organizations that had been founded by stonemasons. If this were the case, it is still unclear why these new members joined. Perhaps they had been lured by the mystique of the rituals or the prospect of gaining hidden knowledge about fields such as geometry. For some, membership may have been a means to recall the values, either real or imagined, of the moribund craft-guild tradition. In any case, by the first decade of the eighteenth century, a network of lodges controlled by nonoperatives existed in both England

and Scotland. These nonoperatives came to be officially known as "accepted" masons because they were not workers in stone. Despite the probable origins of Freemasonry as a craft guild, the new members were primarily from the wealthier and better-educated segments of the community and included professionals and businessmen.[14]

Fraternal societies of all types borrowed much from the structure and practices of Freemasonry. Most obviously, they imitated its system of decentralized but affiliated lodges. They also embraced key elements of the ritual, especially the stress on artisanship and graded degrees. Freemasonry repopularized ritualism for an increasingly secular age by breaking free from the old constraints of craft interests or Roman Catholic doctrine.[15]

British Friendly Societies

The rise of the sickness- and burial-insurance order, known in Great Britain as the friendly society or "box club," also occurred during this period. Some organizations, such as the United General Sea Box of Borrowstounness Friendly Society and the Sea Box Society of St. Andrews, appeared as early as the 1630s and 1640s. The formative stages of development were almost wholly local in character. "Affiliated societies" with multiple lodges, such as the Manchester Unity and the Ancient Order of Foresters, did not emerge until the early nineteenth century.[16]

Freemasonry and friendly societies differed greatly in terms of function and membership composition. The average Mason was either a merchant or professional. Friendly-society members, on the other hand, were more likely to be wage earners or artisans. In addition, Masonic mutual aid tended to be informal, secretive, and geared to special cases while friendly societies focused unabashedly on insurance.[17]

The friendly societies framed their insurance programs long before the advent of modern actuarial tables. They relied on a primitive system of assessment under which each member, regardless of age or occupation, paid an identical premium. The Amicable Society of Patrington in the East Riding was typical in providing "that when a member is sick, lame or blind, and rendered incapable of working . . . he shall be allowed eight shillings per week during his inability to work" and "that upon the death of every free member, notice must be given to the stewards, who, at the next monthly meeting shall pay to the widow or executor ten pounds."[18]

Friendly societies enjoyed almost uninterrupted growth during the eighteenth and nineteenth centuries. Membership surged from at least six hundred thousand in 1793 to as many as four million by 1874. An ever-rising demand for burial insurance by the working and lower middle class fueled much of this expansion. "A pauper funeral," notes E.P. Thompson, "was the ultimate social disgrace. And ceremony bulked large in folk-lore, and preoccupied dying men."[19]

American Fraternal Orders: Initial Development

Not surprisingly, many of these patterns of mutual aid also appeared in the American colonies. The first Masonic lodge opened in Boston in 1733, only sixteen years after the founding of the British grand lodge. Early growth was slow and largely confined to major coastal cities such as Boston and Philadelphia. As in Great Britain, lodges drew membership primarily from the higher social, political, and economic ranks of society.[20]

The Revolution marked a divergence in the evolution of American and British Freemasonry. The presence of prominent members, such as George Washington, John Hancock, and Paul Revere, greatly widened Freemasonry's popular appeal. Initiates flocked to special traveling lodges chartered for the troops. As historian Dorothy Ann Lipson puts it, the war served to "Americanize" Freemasonry. The colonial "brethren" reacted to changing events by staging their own war of separation. They organized grand lodges in each state that were independent from the British structure. American Freemasonry expanded not only in size and numbers but also in membership diversity. The Revolution accelerated a trend, already underway by the 1750s, to broaden the base beyond a narrow upper crust. By the end of the eighteenth century, artisans and skilled workers were important components of the membership. They even formed a majority in some lodges. While American Freemasonry still catered to an elite after the Revolution, it had become a much less exclusive one.[21]

The Revolutionary Era also brought changes in the methods of Masonic social-welfare assistance. In the colonial period, barely a pretense of centralization had existed. Each lodge had enjoyed full authority to raise and disperse all money and establish requirements for recipients. By the 1780s, modifications began to be introduced to this system. The state grand lodges established charity committees to supplement (although never supplant) the local lodges. In 1789, the Pennsylvania Grand Lodge established a fund that was financed through annual assessments of sixty-five cents per member. That same year, the Connecticut Grand Lodge began to deposit three dollars of each initiation fee in a state charity fund.[22]

Although the full extent of Masonic charity will probably never be known, fairly detailed figures exist for selected periods and locations. The Pennsylvania Grand Lodge assisted about one hundred members between 1792 and 1809. It allocated between 57 and 155 dollars annually for this purpose. Such amounts were still negligible compared to the combined totals raised through individual lodges. Between 1798 and 1800 (the only years for which complete figures exist for both the state and local lodges), Masons in Pennsylvania disbursed over 6,000 dollars to needy members. This amount exceeded that of any other private charity in Philadelphia at the time.[23]

Researchers should be leery of drawing broad conclusions from these account-book tallies, no matter how complete they may seem to be. A sizable portion of Masonic mutual aid entailed intangibles such as employment information, temporary lodging, and character references. The underlying premise of such assistance was that brethren should favor their own in any social or economic situation. "You are not charged to do beyond your Ability," summarized an early tract distributed by the fraternity, "only to prefer a poor Brother that is a good Man and true, before any other poor people in the same Circumstances."[24]

American sickness- and burial-insurance orders, much like American Masonic lodges, first developed from British precedents. One clear parallel between the countries was the early primacy of localism. In New England and the rest of the country, it was rare for a "society" to encompass more than a single lodge. It was not until the 1820s that national sickness- and burial-insurance orders of any consequence appeared. A major difference between the countries was that the Americans lagged behind in numbers of organizations. Forty-one mutual-insurance societies (including Masonic lodges) existed in Massachusetts at the beginning of the nineteenth century, compared to just nineteen thirty years earlier. This growth, while impressive, still left the Americans well behind the British total at the time of nearly nine thousand friendly societies.[25]

One possible explanation for these differing levels of growth is the impact of industrialization and urbanization. Most historians agree that fraternal orders developed first and most successfully in towns and cities. According to this view, the migration to cities, combined with increases in disposable income, created a niche for these and other formal associations to form. Richard D. Brown's study of colonial and early national Massachusetts, for example, concludes that voluntary associations did not generally arise until communities had reached population thresholds of between one thousand and two thousand. Another precondition for the emergence of associations, according to Brown, was for one-fourth or more of adult males to be employed in nonagricultural pursuits. The necessity for an urban threshold has been seconded by more recent research for New England as a whole by Conrad Edick Wright.[26]

For many who joined, a lodge affiliation was a means to enhance older and more stable forms of mutual aid based on blood ties, geography, and religion. Hence, as Don Harrison Doyle has asserted, fraternal orders "acted to reinforce, rather than supplant, the family as a social institution. They also supplemented the extended kinship networks that supported the nuclear family." Mary Ann Clawson also stresses the "familial" features of lodges: "Fraternal association provided the ritualized means by which their members could define one another as brothers; biologically unrelated individuals thus used kinship to construct the solidarity necessary to accomplish a variety of tasks."[27] Much like the older kin and geographical networks, early American fraternal societies were often loose and informal in their methods of providing help. A survey of the bylaws and constitutions of six leading societies in Boston during the eighteenth century shows great reluctance to guarantee specific cash benefits for working days lost or funerals. Only one society, the Massachusetts Charitable Mechanic Association, specified an exact sum for burial, and this was forty dollars.[28]

It was the usual practice of these societies to consider applications for aid on a case-by-case basis. The Scots Charitable Society, for instance, allocated funds for such diverse purposes as ship passage, prison bail, and an old-age pension. It also paid regular stipends to a widow who had lost her husband at sea. All of these societies showed little regard for consistency in the amounts they paid in each situation. Extant records of these organizations invariably classify any cash dispersals as "charity" and "relief" rather than "benefits."[29]

The Americans may have been informal in matters of money, but they were models of clarity in formulating sanctions for misconduct. The Boston Marine Society levied specific fines and other punishments for a multitude of offenses including failure to attend funerals of deceased members or "blasphem[ing] the Name of Almighty GOD." It provided the ultimate punishment of expulsion for the "common Drunkard" and for those who "shall at monthly meetings play, or promote the playing of any Cards, Dice, or other Gaming whatsoever."[30]

In some respects, the exactitude of the American societies in the punishment of behavioral infractions and their ambiguity on guarantees of benefits made good economic sense. Actuarial science was still at an embryonic level. Promises to pay uniform sick and death benefits entailed much greater risk than levying fines for infractions such as drunkenness or lack of decorum at meetings. Behavioral restrictions also helped to weed out the poorer risks and heighten feelings of solidarity. Many American societies, after all, had not advanced beyond the formative stage of groping for an identity. It was not a time for reckless departures.

Some historians have argued that American fraternal societies were more likely than their British counterparts to recruit their members from all economic classes. Mary Ann Clawson notes that "the American multi-class fraternal order, with its large membership and popularity among male wage-earners, represents a phenomenon for which there is no exact equivalent in European societies." This view may be only half right. On the one hand, it is certainly true that fraternal orders in the United States rarely discriminated, at least as part of official policy, on the basis of economic class. As early as colonial times, the most prominent groups in Boston, such as the Massachusetts Charitable Society, the Boston Marine Society, and the Hartford Charitable Society, attracted both skilled workers and merchants. As Wright has concluded, lodges in New England "tended to reflect the communities they served." He uncovered evidence that wage earners, primarily from skilled occupations, often represented one-third or more of all members.[31]

The problem with Clawson's characterization is that it may understate the "multi-class" basis of British friendly societies. Historian P. H. J. H. Gosden has found that business owners constituted a majority of over one hundred principal leaders of the Manchester Unity of the Independent Order of Oddfellows and the Ancient Order of Foresters, the two leading affiliated orders in Great Britain during the nineteenth century. It may be true that wage earners were better represented among the rank and file in the British societies, but even this remains unproved.[32]

The Odd Fellows: The First National Insurance Order

Much like Freemasonry, the Odd Fellows began in the United States as a British import. In 1819, an immigrant opened a lodge of the Manchester Unity of the Independent Order of Odd Fellows in Baltimore. It formed the basis for the first "affiliated order" in the United States. Eleven years later, lodges of the Odd Fellows had appeared in four states and increased to over six thousand members. The Americans seceded in 1843 and formed a wholly separate organization called the Independent Order of Odd Fellows. Although other British friendly societies, such as the Foresters, Rechabites, and Druids, also had entered the fray by this time, they had a limited impact by comparison.[33]

It is not too difficult to find evidence of continuity in the practices of American sickness- and burial-insurance orders between the colonial and antebellum periods. Historical studies of Albany, Providence, and Kingston, New York, have confirmed that American Odd Fellowship, much like its eighteenth-century predecessors, drew liberally from all economic classes. Moreover, a substantial segment of skilled workers, in Albany and perhaps elsewhere, obtained leadership positions. According to Stuart Blumin, Odd Fellowship in the United States during these years was "a distinctively working-class movement" that only later solicited recruits from middle and professional ranks.[34]

The Independent Order of Odd Fellows was a fraternal trendsetter for the United States in several respects. It initiated the first major departure from the often haphazard grants of previous societies by using a clear schedule of guaranteed benefits. Under this new system, each member when taken sick could claim a regular stipend per week (usually three to six dollars) to compensate for working days lost. In addition, the Odd Fellows helped to revise the language of American fraternalism. Prior to this time, most societies had favored the words "charity" and "relief" to describe the aid they provided. The Odd Fellows, by contrast, preferred the terms "benefit" and "right." Hence, as one member declared, money was "not paid or received as charity: it is every Brother's right, and paid to every one when sick, whether he be high or low, rich or poor." This was not a philosophy of unconditional entitlement, however. The Odd Fellows followed in the footsteps of colonial fraternal societies in vowing to withhold aid for excessive drunkenness, profanity, adultery, or disruptive behavior.[35]

The decades before and just after the Civil War were ones of sustained expansion for the Independent Order of Odd Fellows. Between 1830 and 1877, the membership rose from about 3,000 to 456,000. Total aid dispensed during these years amounted to over sixty-nine million dollars (at more than one billion dollars by today's standards). Sick and funeral benefits constituted a majority of this spending, but lodges also devoted substantial sums to other purposes. In 1855, for example, the Grand Lodge of Maryland provided aid to nine hundred orphans of deceased members.[36]

The geographically extended structure of the Odd Fellows allowed mobile members to retain benefits throughout the country. It also facilitated a kind of "coinsurance" to mitigate local crises such as natural disasters or epidemics. In 1855, members in Massachusetts contributed over eight hundred dollars to relieve lodges in Pittsburgh that had exhausted their funds because of a fire; ten years later they provided four hundred dollars of aid to lodges in Virginia during a breakout of yellow fever.[37]

At the same time, the greater reliance on national systems also opened the door to abuse and fraud. By the antebellum period, publications of American Odd Fellowship began to warn of traveling impostors who would file false claims. This problem had been less prevalent among sickness- and burial-insurance orders of the eighteenth century, which could more readily rely on local knowledge to root out suspicious characters. To cope with these dangers, the national organization required that members who were moving first obtain transfer or "clearance" cards. At the state level, grand lodges established boards of relief to carefully investigate itinerants who petitioned for aid. According to an article in the *Emblem,* a leading voice of American Odd Fellowship, each state board was a "sort of detective police force" and "scarecrow" to frighten off impostors, thus leaving more for the deserving.[38]

Another device used by the Odd Fellows to short-circuit fraud was the ritual itself. "Passwords and signs," asserted G. W. Clinton, a past grand president, "the later common to the whole Order, and the former ever-changing and ever-circulating, guard against the impositions of the unworthy, assure us our rights, and open the hearts of our brethren to us." The increasingly elaborate amalgam of grips, degrees, regalia, and pageantry was a world apart from the Spartan ritualistic forms of eighteenth-century sickness- and burial-insurance orders. In certain respects, the successful climb up the degree ladder was the antebellum equivalent of building a good credit rating. As a corollary, of course, the attention to degrees served to reinforce those *fraternal* bonds of trust and solidarity that could cut across community, class, or ethnic ties.[39]

The National Life Insurance Order

The formation of the Ancient Order of United Workmen (AOUW) in 1868 signaled the onset of a new phase in American fraternal development. The AOUW was the first notable national life-insurance order. The founder, John Jordan Upchurch, a master mechanic on the Pennsylvania Railroad and ardent Mason, certainly had not planned it that way. Instead, he had envisioned the AOUW as a forum that would unite "through the medium of the lodge affiliation employer and employee and under solemn bond of helpful co-operation, adjust differences that might arise between them and avoid strikes." Had Upchurch achieved his original goal, the AOUW would have become a kind of conservative version of the Knights of Labor.[40]

The AOUW's life-insurance plan, which had started as an incidental feature to attract members, quickly moved to center stage. Adopted in 1868, it guaranteed a death benefit of one thousand (later raised to two thousand) dollars. Funding came from a one-dollar per capita assessment on each member. It would have been beyond the capacity of antebellum societies to pay out this kind of money because no individual lodge had the necessary resources. The AOUW responded to this problem by spreading the burden. It centralized the dispersal of funds into state (and later) national organizations. As a result, the membership of the AOUW expanded rapidly and finally crested at 450,000 in 1902.[41]

Before the Civil War, sickness insurance had been the major focus of fraternal societies. Individual lodges had paid death benefits, but the amount in each case had rarely exceeded 150 dollars—roughly the cost of a funeral. The AOUW reversed these priorities. Although many lodges provided sickness benefits, this feature was never more than a secondary concern.[42]

The next three decades brought a full flowering of similar national life-insurance orders. Hundreds of new organizations, such as the Royal Arcanum, the Knights of Honor, the Order of the Iron Hall, and the Modern Woodmen of America, sprang up across the county. Many older societies that had specialized in sickness and burial policies, such as the Knights of Pythias and Improved Order of Redmen, followed suit with their own national life-insurance plans. By 1908, the two hundred leading societies had paid well over one billion dollars in death benefits.[43]

Membership in these societies grew rapidly during these years. According to *Everybody's Magazine,* the ranks of fraternalism had become nothing less than an "enormous army." The foot soldiers were "the middle-class workmen, the salaried clerk, the farmer, the artisan, the country merchant, and the laborer," all attempting to "insure their helpless broods against abject poverty. Rich men insure in the big [commercial life] companies to create an estate; poor men insure in fraternal orders to create bread and meat. It is an insurance against want, the poorhouse, charity, and degradation."[44]

The combined membership of fraternal organizations in the United States during this period will never be known for sure. The constituent organizations of the National Fraternal Congress (NFC), the major clearinghouse for life-insurance societies, had a combined membership of one-half million in 1886; by 1920, it was over nine million. The U.S. population in 1920 was just over one hundred million people. Even in its best years, however, the NFC failed to reach significant segments of the fraternal population, including blacks and many of those who subscribed to local sick-benefit organizations. In 1920, about eighteen million Americans belonged to lodges, in other words, nearly 30 percent of all adults over age twenty.[45]

The life-insurance order was a peculiarly American institution, although it soon spread throughout Canada. Nothing quite like it appeared in Great Britain until much later and then in a very limited form. During the late nineteenth century, friendly societies continued to specialize in sickness and burial insurance much like American fraternals had in the past. Moreover, commercial companies in Great Britain still thoroughly dominated the life-insurance market after the 1860s, while in the United States they faced stiff fraternal competition.[46]

American fraternal life-insurance societies had the good fortune to arrive on the scene at a time when commercial companies faced especially bad publicity. A spate of bankruptcies associated with financial panics in the 1870s had shaken consumer confidence. By one estimate, the unrecovered losses suffered by policyholders in commercial companies during this period totaled thirty-five million dollars. In addition, the assessment approach of fraternal organizations allowed rates low enough to undercut commercial insurance companies—that is, at least initially. Most members paid a flat premium that did not vary on the basis of age or health. Many societies skirted the common commercial practice of accumulating a sufficient reserve. While most fraternal orders eventually abandoned the crude assessment method as untenable, it gave them a leg up in the market in the meantime. By 1895, half the life-insurance policies in force were on the fraternal plan. As one commentator put it at the time, the United States had entered an unprecedented "golden age of fraternity."[47]

The interest shown by fraternal orders in life insurance, while certainly considerable, never became all-encompassing. At the local level especially, sickness and burial societies still predominated. In 1891, a detailed study conducted by the Connecticut Bureau of Labor Statistics found that there were 494,322 members of fraternal insurance societies in the state. More than 60 percent belonged to sickness and burial orders, compared to 28 percent in life-insurance societies. Almost all the life-insurance orders were affiliates of centralized national organizations such as the Royal Arcanum and Legion and Honor. Over 70 percent of these societies entrusted the payment of death benefits to an office outside of the state. By contrast, an amazing 99 percent of sickness- and funeral-benefit societies assigned this responsibility to local or state lodges. Even the national sickness and burial orders, such as the Ancient Order of Foresters, the Ancient Order of Hibernians, the Independent Order of Odd Fellows, the Grand United Order of Galilean Fishermen, and the Deutscher Order Harugari, relied almost wholly on local and state affiliates to raise and disperse benefit money.[48]

The study by the Connecticut Bureau of Labor Statistics, cited earlier, found that the membership of all fraternal insurance orders relative to general population (men, women, and children) was 15 percent. It calculated that "if to the membership reported should be added the number in the Masonic societies, the Elks, the Patrons of Husbandry, and other societies, not co-operative benefit, and therefore not included herein, the total would be in excess of the total male adult population of the state." This figure, however, is so large because it does not eliminate individuals who had multiple memberships. A fairly safe bet is that fraternal membership encompassed one-third or more of the voting-age male population at the time.[49]

The success of fraternal societies coincided with an intense American fascination with ritualism. No class or ethnic group was immune. Ritualistic trappings, including grips, degrees, and passwords, were used by groups as diverse as the Knights of Labor, the Knights of the Ku Klux Klan, the Farmer's Alliance, the Union League, the American Protective Association, the Tammany Societies, the Church of Latter Day Saints, and the Patrons of Husbandry. Most were variants on the Masonic model. The linkage was especially close in the Knights of Labor, the Patrons of Husbandry, and the modern Ku Klux Klan, which had been founded by Masons.[50]

Conclusion

At the beginning of the twentieth century, fraternal societies seemed headed for a bright future. They had achieved a level of development that was striking when compared to the past. In 1800, the fraternal scene (with the possible exception of Freemasonry) had been characterized by small and localized societies with meager budgets and haphazard schedules of benefits. In 1900, Americans increasingly flocked to far-flung national organizations, characterized by multiple lodges and hefty death and sick benefits. Observers had good reason to be optimistic about the prospects for fraternalism in the coming decades of the twentieth century. As Charles Moreau Harger commented in the *Atlantic Monthly,* "[S]o rapidly does [the fraternal order] increase in popularity that it shows little indication of ever wielding less power over men's destinies than it does today."[51]

While this fraternal golden age continued for a time, it ended much sooner than Harger had expected. In 1906, member societies of the National Fraternal Congress represented 91,434 lodges; by 1925, this figure had peaked at 120,000 lodges. After that, the number of lodges leveled off and fell. The pace of descent accelerated rapidly during the Depression and continued unabated after World War II. An impressive 52,655 lodges still remain, but their emphasis on mutual aid has been greatly reduced. Many now exist primarily as social organizations.[52]

While it is not the goal of this chapter to examine the reasons for the decline of fraternal societies, several possibilities immediately come to mind. Among these are changing social tastes; restrictive governmental regulation; commercial and employer competition in the provision of services; and the opposition of medical societies, which fought fraternal efforts to offer health care. There was another, much more subtle, factor at work: the rise of the modern welfare state. Mutual aid, throughout history, had been a creature of necessity. Government, by taking away social responsibilities that were once the ken of voluntary institutions, undermined much of this necessity. Much that transcended monetary calculations was lost in the exchange. There has yet to arise a modern analogue to the fraternal society either as a provider of services, such as low-cost medical care, or as a device to encourage the spread of the survival values of thrift, neighborhood cooperation, and individual responsibility.[53]

NOTES

From *Social Philosophy and Policy* 14 (summer 1997): 20–38. Reprinted with the permission of Cambridge University Press.

    1. Levitan 1990, 5–6; <www.census.gov/hhes/www/povty98.html>.

    2. *Charities and Commons* (1906), 488–91; U.S. Department of Labor 1933, 8; U.S. Department of Human Services 2000, 3.

    3. Buffum 1935, 5.

4. Tocqueville 1981, 403–4.

5. Flynn 1989, 5, 13, 23, 33, 40, 43; Weissman 1982, 66–81; C. Black 1989, 35, 150; Brigden 1984, 98; Scarisbrick 1984, 19; Unwin 1908, 122, 123.

6. Flynn 1989, 37–39, 44, 49, 51–58; Scarisbrick 1984, 22; C. Black 1989, 14, 163, 184, 223–33; Mollat 1986, 283; Weissman 1982, ix.

7. Mackenney 1987, 71–73; C. Black 1989, 127; Flynn 1989, 41; and McRee 1993, 207. "Unlike the modern welfare state," writes Christopher Black (1989, 281), "involvement with confraternities satisfied more than basic physical needs. For donors and recipients, for those praying and those being prayed for, for comforters and patients, the confraternities could satisfy the needs for fraternity, social solidarity and spiritual comfort in this world as they contemplated the possibilities of joining the ultimate fraternity of Christ and his saints."

8. Brigden 1984, 94; Flynn 1989, 16; C. Black 1989, 270.

9. One of the founders of Londonderry, for example, was a craft guild. See A. Black 1984, 55–65, 151; Mackenney 1987, 7; and Epstein 1991, 157–58.

10. Ross 1976, 175, 194. Ben R. McRee (1993, 224) writes that confraternities even at their apex constituted "but one link in the chain of medieval poor relief," which included "hospitals, help-ales, monastic alms, family aid, individual acts of charity, handouts to mourners at funeral and obit services, and parish assistance."

11. Flynn 1989, 138–39; C. Black 1989, 22; A. Black 1984, 123, 128, 167; Ross 1976, 138–39; Brigden 1984, 101–2; Scarisbrick 1984, 36–37. A good measure of the waning health of English confraternities and guilds was a fall-off in bequests from wills, a major source of funds. From 1522 to 1539, 23.6 percent of wills in London included such bequests, but between 1539 and 1547 this figure declined to just 8.5 percent. See Brigden 1984, 101.

12. Brigden 1984, 104–7. A leading form of organized mutual aid during this period was the "help ale" (or cooperative feast). While the grand totals of will bequests to charity of all types continued to increase after the Chanceries Act, it did not recover in per capita terms until the 1650s. See Stack 1988, 164–65.

13. Hamill 1986, 15–16, 21; and Lipson 1977, 35–37. For another recent study, see Jacob 1991.

14. Hamill 1986, 27–40; Stevenson 1988, 7, 22, 123–24, 156, 197–98, 216–33. Originally "free mason" was a contraction of "freestone mason." The term referred to a specialist "who worked in freestone—usually limestone—capable of being immediately carved for decorative purposes" (Hamill 1986, 27).

15. Schmidt 1980, 119–39; Stevenson 1988, 228–33.

16. Thompson 1966, 418–19; Gosden 1973, 6, 27–30.

17. Gosden 1967, 71–93; Lipson 1977, 201.

18. Gosden 1967, 17, 230; Thompson 1966, 421.

19. Baernreither 1966, 162; Thompson 1966, 419.

20. Lipson 1977, 48–49.

21. Lipson 1977, 50–62; Wright 1992, 106; Bullock 1990, 360–63; Wright 1992, 218–19; and Huss 1986, 286–91. Bullock (1990, 348–49) argues persuasively that the schism between the "modern" and "ancient" factions of American Freemasonry speeded the occupational shift in the composition of the membership. The moderns drew almost wholly from the mercantile and professional classes

while the ancients attracted large numbers of artisans. The Revolution served to discredit the moderns, who tended to be Tories, thus assuring the spread of the more inclusive ancients. The split had originated in England in the 1730s after the ancients had accused the moderns of corrupting the original meaning of the ritual.

22. Huss 1986, 61; Lipson 1977, 210.

23. Huss 1986, 62–63.

24. Lipson 1977, 207; Bullock 1989, 368.

25. Wright 1992, 63, 66; Gosden 1967, 5.

26. Brown 1973, 69–70; Wright 1992, 55–56.

27. Davids 1987, 47; Doyle 1978, 189; Clawson 1989, 25.

28. These were the Scots Charitable Society of Boston, the Massachusetts Charitable Mechanic Association, the Charitable Irish Society of Boston, the Boston Marine Society, the Episcopal Charitable Society of Boston, and the Massachusetts Charitable Society. Copies of the original bylaws from the eighteenth century can be found in Scots' Charitable Society 1986, 36–40; Buckingham 1853, 6–9; Charitable Irish Society 1876, 22–26; Baker 1982, 302–3, 308–9; *Articles and Rules of the Episcopal Charitable Society* 1724; and Massachusetts Charitable Society 1762.

29. Scots' Charitable Society 1986, 22, 24–25, 29.

30. Baker 1982, 302–3.

31. Clawson 1989, 107; Wright 1992, 209, 213–19.

32. Gosden 1967, 88–93, 224–28.

33. Stevens 1907, 113; Greenberg 1985, 89–93; Ridgely 1878, 234; and Schmidt 1980, 243–45. American Freemasonry never fit the definition of an affiliated order. State lodges were the highest level of authority, and proposals to establish a national grand lodge after the Revolution never advanced beyond the planning stage. It would be more proper to characterize Freemasonry in the United States as a confederacy of state grand lodges rather than as a distinct organization.

34. Gilkeson 1986, 156; Greenberg 1985, 93; Blumin 1989, 223–25. At the same time, Blumin (1989, 225) warns against too readily labeling American Odd Fellowship during its subsequent history as "middle class." He finds no evidence that "bourgeois values were brought to the order by businessmen and taught to workers" and asserts that "it is possible to find within the repeated assertion of a class-free brotherhood and hierarchy of merit a hint of the old working-class radicalism, if not of the Ricardian then at least of the 'Jack's as good as his master' variety."

35. *Gavel* (January 1845), 128. Expanding on this point, another article comments that "by observing the rule of life prescribed by Odd Fellowship, we shall be honest, frugal, temperate, and industrious, and thereby be most likely to secure enough to enable us to be as charitable as others, aside from our dues to the Lodge" (*Gavel* [February 1845], 154).

36. Ridgely 1878, 16, 233; *Gavel* (September 1845), 64; *Emblem: An Odd Fellows Magazine* (1856), 444; *Gavel* (May 1846), 284–86. To translate this into 2001 dollars, I used the dollar conversion calculator of the *Columbia Journalism Review,* which can be found at <http://www.cjr.org/resources/inflater.asp>.

37. *Gavel* (May 1846), 287–88; *Emblem: An Odd Fellows Magazine* (1855), 201.

38. *Emblem: An Odd Fellows Magazine* (1855), 53–54.
39. *Gavel* (September 1845), 29. As might be expected, of course, the widespread appeal of ritualism during this period was multifaceted and defies simple explanations. For a provocative discussion of the role of psychological factors, including gender, see Carnes 1989.
40. Sackett 1914, 25. The Knights of Labor was founded in 1869 only a year after the AOUW. For a discussion of some similarities between these organizations, see Clawson 1989, 138–43.
41. Sackett 1914, 27, 130–33; Basye 1919, 10–14. Beginning in the 1870s, the AOUW slowly shifted away from an assessment approach in favor of graded rates for new members. Not until the turn of the century, however, did it complete the transition (Sackett 1914, 147–96).
42. Landis 1914, 105, 107.
43. *Fraternal Monitor* (February 1, 1908), 22; Basye 1919, 16; Stalson 1969, 553.
44. Dickson and Mantz 1910, 776. By this time, large commercial legal-reserve companies, such as the Equitable and Metropolitan, had been well established for decades.
45. Beito 1993, 420–21. The NFC had been formed in 1886 at the instigation of the Ancient Order of United Workmen and eventually represented the leading life-insurance orders. Some other early members were the Knights of Columbus, the Royal Arcanum, and the Knights of Pythias. The NFC did not include representatives from secret orders, such as the Masons and the Elks (Basye 1919, 71–72).
46. Landis 1914, 107; Landis 1904, 481; Landis 1900, 67, 71; *Life Insurance Independent* (1904), 235; *Life Insurance Independent* (1905), 93; Basye 1919, 26. After the turn of the century, some leading British friendly societies experimented with life (as opposed to simple burial) insurance. By 1908, for example, the Manchester Unity offered a policy that was equivalent to one thousand U.S. dollars. Even so, such examples were comparatively rare. See *Fraternal Monitor* (September 1, 1908), 20.
47. De Raismes Kip 1953, 30–31; Stalson 1969, 451–52, 553; Basye 1919, 29; Myers 1937, 682–83; Cheapest Insurance 1906, 7398; Landis 1914, 88; Rotman Zelizer 1983, 93; Carnes 1989, 1.
48. Connecticut Bureau of Labor Statistics 1892, 71, 617.
49. Connecticut Bureau of Labor Statistics 1892, 71, 617. The national estimate is based on an extensive but nevertheless incomplete tabulation of fraternal membership by Albert S. Stevens (1907, 114).
50. Stevens 1907, vi–vii, 70–72, 388–94; Carnes 1989, 6–9; Gist 1940, 32–33, 48; Schmidt 1980, 38, 197; Clawson 1989, 136–38; and McMath 1993, 58–59, 63, 70. Historian Michael W. Fitzgerald (1989, 114) writes that the ritual of the Union League, an organization dedicated to protecting the civil rights of blacks in the South during Reconstruction, "resembled that of the Masons from which it clearly derived; like those of many fraternal organizations, it extoled civic virtue, universal brotherhood, and other worthy causes."
51. Harger 1906, 494.

52. *Statistics of Fraternal Benefit Societies* (1906), 86.
53. Also see Beito 1997.

REFERENCES

Articles and Rules of the Episcopal Charitable Society in Boston. 1724. Worcester, Mass.: American Antiquarian Society, Early American Imprints, 1639–1800.
Baernreither, J. M. [1889] 1966. *English Associations of Working Men.* Detroit: Gale Research Co.
Baker, W. A. 1982. *A History of the Boston Marine Society, 1742–1981.* Boston: Boston Marine Society.
Basye, W. 1919. *History and Operation of Fraternal Insurance.* Rochester: Fraternal Monitor.
Beito, D. T. 1993. Mutual Aid, State Welfare, and Organized Charity: Fraternal Societies and the "Deserving" and "Undeserving" Poor. *Journal of Policy History* 5: 419–34.
———. 1997. The "Lodge Practice Evil" Reconsidered: Medical Care Through Fraternal Societies, 1900–1930. *Journal of Urban History* 23 (July): 569–600.
Black, A. 1984. *Guilds and Civil Society in European Political Thought From the Twelfth Century to the Present.* Ithaca: Cornell University Press.
Black, C. 1989. *Italian Confraternities in the Sixteenth Century.* Cambridge: Cambridge University Press.
Blumin, S. M. 1989. *The Emergence of the Middle Class: Social Experience in the American City, 1760–1900.* Cambridge: Cambridge University Press.
Brigden, S. 1984. Religion and Social Obligation in Early Sixteenth-Century London. *Past and Present* 103 (March): 67–112.
Brown, R. D. 1973. The Emergence of Voluntary Associations in Massachusetts, 1760–1830. *The Journal of Voluntary Action Research* 2 (April): 64–73.
Buckingham, J. T. 1853. *Annals of the Massachusetts Charitable Mechanic Association.* Boston: Press of Crocker and Brewster.
Buffum, E. E. 1935. *Modern Woodmen of America: A History.* Vol. 2. Rock Island, Ill.: Modern Woodmen of America.
Bullock, S. C. 1989. A Pure and Sublime System: The Appeal of Post-Revolutionary Freemasonry. *Journal of the Early Republic* 9 (fall): 359–73.
———. 1990. The Revolutionary Transformation of American Freemasonry, 1752–1792. *William and Mary Quarterly* 47 (July): 347–69.
Carnes, M. C. 1989. *Secret Ritual and Manhood in Victorian America.* New Haven: Yale University Press.
Charitable Irish Society of Boston. 1876. *The Constitution and By-Laws of the Charitable Irish Society of Boston.* Boston: James F. Cotter and Company.
Cheapest Insurance. 1906. *World's Work* 11 (April).
Clawson, M. A. 1989. *Constructing Brotherhood: Class, Gender, and Fraternalism.* Princeton: Princeton University Press.
Connecticut Bureau of Labor Statistics. 1892. *Annual Report.* Part 3.
Davids, K. 1987. Towards an Ecology of Associations. New School for Social Research, Working Paper No. 54.

De Raismes Kip, R. 1953. *Fraternal Life Insurance in America.* Philadelphia: College Offset Press.

Dickson, H., and I. P. Mantz. 1910. Will the Widow Get Her Money? The Weakness in Fraternal Life Insurance and How It May Be Cured. *Everybody's Magazine* 22 (June): 775–86.

Doyle, D. H. 1978. *The Social Order of a Frontier Community: Jacksonville, Illinois, 1825–1870.* Urbana: University of Illinois Press.

Epstein, S. A. 1991. *Wage Labor and Guilds in Medieval Europe.* Chapel Hill: University of North Carolina Press.

Fitzgerald, M. W. 1989. *The Union League Movement in the Deep South: Politics and Agricultural Change During Reconstruction.* Baton Rouge: Louisiana State University Press.

Flynn, M. 1989. *Sacred Charity: Confraternities and Social Welfare in Spain, 1400–1700.* New York: Cornell University Press.

Gilkeson, J. 1986. *Middle-Class Providence, 1820–1940.* Princeton: Princeton University Press.

Gist, N. P. 1940. Secret Societies: A Cultural Study of Fraternalism in the United States. *University of Missouri Studies* 15 (October 1).

Gosden, P. H. J. H. 1967. *The Friendly Societies in England.* New York: Augustus M. Kelly.

———. 1973. *Self Help: Voluntary Associations in the 19th Century.* London: B. T. Batsford.

Greenberg, B. 1985. *Worker and Community: Response to Industrialization in a Nineteenth-Century American City, Albany, New York, 1850–1884.* Albany: State University of New York Press.

Hamill, J. 1986. *The Craft: A History of English Freemasonry.* Great Britain: Crucible.

Harger, C. M. 1906. The Lodge. *Atlantic Monthly* 97 (April): 488–94.

Huss, W. A. 1986. *The Master Builders: A History of the Grand Lodge of Free and Accepted Masons of Pennsylvania.* Vol. 1, *1731–1873.* Philadelphia: Grand Lodge F and A. M. of Pennsylvania.

Jacob, M. C. 1991. *Living the Enlightenment: Freemasonry and Politics in Eighteenth-Century Europe.* New York: Oxford University Press.

Landis, A. 1900. *Friendly Societies and Fraternal Orders.* Winchester, Tenn.: Abb Landis.

———. 1904. Life Insurance by Fraternal Orders. *Annals of the American Academy of Political and Social Science* 24 (November): 55–59.

———. 1914. *Life Insurance.* Nashville: Abb Landis.

Levitan, S. A. 1990. *Programs in Aid of the Poor.* Baltimore: Johns Hopkins University Press.

Lipson, D. A. 1977. *Freemasonry in Federalist Connecticut.* Princeton: Princeton University Press.

Mackenney, R. 1987. *Tradesmen and Traders: The World of Guilds in Venice and Europe.* Totowa, N.J.: Barnes and Noble Books.

Massachusetts Charitable Society. 1762. *Rules and Articles.* Worcester, Mass.: American Antiquarian Society, Early American Imprints, 1639–1800.

McMath, R. C. 1993. *American Populism: A Social History, 1877–1898.* New York: Hill and Wang.

McRee, B. R. 1993. Charity and Gild Solidarity in Late Medieval England. *Journal of British Studies* 32 (July): 195–223.

Mollat, M. 1986. *The Poor in the Middle Ages: An Essay in Social History.* New Haven: Yale University Press.

Myers, R. J. 1937. The Effect of the Social Security Act on the Life Insurance Needs of Labor. *Journal of Political Economy* 45 (October): 681–86.

Ridgely, J. L. 1878. *History of American Odd Fellowship: The First Decade.* Baltimore: James L. Ridgely.

Ross, J. C. 1976. *An Assembly of Good Fellows: Voluntary Associations in History.* Westport, Conn.: Greenwood Press.

Rotman Zelizer, V. 1983. *Morals and Markets: The Development of Life Insurance in the United States.* New Brunswick, N.J.: Transaction Books.

Sackett, M. W. 1914. *Early History of Fraternal Beneficiary Societies in America.* Meadville, Pa.: Tribune Publishing Company.

Scarisbrick, J. J. 1984. *The Reformation and the English People.* Oxford: Basil Blackwell.

Schmidt, A. J. 1980. *Fraternal Organizations.* Westport, Conn.: Greenwood Press.

Scots' Charitable Society of Boston. 1986. *The Constitution and By-Laws of the Scots' Charitable Society of Boston.* Boston: Press of Farrington Printing Company.

Stack, P. 1988. *Poverty and Policy in Tudor and Stuart England.* London: Longman.

Stalson, J. O. 1969. *Marketing Life Insurance: Its History in America.* Bryn Mawr: McCahan Foundation.

Stevens, A. S. 1907. *The Cyclopedia of Fraternities.* 1907. New York: E. B. Treat and Company.

Stevenson, D. 1988. *The Origins of Freemasonry: Scotland's Century, 1590–1710.* Cambridge: Cambridge University Press.

Thompson, E. P. 1966. *The Making of the English Working Class.* New York: Vintage Books.

Tocqueville, A. de. [1850] 1981. *Democracy in America.* New York: Random House.

Unwin, G. 1908. *The Gilds and Companies of London.* London: Methuen and Company.

U.S. Department of Human Services. 2000. *Annual Report to Congress.* Available at <http://aspe.hhs.gov/hsp/indicators00/index.htm>.

U.S. Department of Labor. 1933. *Mother's Aid, 1931.* Washington, D.C.: Government Printing Office.

Weissman, R. F. E. 1982. *Ritual Brotherhood in Renaissance Florence.* New York: Academic Press.

Wright, C. E. 1992. *The Transformation of Charity in Postrevolutionary New England.* Boston: Northeastern University Press.

9

Medical Care through Mutual Aid

The Friendly Societies of Great Britain

David G. Green

Most histories of welfare provision tend to equate the improvement of welfare services with the growth of government involvement. Step by step, the welfare state is said to have filled the gaps supposedly left by the market. More careful examination of the evidence from both Britain and Australia, however, shows that the reality was very different. People in need because of their inability to earn enough to support themselves, whether temporarily or permanently, were supported in a rich variety of ways. Family and neighbors played their part, but because their help was informal and undocumented, historians have tended to underestimate it. Charity was also important, and historians have often supposed that it dominated organized welfare before the welfare state, but mutual aid was by far the most important way in which people met the needs of their fellows.

In both Britain and Australia, the friendly societies were the most important providers of social welfare during the nineteenth and early twentieth centuries.[1] They were self-governing mutual-benefit associations founded by manual workers to provide against hard times. In 1793, the first act of Parliament dealing specifically with friendly societies described them as organizations "of good fellowship for the purpose of raising from time to time, by subscriptions of the several members . . . a stock or fund for the mutual relief and maintenance of all and every the members thereof, in old age, sickness, and infirmity, or for the relief of the widows and children of deceased members."[2] Of course, friendly societies existed long before the enactment of this law. The oldest, the Incorporation of Carters, was founded in 1555 at Leith in Scotland, but it was not until the eighteenth century that the number of societies expanded rapidly. By 1801 Sir Frederick Eden estimated that there were about 7,200 societies with around 648,000 adult male members out of a total population of about 9 million. This can be compared with a figure based on the Poor Law return for 1803, which estimated that there were 9,672 societies with 704,350 members in England and Wales alone.[3]

When the British government introduced compulsory social insurance for 12 million persons under the 1911 National Insurance Act, registered and unregistered voluntary insurance associations—chiefly the friendly societies—already covered at least 9 million individuals. In 1910, the last full year before the 1911 act, there were 6.6 million members of registered friendly societies, quite apart from those in unregistered societies. Friendly-society membership dwarfed that of the other characteristic organizations of the working classes. There were 2.5 million members of registered trade unions in 1910 and 2.5 million members of cooperative societies.

The rate of growth of the friendly societies during the thirty years before national insurance had been accelerating.[4] In 1877, registered membership had been 2.8 million. Ten years later it was 3.6 million, having increased at an average of 90,000 a year. In 1897 it reached 4.8 million, having increased on average by 120,000 a year. And by 1910 it was 6.6 million, having increased at an annual average rate since 1897 of 140,000.

In Australia, a country with a frontier tradition not very different from that of the United States, mutual aid was also strong. At roughly the same time, in 1913, 46 percent of Australians were also benefiting from friendly-society services, some 2.2 million out of a total population of 4.8 million.[5]

In America, too, there were many mutual-aid associations, often branches of British societies, established by nineteenth-century migrants from the British Isles. No systematic study of American mutual aid has so far been carried out, but evidence available in Britain suggests that there was a wide network of branches affiliated with British parent bodies.

The Ancient Order of Foresters, for instance, had sixty-three branches throughout the United States as late as 1933 and had built Foresters' Halls in places as far apart as Waterby, Connecticut; Atlantic

Mine, Michigan; Murray, Utah; Gloversville, New York; Lake Forest, Illinois; Mendocino City, California; New Orleans; Chicago; Denver; Berkeley; and Honolulu.[6]

What Services Did the Friendly Societies Provide?

The common element binding the various services provided by friendly societies was independence. They provided all those services that enabled families to be self-supporting. During the nineteenth century and until early in the twentieth century, most families took pride in being self-supporting, but wages were such that if the breadwinner fell ill or died, hardship was the invariable result. The philosophy forged by this harsh reality was one of mutual aid. By the early years of the twentieth century the friendly societies had a long record of providing benefits in cash and kind, including sick pay when the breadwinner was unable to bring home a wage due to illness, accident, or old age; medical care for both the member and his family; a death grant sufficient to provide a decent funeral; and financial and practical support for widows and orphans of deceased members. Medical services were usually provided by the lodge or branch doctor, who was often appointed by a vote of the members. In addition, every large town in England also had its medical institute, offering the services now provided by health centers and no-wait clinics. Finally, the national societies with branches provided a support network for men traveling in search of work.

Self-Reliance and Mutual Support

British social historians have often claimed that fear of the poor law played a major part in molding working-class attitudes to work and welfare. G. D. H. Cole, for instance, states that the chief motive for thrift was fear of the workhouse.[7] The evidence does not support his conclusion, which makes the common mistake of looking upon members of the working class as passive victims of events. During the second half of the nineteenth century, even while the poor law in Britain was becoming less harsh and the use of outdoor relief in place of workhouse confinement was expanding, the number of paupers steadily diminished. This suggests that it was not so much fear but self-respect that kept men away from the poor law in the latter half of the nineteenth century.

This message was rammed home time and again by the spokespersons for the organized working classes in both Britain and Australia. Arguing against proposals for a compulsory state pension scheme in 1882, the Ancient Order of Foresters, the second-largest friendly society in England with over 600,000 members, pointed out that thrift had succeeded in considerably reducing the number of paupers. The increased facilities for thrift, it asserted, "afforded to the British Workman by his own peculiar organisations—Friendly Societies and Trade Unions," had done much during the previous thirty years to reduce pauperism. The Foresters looked forward to a time when pauperism would be reduced to those suffering from "insanity and contagion."[8] The Royal Commission on the Aged Poor of 1895 confirmed the downward trend (see table 9.1).

The *Foresters' Miscellany* was still opposing the introduction of a state pension scheme in the 1890s:

> The aim of the working class ought to be to bring about economic conditions in which there should be no need for the distribution of state alms. The establishment of a great scheme of state pensions would legalise and stamp as a permanent feature of our social life the chronic poverty of the age. The desire of the best reformers is to remove the conditions that make that poverty so that every citizen shall have a fair chance not only of earning a decent wage for today but such a wage as shall enable him to provide for the future. . . .[9]

Today we are accustomed to thinking in terms of a definite retirement age, but until the turn of the twentieth century most men worked

TABLE 9.1.   Receipt of Poor Relief, 1849–92

Year	Number of Indoor Poor	Number per 1,000 of Population	Number of Outdoor Poor	Number per 1,000 of Population	Total	Number per 1,000 of Population
1849	133,513	7.7	955,146	55.0	1,088,659	62.7
1852	111,323	6.2	804,352	44.7	915,675	50.9
1862	132,236	6.6	784,906	39.0	917,142	45.6
1872	149,200	6.6	828,000	36.3	977,200	42.9
1882	183,374	7.1	604,915	23.2	788,289	30.3
1892	186,607	6.4	558,150	19.2	744,757	25.6

Source: Royal Commission on the Aged Poor 1895, 1:ix.

Note: Indoor relief was conditional upon residence in a workhouse; outdoor relief was the equivalent of modern cash benefits and paid to recipients in their own homes.

until they were no longer able to do so. When a man grew so old that he could not work at all, he received permanent sick pay from his friendly society. As wages increased, so too did the permanent sick pay, or pension, of the friendly societies, but just as a spontaneous solution to the poverty of old age was in sight, along came the state to impose its own remedy.

Working-class leaders in Australia were no less vehement in their hostility to state pensions, as the royal commissions set up in the Australian states of New South Wales and Victoria discovered. The grand secretary of the Independent Order of Oddfellows (a society whose headquarters was in the United States but that had Australian branches) told the New South Wales select committee that a government scheme of old-age pensions would be "repulsive" to his members because it would infringe on the cooperative principle: "As far as I am able to gauge the opinions of the societies," the committee's report concludes, their members thought such a scheme would be "repulsive" because "anything in the form of Government State aid would involve Government supervision in some shape or other."[10]

The Royal Commission on the Friendly Societies established in Victoria contemplated the introduction of a government-sickness insurance scheme in 1876 but decided against it. They shared the view of an earlier English Royal Commission that it would be "difficult, if not impossible, to organise any system of Government sick insurance which would not carry with it something of the appearance of a relief system." This objection, "strong in its application to English working-men anywhere," would in Australia "be absolutely fatal to the success of any such proposal."[11]

Character Building

The friendly societies knew only too well that they had to cultivate the philosophy of self-help and mutual support that guided them, and great effort was put into maintaining this culture of self-reliance and fraternal help. Initiation ceremonies were didactic in design and encouraged the member to make joining the society a moment of self-criticism. The Grand United Order of Oddfellows, for instance, addressed new members as follows: "It is desired that you should make the event of your Initiation a time for strict self-examination; and if you should find anything in your past life to amend, I solemnly charge you to set about that duty without delay,—let no immoral practice, idle action, or low and vulgar pursuit, be retained by you."[12] Teaching did not end with initiation. Membership consisted of a process of progression through a series of "degrees" during which the society taught values such as hard work, liberty, tolerance toward others, and fraternalism toward fellow members. Grand United had three such degrees and Manchester Unity four, while the Ancient Order of Foresters offered members a series of seven "lectures."

Among the values promoted was democracy. The prevailing ethic in the earliest societies was that everyone should have an equal say. And since it was possible for all the members to meet in one place the normal practice was for decisions to be taken in a general assembly of all members. These early meetings were not only to reach decisions but also for enjoyment. This is reflected in the rules of the early clubs, which provided both for the maintenance of order and for the distribution of refreshments to members.

As in the early trade unions, the principal means of maintaining order was to invest the chairman of a meeting with disciplinary power. In the early years in both Britain and Australia, it was usual for the clubs to meet in a public house in a room lent free by the landlord. It was assumed that each man would do his share of drinking, and the rules often prescribed the sum to be spent on drinks at each meeting. In the Friendly Society of Ironfounders, for example, the monthly contribution in 1809 was a shilling "to the box" and threepence for liquor "to be spent whether present or not."[13]

The societies sharply contrasted themselves with charities. Charity involved one set of people helping another set, whereas mutual aid was putting money aside in a common fund and helping each other when the need arose. The benefits were rights:

> For certain benefits in sickness . . . all the Brethren in common subscribe to one fund. That fund is our Bank; and to draw therefrom is the independent and manly right of every Member, whenever the contingency for which the funds are subscribed may arise, as freely as if the fund was in the hand of their own banker, and they had but to issue a cheque for the amount. These are not BENEVOLENCES—they are rights.[14]

These words enable us to understand why the appeal to "rights" was popular in the early years of the welfare state. But in the voluntary associations that predated the welfare state the link between personal payment and entitlement was clear. Once the state intervened, "rights" increasingly became claims to benefits at the expense of *other* people and no longer the just entitlement of shared responsibility.

Collectivism without the State

During the nineteenth century the local benefit clubs began to form federations to put their finances onto a sounder footing. Gradually a three-tier federal structure emerged—branch, district, and unity—permitting significant local autonomy with final authority vested in an annual or biennial assembly. Each annual assembly was empowered to make, annul, or amend the rules of the order. And each concluded with the election of the president and the executive committee, which usually comprised the chief officers and between six and twelve other members.

The most important official was the permanent secretary. Although grand secretaries were very influential, they were never the dictators that trade-union general secretaries often became. The societies prided themselves on the absence of barriers to the advancement of any member to senior office: "We in the Manchester Unity are essentially a democratic body; we believe in the governing of the people by the people; we recognise the equality of members, and the power is given to the humblest member in any Lodge to win his way, by dint of perseverance and honest, hard work, to the highest and most responsible position."[15] Just as labor parties in Western countries demanded that parliamentarians should be paid to permit wage earners to compete on equal terms, so the friendly societies ensured that want of cash did not deter their members from holding the highest offices. By the 1920s Manchester Unity in New South Wales, for instance, was paying its grand lodge officers thirty shillings per day when on official business, so that the position of grand master "should be open to the most humble members of the society."[16]

Later many societies introduced an intermediate level of organization between local branches and the unity level. Gradually they found it advisable to spread the funeral-fund liability more widely than among members of each branch, where even a few deaths in quick succession could exhaust a small fund. Each district took its authority from the central body but was governed by a committee of representatives from the individual branches. Some branches, however, disliked the additional control that the district system entailed and refused to affiliate.

In the Ancient Order of Foresters in Victoria the districts were founded before the statewide unity. Branches often seceded from districts. For example, three out of the thirteen branches in the Ballarat District had seceded by 1875.[17] The desire for branch autonomy was so strong that attempts to establish a central organization in the state of Victoria met strong resistance. The branches in the Melbourne district refused to join, and others found maintaining a link with the English headquarters more conducive to autonomy.[18]

Participatory Democracy

Once the friendly societies had become federations, pressures toward centralization began to emerge. Within the branches there was always the possibility that the leading office holders or some clique of members would come to dominate. There was also the constant danger that power might pass from the branches to the district or unity levels. The friendly societies responded by experimenting with a number of devices intended to (a) maximize the control over society affairs exercised by individual members assembled in the local branch meeting and to (b) secure the independence of branches from the superior district and unity levels in each society.

The view of the Foresters was that all lawful authority originated "with and from the Members at large." In the branch all Foresters met "on terms of perfect equality": "No office is too high for the poorest to aspire to; no duty too humble for the richest to stoop to. Intelligence to govern, ability to exercise authority with becoming humility, yet with the requisite firmness, and personal demeanour to ensure respect are all the qualifications for office required; and these are in the power of every Member to acquire."[19] As in the early trade unions, the rules gave the branch chairman the power to impose fines for misconduct, but while the societies recognized the need for discipline in their meetings, they also sought to prevent presiding officers from abusing their power. Most societies impressed their expectations on a new chairman by requiring him to swear an oath at his installation ceremony. In addition, rules also laid down what a chairman could and could not do. In the Bendigo district of Victoria, for example, the Foresters provided for an officer to be instantly deposed to "check insolent demeanour" and "to prevent any abuse of power."[20]

In several societies the branch devoted part of its opening ceremony, carried out at every fortnightly or monthly meeting, to reminding officeholders of their obligations. At the beginning of every meeting, officeholders were required solemnly to state their duties. In Grand United, for instance, the financial secretary had to pledge to "keep a fair and impartial account betwixt every brother and the Lodge, to minute transactions, to keep the accounts clear and intelligible and to balance such accounts when required by you or the Lodge."[21]

In Grand United the "inferior" offices—each held by rotation—were the left and right supporters to the noble grand, the left and right supporters to the vice grand, the warden, the conductor, and the outside and inside guardians. The duty of the supporters was "to assist in opening and closing, and in the preservation of order during the meeting." The warden had care of all regalia and other branch property and was also required "to keep the branch as comfortable as possible during branch hours, and assist the conductor on the initiation of members" and to "examine the room, previous to opening, and see that no irregular member or improper persons shall be present." The conductor's duty was to introduce members for initiation. The outside and inside guardians were required to see that no "irregular, intoxicated, or improperly dressed members, or one who may not have the password, gain admittance" without the permission of the noble grand.[22]

With the exception of the branch secretary, who held office at the pleasure of the lodge, it was customary for senior positions to change hands at each election, usually held every six months.

It was on the shoulders of the branch secretary that the most important duties fell. The branch secretary was elected at a specially summoned meeting and thereafter held office at the pleasure of the lodge. Lodges usually tried to find competent persons and keep them in this position. Sometimes they found it difficult to find a capable secretary, particularly in branches composed of members skilled in manual occupations but with no training in administrative work. This was one of the costs of self-organization.

The branch secretary was often paid a small honorarium, but the payment came nowhere near compensating for work done.[23] The fact that secretaries were paid, however, made it easier to insist that they perform well. Societies did not hesitate to fine secretaries who did not.

Each lodge also had three major offices: the noble grand or chairman, the vice grand or vice chairman, and the immediate past noble grand. All members were expected to seek to occupy these positions—to "go through the chairs" as it was called. To do so they had to prove themselves by holding minor offices and by taking the degrees of the order.

But mere turn-taking was not enough. The holding of office also allowed members to learn new skills, and for many manual workers, the lodge offered opportunities for self-development lacking at the workplace. But the policy of changing the chairman every six months also carried with it certain risks. The lodge might find its meetings being presided over incompetently. To overcome this danger, each chairman appointed two supporters, a right and a left supporter. They would sit on either side of the chairman at meetings and offer advice as the meeting proceeded. Traditionally, the chairman chose an experienced right supporter, a member who had previously held the office and who was acknowledged as being well informed about the rules and procedures. In this fashion a high level of sharing of office was combined with efficient performance.

The federal structure of the societies meant that they had a large enough national structure to offer members real security, while the preservation of substantial powers within branches allowed members to feel a real sense of belonging. The Prudential Assurance Company, the largest British commercial assurance company at the time, had to abandon the payment of sickness benefits because, as its secretary told the Royal Commission on Friendly Societies in 1873, "after five years' experience we found we were unable to cope with the fraud that was practised." Large insurers face the same problems that governments have encountered in the provision of welfare benefits. If they are seen as anonymous, then no harm is apparently done by making a fraudulent claim. Low-paid workers intent on self-reliance, however, could not afford to tolerate fraud and sought to overcome it by ensuring the genuine participation of members in office-holding and decision-making. By modern standards it may seem quaint and even faintly ridiculous to take it in turns to be the vice chairman (vice grand), the chairman (noble grand), and the immediate past noble grand, not to mention the left supporter and the right supporter, but people determined not to look to the government to solve their problems and with nothing to fall back on but their own energy and strength had to stick together. This necessity meant that every member was important and had to be treated as such.

Who Were the Members?

There were three membership qualifications: age, health, and good character. Lodges rarely applied the good-character rule, and when they did, it was invariably to exclude criminals. For example, Court Perseverance of the Foresters, based in Melbourne, was told at its meeting in August 1859 that one of the candidates nominated for membership that night had been involved in fraud. He had been employed as a foreman, and one of his duties had been to pay laborers in his charge fourteen shillings per day. Instead of paying the men fourteen shillings, he had paid them thirteen and pocketed the remainder. The branch required that a signed statement of the accusation be produced. This statement was further verified by two others present at the meeting, and as a result, the foreman's application was rejected.[24]

The age and health requirements served to ensure that everyone joined the fund on roughly equal terms. But in reality these qualifications were not always enforced. The age requirement often seems to have been ignored, and enforcement of the health requirement varied considerably from place to place. The British Medical Association branch in New South Wales took the view that medical examinations were "unsatisfactory and insufficient."[25] A second doctor told the New South Wales Royal Commission that the friendly societies were "anxious, not to get healthy lives, but increased members." He claimed to have been "pooh-poohed" on several occasions for rejecting candidates.[26] Another doctor said he rejected about 5 percent of applicants.

Some scholars have complained that the friendly societies excluded the low paid, but I can find no evidence of this. The membership qualifications had nothing to do with earnings or occupation, even though it was well known that some occupations drew more heavily on the sick fund than others. This issue was hotly debated in Grand United in New South Wales between 1923 and 1931. The executive committee of Grand United proposed to the 1923 annual meeting that because miners' sick pay was so high, they should contribute two pence per week more than other members. The notion was "very vigorously opposed" and defeated. Later, in 1930, a move was made to restrict the payment of sick pay to miners in cases where they were also receiving workers' compensation payments of two pounds per week or more. The resolution was carried, but its opponents did not give up, and between the 1930 and the 1931 annual meetings they engaged in vigorous lobbying. Both the miners and the nonmining members who supported them regarded the measure as "class legislation" and against the principle of "the strong helping the weak." The decision was overturned at the 1931 annual meeting by a vote of two to one.[27]

Historians have sometimes claimed that the societies were joined primarily by high-paid skilled workers in regular work, but in reality the societies went to considerable lengths to help members who fell on hard times or lost their jobs. Usually they were helped out of general revenues, but special benevolent funds were organized for them. By 1898, fifty of the eighty Foresters' branches in the Melbourne district had benevolent funds. In the branch at Fitzroy each member contributed one shilling per year. The fund was used to pay the contributions of members unable to meet their obligations through "want of work" or illness and to make grants of up to 10 pounds to those in distress. According to its secretary, "No member . . . need ever leave the [branch] through want of work."[28]

Equality and the "Rule of Law"

The friendly societies originated as local clubs that made their common decisions in a general assembly of members. But as we have seen, over the years it became necessary to appoint office holders. Later federations of local clubs emerged. Throughout the period of these changes the spirit of participatory democracy remained alive, and the chief device used to keep it alive was the rulebook. Just as Americans hold the Constitution in high esteem, so the friendly society rulebook was almost an object of reverence to the manual workers who made up the membership.

   This reverence for friendly societies' laws emerges in this announcement by the South Australian Oddfellows, made soon after their foundation in Adelaide:

   What has Oddfellowship done? With the patronage, in the first instance, of no man of fortune, or of Colonial rank—a few old members of the Manchester Unity—men of no personal influence or importance, armed only with the well digested and strikingly excellent laws of that Society, formed themselves into a small branch, and were joined by one and another, chiefly of the poorer classes.[29]

Every member was equal under the rules. Moreover, the rules were not externally imposed; they had been fashioned over the years by the members themselves: adapted, annulled, and revised regularly as circumstances changed. If the rules imposed constraints, as they must, they were constraints freely accepted by every member.

   Friendly-society members were proud of their rules, or more precisely, they were proud of the principles their rules embodied. The rules laid down the rights and obligations of members and outlined the duties of office holders. To ensure a sharing of the pleasures and burdens of office and to inhibit domination of branches by cliques, they limited the powers of office holders. And the rules maintained the autonomy of the branches from the district and unity levels within each federation. The societies were in a real sense ruled by laws rather than ruled by men.

Medical Care

Medical care in Britain was being provided in a variety of ways at the turn of the twentieth century. Apart from the poor law, these fell into three main categories. First, a large section of the population obtained care free of charge through charities. Particularly in London and the larger towns, they used the outpatient departments of the voluntary hospitals; some used the free dispensaries where these existed. Second, many obtained medical care as private patients and paid a fee to the doctor of their choice. The fees charged varied according to income, with rent taken as the chief test of income. Third, there was a wide variety of prepaid insurance schemes, commonly called contract practice.

Each type of contract practice (sometimes called club practice) was based on the principle of the flat-rate annual contribution, usually payable quarterly but sometimes weekly or fortnightly, entitling the contributor to any number of consultations plus medicines during the period covered. Some such clubs were based at factories, and others were organized by charities; some were run on commercial lines, some by individual doctors, and some by the friendly societies. The most important numerically were the friendly-society schemes.

By the 1830s there were numerous medical clubs throughout the country. As their influence spread, the clubs ran into strong opposition from the organized medical profession, in much the same way that the early American health maintenance organizations were obstructed by the American Medical Association. One of the earliest signs of the conflict came in 1837, when a leading article in the prestigious medical journal the *Lancet* opposed a semicharitable penny club in the Cricklade and Wootton Basset poor-law union.[30]

In the 1830s and 1840s, as well as later, organized medicine had two main criticisms of medical clubs. First, members of the profession charged that medical officers were underpaid because competition among doctors tended to drive fees downward. Second, they claimed that some friendly-society members could afford to pay higher doctor's fees and demanded that a wage limit be imposed to exclude better-paid workers from contract practice.

By the 1890s the *British Medical Journal* and the *Lancet* were openly referring to the "battle of the clubs" and urging all doctors to join the struggle. Some doctors called for an openly trade-union stance and condemned reluctant colleagues as "blacklegs." Doctors in Great Yarmouth were in the forefront of the conflict. They formed a cartel in 1896 and approached local benefit societies for new terms. In October, the local friendly societies reacted angrily and asked the medical men to pledge themselves not to raise their demands again. The doctors refused. The societies retaliated by advertising successfully for alternative practitioners and establishing a medical institute to employ full-time salaried medical officers. This proved costly to Yarmouth's doctors, who estimated their losses at about 2,000 pounds a year in club contributions.[31]

But it was not everywhere that the friendly societies reacted in this manner. Events in Portsmouth illustrate the strong but restrained bargaining power of the mass of patients. The local combination of doctors, the Portsmouth Medical Union, met a variety of responses. For instance, the two medical officers of the Portsmouth Medical Benefit Society, an organization run by dockyard workers and funded by pay-packet deductions, resigned in protest at the low fees. The dock workers found other doctors to fill their places. Some of the dock workers, however, sympathized with the original medical officers and established a new benefit society to employ them on more favorable terms.[32]

A couple of months later, in November 1895, one of Portsmouth's largest Oddfellows lodges held elections for its doctor. The main issue was the proposal to fix juvenile rates at 2s. 6d. per annum for all children aged from three months to fifteen years. The existing medical officer, Doctor Lord, refused to accept the new terms and sought a fee of 4s. 0d. per annum. Three outside competitors stood against him, much to the annoyance of the *British Medical Journal.* One doctor offered to attend juveniles at 2s. 6d., the asking rate; two others offered rates below the societies' own stipulation: 2s. 0d. and 1s. 6d. In the event, Doctor Lord was so well respected that he was decisively reelected at his higher fee.[33] Around the same time, the Rechabites in Portsmouth elected their surgeon. The sitting candidate had offered to serve at 4s. 0d. and was opposed by doctors offering 3s. 6d. and 3s. 0d. On this occasion, the existing medical officer was not reelected, but the members did not choose the cheapest doctor. They preferred the candidate who tendered 3s. 6d.[34] What we see here was not producer- or consumer- dominated health care but rather the diversity and mutual adjustment between producer and consumer that liberty alone permits.

By the end of the nineteenth century, the friendly societies were establishing more and more medical institutes employing salaried doctors. In today's terms the institutes were staff-model health maintenance organizations. In 1896 there were at least thirty-nine medical institutes with over 200,000 members. At least twenty owned their premises, combining surgery, dispensary, and doctor's living accommodation. Annual capitation fees varied but were usually 3s. for men, 4–5s. for wives, and 1s. plus for children. Some charged a single fee for the whole family of 3s. 6d. or more. The largest institute in 1896 was at Derby with 11,604 members, followed by York with 10,328 members and Wolverhampton with 8,735.[35] The medical institutes were proud of their self-governing character. As the preface to the 1896 rules of the Luton Friendly Societies Medical Institute says, the institute "is managed by *working men,* who should best understand their own wants and how to meet them."

After the turn of the century, doctors' rates of pay were increasing slowly by mutual consent from around four shillings to nearer five shillings a year on average, but the friendly societies refused to accept the demand of organized medicine that only low-paid individuals could join. To exclude workers who earned more than 1 pound a week, as some doctors demanded, seemed to many friendly-society members to strike at the whole root of their fraternal philosophy. The Oddfellows, said one leading article in the *South Australian OddFellows' Magazine,* prided themselves on "the entire equality of rank amongst their brethren." The doctors' wage limit would divide the members into two groups, "the opulent and the needy," and to be on the doctor's list would be looked upon as "a mark of social inferiority."[36]

Traveling in Search of Work

Members who needed to travel in search of a job were supported by other branches. In the Manchester Unity, a society with over 700,000 members in the 1890s, a member of twelve months duration who was seeking work obtained a card from his lodge secretary that showed the benefit due in sickness or death. It was valid for six months and entitled him to report to any lodge, which would then pay his traveling expenses. The lodge's costs could be reclaimed from the central funds.[37] Manchester Unity members who found it necessary to move for whatever reason could also transfer to the nearest branch. Just as when members applied to travel in search of work, members' old branches issued them with "clearance" certificates that they could "throw in" to their new lodges. The clearance system operated internationally from early in the nineteenth century.[38] Migrants to Australia, New Zealand, Canada, or the United States of America, for instance, thus found themselves immediately among friends. In the Manchester Unity between 1848 and 1872, 16,086 members were issued traveling documents.[39] As the Chief Registrar of Friendly Societies said to the Royal Commission on Labour in 1892: "The organisation of the affiliated orders therefore lends itself much more than that of the isolated friendly societies to industrial freedom and independence. The working man, who is not satisfied with his lot can leave his place of employment and seek for work elsewhere, and he gets material help while on the search, and finds friends who may give him advice."[40]

Conclusions

A family can face three different types of cash shortage. First, it may need basic income support when simply unable to maintain itself above subsistence level. This may arise even when a family has members working. Second, a family may face a need for contingent income support. This can be a temporary occurrence, when, for instance, the breadwinner experiences a loss of income due to illness or unemployment. Third, a family may face a need for contingent expense coverage. Additional expenses stretching the family budget may be unpredictable, as when, for example, ill health strikes, or predictable, as when a child is born.

Historically governments have usually played the leading role in providing basic income support, laying down a line below which no one should fall. But no less important, before the welfare state, private voluntary organizations took the lead in providing contingent income support and contingent expense coverage. As we have seen, in both Britain and Australia the friendly societies and to a lesser extent the trade unions provided income during sickness, as well as supplying medical services. This was quite apart from the efforts of charitable organizations.

But the friendly societies were not merely benefit societies. They also sought to promote good character, a fact of great importance for classical-liberal thought, which tends to take good conduct and a desire for a better life for granted and consequently to assume that every person will readily become an ambitious, self-reliant, participating citizen. In the 1860s and 1870s, when the poor law was becoming more lenient, the wholesome influence of the friendly societies and other institutions like the Methodist and other nonconformist churches proved sufficient to maintain a strong commitment to liberty and self-reliance. In the years after World War II, when such institutions had lost their influence, welfare leniency produced a different result, measured in family breakdown and growing personal dependency.

Does the history of the friendly societies offer any lessons for modern welfare reformers? Perhaps the most important message is that the friendly societies were not just benefit societies. Unlike state welfare programs, the friendly societies treated people as if they had a moral dimension to their character. Marvin Olasky's (1992) *The Tragedy of American Compassion* describes how nineteenth-century American charities avoided the mistakes of twentieth-century welfare programs. They did not treat the poor as victims of circumstance in need of cash handouts but attended to their moral, spiritual dimensions in the hope of restoring them to full independence and the enjoyment of liberty that followed. Like the mutual-aid associations, they appealed to the better side of human nature, enabling people to face new challenges of self-organization and leadership.

The next generation of welfare reforms should learn from this experience by calling forth the best in people. The neglected history of welfare before the welfare state shows that even at much lower levels of personal prosperity, if we allow sufficient space for human ingenuity, some of the finest welfare institutions known to humankind can flourish.

NOTES

1. For a fuller discussion of Britain's friendly societies, see Green 1993.
2. 33 Geo. III, c. 54, s. I.
3. Gosden 1961, 4–5.
4. Green 1985, 179.
5. Green and Cromwell 1984, 221.
6. *Foresters' Directory* (1933), 365–72.
7. Cole 1948, 154.
8. *Foresters' Miscellany* (1882), 6.
9. Quoted in Hay 1978, 17.

10. New South Wales Parliament Select Committee 1896, questions 605–6, 612.

11. Victorian Royal Commission on the Friendly Societies 1876, vi. See also *Minutes of Evidence,* questions. 552, 611, 11101–1, 2646–67, 4765–66.

12. Green and Cromwell 1984, 17.

13. Webb and Webb 1913, 3–5.

14. Ancient Order of Foresters 1879, 50–51.

15. *Manchester Unity Magazine* (December 20, 1910), 2.

16. Royal Commission on National Insurance, Australia 1924–25, Q. 221.

17. Royal Commission on the Friendly Societies, Victoria 1876, Q. 3545.

18. Royal Commission on the Friendly Societies, Victoria 1876, Qs. 3562–64.

19. Ancient Order of Foresters 1879, 41–42.

20. Ancient Order of Foresters, Bendigo United District 1870, rule 69.

21. Grand United Order of Odd Fellows 1879, 28.

22. Grand United Order of Odd Fellows, Braidwood District 1866, rule 3.

23. Royal Commission on Old-Age Pensions, Australia 1906, Q. 3724.

24. Ancient Order of Foresters 1859–65.

25. Royal Commission on the Working of the Friendly Societies Act 1883, 193–742, Q. 9074.

26. Royal Commission on the Working of the Friendly Societies Act 1883, Qs. 9176–77.

27. Smedley and Ridley 1948, 42, 46.

28. Royal Commission on Old-Age Pensions, Victoria 1898, Q. 3045.

29. *South Australian OddFellows' Magazine* (January 1845), 1.

30. *Lancet* (April 15, 1837), 133.

31. *Lancet* (February 24, 1900), 577; *Lancet* (March 3, 1900), 655–57.

32. *Lancet* (September 21, 1895), 757.

33. *British Medical Journal* (November 23, 1895), 1319; *British Medical Journal* (November 30, 1895), 1368.

34. *British Medical Journal* (September 12, 1896), 684.

35. *Foresters' Directory* (1896).

36. *South Australian OddFellows' Magazine* (April 1897), 101.

37. Siddall 1924, 10.

38. Independent Order of Oddfellows, Manchester Unity 1856, 8.

39. Gosden 1961, 76.

40. Evidence of the Chief Registrar to the Royal Commission on Labour, 1892, Appendix LIII. Quoted in Gosden 1961, appendix A.

REFERENCES

Ancient Order of Foresters. 1859–65. *Minute Book.* Court Perseverance 2727.
———. 1879. Lecture 3.
Ancient Order of Foresters, Bendigo United District. 1870. *Court Laws.*
Cole, G. D. H. 1948. *A Short History of the British Working-Class Movement.* London: Allen and Unwin.

Gosden, P. H. J. H. 1961. *The Friendly Societies in England 1815–1875.* Manchester: Manchester University Press.

Grand United Order of Odd Fellows. 1879. *Ritual.*

Grand United Order of Odd Fellows, Braidwood District. 1866. *Branch Laws.*

Green, D. G. 1985. *Working Class Patients and the Medical Establishment.* London: Gower/Temple Smith.

————— 1993. *Reinventing Civil Society.* London: Institute of Economic Affairs.

Green, D. G., and L. G. Cromwell. 1984. *Mutual Aid or Welfare State.* Sydney: Allen and Unwin.

Hay, J. R. 1978. *The Development of the British Welfare State 1880–1975.* London: Edward Arnold.

Independent Order of Oddfellows, Manchester Unity, New South Wales, Sydney District. 1856. *Quarterly Report.*

New South Wales Parliament Select Committee of the Legislative Assembly. 1896. *Report on State Insurance or Old-Age and Invalidity Pensions.* Vol. 2, *Votes and Proceedings.*

Olasky, M. 1992. *The Tragedy of American Compassion.* Washington, D.C.: Regnery Gateway.

Royal Commission on National Insurance, Australia. 1924–25. *Minutes of Evidence.*

Royal Commission on Old-Age Pensions, Australia. 1906. *Report, Minutes of Evidence.* Vol. 3, *Parliamentary Papers.*

Royal Commission on Old-Age Pensions, Victoria. 1898. *Parliamentary Papers.* Vol. 3, *Minutes of Evidence.*

Royal Commission on the Aged Poor. 1895. *Report.*

Royal Commission on the Friendly Societies, Victoria. 1876. *Minutes of Evidence.*

Royal Commission on the Working of the Friendly Societies Act. 1883. *Notes and Proceedings.* Vol 3.

Siddall, T. W. 1924. *Story of a Century.* Sheffield: Independent Order of Oddfellows, Manchester Unity, Sheffield District.

Smedley, W., and H. Ridley, eds. 1948. *100 Grand United Years.* Sydney: Grand United Order of Odd Fellows.

Victorian Royal Commission on the Friendly Societies. 1876. *Report.*

Webb, S., and B. Webb. 1913. *Industrial Democracy.* London: The Authors.

10

Education in the Voluntary City

James Tooley

It is often assumed that only with government intervention can we obtain high-quality and universal education. In this chapter, I marshal evidence from nineteenth-century England and Wales, nineteenth-century America, and twenty-first century India to show that such an assumption is untenable.

But before examining this evidence, it is worth asking whether governments in developed countries have succeeded in providing high-quality universal education. The answer to this first question, unfortunately, is no. In the United Kingdom, for example, functional illiteracy is common. Even after eleven years of compulsory schooling many people have an inability to cope with the reading and numerical demands of everyday life. In Britain 40 percent of twenty-one year olds *admit* to difficulties with writing and spelling, nearly 30 percent to difficulties with numeracy, and 20 percent to difficulties with reading and writing (Central Statistical Office 1995, 58). Similarly, in a recent survey conducted in Canada, Germany, the Netherlands, Poland, Switzerland (French and German), and the United States—all countries with (de jure) universal schooling—"roughly a fifth of the populations" of all of these countries was "found to be barely literate—unable, for instance, to read and grasp a bus schedule" (Coulson 1999, 9).

Even on the more restricted question of universality, governments have failed. In a typical American inner-city school, for example, a shocking 10 percent of students are absent on a typical day. In schools with high poverty levels, over 12 percent of the students are absent on a typical day. Absentee rates at private schools, even those in high-poverty areas, are less than half the rates at the public schools.[1] Since not every student is absent 10 percent of the time, absentee rates of 10 percent imply that some students receive considerably fewer days of education than is required. The situation in the United Kingdom is similar. Studies suggest that currently one in ten of all young people are not in school and that over 30 percent of students regularly or sometimes play truant (Bentley 1999, 75; O'Keefe 1994). This does not seem like universal schooling after all.

These facts suggest that high-quality universal education is an aspiration that current government systems have failed to meet. Legal universal state schooling does not imply that all are in school, nor does it imply that all receive the benefits of a real education. This is the first very important point to grasp.

The second question to ask is: can we have high-quality universal education without government intervention? Historical evidence from several countries—including the United Kingdom, the United States, and Australia—suggests that before the state provided schools or compelled school attendance, we were fast approaching universal schooling. The data is mainly on schooling, measured as time spent in school, rather than on education more broadly conceived. Nevertheless, data on literacy rates and more anecdotal data on the quality of schooling are also supportive. But in any case, we can be more confident about using data on time spent in school to measure "education" in the nineteenth century than today. If schooling is not compulsory, then it is only likely to be used if it is producing benefits to its customers. Thus the same number of days of schooling in the nineteenth century, when schooling was noncompulsory, is likely to have produced more education than today, when schooling is compulsory.

Lest anyone should think that the Anglo-Saxon phenomenon is unique, there is plenty of evidence to show that France and Germany also had large and successful private educational markets until the state came along and suppressed and supplanted these opportunities (Coulson 1999). Furthermore, my own research on education in developing countries shows an enormous number of students in private education. I discuss this research further later in the chapter. First, let us consider the situation in England and Wales.[2]

Education without the State, Part 1: Nineteenth-Century England and Wales

If asked to consider what "education without the state" was like in Victorian England, many readers would assume that there was very little of it going on for the working classes and that what there was was of a very poor quality. In a recent debate, one learned person threw at me the statistic that there was "70 percent illiteracy" before government got involved in education in 1870. This kind of figure seems to be an exaggeration of the figure that many of us may have been brought up on from history books such as *British History in the Nineteenth Century,* by G. M. Trevelyan (1922), and Arthur Bryant's (1953) *English Saga.* Trevelyan notes that on the eve of the 1870 act that laid the foundations for state education in England and Wales, "Only about half the children in the country were educated at all, and most of these very indifferently. England, for all her wealth, lagged far behind . . . several foreign countries" (354). And Bryant (1953, 125) similarly comments that "[t]he great mass of the nation was illiterate. In 1869 only one British child in two was receiving any education at all."

If it was that bad, then it would seem that the situation in England and Wales certainly would not provide any support to our argument about universal provision without the state. In fact, however, the reality is strikingly different—and we will see in a moment where these historians picked up their misleading statistics.

We owe much of our new insight into the possibilities of education without the state to the seminal work of E. G. West. West's (1994) *Education and the State,* first published by the Institute of Economic Affairs (IEA) London in 1965, provoked an outcry at the time—and even led to a libel trial when the then-editor of the *New Statesman* published a review suggesting that West had concocted his data. The case was won by the directors of the IEA, and showing the touching, greedless innocence of England in the 1960s, they settled for an apology.

As far as the quantity of schooling is concerned, West argues that prior to major state involvement in education in England and Wales through the 1870 Forster Act, school attendance rates and literacy rates were 90 percent or above and that state intervention, far from being required to ensure universal attendance and literacy, merely reinforced a process that had been developing for some time.

Instead of relying on secondhand accounts from historians like Trevelyan and Bryant, West went back to original nineteenth-century sources. (When reading these accounts, remember that the really significant government intervention in education did not occur until 1870, when William Forster introduced state provision through local school boards, although there were small subsidies to a small minority of schools—not larger than 15 percent—from 1833.)[3] James Mill (quoted in West 1994, 170), father of John Stuart Mill, writing in 1813, noted:

From observation and inquiry . . . we can ourselves speak decidedly as to the rapid progress which the love of education is making among the lower orders in England. Even around London, in a circle of fifty miles radius, which is far from the most instructed and virtuous part of the kingdom, there is hardly a village that has not something of a school; and not many children of either sex who are not taught more or less, reading and writing.

This "love of education" was being demonstrated by the working classes a full fifty-seven years before the 1870 act. How were such schools funded? Mill added: "We have met with families in which, for weeks together, not an article of sustenance but potatoes had been used; yet for every child the hard-earned sum was provided to send them to school" (quoted in West 1994, 171). As Arthur Seldon (1990, 255), the intellectual leader of the IEA, points out, reviewing this and other evidence: "Education would have been among the earliest candidates for household budgeting after the staples of everyday life." And a similar picture is revealed today in many developing countries, where parents' priority is their children's schooling, not other consumer goods (see the discussion later in this chapter and Tooley 1999).

But we do not have to be satisfied with Mill's anecdotal observations. Estimates for the Parliamentary Select Committee in 1818 and 1834 show that the number of pupils in schools had increased from 478,000 in 1818 to 1,294,000 in 1834—and all "without any interposition of the Government or public authorities," as Henry Brougham, a Whig statesman, put it in a speech to the House of Lords on May 21, 1835.

Brougham was so impressed by this growth in schooling that he spoke of the "irresistible conclusion" that, given "such a number of schools and such means of education furnished by the parents themselves from their own earnings . . . it behoves us to take the greatest care how we interfere with a system which prospers so well of itself" (quoted in West 1994,173). His fear was that if working-class parents were made to pay new rates and taxes for funding subsidies for state education—and the taxation system was heavily "regressive," hitting working-class people hardest (with 60 percent of taxation falling on food and tobacco around this time)—they would simply be unable to afford to pay for schooling. And so private schools would disappear: "There would be ultimately be no net increase in the growth of schooling but simply a change in the pattern of the existing provision" (West 1994, 173).

The numbers continued to rise, until by 1851, according to the census, there were 2,144,278 children in day schools—of which over 85 percent were in private schools, that is, "schools which derive their income solely from (fee) payments or which are maintained with a view to pecuniary advantage" (quoted in West 1994, 175). It is also important to note that the remaining 15 percent or so were in so-called public schools, but this meant schools "supported *in any degree*" by government subsidies—which were usually rather minimal at this stage (West 1994, 175; emphasis original). Interestingly, David Mitch (1992, 144) has shown that the private schools at this time were not only more popular and at least as effective in promoting literacy and numeracy as the subsidized schools, but they actually spent roughly two-thirds of the amount spent by the subsidized schools per pupil. Private schools today continue to be far more efficient than public schools—that is, they operate at lower costs and produce outputs (education) of equal or greater quality than public schools.

Finally, there was the "mammoth report" of the Newcastle Commission on Popular Education, set up in 1858 and reporting in 1861. Its results estimate that about 95 percent of children were in school for up to six years. The remaining small minority could be accounted for by sick children, children educated at home, and also perhaps an error in estimation (West 1994, 177). Moreover, on the funding of educational opportunities, we find that even in the minority of schools in receipt of some state funding, two-thirds of funding came from nonstate sources, including parents' contributions to fees and church and philanthropic funds (West 1983, 427). Even here the *biggest* part of the school fees were provided by parents.

Moreover, the Newcastle Commission very significantly also reported that the proportion of scholars to the population *as a whole* was now 1:7.7. On this basis, the commission concluded:

> The proportion of children receiving instruction to the whole population is, in our opinion, nearly as high as can be reasonably expected. In Prussia, where it is compulsory, it is 1 in 6.27 . . . in Holland it is 1 in 8.11; in France it is 1 in 9.0. The presence of this proportion of the population in school implies . . . that almost every one receives some amount of school education at some period or other. . . . (Royal Commission on Education 1861, 1:293)

Finally, concerning schools, table 10.1 gives some interesting estimates of net national income spent on day schooling in the period from

1833 to 1965.[4] The estimates are that the percentage of national income spent on the schooling of children under the age of eleven was *superior* in 1833 to the situation that pertained in 1920 and *roughly comparable* to the amount spent in 1965. Only at higher levels was significantly less spent on schooling in 1833 than in 1965, but again this amount was *more* than in 1920.

All these figures are about schooling, of course, and arguments elsewhere suggest that it is important to distinguish between schooling and education, the former sometimes being of little value or even antieducational (Tooley 2000). But there is much data on literacy rates in the nineteenth century to help support the notion that schooling was also actually having a desired educational impact.

First, far from being in the vanguard of promoting literacy, *governments were severely hostile to the growing literacy among the lower classes.* For example, the Licensing Act, passed in 1662, limited the number of legal printers and appointed state and church authorities to censor or eliminate whatever books they found heretical or seditious (Coulson 1999, 92). Under this legislation, in 1663 a printer called Twyn was hanged for the crime of publishing that "the execution of judgment and justice is as well the people's as the magistrate's duty" (Fox Bourne 1887, 28). Aware that such hard-hitting measures were only serving to foster popular dissent, in the eighteenth century the government went for more subtle methods of discouraging reading, with an advertising tax, a stamp tax, and an excise tax on paper all imposed on newspapers. These taxes were only repealed in 1853, 1855, and 1861 respectively (West 1994, 49), all within the period when private schooling was expanding dramatically.

But far from succumbing to the government's efforts to sabotage the spreading of literacy, ordinary people lapped it up, so much so that by the end of the Industrial Revolution, in the 1830s, it was estimated that already "between two-thirds and three-quarters of the working classes" were literate (West 1994, 164). It must be stressed that the only contribution government intervention made to this end was to seek to *curtail* it.

TABLE 10.1. Percentage of Net National Income Spent on Day Schooling, 1833–1965

	1833	1920	1965
Children, all ages	1.0	0.70	2.00
Children, <11 yrs	0.8	0.58	0.86

Source: West 1970, 87.

And why the government was seeking to do this is clear. It is estimated that Thomas Paine's *The Rights of Man*—which Thomas Malthus (1958, 190) complained in 1803 was doing "great mischief among the lower and middle classes of this country"—had sold over a million and a half copies, while William Cobbett—the "original deschooler"—had sold two hundred thousand copies of his radical pamphlet *Address to the Journeymen and Labourers* in just two months (West 1994, 158–59).

By 1826 James Mill noted that among "the lowest people" literacy was now the norm and that reading, writing, and accounts were "requirements now common to the lowest of the people" (quoted in West 1994, 271).

Further comprehensive statistical evidence is offered by West, including records of educational qualifications of criminals, records of workhouse children, workplace literacy returns, and numbers of people signing the marriage register. From these various sources, he concludes that "93 percent of school leavers were already literate when the 1870 board schools first began to operate" (West, 1994, 167).

The picture revealed by West—and now supported by others—is nothing like that of a nation "lagging far behind" foreign countries, as portrayed by Trevelyan, or afflicted with mass illiteracy, as offered by Bryant.[5] If these are the true data, where did these historians get their figures from?

It seems that they got their figures from the architect of the 1870 act himself. When Forster introduced his Education Bill of 1870 into Parliament, oddly he made hardly any reference to the Newcastle Commission's findings, which had taken three years to produce and had used five commissioners and ten assistant commissioners (West 1994, 180). Instead he relied on evidence from a small-scale survey conducted in 1869 over a period of a few months by two inspectors in four industrial towns—Liverpool, Manchester, Leeds, and Birmingham. In Liverpool, for example, Forster argued that out of an estimated 80,000 children of school age, "20,000 of them attend no school whatever, while at least another 20,000 attend schools where they get an education not worth having" (quoted in West 1994, 181). In other words, here we have at least 25 percent and even, if the quality judgment is believed, up to 50 percent of the relevant population not in schooling. Hence the figures used by Trevelyan and Bryant. (Note that they have exaggerated them slightly and ignored caveats.)

At first glance this seems a major discrepancy. And as has been noted, later historians have tended to side with Forster's figures rather than with those of the Newcastle Commission, the suggestion being that the Newcastle Commission was "looking for facts which would paint so favourable a picture as to relieve the government from too embarrassing a growth of educational expenditure in the future" (West, 1994, 181). Now, if one is to "deconstruct" one set of statistics, then one should, in fairness, also deconstruct the other. Perhaps the opposite conclusion could then be levied at Forster's inspectors—that they wanted to paint "so bad a picture" in order to ensure that their own department was entrusted with the expansion of the education system? However, we do not need to engage with the discussion at this level, for there is a more obvious factor that can resolve the dispute. The Newcastle Commission had discovered that a typical child was in school for 5.7 years. But Forster, in calculating his figures, had assumed that the school-age population was in school for *8 years,* in other words, from the ages of five to thirteen.[6] Even if we assume that the school-age period had increased from 5.7 to 6 years by the time of Forster's survey, then we can see that this alone will cause the major discrepancy between the two sets of figures. For instead of Forster's estimated eighty thousand children of school age, we are likely to find a reduced figure of, say, sixty thousand (i.e., six-eighths of eighty thousand) who were *actually* of school age. But this was exactly the figure that Forster's survey *did* find in school! The fallacy that Forster committed would be rather like defining the proper school-leaving age in England today as twenty years and then claiming that, say, 25 percent of "school-age" children were not in school at all.

So the source of the popular misapprehension about the quantity of schooling in England and Wales is easily found—and just as easily dismissed.

Those who might argue that the government needed to intervene in education in England and Wales do have another possible avenue, however. This would be to question the *quality* of schooling offered at the time. This was certainly John Stuart Mill's problem with the private alternative in education in the nineteenth century. Mill wrote, "It is the *quality* which so grievously demands the amending hand of government. And this is the demand which is principally in danger of being obstructed by popular apathy and ignorance" (quoted in Garforth 1980, 114).

When the poverty in Victorian England is taken into account, however, the evidence suggests that the quality of schooling was not on the whole poor (see Tooley 1996, 35–40, for an extensive discussion). Doubts must also be cast on the suggestion, commonly put forward, that government inspection led to a higher quality of education: the inspectors' early official concept of educational efficiency meant "a schooling which scored high marks in divinity and morality" (West 1994, 104). Indeed, some schools were deemed worthless precisely because of failure in moral and religious training. But it is likely that many parents felt that these aspects of education were being largely catered to in the family and in the Sunday Schools.

The conflict between what the public demands in schooling and what the authorities want taught is a recurring one. Often the conflict is over religion or "morals." Germany, France, and the United States, for example, have all been riven by educational disputes centered around religion and morals (Coulson 1999). In other cases, the conflict is over language or teaching materials. Even prior to the Reformation, for example, private schools in Germany arose to supply the public's demand for teaching in German rather than in Latin. In India, as discussed later in this chapter, many parents turn to the private schools for teaching in English while the public schools are required to teach in one of the local languages.

Turning back to the situation in England, it must be noted that inspectors making the criticisms of the private schools are known to have had particular biases. For example, H. S. Tremenheere, in the early 1850s, noted that the people's education enabled them to read "seditious literature without having the moral or intellectual strength to discern its falseness" (quoted in Stephens 1987, 133). This was literature that was "exaggerating the principle of equality before God and the law" and encouraging workers to be antagonistic toward their employers (Stephens 1987, 133). Considering prejudices like these, perhaps we should not be taking these inspectors' reports so seriously but instead be engaged in a critical deconstruction of their motives.

David Mitch (1992, 147–49) has explored the quality of private schooling in Victorian England by attempting to compare literacy rates in private and public (i.e., state) schools. His first statistical analysis showed that enrollment in private schools improved literacy rates for men and women, whereas enrollment in "public" schools (i.e., schools with *any,* however small, state subsidy) had a *negative* impact on male literacy, with the effect on female literacy negligible. Controlling for factors that could have affected these results, such as the differing nature of the clientele in each school, Mitch still found private schools had a significant positive impact, against an insignificant impact for public schools.

It is commonly held that not only did the state need to get involved in the funding and provision of schooling from 1870 but that an essential part of its later intervention was also to introduce the regulation of compulsory schooling. Only in this way could adequate educational opportunities be provided for all. Does the historical evidence support this part of the accepted wisdom?

It seems again that it does not. First, historians note that there were many factors that led to *positive* parental attitudes to schooling and that these were gradually increasing throughout the nineteenth century. The historian W. B. Stephens—interestingly while trying to show that compulsion was *necessary*—notes in passing that not only were there economic benefits to schooling but there were also political and social ones. There was the desire to be respectable in the eyes of "local clergy and others," as well as the attractions of "reading for pleasure and the ability to communicate with relations living at a distance" (Stephens 1987, 49). Moreover, "as schooling *became the norm* the completely unschooled became increasingly untypical, a situation which *must have brought its own pressure to conform*" (Stephens 1987, 50; emphasis added). Stephens further argues that "[f]rom 1840 schooling appears increasingly desirable socially and also functionally advantageous in an increasing number of jobs" (1987, 51). Moreover, "the vast expansion from the 1830s of didactic evangelical and utilitarian publications, of political and commercial literature, and of newspapers, radical and otherwise, attest to a working-class society in which the ability to read must have added to the economic advantages political and social ones" (Stephens 1987, 51).

This trend in schooling norms would have had a considerable bearing on the need for compulsion. If there were social and political, as well as economic, advantages in sending children to school and if there were norms that made this more favorable, then it is likely that the rate of schooling would have continued to increase.

Historians also note that there were negative attitudes of parents that would need state compulsion to overcome. These seem to have been of four kinds. But three of these concern economic factors that may have influenced parental choice about sending children to school—and that were *likely to have disappeared as factors as the wealth of the nation increased.* The first is the actual fees for schooling, while the second is the opportunity costs of sending children to school—that is, the benefits foregone of children's income and assistance around the house that could have been had if children had not gone to school. Both of these are likely to have been quite considerable deterrents to many poor parents. Thirdly, many poor parents were quite suspicious of the economic benefit to be derived from schooling their children and so were not prepared to make the necessary sacrifices for no economic return. A common saying among the working classes was: "The father went down the pit and he made a fortune, his son went to school and lost it" (Stephens 1987, 123). This attitude was reinforced by some employers, who, while promoting schooling, "admitted that their most skilful and best paid workmen were not necessarily those who were literate" (Stephens 1987, 124).

Clearly, as England and Wales grew in wealth, the importance of the first two factors would have rapidly diminished. The third would have been influenced by the demands of employment; as industrialization increased, the demands of employers for a schooled, skilled workforce likewise increased.

The fourth factor influencing parental attitudes toward education is of a different, noneconomic kind. This is that some working-class parents were greedy, lazy, and feckless. But all the evidence suggests that these were a very small minority. The majority of the working class in England—as all the foregoing statistics show—were responsible and concerned for their children's education.[7]

West (1994, 173) memorably remarks that "when the government made its debut in education in 1833 mainly in the role of subsidiser it was as if it jumped into the saddle of a horse that was already galloping." Without government, we suggest, the "horses"—the voluntary-city alternative—would have continued to gallop.

The evidence from England and Wales leads to the extrapolation that with increasing wealth and the overcoming of economic conditions that undermined parental desire for education, universal education could easily have been achieved without the state.

Education without the State, Part 2: America

A similar picture of extensive provision without the state can be found by looking at the situation in America.[8]

Although the states differed somewhat—New England states being early adopters of public education—education was predominantly private in most of the United States from the colonial period until the middle of the nineteenth century. Many schools were run for profit, and these led the nation in moving curricula from a purely classical focus to an emphasis on the practical uses of, for example, mathematics in such areas as finance, accounting, and surveying. Historian Robert Seybolt (1971, 101–2) notes that in the colonial period: "In the hands of private schoolmasters the curriculum expanded rapidly. Their schools were commercial ventures, and, consequently competition was keen. . . . Popular demands, and the element of competition forced them not only to add new courses of instruction, but constantly to improve their methods and techniques of instruction."

Many other private schools were associated with churches or religious organizations, and others were run by charitable organizations on a nonsectarian or ecumenical basis. Involvement by the state governments was infrequent and when it occurred typically involved reimbursement of private schools for the education of poor students—what today we would call a voucher system. Tuition, however, was generally low and affordable to most of the population. Investigating the situation in New York City in the late 1700s, Carl Kaestle (1973, 4–5) found that tuition was "low enough to be within the means of many workers of the middling sort" and that, as a result, "New York, like other American towns of the revolutionary period, had a high literacy rate relative to other places in the world . . . ."

Across America as a whole, it has been estimated that before public schooling got started, at least 75 percent of the population was literate, and probably more: in the 1850 U.S. census, only 10 percent identified themselves as illiterate (Coulson 1999, 84). Particularly fascinating to observe is how little was the impact of either compulsory-attendance laws or, when they came, public schools. In all the American states, schooling was made compulsory between 1852 and 1918. But enrollment of white children did not go up—this government intervention succeeded in *lowering the rate of enrollment by 2.6 percent!* (This figure uses data for the years between 1850 and 1900.) There was an aggregate increase during this time but only because of "the dramatic rise in black enrollment following the abolition of slavery—from 1.9 percent in 1860 to 31.1 percent in 1900" (Coulson 1999, 84).[9] It was not until after 1920 that the schooling enrollment rate again began to increase, when the population became more urban and industrialized. As implied in our discussion of England and Wales, this reduced the demand for child labor and raised the economic value of literacy and education.

As late as 1850, a majority of funds for American education came from private sources. By 1870, however, about two-thirds of all financial resources were publicly provided (Cremin 1980). Led by education reformers like Horace Mann and Henry Barnard, the common- or public-school movement ostensibly sought to promote equal educational opportunity and extend education beyond the affluent.

Yet, as noted earlier, education was already being consumed by the masses in low-cost private schools. At best, and as far as the quantity of education was concerned, all the public schools accomplished was *replacing* the private schools. In a detailed study of Massachusetts, for example, Kaestle and Maris Vinkovis (1980) found that the common-school movement did not lead to increased participation in education. Instead, the percentage of the population under twenty attending school showing little change from 1840 to 1880. As in England and Wales, the public schools crowded out attendance at private schools and did not increase overall attendance.

Historians, moreover, have challenged the Mann view of the common-school movement. Kaestle (1973) argues that the common schools were designed to provide a foundation for preserving and extending Anglo-American Protestant values in the face of a rise in mass immigration, much of it consisting of Roman Catholics from Ireland, Germany, and other countries. An 1851 article on the Irish immigration "problem" from the *Massachusetts Teacher* makes this idea clear:

> [T]he *ignorant* of the old world, have found a rapid and almost a free passage to the new. . . . Will [the influx of foreigners] . . . spread ignorance and vice, crime and disease through our native population? Or can we, by any process, not only preserve ourselves from threatened demoralization but improve and purify and make valuable this new element which is thus forced upon us, and which we cannot shut out if we would? . . . The rising generation must be taught as our own children are taught. We say *must be,* because in many cases this can only be accomplished by coercion. In too many instances the parents are unfit guardians of their own children. If left to their direction the young will be brought up in idle, dissolute, vagrant habits which will make them worse members of their society than their parents are . . . the children must be gathered up and forced into school, and those who resist or impede this plan, whether parents or *priests,* must be held accountable and punished.[10]

Education without the State, Part 3: Twenty-First-Century India

To this picture of education in Victorian England, Wales, and America can be added a strikingly similar picture of education in India today, of educational entrepreneurs meeting the educational needs of the poorest in society without any help—nay, hindered by the state's obstructivism.

Ask people to describe private education in a developing country like India, and most present, I find, a picture of a few elite schools catering to the wealthier sectors of society. The reality could not be further from the truth. What the situation in countries like India reveals is the extent to which the private sector can step in to cater to demand when state provision is either inadequate or nonexistent. It reveals the nature of the voluntary city at its most honorable.

Any visitor to the "slums" of any major city in India will be struck by the sheer number of private schools—there seems to be one on almost every street corner or down every alleyway. In India as a whole 17 percent of all kindergarten, primary, and secondary schools are in the private sector.[11] Many schools have grouped themselves together in voluntary federations. One such, the largest in the state of Andhra Pradesh, is the Federation of Private Schools Management, Hyderabad. The federation was formed in 1997 by a group of unaided private-school correspondents and principals. Their schools saw the benefits of sharing course materials, addressing common problems together, and engaging in quality control and mutual support. They also perceived the usefulness of having an organization through which to address officials in government about their concerns—for their common view was that government was putting considerable bureaucratic hurdles in the way of the successful development of private education. The federation includes five hundred schools—which it claims is approximately 10 percent of the total of unaided private schools in Andhra Pradesh and almost 50 percent of the total in Hyderabad. Of these five hundred schools, 40 percent are recognized by government and 60 percent are not. In fact, such private unaided schools take up about 11 percent of total pupil enrollment in the state of Andhra Pradesh.

To give a flavor of the educational opportunities that we are discussing here, this section gives some figures from a recent study I undertook for the International Finance Corporation (IFC) on this sector. Through this discussion, we can illustrate major themes about the current role of the private sector in many developing countries, as it steps in to provide parents with a sanctuary against the inadequacies of state provision.

The Federation of Private Schools Management, Hyderabad

The data in tables 10.2 and 10.3 concern thirteen schools belonging to the federation, chosen opportunistically from a much larger sample of schools that were interested in having me visit. I interviewed the princi-

TABLE 10.2.   Andhra Pradesh Private School: Pupils and Fees

	Dawn School	Sir Bickthall	Little Nightingale	Crescent Girls' School	Iqra	Peace High School	Firdaus Flowers	Magnifca	Vidya Bharathi	Little's Century	Sidhartha	MA Ideal	Sharda Vidyalam
Number of pupils	2000	100	400	300	375	400	600	700	1700	350	340	1000	110
Scholarships	300	0	50	1	0	50	40	100	25	70	68	200	11
Fee-paying pupils	1700	100	350	299	375	350	560	600	1675	280	272	800	99
Monthly fees (rupees)	150–200	50–60	30–40	25–35	45–85	50–100	70–155	80–100	80–160	35–45	40–100	40–90	30–40
Monthly fees (US$)	3.57–4.76	1.19–1.43	0.71–0.95	0.60–0.83	1.07–2.02	1.19–2.38	1.67–3.69	1.90–2.38	1.90–3.81	0.83–1.07	0.95–2.38	0.95–2.14	0.71–0.95

TABLE 10.3. Andhra Pradesh Private School: Teachers, Salaries, and Teacher-Pupil Ratio

	Dawn School	Sir Bickthall	Little Nightingale	Crescent Girls' School	Iqra	Peace High School	Firdaus Flowers	Magnifca	Vidya Bharathi	Little's Century	Sidhartha	MA Ideal	Sharda Vidyalam
Teachers	70	3	12	13	14	14	25	20	50	17	13	30	5
Teacher-pupil ratio	1:29	1:33	1:33	1:23	1:27	1:29	1:24	1:35	1:34	1:21	1:26	1:33	1:22
Monthly salaries (rupees)	2000–5000	2500–3000	500–2000	1000–1500	1000–2000	Average: 1071	800–3000	1200–2200	3000–5000	800–1200	700–1400	800–2200	400–600
Monthly salaries (US$)	47.6–119.0	59.5–71.4	11.9–47.6	23.8–35.7	23.8–47.6	Average: 25.5	19.0–71.4	28.6–52.4	71.4–119.0	19.0–28.6	16.7–33.3	19.0–52.4	9.5–14.2

pal, the school correspondent (essentially the secretary of the education society that runs the school, who is responsible for interactions with government), teachers, and parents, using semistructured interview protocols designed to triangulate as far as possible information gleaned from one source with other sources. The first twelve of these schools are in various locations around Hyderabad including Bahadupina, Malakpet, Ziaguda, and Ranga Reddy. The thirteenth is in a small rural farming village under Pargi Mandal, about one hundred kilometers from Hyderabad.

Pupil Numbers, Number of Free Scholarships,
and Pupil Fees

Schools ranged in size from one hundred students—in a school that had just opened and was seeking to grow—to two thousand, the largest. Pupil fees vary according to the grade level of the child. The lowest fees charged were in the Crescent Girls' School, ranging from 25 to 35 Rs. per month (about U.S. $.60 to $.83 per month). The highest fees were in the Dawn School, ranging from 150 to 200 Rs. per month (about U.S. $3.57 to $4.76 per month).

A very important feature of all but three of the schools is that they have a significant number of *scholarships*—that is, free places to the poorest students. The free places are allocated by the school correspondent on the basis of claims of need checked informally in the community. Five of the schools had between 15 and 20 percent of students on scholarship. Hence, although these are schools for the poor, the very poorest can come to them for free.

Number of Teachers, Teacher-Pupil Ratio, Teacher Pay,
and Qualifications

The smallest school had three teachers, the largest seventy. For all of the schools, the teacher-pupil ratio varied from 1:22 to 1:35. (This is one of the noted features of the private schools, that their teacher-pupil ratio is much lower than in the government schools; see the discussion later in this chapter.)

In a state school, the average teacher pay varied from 4,000 Rs. to 9,000 Rs. per month, depending on qualifications (U.S. $95 to $214 per month). In the unaided private schools pay was significantly lower, from as low as 400 to 600 Rs. per month in the rural school (U.S. $9.50 to $14.20 per month) to a high of 2,000 to 5,000 Rs. per month in the city (U.S. $47.60 to $119.00).

As far as teacher qualifications are concerned, all of the schools had teachers qualified at least to the intermediate (grade 12) level, and the great majority of schools had either many or all graduates. Some schools had teachers with master's degrees, and one a teacher with a Ph.D.

Governing Structure and Management

The governing structure for all thirteen of the schools is technically the same; each is managed by an associated educational, religious, or charitable society, as constituted under the 1860 act and as required for the schools to be recognized by government under the Andhra Pradesh 1982 Education Act. (This and other regulations stipulate that if a school is to be recognized, then it must be such a society and not run for profit.) However, it is very important to note that this does not mean that any school was run as a "charity," funded by charitable donations—without exception, all of the schools were run on *commercial business principles,* in the sense that they were self-financing, without exception gaining *all* of their income from student fees, commercial loans, or sales of goods. Most of the schools, as noted later, also made a small surplus that was, in principle, reinvested in the school.

This said, it is also the case that all of the correspondents and principals interviewed claimed to be motivated by a concern for the poor communities in which they worked. Many described themselves as "social workers" and clearly derived considerable status from being willing to help in areas that were not on the face of it particularly promising. Typical of the comments is this one from Mohamed Wajid, director and correspondent of the Peace High School: "These people belong to a slum area, they totally depend upon us, they totally trust us." His mother had "forced" him to take over the school when she was ready to retire: "She showed me pictures of the poor people living here, and reminded me that life must not be lived for oneself, life must be lived for others. So she made me take over the running of her school."

Government Recognition

Only two out of the thirteen schools (15 percent) had full recognition from the government (Dawn and Vidya Bharathi). Two more had recognition up to grade 7, one of which (MA Ideal) was hopeful of obtaining recognition for grades 8 through 10 when its new building was completed; the other (Firdaus Flowers), however, could not meet the appropriate requirements. One more (Crescent Girls') was, rather mysteriously, only awarded annual temporary recognition. The other eight were not recognized, and although some of these described themselves as "seeking" recognition, this usually seemed to be a euphemism for stating that they were also unable to fulfill the requirements.

There are two major perceived problems for parents when schools are not recognized. First, very importantly, only at government-recognized schools can students sit their school examinations (grades 7 and 10). However, the schools in the federation (and more widely) have found a neat way around this—there is nothing in the statutory regulations to stop schools that are unrecognized from sending their students to a recognized school as "private candidates" for the purpose of taking examinations. This loophole is used to great effect within the federation. So, for example, one of the most prestigious schools in the state, the venerated seventy-five-year-old establishment Idara I Millia in Old Malakpet, sends its students to the Dawn School to take their examinations, itself not being recognized. (In its case, it has not sought recognition, not wanting all that comes with this, including having to deal with what it terms "corrupt education officers" and "incompetent regulations.")

However, this process costs more for parents. For students to take an examination in their own school costs 50 Rs. per entry (about U.S. $1.20), but as "private" candidates, they have to pay five times this, 250 Rs. per entry. (For some of the schools this is almost equivalent to the *annual* student fee.) This is a major disadvantage for parents. The *second* disadvantage is that students have "private" candidate stamped on their certificates, not the name of a school. Not only do some high schools, colleges, and universities look down on this status and prefer candidates with a named—especially a named *known*—school, but it also is an inconvenience, as most high schools or colleges will ask for other proof of residence and identity when a "private" candidate applies for entry, whereas with an ordinary certificate this is not required.

As noted, some of the schools were having problems acquiring recognition. Crescent Girls' has had temporary recognition since May 6, 1978; since that date, the school has been annually submitting proposals for full recognition but has still not secured it. To make matters worse—and apparently this is not unique to this school—no one is sure what the problem is, as the school seems to satisfy all the requirements, including trained teachers, a suitable-sized plot, and a playground. The suspicion is that the school's application has simply gotten lost inside the labyrinth of the ministry of education. This clearly has affected morale at the school and recruitment of pupils.

For other of the schools, three conditions in particular were described as onerous and difficult to meet. The statutory rules state that a school must have a playground of one thousand square yards—clearly beyond the reach of most such poor schools in the slums, given availability and cost of land. There is also a requirement for government-trained teachers within the school. But teacher-training colleges only offer vernacular-medium teaching certificates for primary schools, and most of the private schools are English-medium. So although there are no state-offered qualifications for teachers *to* take, the government refuses to recognize schools that do not have state-qualified teachers! A catch-22. Finally, the society must deposit a "corpus" or endowment fund of 25,000 Rs. (U.S. $600) or 50,000 Rs. (U.S. $1,200), depending on the level of the school, in a stipulated bank account. In itself, this fund is extremely hard to find for many schools—for at least seven of the schools this amount is greater than their annual surplus. But also, officials are apparently confused about whether or not this sum can be used by the school. The confusion probably arises because the 1987 act brought in a category of unaided private schools called *registered* schools, for which this sum of money *cannot* be touched, whereas for *recognized* status (which is what the schools are seeking), the law says that it can be. However, perhaps because of the confusing nature of these rules to the officials concerned, several of the schools have had bureaucrats prohibiting access to this money. This is a further deterrent to those schools that might otherwise seek recognition.

Language Medium

A key advantage of the private schools, it was pointed out by parents, is that they are able to teach in English—which the market clearly seeks. Of the thirteen schools, only one was Urdu-medium and one Telegu-medium (the rural school). An amendment to the Indian Constitution rules that all states must teach children in their mother tongue, but most parents seem to feel that the family can adequately teach this and that familiarity with English is needed for the wider world.

Why Do Poorer Parents Send Their Children to Unaided Private Schools?

In all the "slum" areas and in a majority of the villages in Andhra Pradesh and in India as a whole, there are government schools available for poorer parents. At these schools, tuition is free, and at many free rice is provided at lunchtime. So why do parents prefer to send their children to these private schools, which, however cheap, are certainly not free? And are they justified in doing so?

To answer these questions fully requires much more detailed research, including research on the academic and social effectiveness of these schools vis-à-vis government schools. However, some recent research—the Public Report on Basic Education in India (PROBE) report (PROBE Team 1999)—suggests hypotheses about why parents do prefer these schools, hypotheses that are certainly backed up by the informal discussions conducted as part of this project.

The PROBE Research

The PROBE team notes the two conditions that cause private schools to be attractive to parents: the breakdown of government schools and parental ability to pay.[12] According to the PROBE team the first reason is "more decisive" than the second; they discuss the situation in Himachal Pradesh and Bihar as evidence. In the former region, parents have purchasing power but the state schools are good, so there are many fewer private schools: "In central Bihar, by contrast, poverty is endemic, yet private schools can be found in many villages . . . due to the dysfunctional state of government schools. When asked why a private school had been opened in the village, private-school teachers usually mentioned either the absence of a government school or its malfunctioning" (PROBE Team 1999, 102).

The report outlines some of the "malfunctioning" that is taking place in government schools for the poor in the four states, Bihar, Madhya Pradesh, Rajasthan, and Uttar Pradesh. The schools suffer from poor *physical facilities* and high *pupil-teacher ratios,* but what is most disturbing is the *low level of teaching activity* taking place in them. When researchers called unannounced on their random sample, only in 53 percent of the schools was there any "teaching activity" going on (PROBE Team 1999, 47). In fully 33 percent, the head teacher was absent. But even these figures *over*estimate what was taking place, because they include only those schools that were actually open when the researchers visited. Moreover, the researchers usually visited in the late morning, which was the time of peak school activity. Finally, "teaching activity" is construed broadly to include children reading aloud or being supervised doing their own written work. The investigators found a particularly alarming pattern—that children in the first class seem to be "systematically neglected" in these schools: "When teachers are unable or unwilling to teach all the children, they typically concentrate their efforts on the older children" because such children are easier and less demanding to teach and also because grade 5 examination results are sometimes taken seriously (PROBE Team 1999, 48).

The report gives some touching examples of parents who are struggling against their odds to keep children in school but whose children who are clearly learning next to nothing. Children's work is "at best casually checked" (PROBE Team 1999, 48). Moreover:

> The PROBE survey came across many instances where an element of plain negligence was . . . involved. These include several cases of irresponsible teachers keeping a school closed or non-functional for months at a time; a school where the teacher was drunk, while only one-sixth of the children enrolled were present; other drunk teachers, some of who expect pupils to bring them *daru* [drink]; a headteacher who asks the children to do domestic chores, including looking after the baby; several cases of teachers sleeping at school; . . . a headteacher who comes to school once a week; another headteacher who did not know the name of a single child in the school. . . . etc., etc. (PROBE Team 1999, 63)

Significantly, the low level of teaching activity occurred even in those schools with relatively good infrastructure, teaching aids, and pupil-teacher ratio. Even in such schools, "[i]nactive teachers were found engaged in a variety of pastimes such as sipping tea, reading comics or eating peanuts, when they were not just sitting idle. Generally, teaching activity has been reduced to a minimum, in terms of both time and effort. And this pattern is not confined to a minority of irresponsible teachers—it has become a way of life in the profession" (PROBE Team 1999, 63).

But all of this highlights the underlying problem in the public schools: the "deep *lack of accountability* in the schooling system" (PROBE Team 1999, 54; emphasis original). For these problems were *not* found in the private schools. The PROBE team found a considerably higher level of teaching activity taking place in the private schools, even though the work environment in these is not better. In the private schools, teachers were teaching, even though they are paid significantly less than in the state schools:

> This feature of private schools brings out the key role of *accountability* in the schooling system. In a private school, the teachers are accountable to the manager (who can fire them), and, through him or her, to the parents (who can withdraw their children). In a government school, the chain of accountability is much weaker, as teachers have a permanent job with salaries and promotions unrelated to performance. This contrast is perceived with crys-

tal clarity by the vast majority of parents. (PROBE Team 1999, 64; emphasis original)

The report continues: "As parents see it, the main advantage of private schools is that, being more accountable, they have higher levels of teaching activity. This is confirmed by the PROBE survey: in most of the private schools we visited, there was feverish classroom activity" (PROBE Team 1999, 102). Moreover, when the team interviewed their large sample of parents, "[m]ost parents stated that, if the costs of sending a child to a government and private school were the *same,* they would rather send their children to a private school" (PROBE Team 1999, 102; emphasis original).

Concerning comparisons between private and public schools, some general points are made that are of considerable interest in this context:

Premises. Usually, the team found, the private-school premises were no better than those of the government schools in terms of availability of facilities, "but the *utilization* of these facilities tends to be more efficient" (PROBE Team 1999, 104; emphasis original).

Teachers. Regarding teachers, the report notes that the formal educational qualifications "are similar to those of government teachers, but most of them (80 percent) are untrained" (PROBE Team 1999, 104). In fact in private schools, 57 percent of teachers are graduates, compared with 45 percent in public schools—which is significantly less (Probe Team 1999, 104). It is certainly true that over three times as many teachers in the government schools are trained than in the private schools. But given the comments thus far, one wonders whether having trained teachers is of any significant benefit.

Teaching methods. Although the same kinds of teaching methods are commonly used in government and private schools—with recitation, memorization, and copying from textbooks common—there is a big difference in the way children are monitored: "Class-1 children, much neglected in government schools . . . receive close attention in private schools, *perhaps because private-school teachers are keen to retain their "clients," and know that a neglected class-1 child can easily drop out*" (PROBE Team 1999, 104; emphasis added). Pupil-teacher ratios are also much lower in private schools, at 25:1 compared to 50:1 (this ratio is 23:1 in unrecognized schools). There is also a greater emphasis on order and discipline in the private schools.

English medium. This is a "big selling point of private schools," with seventeen of the forty-one private schools English-medium (PROBE Team 1999, 104).

Attendance. In private schools, 84 percent of children enrolled were present at the time of the PROBE survey, whereas the figure was only 69 percent for government schools.

PROBE Conclusions

The findings of the PROBE report and my own research suggest the following conclusion: poor parents are willing to pay for their children to attend private schools because they perceive the quality of the private schools to be higher than that of the government schools. On average, the quality is higher in the private schools in terms of the amount of teaching activity (time spent teaching), the quality of instruction, and the subjects that are taught (the private schools being more receptive to parental demands regarding subject matter). The quality is higher because of the accountability of private schools to parents.

Statistical studies show that the higher quality of private schools in terms of quantity and quality of teaching and subject matter translates into greater student achievement. Govinda and Varghese 1993 and Kingdon 1996, for example, study the achievement of students on standardized tests in public and private schools in the states of Madhya Pradesh and Uttar Pradesh respectively. After controlling for other factors that might explain differential student achievement, both studies find that students in private schools perform better than their public-school equivalents. Moreover, private schools perform better at lower cost and thus are significantly more efficient than government-run schools.

These conclusions hold true not just in India but in many other developing countries (and also of course in the historical studies of England and Wales and of America, as discussed earlier). India is hardly alone in having a private educational market. Indeed the market is even larger in many other developing countries. In Colombia, 28 percent of total enrollment in kindergarten and primary education is in the private sector, increasing to 40 percent at the secondary-school level. In the Brazilian state of San Paulo (representing 25 percent of the total population) almost 20 percent of high-school-age children are taught in private schools. One chain of schools in Brazil, Objectivo, teaches approximately five hundred thousand students from preschool through to university preparation. Objectivo even has its own associated university, Universidade Paulista (UNIP). In Argentina and Côte d'Ivoire 30 percent and 57 percent respectively of secondary-school enrollment is in the private sector; Indonesia has 23 percent private primary- and secondary-school students and currently a massive 94 percent of higher-education students in private schools. And these students are not just from the elite but stretch right down to lower socio-economic groups (Tooley 1999).

Furthermore, statistical studies of public and private schools in Colombia, the Dominican Republic, the Phillippines, Tanzania, and Thailand show that, as in India, the higher quality of private schools translates into higher student achievement. Jimenez and Lockheed 1996; Jimenez, Lockheed, and Paqueo 1991; and Jimenez, Lockheed, and Wattanawaha 1988 all find that even after controlling for other factors, students in private schools perform significantly better on standard achievement tests than their public-school counterparts. Furthermore, and once again, private schools in these countries produce higher-achieving students at lower cost than do public schools.

Conclusions

A broad range of evidence from Victorian England and Wales and nineteenth-century America shows how near-universal schooling was achieved before the state intervened in education. The evidence suggests that the impact of state intervention was to curb what was already flourishing—so much so that the picture of education in this and previous centuries seems far bleaker than it would have been had the private alternative not been suppressed and supplanted.

In present-day India state education is singularly failing to meet the needs of the poorest citizens. (Much the same could be said of state education in America and Britain.) Private schools have arisen to fill the gaps left by state education despite the fact that governments put all sorts of roadblocks in the way of their flourishing. Why do parents, given the availability of free state education, send their children to private schools? The PROBE research unequivocally answers this question: the parents are refugees from a state sector that has failed them. Teachers in the public sector showed a cavalier lack of interest in teaching. Private schools were better. The burgeoning private-educational sector in Brazil, Colombia, Argentina, Russia, and elsewhere demonstrates the widespread desire for better schools.

In India and elsewhere around the world the factor that gives private schools their edge, and that will *always* give private schools their edge, is their *accountability*. Private schools are concerned that they keep parents' custom and so ensure that what is provided within the schools is desirable to them.

In short, education is not something that we need the state to provide, nor is it something that we should wish the state to provide. If we want an educational system that lifts people out of poverty, is responsive to demand, and is successful and innovative, we must look instead to the voluntary city.

NOTES

1. For data on U.S. absentee rates see "The Condition of Education 1996," supplemental table 42-1, produced by the National Center for Education Statistics and available on the web at <http://nces.ed.gov>.

Note also that the typical private school in the United States operates more days in the year and more hours per day than the typical public school (although the differences are not large).

2. In the United Kingdom, there are three education systems—in England and Wales, in Northern Ireland, and in Scotland.

3. Universal compulsion did not come until 1880, with attendance up to age eleven made compulsory in 1893 and raised to age twelve in 1899. Elementary-school fees were completely abolished only in 1918.

4. The 1833 figures are based in part on Lord Kerry's 1833 report. The Manchester Statistical Society reported that these figures somewhat *under*estimated the provision of education. The Kerry figures were for 1,276,947 day-school scholars—a figure that West 1994 corrects upward, bearing in mind the Manchester Statistical Society's report, to between 1,596,184 and 1,915,420. He then notes the average weekly school fees of 8 1/2 d. for boys, 10 1/2 d. for girls, and 4 d. for dame schools and assumes a 34-week school year and 80 percent attendance rates (given lower 1851 estimates for this). Hence the annual cost of 34 weeks x 9 d. (the weighted average fee) = £1 5s. 6d. With the estimates of pupil numbers from the Kerry report, this would amount to somewhere in the range of £2,040,000 to £2,422,500. West then includes Sunday schools and raises the total to between £2,450,000 and £2,900,000. Finally, educational provision in factories gives a figure of about £3,000,000. With gross national income in England in 1833 estimated at £310,000,000, this yields the figure of approximately 1 percent.

5. See Tooley 1996 for a review of the debate aroused by West's work and the current consensus.

6. Of course this is less schooling than we consider desirable today, but note that the school-leaving age was not even raised to twelve until 1899.

7. A parallel argument can be made concerning higher education; see Seville and Tooley 1997.

8. Readers interested in further details on these and other countries could begin with Andrew Coulson's (1999) excellent introduction, *Market Education,* and follow up the comprehensive sources in his references. See also for review High and Ellig 1988. For a similar picture with regard to Australia see West 1992.

9. Figures are for five to seventeen year olds and are from the U.S. Bureau of the Census 1975, H419, 368.

10. Emphasis original. Quoted in Coulson 1999, 79–80, which cites "Immigration," *Massachusetts Teacher* (1851), in Cohen 1974, 995–97.

11. The private sector in India is also heavily involved in higher education, especially vocational education. NIIT, for example, is the leading supplier of computer education with over four hundred centers and five hundred thousand graduates. Firms in India now advertise for a GNIIT—a graduate of NIIT. For more see Tooley 1999.

12. The relevant parts of the *Public Report on Basic Education in India* (Probe Team 1999) look at primary education in four states—Bihar, Madhya Pradesh, Uttar Pradesh, and Rajasthan—where educational provision is similar enough to that in Andhra Pradesh to warrant comparisons and to raise hypotheses regarding the earlier question. In these four states, the fieldwork surveyed a sample of 188 villages, more or less selected as a random sample from all villages in the 300 to 3,000 population range. Within these 188 villages, there were a total of 195 government schools and 41 private schools. Teachers, parents, and children from all of these schools were interviewed (a total of 1,221 households; 2,820 six- to fourteen-year-old children; 650 government-school teachers; and 186 private-school teachers).

REFERENCES

Bentley, T. 1999. *Learning beyond the Classroom.* London: Routledge.
Bryant, A. W. M. 1953. *English Saga: 1810–1940.* London: Collins.
Central Statistical Office. 1995. *Social Trends: 1995 Edition.* London: HMSO.
Cohen, S., ed. 1974. *Education in the United States: A Documentary History.* New York: Random House.
Coulson, A. 1999. *Market Education: The Unknown History.* London: Transaction Publishers.
Cremin, L. A. 1980. *American Education: The National Experience, 1783–1876.* New York: Harper and Row.
Department for Education and Employment and Office for Standards in Education (DfEE) and Ofsted. 1999. *Departmental Report: The Government's Expenditure Plans 1999–00 to 2001–02.* London: HMSO.
Fox Bourne, H. R. 1887. *English Newspapers: Chapters in the History of Journalism.* London: Chatto and Windus.
Gardner, P. 1984. *The Lost Elementary Schools of Victorian England: The People's Education.* London: Croom Helm.
Garforth, F. W. 1980. *Educative Democracy: John Stuart Mill on Education in Society.* Oxford: Oxford University Press.
Govinda, R., and N. V. Varghese. 1993. *Quality of Primary Schooling in India: A Case Study of Madhya Pradesh.* Paris: National Institute of Educational Planning.
High, J., and J. Ellig. 1988. The Private Supply of Education: Some Historical Evidence. In *The Theory of Market Failure,* ed. T. Cowen. Fairfax, Va.: George Mason University Press.

Jimenez, E., and M. Lockheed. 1996. *Public and Private Secondary Education in Developing Countries: A Comparative Study.* Washington, D.C.: World Bank.

Jimenez, E., M. Lockheed, and V. Paqueo. 1991. The Relative Efficiency of Private and Public Schools in Developing Countries. *World Bank Research Observer* 6:205–18.

Jimenez, E., M. Lockheed, and N. Wattanawaha. 1988. The Relative Efficiency of Public and Private Schools: The Case of Thailand. *World Bank Economic Review* 2:139–64.

Kaestle, C. 1973. *Evolution of an Urban School System: New York City, 1750–1850.* Cambridge: Harvard University Press.

————. 1983. *Pillars of the Republic: Common School and American Society, 1780–1860.* New York: Hill and Wang.

Kaestle, C., and M. Vinovskis. 1980. *Education and Social Change in Nineteenth-Century Massachusetts.* Cambridge: Harvard University Press.

Kingdon, G. 1996. The Quality and Efficiency of Private and Public Education: A Case Study of Urban India. *Oxford Bulletin of Economics and Statistics* 58 (1): 57–81.

Malthus, T. R. [1798] 1958. *Essays on Population.* New York: Dent/Dutton.

Mitch, D. F. 1992. *The Rise of Popular Literacy in Victorian England: The Influence of Private Choice and Public Policy.* Philadelphia: University of Pennsylvania Press

O'Keefe, D. J. 1994. *Truancy in English Secondary Schools.* London: HMSO.

Paine, T. [1791] 1987. Rights of Man. In *The Thomas Paine Reader,* ed. Michael Foot. New York: Penguin.

PROBE Team. 1999. *Public Report on Basic Education in India.* Oxford: Oxford University Press.

Royal Commission on Education. 1861. *Report of the Commissioners Appointed to Enquire into The State of Popular Education in England.*

Seldon, A. 1990. *Capitalism.* Oxford: Basil Blackwell.

Seville, A., and J. Tooley. 1997. *The Higher Education Debate: Challenging the Assumptions.* London: Institue of Economic Affairs.

Seybolt, R. F. [1925] 1971. *Source Studies in American Colonial Education: The Private School.* New York: Arno Press.

Stephens, W. B. 1987. *Education, Literacy and Society 1830–70: The Geography of Diversity in Provincial England.* Manchester: Manchester University Press.

Tooley, J. 1996. *Education without the State.* London: Institute of Economic Affairs.

————. 1999. *The Global Education Industry: Lessons from Private Education in Developing Countries.* London: Institute of Economic Affairs/International Finance Corporation.

————. 2000. *Reclaiming Education.* London: Continuum.

Trevelyan, G. M. 1922. *British History in the Nineteenth Century, 1782–1901.* London: Longmans and Co.

U.S. Bureau of the Census. 1975. *Historical Statistics of the United States: Colonial Times to 1970.* Washington D.C.: U.S. Government Printing Office.

West, E. G. 1970. Resource Allocation and Growth in Early-Nineteenth Century British Education. *Economic History Review* 23:68–95.

———. 1975. Educational Slowdown and Public Intervention in Nineteenth-Century England: A Study in the Economics of Bureaucracy. *Explorations in Economic History* 12:61–87.

———. 1983. Nineteenth-Century Educational History: The Kiesling Critique. *Economic History Review* 36:426–34.

———. 1992. The Benthamites as Educational Engineers: The Reputation and the Record. *History of Political Economy* 24 (3): 595–622.

———. 1994. *Education and the State.* 3d ed. Indianapolis: Liberty Fund.

3

The Voluntary City
and Community

Introduction to
Part 3

The Voluntary City and Community

Jane Jacobs's well-founded attack on Modernist planning implicitly suggests that public officials would do a much better job if shown the way. This was probably asking too much. Many Americans have lost faith in public provision of services in favor of market alternatives and private local governance. Millions now live in communities governed by homeowners' associations.

Fred E. Foldvary (chapter 11) presents the theory of proprietary communities and some history of the concept. Foldvary reminds us that economic necessity and a lack of subsidies force developers to learn to supply public goods in efficient doses. These are, after all, really "territorial" goods rather than public goods in the pure economic sense.

Among the services a consumer buys when purchasing a home is the associated political structure. Consumers shop for governance rules as they shop for any other set of residential features. Donald J. Boudreaux and Randall G. Holcombe (chapter 12) analyze the theory of competitive governance and report on the political constitutions that evolve from the market process. The governance structures that arise spontaneously in the market are not typically the same as those found in conventional cities and towns. In condominium associations, for example, rather than one person–one vote, votes may be allocated according to condominium size or value. At first sight the rejection of one person–one vote is scandalous. Yet on second glance the idea is familiar to anyone who owns corporate stock where votes are allocated according to one vote per share.[1] Should condominium and other homeowner associations be governed more like corporations or small towns?[2] Are there principles that explain how votes are or should be allocated in different contexts? Boudreaux and Holcombe do not have all the answers, but the questions their chapter raises are profound and at times disturbing.

Robert Reich (cited in chapter 13), former secretary of labor, writes that "condominiums and the omnipresent residential communities dun their members to undertake work that financially strapped local governments can no longer afford to do well—maintaining roads, mending sidewalks, pruning trees, repairing street lights, cleaning swimming pools, paying for lifeguards, and, notably, hiring security guards to protect life and property." For Reich, however, such communities are a problem, even a plague, as they represent a "secession of the successful" from society. To prevent such secession, Reich and others want to restrict proprietary communities and bring them back within political governance.

Robert H. Nelson (chapter 13), however, has an alternate take on the same phenomena. Nelson writes:

> The criticisms of private neighborhoods, although now heard with growing frequency, may have matters almost exactly backward. The real inequality may not be in the social divisions resulting from economically and socially segregated patterns of living in the suburbs. The fact that so many people, including people with many options, choose this style of private living is strong evidence that it has much to offer. Rather, the greatest inequality may be in the denial of a similar private opportunity to people in the inner city.

Thus, appropriately, Nelson spells out how the advantages of proprietary communities can be had in older established neighborhoods, where most people still reside. The proposed residential improvement districts (RIDs) would give inner-city residents greater control over their neighborhoods, enhance personal safety, and make possible a more efficient use of land and other local resources. As Nelson concludes, "[T]he general adoption of collective private ownership of residential property could offer social benefits as great as those experienced in the twentieth century as a result of widespread corporate ownership of business property. . . . [S]tate governments should facilitate this evolution rather than obstruct it."

Looking to the future, Spencer Heath MacCallum suggests that common interest developments (CIDs) are really way stations on the way to a hotel model of residential provision. Private communities may have their advantages, but as currently structured they are still political communities. Political communities, MacCallum suggests, inevitably involve wealth redistribution, potential exploitation, and wealth-draining battles for control. (Note that Boudreaux and Holcombe agree but argue that the scope for such activities is reduced in private communities that have well-designed constitutions; see also Barzel and Sass 1990.) A hotel, in contrast, is a private *nonpolitical* community. A hotel, MacCallum writes, is a miniature city, albeit one arranged vertically and with a high population turnover. There is no reason, moreover, why the hotel model should not be applied to residential homes leased for long periods of time. The thought is intriguing, but MacCallum acknowledges that the failure (as of this writing) of developers to build on this model is something of a puzzle. Even if MacCallum is wrong about the benefits of the hotel model, however, explaining why may help us to understand the virtues of other systems of residential development.

NOTES

1. One vote per share is typical although not universal. Occasionally firms issue shares without votes. In addition, corporate voting is not always by majority rule.

2. Robert H. Nelson (chapter 13) also raises the issue of whether proprietary communities are more like corporations or towns. He notes that in the early history of the United States cities used voting systems based upon property value just as corporations do today.

REFERENCE

Barzel, Y., and T. R. Sass. 1990. The Allocation of Resources by Voting. *Quarterly Journal of Economics* 105 (3): 745–71.

11

Proprietary Communities and Community Associations

Fred E. Foldvary

Do community goods and services such as streets, parks, and garbage collection have to be provided by government? The prevailing view is that they do, because private companies cannot do so profitably. According to this "market-failure" view, since people benefit from civic services whether they pay for them or not, many will be "free riders," not paying for the services unless they are forced to.

This chapter shows that private communities are in fact providing services similar to those of cities—the market-failure argument is not just theoretically but factually incorrect. Proprietary communities and community associations that are providing services voluntarily by contract include condominiums, residential associations, cooperatives, hotels, shopping centers, land trusts, and marinas.

Spencer Heath was a pioneer in studying and originating the concept of proprietary-community administration, so we turn first to Heath's work. We will then examine the works of Spencer Heath MacCallum, Heath's grandson, who continued this line of thought, and then take a look at community associations.

Heath on Proprietary Communities

Heath's main work, *Citadel, Market and Altar* (1957), appeared, ironically, shortly after the famous Samuelson and Tiebout models on public goods but evidently did not attract academic attention. (Paul

258

Samuelson [1954] laid out mathematically the distinction between public and private goods and then went on to assert that public goods are inherently subject to market failure, a doctrine subsequently disputed, for example, by Foldvary 1994. Charles Tiebout [1956] pioneered the concept of public goods provided by competing local communities, which would eliminate market failure at least for such communities.)

Heath had developed his concepts over twenty years earlier in a manuscript entitled *Politics versus Proprietorship* (1936) and subtitled *A Fragmentary Study of Social and Economic Phenomena with Particular Reference to the Public Administrative Functions Belonging to Proprietorship in Land—Proprietorship as a Creative Social Agency.* This is a collection of his papers that Heath compiled and distributed "as a record of the development and earliest expression" of this work (Heath 1936, iii).

In one paper, "Creative Association," Heath wrote that the value of public services is manifested as the rent "which attaches to exclusive locations in proportion to benefits received by or at these locations" (Heath 1936, 2). This central idea he obtained from Henry George, and the major essay in the 1936 collection is entitled "Henry George: A Further Application of his General Principles." Heath saw himself as extending the concepts of George and quotes from the preface to the fourth edition of *Progress and Poverty* (George 1975, xi): "What I have most endeavored to do is to establish general principles, trusting to my readers to carry further their applications where this is needed."

Economists since George have recognized that land rent is the most efficient way to finance most civic services, because it has little excess burden, because it returns to government the capitalized land value derived from the public goods it provides, and because it complements marginal-cost pricing (Gaffney 1994; Tideman 1985; Tideman 1990; Vickrey 1977).

But though Heath's theory of rent is adopted from George, Heath turns George's political program on its head. Whereas George regards the landowner qua landowner as a passive receiver of rent that he has no part in creating, to Heath the title holder can also be an entrepreneur with the potential of becoming "a producer of and a restorer of land values" (Heath 1936, 14). Since George himself (1975, 343) agrees that the value of improvements to land, such as clearing a forest or draining a swamp, belongs to the one doing the work, Heath does not directly contradict George, but he takes George's concepts in a new direction, toward a society whose collective goods are provided by entrepreneurs who create location-specific capital goods that generate the rents that finance the goods. George (1975, 452) recognizes that as persons, landowners are typically also laborers and owners of capital goods, but he does not envision the owner's role as a creator of land value. "The great Henry George," wrote Heath, did not discern "this natural, at once private and public function, of landowners to invest their rents and also apply their services in the administration of public affairs and to receive in compensation for their services all the increase of rent above the cost of government" (Heath 1936, 15).

Heath appeals to the historical example of medieval Europe, where "it was a frequent practice for lords of the land to organize free communities" (Heath 1936, 16). The lords advertised for inhabitants, who received protection and services in exchange for the payment of rent. David T. Beito (1988), in his analysis of urban voluntary associations, also refers to historical studies by Thierry and Pirenne on the voluntary character of medieval cities. Each member of a "sworn commune" took a public oath to obey the city charter, agreements that "are the root of the restrictive covenants of modern times" (Beito 1988, 2). Violators of the peace would be expelled from the city walls. Merchants dominated the leadership of the communes, and voluntary associations provided collective goods such as roads and defense.

H. Berman (1983, 362) in his studies of medieval towns also found that they "did not simply emerge" but were founded and that their charters generally established liberties and self-government. These "new municipal governments of Europe were the first purely secular political bodies, the first modern secular states" (Berman 1983, 389). The "commune" was based on a covenant; the city charter was a social contract: "[I]t must, indeed, have been one of the principal historical sources from which the modern contract theory of government emerged" (Berman, 1983, 393). The community was a "corporation (universitas)," a corporation being a "body of people sharing common legal functions and acting as a legal entity," much like modern civic associations (Berman 1983, 393).

As Heath notes, these free cities were later absorbed by the emerging national states. In the present time, "what vitiates capitalism . . . is not its growth but its immaturity; that the use of [private] capital . . . has not been properly extended to community goods" (Heath 1936, 20). The payment for such goods by rent would constitute a "welding of the particular interest with the general interest" (Heath 1936, 21). The concept of the proprietary provision of community goods can be developed "with reference to the general sovereignty extending to the entire territory and the particular or residual sovereignty reposed in those who hold particular parcels of the territory by delegation of sovereign power" (Heath 1936, 23).

In another paper, "Outline of the Economic, Political, and Proprietary Departments of Society," Heath views his concepts as a refinement of those of George:

> The proposal of Henry George to deprive the service department of society[,] that is, the political authority, of all its power of predatory taxation and thus restore the proprietary department to its function of disbursing the public revenue of rent to those public servants who collectively constitute the political department, carries with it the necessary implication that the proprietary department eventually will take on and exercise its full administrative functions over all the public services. (Heath 1936, 65–66)

Heath adds, "[T]he balance of rent not required for these purposes will be the clear earnings of the proprietors who have administered and supervised the enterprise" (Heath 1936, 65–66). This "rent" is really not a return to the value as provided by nature but a rental return to infrastructure, capital goods that attach to land. Hence, its retention by the entrepreneur is fully consistent with the Georgist doctrine of not taxing the products of human action.

Heath lumps together the site rent generated by civic goods with that due to natural conditions or population. Only rents generated by the former are really "clear earnings," and George's emphasis on site rents as a nondestructive source of community funds is based on the latter. What George did not envision was the possibility that governance and the provision of civic goods could be proprietary or contractual.

Heath's concept was expanded in his book *Citadel, Market and Altar* (1957). The historical appeal this time is to "Saxon England," in which community services were paid from ground rent by freeholders to the landlords: "And it was only from the hand of a public authority acting as *owner* of the community, and not as ruler over the persons and properties of its inhabitants, that these community services could be obtained by voluntary contract and for market value received" (Heath 1957, 77). Anglo-Saxon community organization, culminating in the "Alfredian Renaissance," was proprietary government, and "there was no public revenue but rent" (Heath 1957, 80).

Lysander Spooner (n.d., 145) also describes the Anglo-Saxon system as one in which "the state rested for support on the land, and not upon taxation levied upon the people personally." Freeholders held their lands on the condition of paying rents, in part by rendering military and civil services (Spooner n.d., 146), jury duty being among the latter.

Although there is no present-day example of nationwide proprietary administration, "[i]n a modern hotel community . . . the pattern is plain. It is an organized community with such services in common as policing, water, drainage, heat, light and power, communications and transportation, even educational and recreational facilities such as libraries, musical and literary entertainment, swimming pools, gardens and golf courses, with courteous services by the community officers and employees" (Heath 1957, 82).

As to its operation, "[t]he entire community is operated *for* and not by its inhabitants. Other than good behavior, they have no obligation beyond making the agreed or customary payments for the services they receive. And what they pay is voluntary, very different from taxation" (Heath 1957, 82). Moreover, the payment is limited "by the competition of the market" (Heath 1957, 82). Long-term residents in a hotel may have a contract obligating them to make payments, but one becomes a resident by making a voluntary contractual agreement. The agreement obligates the hotel proprietor to certain payment rates, unlike governments, which may arbitrarily change tax rates without being bound by any contractual agreements.

Heath states that "in all respects a public community is, in principle, the same as a hotel" (Heath 1957, 146). When the proprietary concept is broadened to a larger community, the owners give "not mere occupancy alone, but positive and protective public services as well, for sake of the new rents and higher values that will accrue . . ." (Heath 1957, 96). He foresaw "proprietary community-service authorities, organized as local community proprietors over extensive areas, comprising many communities and establishing associative relationships among themselves in order to provide wider services on a regional, a national and eventually on an international and world-wide scale" (Heath 1957, 96).

Unlike sovereign governance, proprietary administration is subject to a market discipline. As Heath puts it, "[T]he slightest neglect of the public interest or lapse in the form of corruption or oppression would itself penalize them by decline in rents and values" (Heath 1957, 135). This is relative to public governments, where, as Heath recognizes, ownership and management are separate: "Political public officers, unlike the owners of land, have no ownership hence no business interest in the public values" (Heath 1957, 172).

Actually, Heath's theory depends on competitive conditions. A "neglect" is still possible when a proprietary community has some degree of monopoly or when neglect affects only a few parties and therefore has little effect on rent. If the proprietor owns the land and the tenants own their buildings, the proprietor can in the short run increase rents or reduce services relative to rents, which decreases the value of the buildings below the value of the construction, since new entrants would capitalize the increased cost into lower purchasing bids. Without upkeep, the community would eventually decay. This deterioration and site exploitation can be avoided through increased mobility and contractual constraints. Leases can specify performance standards for services and guarantee the resale value of the buildings. If the owner owns the buildings, then the tenants' investments in inventories and fixtures are not nearly as site specific.

Heath recognizes that there are economies of scale in the provision of some public goods. Industry needs "public rights of way for communications and exchange, and other common services that can be supplied only by or under a united public authority, either political or proprietary" (Heath, 1957, 160). For this to be the case, "it is only necessary that the site-owning interests, or substantial portions of it duly organized in corporate or similarly effective form, merge their separate titles and interests and take in exchange corresponding undivided interests in the whole" (Heath 1957, 135).

Some owners could hold out, "but they and their unincluded properties will naturally receive second consideration in all matters of public benefit or preferment. Unfranchised as owners, their influence and advantages all will be of second rate," many of the benefits being excludable (Heath 1957, 136).

Heath notes that owners of enterprises "cannot afford to have their capital tied up" in assets not relevant to their chief operations (Heath 1957, 154). Businesses and professionals seldom own the premises they occupy, which require specialized administrative services. Hence, specialized firms arise that own land and provide public-goods services. They not only provide for administration over the sites and various services but also strive to "keep up the public demand" for that space, including protecting the tenants from theft and injury and keeping them comfortable (Heath 1957, 155). The rents generated by the sites depend on the prosperity of the enterprises on the sites. As examples of specialized firms serving sites, Heath includes apartment housing, professional buildings, and shopping centers.

MacCallum on Proprietary Communities

Spencer Heath MacCallum, pursuing the concepts pioneered by his grandfather, wrote his thesis on "Proprietary Community" in 1961, merging themes from anthropology, economics, and real-estate studies. In "The Social Nature of Ownership" (1965), MacCallum considers the relationship between property and society. He notes that "propriety" and "property" were interchangeable terms in sixteenth- and seventeenth-century usage, the former having connotations of customary aspects. "Property" comes from the Latin term "proprius," meaning "self" or "one's own," but legal ownership also involves the recognition by others of jurisdiction and hence "is a social phenomenon" (MacCallum 1965, 53). This is consistent, states MacCallum, with W. E. Moore's definition of property as consisting of rights (MacCallum 1965, 54).

But ubiquitous social characteristics do not imply a need for sovereign governance. "It can be argued today," states MacCallum, "that there are no longer any political functions being performed at the municipal level and upward in our society that differ substantially from those that we can observe being performed on a smaller scale entirely within the context of normal property relations" (MacCallum 1965, 57). This is the central theme of the work of MacCallum and Heath, and MacCallum extends it in his concept of the "entrecom," or entrepreneurial community (see MacCallum's chapter in this volume).

More specifically, "in the United States and Canada there has been a major development since World War II of a distinctive form of association based on the organized ownership and unified administration of land" (MacCallum 1965, 57). Examples include "shopping centers, industrial parks, professional and research centers, marinas, mobile home parks, medical centers, and scores of multifunctional building complexes, such as Prudential Center, Century City, Gateway Center and so forth of which Rockefeller Center was the prototype" (MacCallum 1965, 57–58). These have been evolving to include complementary land uses, such as the type of use that occurs in shopping centers with many different enterprises (e.g., banks and theaters) besides retail stores. Such clusters have on a smaller scale "all of the functional requirements of municipalities" (MacCallum 1965, 58).

One of the largest proprietary communities in the world today is Walt Disney World, which has achieved a high degree of self-governance and provides transit, security, trash collection, streets, parks, and other civic goods and services and encompasses within itself subsidiary proprietary communities such as hotels and even a town (see Foldvary 1994).

MacCallum notes that property is a "far more versatile institution than is commonly imagined" (MacCallum 1965, 58). In the public field, contemporary society "suffers a schizophrenia" whereby "the same agency that provides wanted public services also performs such public disservices" in "cannibalizing the society" (MacCallum 1965, 58). Government becomes ambiguous, both benign in its services and yet also a threat to society: "The modern dilemma is that we have a continually growing need for community service that we know no way of getting except through the technique of sovereignty, which in turn exists by . . . the abrogation of ownership" (MacCallum 1965, 58).

The public-goods literature posits the dominant view that only state agencies can override the free-rider problem inherent in collective goods, and the public-choice literature on "rent seeking" or transfer seeking posits the problem of government failure. But MacCallum offers a way out of this dismal-science dilemma, that of proprietary governance.

In *The Art of Community* (1970), based on his thesis, MacCallum examines the proprietary community as a vehicle that resolves the twin public-goods dilemmas, free riding and transfer seeking, by combining governance with market. He observes that "an empirical art of community has developed within Western society since mid-century . . . in the real-estate field, outside the cognizance of the social sciences" (1970, 1). The proprietary community fulfills Knut Wicksell's proposition that government can be a positive-sum participant in the economic process if it adheres to the market rules of property and contract (Wagner 1988, 161).

By "proprietary" MacCallum means property under a "single ownership" (1970, 55)—the "entrecom" as opposed to fractionated titles, such as occurs both in sovereign governance and with civic associations.

MacCallum first examines hotels as communities. He observes that there is, as noted earlier by Heath (1957), a homology between hotels and cities: "The hotel has its public and private areas, corridors for streets, and a lobby for its town square. In the lobby is the municipal park with its sculpture, fountains, and plantings. . . . Its public transit system, as it happens, operates vertically instead of horizontally" (MacCallum 1970, 2). One can add that major hotels also often operate a horizontal public-transit system in the form of vans or shuttles to airports, parking lots, and downtown locations.

Like cities, hotels provide utilities such as electricity, water, and sewerage. The administration provides for security and fire protection.

Some hotels provide chapels, concerts, child care, and "community-wide credit arrangements" (MacCallum 1970, 2).

MacCallum (1970, 3) defines a community as "an occupation by two or more persons of a place divided into private and public areas according to a system of relations which defines and allocates responsibility for the performance of all activities that might be required for its continuity." Hence the basic ingredients are persons, space, goods, and rules. Besides hotels, examples of communities given by MacCallum include office buildings, theaters during a performance, apartment houses, trailer camps, restaurants, and private residences with more than one inhabitant. "Airplanes, ships, and trains in transit," he notes, "meet the requirements of the definition" (1970, 4).

The principle on which a hotel is organized is contract. MacCallum (1970, 5) states that "[t]he manner of the relationship of each toward others is specified in the terms of the individual contracts, the sum of which at any time is the social charter or constitution of the community."

This "constitution" refers to the makeup and basic laws of the organization. The field of constitutional economics studies a "choice of constraints" rather than "choice within constraints" (Buchanan 1987, 58). The constitution of a hotel would be its articles of incorporation, and its agreements with its staff and guests would constitute its law. Indeed, in the commercial law that developed in medieval Europe, contract law referred not to law about contracts but to that "law" that contracting parties bring into existence by their agreement (Benson 1990, 32).

Much of the contractual nature of a hotel, such as the relations of the guests to one another, is tacit: "A contract is nothing more than an agreement, a meeting of minds, and it is enough for such a purpose that much of it be unwritten" (MacCallum 1970, 5).

The modern hotel, with its services, is an American invention (MacCallum 1970, 9). The word "hotel" is a French import meaning "large house" or "town hall," and one of the first uses of the term in the United States was at the City Hotel in New York, built in 1794, the first inn to be financed by a stock company. The Tremont House in Boston, completed in 1829, was the first to provide "hotel service" (MacCallum 1970, 10). It became a model copied in many American towns. In the frontier, the public hall of the inn was often the only place to entertain and became the center of community life. The hotel industry since World War II has been characterized by chain and franchise operation and professional management. The trend now is to combine hotel accommodation with office space and shopping facilities, "aiming at a more balanced and complementary use of land" (MacCallum 1970, 14).

MacCallum points out that proprietary communities are special-purpose organizations, although they have developed a "generalizing trend" away from their original character as shopping centers to include, for example, office buildings (1970, 7). Shopping centers are a recent development, their number rising from little more than one hundred before 1950 to many thousands today. Developers of shopping centers found that since the developments increased site values in the vicinity, they could appropriate these value increments by buying more land than strictly needed for the center. They then became involved in developing the surrounding area (Galantay 1975, 72).

In the early 1900s, a few land developers realized that the value of a development could be increased if land uses could be clustered according to some plan "instead of being strung out haphazardly" (MacCallum 1970, 15). Edward Bouton of Baltimore is credited with the first shopping center, in 1907. The automobile made it feasible to have a community of shops offset from the street, with integrated parking.

In an analysis of firm-location decisions, Marc Dudey (1990) determines that firms may choose to cluster together to facilitate convenient price comparison. After World War II, regional shopping centers began to substitute for downtown facilities, offering major department stores and a careful selection of tenants, including competing stores to provide comparison shopping (MacCallum 1970, 16). "Planned competition" is no longer an oxymoron.

Another evolutionary step was service-oriented center management, following the example of "hotel service," serving the tenants as well as the customers. At the same time, merchants' associations evolved in a symbiotic relationship with the management, the owner of the center having a role in coordination and promotion (MacCallum 1970, 17). Shopping-center management is community governance, coordinating many interests (MacCallum 1970, 19).

Industrial estates and parks began at the end of the nineteenth century and have a history of growth similar to that of shopping centers. An industrial park consists of a subdivision of land used by a community of industries, whereas an industrial estate—the preferred pattern in Great Britain—is a tract of land leased to industries according to some overall plan. Many developers began with the intention of selling sites but ended up leasing sites due to the preferences of the occupants. Though industrial parks typically include restrictive covenants, they have often been inflexible and difficult to enforce. With the estate leasehold system, the owner has an interest in the future land value and has both the incentive and the power to enforce the covenants, as well as the ability to modify any covenants that prove to be burdensome as the needs of the enterprises change (MacCallum 1970, 23–24). Land economist Richard Ratcliff (1949, 415) has noted that once lots are sold into individual ownership, it becomes impractical to replan or resubdivide. This difficulty, notes MacCallum, has not yet become a major problem due to the newness of industrial parks; realtors have not drawn attention to it because it would be "knocking the merchandise," their interest being sales.

As with shopping centers, the owner or association of an industrial park or estate offers services such as ground and building maintenance, financing, publicity, warehousing, trucking, banking, medical and club facilities, and police and fire protection. The services of a developer include planning for complementary land uses such as warehousing, computing services, hotels, restaurants, banking, and recreation. There is potential for an expansion of services into areas such as waste disposal.

The mobile-home park represents another type of proprietary community, "the first substantial use of ground lease for single-family homes" (MacCallum 1970, 28) and also the first successful use of factory-constructed homes. Mobile homes are larger than trailers and require special equipment to move. Trailer parks developed from automobile campgrounds. The mobile-home park mutated from these campgrounds after World War II, providing residential rather than recreational services. Mobile-home parks have been restricted by a shortage of sites due to zoning ordinances. The zoning protects the existing operations from competition, to the general detriment of the industry, and reduces the mobility of the homes.

Mobile-home parks offer services such as landscaping, parking, utilities (including central television antennas), laundries, recreation, and community meeting rooms. According to MacCallum, a major determinant of the quality of life in these communities is management, including fostering a community spirit, with good relations among the residents (1970, 30).

Mobile-home parks again offer a contrast between associations of landowners and leaseholds under one owner. (See MacCallum's chapter in this volume for an expansion of this theme.) Some older parks, sold as subdivisions, "their land pattern frozen by fragmentation of title," became obsolete as the homes grew larger (MacCallum 1970, 31). "This," MacCallum notes, "is the problem in miniature of all cities, which are simply larger, agglomerate subdivisions"; under unified ownership, obsolescence can be "programmed out systematically" (1970, 32).

Another type of proprietary community is a "real-estate complex," such as Rockefeller Center in New York City, combining many different land uses. Other types include medical clinics, campgrounds, and marinas. MacCallum also forecasts the growth of "new towns," developed on the leasehold plan, combining residential and commercial areas. Though many private new towns have developed, they have been divided into lots sold to individual owners.

As noted by MacCallum (1970, 35), all of these forms of proprietary community are enterprises in which land is improved in exchange for compensation in the form of rent. The improvements are capital goods, and the return is actually the yield from these capital goods, but the returns take the form of rentals paid by users of particular sites and goods, induced by the value of the services—the collective goods—offered to the sites. The rents are paid for rights of occupancy, the "quiet possession" of some space serviced by these goods. The public goods are financed as tie-ins to the space used by the user. In the case of hotels, the value of the land beneath a building is not necessarily increased by the existence of the hotel, but in an analogous way, the rooms become sites whose value depends on the constructed environment.

As MacCallum puts it, "Multi-story buildings are but so much increased land area stacked vertically in one place. The layers being sheltered by one another and screened and consequently 'indoor' does not change its nature, for land use must be planned whether the land is dispersed or piled up—whether it lies in one plane or in successive planes" (1970, 35). Actually, the land volume per se is not increased; the three-dimensional air space is made useful, just as the clearing and leveling of land make surface sites useful. The increase in rent derives from the increased usefulness of the vertical space, just as making the surface more useful increases its site rent.

The trend toward a larger size of projects and more varied land uses within them requires both more comprehensive planning and greater control and coordination in operation. MacCallum (1970, 39) also notes the growing trend of the retention of land ownership by one agency for continuing administration. This could slow the overall process of subdivision and in particular cases even reverse it as sites are assembled for effective management. The real-estate industry is thereby being transformed from an industry focused on selling sites to one focused on long-term ownership and management. Real-estate developers have realized that the environment surrounding a site is a key to determining its land value. They have also realized that a neighborhood can deteriorate after the sites are sold off unless there is some provision for the continuing coordination of land uses (MacCallum 1970, 42). The expected future status of a neighborhood is reflected in its present land value.

The "new town" movement is part of the trend toward larger projects, variety, and private governance. Developers of housing sought a product for customers desiring amenities as well housing, thus creating "new towns" (Galantay 1975, 72). Among towns created entirely with private funding are Lake Havasu City, Arizona, and Irvine Ranch, California (Christensen 1978, 281). Many unincorporated towns governed by residential associations, such as Reston, Virginia, have been built with private funds as well.

Neither zoning nor covenants, MacCallum states, is sufficiently flexible for the coordination of land uses. John Mowbray, a past president of the Urban Land Institute, called zoning "unwieldy," encompassing many nuisances. Zoning is difficult to change by a landowner yet subject to change at any time by the city (MacCallum 1970, 43). (Robert H. Nelson, in his chapter in this volume, expands on this theme.)

Private covenants have been used widely with some success, but if there is no organization enforcing them, individual homeowners often hesitate to call attention to infractions of their neighbors. Residential associations offer one form of governance and leaseholds by one owner another. Leaseholds have been slow to develop in the United States due to the historical role of landlords as little more than rent collectors. Another reason MacCallum offers is the prestige of land ownership, which he believes may be largely due to government interventions. However, says MacCallum, the "tide has turned" for commercial realty, and mobile-home parks provide an example of residential land (1970, 44).

MacCallum (1970, 46) states that so long as projects are subdivided and sold, they are being planned "for the present and inadequately for the future. Obsolescence begins with their subdivision into parts." Though in many large recent projects some parts such as commercial areas have been kept under single ownership, only in a few have entire communities remained under a single proprietor for ongoing management on a leasehold basis. But real estate is developing into an industry whose product is the creation and maintenance of "human environment" (MacCallum 1970, 48). "The objective," MacCallum says, "is to optimize the total environment of each site within a system of sites in order to maximize the combined rents they will command" (1970, 50).

Rent, therefore, provides a "quantitative measure of the successful functioning of the community. . . . *Pathology is signaled by a declining income line*" (MacCallum 1970, 50; emphasis original). As Gaffney

(1989, 4) puts it, urban blight is a failure to maintain urban capital goods. Such social pathology can occur due to a lack of community organization when land titles in a neighborhood are "fractionated." In a typical town under a sovereign government, titles are "scattered," and there is potential for conflicts of interest (MacCallum 1970, 55). Various proposals affect land values unevenly. Divided interests and the lack of a leadership not identified with special interests "[show] up clearly in the older downtown business districts, as compared with merchants in shopping centers," characterized by a single landlord (MacCallum 1970, 57). A proprietary ownership, with primary residual ownership, can provide for effective organization and realize the "functional role of real estate" (MacCallum 1970, 55). A merchant in a shopping center buys not only a site and associated public goods but also leadership, in other words, effective governance (MacCallum 1970, 59). An entrepreneur creating a community needs to provide for land planning, selection of tenants or club members, and leadership (MacCallum 1970, 63).

The theory of governance can be applied here, since the site-specific investments and ongoing relationships with tenants, members, and customers would induce complex contracts and flexible conflict resolution. The long-term nature of the real-estate improvements and their fixed location induce the governance of the development. Opportunistic tenants can ruin the investment of the owner, and the tenant desires to be protected from opportunism by the owner. Although there can be competition among many communities, once a tenant becomes located in one, his or her investment becomes site specific, and the result is seen in the contracts and law for real estate–based relationships, which are especially complex.

Proprietary administration fulfills the needs of community life and therein provides an "alternative to tax-supported institutions" (MacCallum 1970, 63). This is most effective, says MacCallum, under a single land title (whether that title vests in a person or a corporation) rather than under fractionated ownership by a civic association of owners. The popularity of subdivisions is, he states, due to fiscal interventions such as Federal Housing Administration (FHA) subsidies and tax laws (MacCallum 1970, 83).

MacCallum may be overlooking some of the economic and cultural values of living in a democratically run community. Democratic governance can foster a sense of community and induce volunteer efforts, as shown by communities such as Arden, Delaware (Foldrary, 1994). When the land and buildings are under separate title, the site owner can exploit the building owners unless there are contractual protections. At any rate, in a world of private communities, there would be competition among both types of governance, and the relative merits of either would be demonstrated by the market process.

As Samuelson (1954; 1955) states, and as is echoed in much of the public-goods literature, the provision of many public goods requires governance, but it does not follow that such governance need preclude a decentralized pricing system or market process if, as MacCallum argues, proprietary governance can deliver the goods as well as or better than sovereign governance.

MacCallum observes a trend at the local level toward "social reintegration in the proprietary pattern, a trend that has not sprung from any conscious design" (1970, 95). Here he echoes Friedrich Hayek (1967, 96), who writes of evolving institutions, in terminology originally used by Adam Ferguson, as "the results of human action but not of human design." Though each particular local proprietary community is individually designed and planned, a nexus of proprietary communities is evolving despite "recurrent crises of civic affairs" (MacCallum 1970, 95).

As noted by MacCallum, the revolutions of the eighteenth century purged land ownership of sovereignty, divorcing the landed nobility from government. Land could then be transferred like other types of property. The function of landowners was thereafter at first distributive, with civic improvements financed by governments via taxes rather than by the landlords. But in the twentieth century, land owners and developers began "to assume responsibility for some of the public improvements of land. . . . Such a development has become increasingly necessary as sovereignty has failed to meet the advancing demand" for such improvements as well as for localized governance (MacCallum 1970, 101). Indeed, many cities have shifted the responsibility for developing and paying for local civic goods to developers. The trend of increasing landowner responsibility is a function of developers retaining their interest intact in their properties after development, in other words, of developing income properties instead of subdividing land.

Some developments continue to grow after becoming established. Rockefeller Center, for example, has expanded by purchasing or administering adjacent sites. Architect Arthur Holden suggested in the 1930s that landowners could form an owning and managing corporation, pooling their titles in exchange for shares in the corporation with a higher total value. The corporation could then redevelop the area, and each owner would also obtain a more liquid investment (MacCallum 1970, 102).

MacCallum foresees, as Heath did, that as islands of profitable proprietary administration grow in number and size, they will tend to federate their interests to gain regional advantages, make goods collective over a greater area (MacCallum 1970, 103). A proprietary "art of community" could replace much of sovereign governance.

Civic Associations

A civic association is a voluntary association that provides community services to its members. These contractual communities include residential, industrial, and retail purposes.

A residential community association (RCA) or residential association is an organization that provides collective goods for a membership of residents in some geographical neighborhood. Such associations are governed by real-estate contract law and by their internal private rules, such as conditions, covenants, and restrictions (CC&Rs). Civic associations can also be neighborhood associations providing local public services such as safety, cleanliness, and community property improvements.

RCAs are of three legal types. In a cooperative, instead of owning a particular unit, a member has shares in a corporation that owns the real estate and assigns rights to occupy a unit. In a condominium, a member has title to a particular unit and, tied to that unit, a fractional ownership of the common space and facilities in common interest with the other owners. While the condominium association manages the common property for the owners, the association itself does not own the property. In the third type, a homeowners' association (HOA), a member has title only to a unit, such as a lot, that is tied into the association membership. The HOA itself owns the common elements. In practice, condominiums and HOAs operate similarly, except that the assessments and voting share of a condominium owner are typically proportional to his or her share of the common property, whereas in HOAs, assessments and voting can take any form.

Stephen E. Barton and Carol J. Silverman (1989) note that RCAs have moved politics into a setting of private governments that (as MacCallum notes in his contribution to this volume) share many of the characteristics of public-sector politics. Politics, in terms of coordinating common interests, are inherent when people associate, as they do after joining an RCA. It is this political aspect, with its potential for conflict, that MacCallum criticizes.

Despite such political concerns, Dean J. Miller (1989) reports that few RCAs have failed, even when they have had severe management problems. Many such troubles occur when the developer turns over the facilities to the RCA, which discovers deficiencies and unexpected costs. The developer should be liable for such costs, and in a proper market, any such liabilities should be disclosed.

The earliest known use of deed-related associations took place in the mid 1700s in London. Lord Leicester established a park in Leicester Square, and adjacent property owners agreed to an assessment to fund it, which benefited them by increasing their property values (Frazier 1980, 96). Another private community in Great Britain was Victoria Park, near Manchester, which was laid out in 1837 and operated privately until 1954. The sale of its lots carried with it "certain conditions, the 'laws' of the Park, which would protect its amenities" (Spiers 1976, 13). Besides annual "rates," Victoria Park levied tolls on some of its roads.

Ebenezer Howard developed a theory of civic associations in *Garden Cities of To-Morrow* (1965). Howard envisioned a "voluntary plan of public finance" using leaseholds of land: "One essential feature of the plan is that all ground rents, which are to be based upon the annual value of the land, shall be paid to the trustees, who, after providing for interest and sinking fund, will hand the balance to the Central Council of the new municipality, to be employed by such Council in the creation and maintenance of all necessary public works—roads, schools, parks, etc." (Howard 1965, 51). Howard credits Thomas Spence with having thought of the concept in 1775 of assembling landed property and letting it out on leaseholds (1965, 119–23).

Residential land trusts implement Spence's concept, and some have been established explicitly to base community financing on ground rents. The village of Arden, Delaware, founded in 1900, is financed by the leasehold rents paid to a nonprofit trust that owns the land, and the rents pay for the village expenses as well as the county property tax. There are about fifty operating urban community land trusts in the United States and over eight hundred land trusts of various types (Naureckas 1990, 115). The Arden-type land trust combines a unified landowner with democratic governance regarding expenditures and local rules.

Howard envisioned combining the qualities of city and country environments: "Human society and the beauty of nature are meant to be enjoyed together. . . . Town and country *must be married*" (1965, 48; emphasis original). Howard credits the idea of combining city and country to James Buckingham in 1849 (1965, 125). The architecture of the Garden City would be varied, but there would be a "general observance of street line or harmonious departure from it," over which the municipal authority would have control (Howard 1965, 54). The town would have a unity of design, planned as a whole (Howard 1965, 76). There would be a cluster of towns around a central city. To the lease holders, the town would issue a prospectus indicating the scope of operations. A board of management, elected by leaseholders, would govern the city. The extent of town services would be limited by the willingness of leaseholders to pay the rents (Howard 1965, 91). Howard envisioned charitable institutions in the community sponsored by public-spirited residents. Arden-type land trusts and residential associations such as Reston in Virginia and Columbia in Maryland have implemented Howard's plan to a remarkable degree.

As pointed out by Christensen (1978, 116), communities, especially cities, have been a focus of utopian thought, where "utopian" has connotations of being impractical or unattainable. However, as Christensen notes, the goal has often been not perfection but reform, focused on changing the institutions rather than human nature (1978, 117). Howard's primary goal was the reform of economic arrangements rather than mere architectural innovation (1965, 122). The Garden City was to be a model for a large-scale reform of society. Howard's emphasis is on the city rather than the garden (1965, 128), with a view toward decentralizing government (1965, 147). Likewise, MacCallum has economywide reforms in mind, with the proprietary community a building block as well as a prototype of institutional innovations. Howard recognized two camps of reformers: those who advocated increased production and greater efficiency and those who urged a more equitable distribution of wealth. The Garden City approach merged both goals, in Howard's view (1965, 130).

Howard was responsible for the creation of two towns in England—Letchworth and Welwyn, which were successful but, as MacCallum (1972, 21) states, "ironically provided the model for the present Satellite Towns program in England under which they were themselves nationalized." The two towns, says MacCallum, "fell far short of their potential" due to the setting up of a government "without any equity interest in its administration," using a democratic nonprofit trust (1972, 21).

Early examples of developments with RCAs in the United States are Louisburg Square in Boston and Gramercy Park in New York City, both established in the early 1800s. Louisburg Square, established in 1828, was the first HOA in the United States, made up of townhouses. In St. Louis, neighborhoods with privately owned streets were developed within the city (see Foldvary 1994). A few other cities have privatized streets; one could compose a song about the "private streets of

Laredo," of which 150 blocks were sold to private enterprises and organizations during the period from 1982 to 1985 (Fitzgerald 1988, 163–64).

By the end of the 1800s, developers were incorporating RCAs into deeds to support common areas and maintain architectural standards. In 1891, for example, an RCA organized in conjunction with a 1230-acre development by Edward Bouton in Baltimore provided water, roads, and sewers (Frazier 1980, 97). The first housing cooperative in the United States was established in New York City in 1918, and the first condominium, the Greystoke, was constructed in Salt Lake City in 1962 (*Community Associations Factbook* 1988). Large-scale development began to replace lot-by-lot subdivisions during the 1960s (Dean 1989, 4). During the 1970s, RCAs were mainly in California, New York, and Florida, but since then they have been spreading throughout the country.

Residential associations have themselves associated, like many industries. The Greater Boston Association of RCA Presidents was formed to promote RCA political concerns (Dean 1989, 6), and RCAs have formed alliances in other cities.

The Community Associations Institute (CAI), with headquarters in Alexandria, Virginia, was established in 1973 by the Urban Land Institute and the National Association of Homebuilders to serve condominium, cooperative, and homeowner associations. Members may be either individuals (e.g., board members) or RCAs; there are now ten thousand members. The CAI offers over two hundred publications and seminars on creating, managing, and marketing RCAs and sells videotapes such as one describing "Serving on the Board." It also offers a training program for community association managers, a recognized distinct profession. One of its publications, *The Homeowners Association Manual* (Dunbar 1988), is a guide to running and participating in a RCA. The CAI also publishes information jointly with the Urban Land Institute, such as *Condominium and Homeowner Associations That Work* (Wolfe 1978).

One of its affiliates is the Community Associations Institute Research Foundation, formed in 1975, which gathers and distributes information about operating an RCA. It conducts surveys, publishes practical information, and conducts other research. The foundation has a "loaner-file program" that for a modest fee loans out packages of information for two weeks on legal issues, management, association newsletters, maintenance, municipal relations, and development.

Housing cooperatives also have an association, the National Association of Housing Cooperatives, organized in 1950. In 1991, the association created the Center for Cooperative Housing, which offers services to cooperatives.

RCAs were once largely limited to retirement, luxury, and resort developments but are now available to "all income levels" (*Community Associations Factbook* 1988, 2). The growth and success of community associations also turn the market-failure argument on its head, since much suboptimal provision of collective goods by contractual processes can be traced to interventions by sovereign governments rather than a failure of voluntary efforts. Members of RCAs are required to pay taxes for municipal services whether or not they provide local private substitutes. In addition, the amortization funds and the common property of RCAs have been subject to property and income taxation (Frazier 1980, 92). The CAI recognizes that although RCAs perform many of the functions of government, their members "also pay local government property taxes for similar services received by other homeowners, but not by the community association resident. . . . Increasingly, community associations are voicing their concern. . ." (*Community Associations Factbook* 1988, 15).

The use of RCAs gives developers a competitive advantage, enabling them to offer cost savings relative to autonomous housing. By clustering and stacking units, developers reduce construction costs per unit and make more efficient use of land. Clusters save costs in building streets and utilities, leave more open space, and facilitate the production of an environment and amenities beyond those that local governmental officials wish to provide and maintain. A planned community also enables a developer to use a more flexible type of zoning, while offering buyers a wider range of choices (Dean 1989, 4).

Local governments benefit as well by receiving tax revenues without having to supply and maintain infrastructure. RCAs do not usually obtain reduced tax liabilities for services that substitute for those provided by local government. Moreover, RCA owners pay a property tax on any higher land values that are due to their own services. In some cases, the amenities themselves are taxed (Dean 1989, 5). The implicit stream of income flowing to local government from RCAs induces the government to enact paternalistic legal measures, such as accounting requirements, to protect its "investment" by keeping the RCAs well managed, since if they were to cease operation, responsibility for local goods such as parks could be shifted to the government.

Since the association assessments are not currently deductible from income taxes, the federal government and some state governments also benefit from the substitution of privately provided services for those paid from tax-deductible sources.

Among the facilities operated by RCAs are swimming pools (in 69 percent of RCAs), community meeting places (in 46 percent), tennis courts (in 41 percent), playgrounds (in 28 percent), parks or nature areas (in 20 percent), exercise facilities (in 17 percent), lakes (in 16 percent), and golf courses (in 4 percent). Services offered include landscaping (in 94 percent), exterior building maintenance (in 82 percent), parking (in 79 percent), garbage removal (in 74 percent), water and sewerage (in 68 percent), private streets (in 62 percent), sidewalk maintenance (in 59 percent), exterior lighting (in 56 percent), passive security (in 39 percent), and active security and protection (in 33 percent) (*Community Associations Factbook* 1988, 9). All RCAs provide rules enforcement. Many RCAs, especially the larger ones, hire a professional manager or management company. Hence, RCAs offer a combination of community goods and lower-cost individual goods (housing).

Contrary to the practice of many sovereign governments, which issue debt to finance capital goods and projects or even operating expenses, it is typical for many RCAs to have a reserve fund for future repairs and other capital goods. The CAI's *Homeowners Association Manual,* mentioned earlier, recommends that RCAs have a separate capital budget, backed by studies of the useful life of the capital goods (Dunbar 1988, 90). Some 82 percent of nonconverted condominiums (99 percent of converted ones) and 96 percent of HOAs have reserves, the average HOA having $119 set aside per unit and the average non-converted condominium having $407 set aside (*Community Associations Factbook* 1988, 12).

With many condominiums now aging, reserve funds are vital to the continuing financial viability of these associations. As Wagner (1986, 209) notes, "When property comprises the tax base, liability for debt amortization rests on property owners in proportion to their ownership shares. . . . Hence, debt choices are capitalized into property values." Wagner adds that this is nevertheless not equivalent to a personal debt choice. In residential associations, however, when the voters are also the property owners, the evidence of these reserves shows that debt tends to be avoided and replaced with advance funding, although reserve funds may also reflect the difficulty and higher costs to the associations of borrowing funds. Also, unlike sovereign municipal bonds, RCA interest income is taxable. Since the capital stock is being consumed— in other words, depreciates—it is economically appropriate for that consumption to be funded concurrently. The annual placement of funds into a reserve account is not an arbitrary savings account for funds left over after expenses but a payment for an annual expense that accrues.

The growth of neighborhood associations in recent decades is due in some degree to the decline of other voluntary or quasigovernmental clubs. Political party machines formerly established neighborhood clubs. Precinct captains organized a local provision of public goods and also facilitated the local provision of municipal goods in return for political support. Beginning with the New Deal, government programs and transfer payments reduced the power of these political clubs. Civic associations arose to replace the lost services, providing items such as street lamps, miniparks, tutoring, and emergency medical and fire protection. In New York City there were one thousand block associations in 1980 (Frazier 1980, 94).

The fact that RCAs provide services that supplement if not replace those of government is evidence of both the feasibility of and the preference for such services. One would expect members of RCAs to be content with this arrangement, since otherwise there would be more exit from them as information, however opaque, does spread. Surveys of RCAs confirm this theoretical expectation; one study of 233 associations, conducted by the Urban Land Institute, shows a 91 percent favorable response to deed stipulations. The enforcement of deed stipulations has also been effective; researchers have found little physical deterioration in RCA housing (Frazier 1980, 98).

On the cost side, in a study by Robert Deacon of twenty-three associations and forty-one comparable towns, associations are reported as paying 58 percent of what governments would spend for similar police services and 70 percent of similar sovereign expenditures for street maintenance (Frazier 1980, 100). One factor accounting for the less efficient government service is the independent civil service, which is less responsive to the residents (Frazier 1980, 100).

Contractual Constitutions and Law

A "constitution" can be considered to be a subset of the set of rules in a club such that no rule in the subset is entirely dependent upon or authorized by another rule in the superset (including the subset). In other words, all the rules of the club are derived from the rules of the constitution, and the constitutional rules themselves are not derived from other rules.

A constitution is therefore the supreme body of rules for governance. These rules can be formal, as in a written document, or tacit, following tradition or the desires of those in power. The actual constitution is then a combination of the tacit and formal rules. All governance
has rules and therefore necessarily has some supreme set of rules, or a
constitution.

James Buchanan (1990, 3; emphasis original) has written, as noted
earlier, that "[c]onstitutional economics directs analytical attention to
the *choice among constraints.*" Actual restraints may well differ from
the merely formal ones, and government agents may interpret them to
the degree that the formal rules become a mere formality. The formal
constitution of a contractual community may be less subject to being
overridden by tacit rules, since typically an association can be sued in a
sovereign court, whereas a sovereign government often claims immunity from suits. However, if the government intervenes in suits against
contractual communities or itself violates previous agreements it had
with them, the formal rules of associations obviously become overridden as well. In a world of contractual communities, under noninter-
ventionist sovereign governments, the ability to sue for significant violations of a constitution would seem to keep the actual and formal
constitutions closely related.

The constitutions of sovereign governments are typically decided
upon by a committee of representatives or by a previous government that
presents it to a legislative body for approval. In associations or proprietary governance, a constitution is often drawn up by the proprietor or
developer of the community. Donald J. Boudreaux and Randall G. Holcombe (1989, 266) analyze this practice, which economizes on the production of constitutional rules, avoiding the transaction costs involved
when a large number of persons attempt to create rules. Approval of the
constitution is then expressed by entry into the community.

Boudreaux and Holcombe state that purchasers generally prefer
that rules be "inflexible and difficult to change" (1989, 274). Inflexibil-
ity is a benefit, however, only for the most fundamental rules of an
association. In the Vandeventer private neighborhood of St. Louis, the
charter required unanimous consent for amendments, which proved to
be too inflexible as the surrounding area developed into commercial
use. However, many residential associations do have unanimity clauses
for changes that affect the basic investment of the owners, such as the
percentage of common interest of each unit in a condominium.

Yoram Barzel and Tim R. Sass (1990) analyze voting systems in
condominiums. Their results show that developers of "voting organi-

zations" provide constitutions that maximize the expected value of the unit shares by minimizing the feasibility of wealth transfers and the costs of decision-making (cf. Buchanan and Tullock 1962). Constitutional constraints prevent a faction from transferring wealth from the other members. Voting rules for condominiums run as investments are less restrictive and less inclusive than those of owner-residents. Wealth transfers are minimized by matching assessments with benefits and by developers' providing the major structures before transferring title to the association, which subsequently manages them with generally little discretion for creating major new goods.

MacCallum (1971, 6) notes that "the formal written law" of a proprietary community under one landlord "is simply the totality of the leases in effect at a given time." The lease thus becomes an "instrument of social policy," including also obligations of lessees to their neighbors. A second level of proprietary law is that of its subgroups, contracts made by the landlord or the lessees with their employees, contractors, and suppliers (1971, 7). A third group of persons, the visitors to the community or "business invitees" (e.g., customers), are also subject to both levels of this law (such as dress codes, pet restrictions, and denial of access ["keep off the grass"]). MacCallum observes that the typically desired decision-making process of the governance of such retail communities—for example, by merchants' councils—is by consensus rather than majority voting. If a measure can only be obtained by a majority vote, then, as one participant stated, "we don't want it" (1971, 10).

The principle of constitutional constraints was implemented by MacCallum (1977) in writing a constitution for "Orbis," put forth as a hypothetical community in space. The same economic principles apply to a space colony as to earthly proprietary communities, the colony being a type of artificial surface site, as are ships and airplanes. The owner would foster an environment, and the tenants would pay "ground rent" exclusive of the tenants' improvements (1977, 43). A tenant would be able to transfer a leasehold.

The problem of "site exploitation," the potential for an owner of sites to extract rents above what a newcomer would willingly pay, is dealt with for Orbis by governance constraints, as theorized by Boudreaux and Holcombe. First, if the owner decides to replace a tenant in order to change the site use, the tenant is reimbursed for the value of his fixed improvements and is compensated for other losses (MacCallum 1977, 42). Secondly, when the rental charge is revised, it is set "to an amount estimated to be equal to the then market rate of said site," less a 10 percent reduction for a preferred tenant, as appraised by three disinterested parties (MacCallum 1977, 44).

This second protection guards against arbitrary rental charges but not against an extravagant owner who spends the rental funds for his or her personal benefit, thereby reducing the market rent of the sites. Hence there is a third provision by which the owner pledges to conduct business such that the total site value as income property is maximized (MacCallum 1977, 43). This implies that only those expenditures are made that increase site value or at least do not decrease it, preventing site exploitation on the expenditure side.

This application to space colonies demonstrates the universality of the proprietary principles set forth by Heath and MacCallum. The same constitution could be used, for example, in creating a new proprietary colony on earth. The possibility of the private-sector provision of all civic goods in a space craft or on ships, which are effectively seagoing cities, demonstrates the general feasibility of a market-process public-goods finance.

Community and Entrepreneurship

The typical case made for market failure in the production of collective goods is that individuals may have no incentive to contribute to the provision of the good. This case, besides homogenizing collective goods and ignoring private governance, makes an institutional assumption about the nature of the society. It posits that there is no existing community, that households exist in an atomistic relationship. If an entrepreneur wishes to build a dam, he or she must contract with each household separately. Such an assumption does lead to theoretical insights, but empirically, such atomistic communities do not exist. It would therefore make sense to also have a theory that presumes the existence of community. The evolution of human society is one of changing but continuously existing communities. New communities evolve from previously existing ones. A realistic theory of public goods must recognize that society is always, already, in community.

If a community necessarily exists, then the question of the provision of civic goods is transformed from whether the market can fail to that of the nature of the community. If the community has a sovereign government providing the goods, the alternative of voluntary provision concerns not the possibility of market failure but that of the devolution of power and authority from the sovereign government to contractual governance that can provide the same goods.

Gordon Tullock (1994) theorizes that many services can be devolved to the neighborhood level, which could become a predominant level of government if policy permits. He notes that small-scale government is more in accord with individual preferences and that the Fairfield company, a developer in Arizona, has designed its communities to attract different types of residents in each (1994, 14). Robert Nelson (1989) suggests that a neighborhood association could have the option of selling part or all of the neighborhood, retaining flexible responses to changes in the real-estate market and enabling the neighborhood to profit from new development.

An intentional community can be created anew, but within the framework of previously existing contractual and sovereign communities. A ship at sea, for example, sails under the flag of some sovereign country. The creation of a new ship includes many civic goods within the ship, yet it is not claimed that there will be a prisoner's dilemma about funding the goods. The owner need not worry about individual demand revelation, so long as the expected total demand covers costs. The owner ties in the collectively consumed services to the rent paid for a cabin, and the existence of many different types of ships provides for competitive pricing.

The example of a dam serving a valley therefore poses less of a problem for contractual provision when it is realized that the residents in the valley must be *already in community.* If the valley consists of several communities, the coordination problem is still vastly reduced from the atomistic case. An entrepreneur wishing to build the dam need only contract with a few community associations rather than with the individual households. Furthermore, the communities themselves may have formed a greater community with intercommunity agreements.

Whereas the earlier discussion is centered around territorial communities, Tullock (1985) proposes nonterritorial constitutions for contractual associations. He notes the example of the Millet system of the old Turkish empire, under which autonomous non-Muslim religious communities were formed. Tullock proposes associations with quasi governmental power, which would be without a specific geographic location. They would provide services that are not geographical in scope, somewhat like those that churches provide today. Aspects of law that these "sociological" associations could assume might include those concerned with family, probate, and contract.

The provision of a civic good is typically theorized as an isolated good, but in reality, a community offers a package of goods, and potential members have the choice of accepting or rejecting the package. If one of the communities refuses to contribute toward a dam, then the others can confront it with withdrawal from the greater community and the loss of the package of goods that the dam offers. Some inter-community agreements would be typically excludable; for example, law enforcement officers can enter another community in pursuit of crimi-nals, and refusing communities can be cut off from trade, mutual law enforcement, and other benefits. The refusal of one community to cooperate in the provision of a common good, when it is recognized that they in fact wish to benefit from the good, would involve the loss of goodwill, which itself is a public good. Hence, the refusal of one community to participate in the provision of a public good would not be costless, as Heath points out.

A community is not a set of atomistic members who happen to be located within some boundary line but a web of relationships. Emo-tional attachments and networks of relationships may create benevolent sympathy for persons in the community and for the community as a whole, and this sympathy can be tapped for the voluntary provision of nonexcludable civic goods. A community therefore has the feasibility of providing for club goods by catallactic (commercial exchange) means and for nonexcludable goods by sympathetic means as well as by tie-ins to club and private goods. This feasibility does not make the provision of nonexcludable collective goods automatic or inevitable, but possible. What transforms the possibility into actuality is entrepreneurship.

Douglas Den Uyl (1985, 33) states that leaders reduce the number of "prisoner's dilemma" games where most of the people do not get what would benefit them the most. The entrepreneur not only creates civic goods but also generates institutions—traditions, festivals— that elicit sympathy for the community. Sympathy itself is a public good generated by entrepreneurship.

Daniel Klein (1990, 799), describing the turnpikes constructed in the nineteenth-century United States, notes that many of these efforts were not profitable and that the "investors" knew this in advance, which seems counter to a "straight application of the simple public-goods model." He notes that in early nineteenth-century New England, there was no sharp distinction between private and public works.

The free-rider problem was overcome by the culture and gover-nance structure of the early American towns. They were largely self-governing, and there was a high degree of participation in the govern-ment by the residents. Church congregations provided schools, libraries, and poor relief (Klein 1990, 800). These social relationships constituted what Coleman (1990) calls "social capital." Cooperative societies flourished during this era, providing religious, scientific, and civic services. Some turnpike companies explicitly called themselves "societies" (Klein 1990, 802).

The main incentive at work for the turnpikes, in Klein's theory, was negative: a failure to cooperate would be noticed. Social pressure was applied to obtain cooperation in these communities of up to a few thousand persons (Klein 1990, 803). At town meetings to decide on the turnpikes, important residents were expected to participate. Stock pledges were made in public. Committees were formed to solicit subscriptions.

The motive to contribute was not, however, entirely negative, since recognition and approval from others have positive utility. Moreover, whereas social pressure could elicit payments from members of a community, the instigators of the project did not themselves act out of social pressure.

As stated by Klein (1990, 809), "The ability of voluntary association to provide infrastructure, education, security, and poor relief depends on the exercise and spontaneous development of certain institutions, activities, and sentiments." But entrepreneurship was also required, which raises a question. Why did the entrepreneurs initiate the projects in the first place? Social pressure cannot explain the initiation of a project. Since leaders did not always believe that their private gain would be greater than the costs, there must have been some element of benevolent sympathy in their acts.

Conclusion

The existence of proprietary communities and associations implies that market-failure doctrines about public goods, such as that the decentralized price system cannot be used or that market mechanisms will not provide goods "optimally," are not warranted. Much of the literature on public goods overlooks the feasibility and actual practice of private governance, both proprietary administration and association governance. The market-failure argument also overlooks the spatial aspect of communities—that territorial public goods generate rent, which eliminates users as free riders since they have to pay for space, and that rent enables private providers to finance goods.

Consensual communities eliminate the false alternative of government versus markets in the provision of public goods, as contractual communities unite governance with market competition in the provision of public goods. A theory of public goods consistent with historical experience needs to recognize that society is always in community and that the realistic choice in the provision of civic goods is not market versus government, but whether the governance that provides the collective goods is imposed or voluntary.

◆

NOTE

This chapter first appeared in *Public Goods and Private Communities: The Market Provision of Social Services,* 86–113. (Cheltenham: Edward Elgar, 1994). Reprinted by permission of Edward Elgar Publishing.

REFERENCES

Barton, S. E., and C. J. Silverman. 1989. The Political Life of Mandatory Homeowners' Associations. In *Residential Community Associations: Private Governments in the Intergovernmental System?* ed. D. Dean. Washington, D.C.: Advisory Commission on Intergovernmental Relations.
Barzel, Y., and T. R. Sass. 1990. The Allocation of Resources by Voting. *Quarterly Journal of Economics* 90 (3): 745–71.
Beito, D. T. 1988. Voluntary Association and the Life of the City. *Humane Studies Review* 6 (1): 1–2, 17–22.
Benson, B. L. 1990. *The Enterprise of Law: Justice Without the State.* San Francisco: Pacific Research Institute for Public Policy.
Berman, H. J. 1983. *Law and Revolution: The Foundation of the Western Legal Tradition.* Cambridge: Harvard University Press.
Boudreaux, D. J., and R. G. Holcombe. 1989. Government by Contract. *Public Finance Quarterly* 17 (3): 264–80.
Buchanan, J. M. 1987. Constitutional Economics. In *The New Palgrave,* ed. J. Eatwell, M. Milgate, and P. Newman. London: Macmillan.
———. 1990. The Domain of Constitutional Economics. *Constitutional Political Economy* 1 (1): 1–18.
Buchanan, J. M., and G. Tullock. 1962. *The Calculus of Consent.* Ann Arbor: University of Michigan Press.
Christensen, C. A. 1978. The American Garden City: Concepts and Assumptions. Ph.D. diss., University of Minnesota.
Coleman, J. 1990. Constitutional Contractarianism. *Constitutional Political Economy* 1 (2): 135–48.
Community Associations Factbook. 1988. Alexandria, Va.: Community Associations Institute.
Dean, D., ed. 1989. *Residential Community Associations: Private Governments in the Intergovernmental System?* Washington, D.C.: Advisory Commission on Intergovernmental Relations.
Den Uyl, D. J. 1985. *Studia Spinoza: Spinoza's Philosophy of Society.* N.p.

Dudey, M. 1990. Competition by Choice: The Effect of Consumer Search on Firm Location Decisions. *American Economic Review* 80 (5): 1092–1104.

Dunbar, P. M. 1988. *The Homeowners Association Manual.* 2d ed. Clearwater, Fl.: Suncoast Professional Publishing Corporation, and Alexandria, Va.: Community Associations Instutute.

Fitzgerald, R. 1988. *When Government Goes Private.* New York: Universe Books.

Foldvary, F. 1994. *Public Goods and Private Communities.* Aldershot, U.K.: Edward Elgar Publishing.

Frazier, M. 1980. Privatizing the City. *Policy Review* 12 (spring): 91–108.

Gaffney, M. 1989. The Role of Ground Rent in Urban Decay and Revival. Business Research Institute, St. Johns University, Distinguished Papers, No. 89F-1.

———. 1994. Land as a Distinctive Factor of Production. In *Land and Taxation,* ed. N. Tideman. London: Shepheard-Walwyn.

Galantay, E. Y. 1975. *New Towns: Antiquity to Present.* New York: George Braziller.

George, H. [1879] 1975. *Progress and Poverty.* New York: Robert Schalkenbach.

Hayek, F. A. 1967. The Results of Human Action but not of Human Design. In *Studies in Philosophy, Politics and Economics.* Chicago: University of Chicago Press: 96–105.

Heath, S. 1936. *Politics versus Proprietorship.* N.p.

———. 1957. *Citadel, Market and Altar.* Baltimore: Science of Society Foundation.

Howard, E. [1902] 1965. *Garden Cities of To-Morrow.* Cambridge: MIT. Press.

Klein, D. B. 1990. The Voluntary Provision of Public Goods? The Turnpike Companies of Early America. *Economic Inquiry* 28 (4): 788–812.

MacCallum, S. 1965. The Social Nature of Ownership. *Modern Age* 9 (1): 49–61.

———. 1970. *The Art of Community.* Menlo Park, Calif.: Institute for Humane Studies.

———. 1971. Jural Behavior in American Shopping Centers: Initial Views on the Proprietary Community. *Human Organization* 30 (1): 3–10.

———. 1972. Associated Individualism: a Victorian Dream of Freedom. *Reason* 4 (1): 17–24.

———. 1977. Drafting a Constitution for ORBIS. *Rampart Individualist* 1 (1/ 2): 35–52.

Miller, D. J. 1989. Life Cycle of an RCA. In *Residential Community Associations: Private Governments in the Intergovernmental System?* ed. D. Dean. Washington, D.C.: Advisory Commission on Intergovernmental Relations: 39–44.

Naureckas, J. 1990. Land Trusts Offer American Land Reform. In *Intentional Communities,* ed. D. Questenberry, 114–15. Evansville, Ind.: Fellowship for Intentional Community, and Stelle, Ill.: Communities Publications Cooperative.

Nelson, R. H. 1989. The Privatization of Local Government: From Zoning to RCAs. In *Residential Community Associations: Private Governments in the Intergovernmental System?* ed. D. Dean. Washington, D.C.: Advisory Commission on Intergovernmental Relations.

Parks, R. B., and R. J. Oakerson. 1988. *Metropolitan Organization: The St. Louis Case.* Washington, D.C.: Advisory Commission on Intergovernmental Relations.

Ratcliff, R. U. 1949. *Urban Land Economics.* New York: McGraw-Hill.

Samuelson, P. A. 1954. The Pure Theory of Public Expenditure. *Review of Economics and Statistics* 36 (4): 387–89.

———. 1955. Diagrammatic Exposition of a Theory of Public Expenditure. *Review of Economics and Statistics* 37 (4): 350–56.

Spiers, M. 1976. *Victoria Park: A Nineteenth-Century Suburb in its Social and Administrative Context.* Manchester, U.K.: Cletham Society.

Spooner, L. [1852] n.d.. *An Essay on the Trial by Jury.* Mesa: Arizona Caucus Club.

Tideman, T. N. 1985. Efficient Local Public Goods Without Compulsory Taxes. In *Perspectives on Local Public Finance and Public Policy,* vol. 2, ed. J. M. Quigley, 181–202. Greenwich, Conn.: JAI Press.

———. 1990. Integrating Land-Value Taxation with the Internalization of Spatial Externalities. *Land Economics* 66 (3): 341–55.

Tiebout, C. M. 1956. A Pure Theory of Local Expenditure. *Journal of Political Economy* 64:416–24.

Tullock, G. 1985. A New Proposal for Decentralizing Government Activity. In *Rationale Wirtschaftspolitik in komplexen Gesellschaftern,* ed. H. Milde and H. G. Monissen, 139–48. Stuttgart: Verlag W. Kohlhammer.

———. 1994. *The New Federalist.* Vancouver: Fraser Institute.

Vickrey, W. 1977. The City as a Firm. In *Economics of Public Services.* ed. M. S. Feldstein and R. P. Inman, 334–43. London: Macmillan.

Wagner, R. E. 1986. Liability Rules, Fiscal Institutions and the Debt. In *Deficits,* ed. J. M. Buchanan, C. K. Rowley, and R. D. Tollison, 199–217. New York: Blackwell.

———. 1988. The Calculus of Consent: A Wicksellian Retrospective. *Public Choice* 56:153–66.

Wolfe, D. B. 1978. *Condominium and Homeowner Associations That Work.* Washington, D.C.: Urban Land Institute.

12

Contractual Governments in Theory and Practice

Donald J. Boudreaux and Randall G. Holcombe

Homeowners' associations with many of the characteristics of local governments govern many communities in the United States. While specific characteristics vary greatly from case to case, it is not uncommon to find associations that provide public goods such as roads, parks, golf courses, swimming pools, and police protection in the form of private security guards; that tax residents to pay for these goods; that are governed by officials elected by the homeowners; and that have provisions for making constitutional changes in the association rules. We have two goals in this chapter: to explain theoretical reasons that make such contractual governments desirable and to describe several examples of their operation in the real world.

The great variety in contractual governments is easily understandable: different people prefer different types of government just like they prefer different types of homes, cars, music, or food. But there are many local governments already in existence, so the question arises as to why contractual governments might be desirable instead of—or in addition to—traditional local governments. The answer lies not in the goods and services contractual governments provide but in the rules they follow to produce those goods and services. All types of local governments produce goods and services, but how well these match the desires of the residents depends upon the rules the government follows to decide which activities to pursue and how to pursue them. These rules make up the government's constitution.

The Theory of Local Governments

In 1956, Charles Tiebout made an important contribution to the theory of local government when he described how intergovernmental competition allows individuals to choose to live under a local government that provides the type of public-sector output they desire. Governments will respond to the preferences of their residents by differentiating their products, and people with similar public-sector demands will tend to live in the same locality. While many factors can prevent this type of intergovernmental competition from working perfectly, the ability to move out of the jurisdiction of a less desirable local government to that of a more desirable one encourages greater efficiency.

The Tiebout mechanism of "voting with your feet" to produce efficiency has two important limitations.[1] First, locational choices are costly to reverse. Individuals moving into an area may have a wide array of locational alternatives, but once located, they can relocate only by incurring significant costs. Second, while individuals have a large incentive to choose their location with some care—thus making intergovernmental differences important to the location decision—once having chosen a location, they have little incentive to expend much effort participating in the local public decision-making process. Such a situation discourages responsive government both because citizens lack strong incentives to convey their preferences and because local officials have limited motivation to respond. Gordon Tullock (1970; 1971) makes this point and goes on to note that Tiebout-like competition would be stronger if governments were privately owned and operated. Tiebout competition has a limited ability to curb inefficient government because the expected value of future taxes and public-sector production tends to be capitalized into the value of real property. Dennis Epple and Allan Zelenitz (1981) argue that residents in Tiebout governments require a political voice in addition to mobility even if moving is costless, because landowners cannot move their land. A different problem for residents occurs, though, when taxes and expenditures change in such a way that maintains the value of property but makes it more desirable for one type of resident and less desirable for another. In Tiebout's model, individuals can move without suffering a loss in the process; Tiebout depicts moving as nothing more than a sorting process. When moving is costly, however, residents have a stake in local government activity over and above the extent to which it affects property values. They find constitutional rules to be desirable because relocation is costly. Constitutional rules are a method of assuring residents that governmental policy can change only through an orderly and clearly defined process. Constitutions and intergovernmental competition are substitutes for each other. If there are competitive governments and if movement among them is costless, then the residents do not need a constitution. A constitution is a way of protecting an individual's locational investment when moving is costly. This observation explains why constitutional rules are desirable even with competitive local governments.

Local governments do have constitutional rules. Because contractual governments exist both independently of and within local governments, the next issue to consider is what they offer that traditional municipal governments cannot. One answer, undoubtedly relevant in many cases, is that some public goods would be optimally provided at a level of aggregation not coinciding with an existing local government, so a contractual government is formed to produce the optimal sharing group. This explanation is along the lines of the work of James M. Buchanan (1965), who examines public goods in terms of the optimal sharing group. Another reason is that contractual governments provide an environment more conducive to the development of optimal constitutional rules.

The Formation of Contractual Governments

The typical contractual government arises when a single subdivider creates a constitution that governs the property and then sells ownership to a large number of individuals with the requirement that they must abide by these constitutional rules. The original owner creates the contractual government with the intention of increasing the value of the individual parcels that later will be sold. Condominium associations and homeowners' associations are typical contractual governments. In condominiums, oversight of common property provides an obvious motivation, but contractual governments increasingly exist in neighborhoods of detached single-family homes, which traditionally have not been subject to any type of government below the municipal level.

In some neighborhoods, a municipal government existed prior to the development of the area, and the subdivider created a contractual government to produce public goods not offered by the municipality. Developers frequently do this through restrictive covenants governing certain characteristics for homes, such as minimum number of square feet, exterior construction and appearance, and the location and types of fences allowed. These covenants are like zoning laws but tend to be much more specific and restrictive. Developers also might create public goods, such as neighborhood swimming pools or security guards, paid for by an assessment on the property owners and administered by a homeowners' association. The association will have a constitution, will be run by elected members, and will have the power to tax residents to pay for the public goods it produces. In other areas a developer creates a homeowners' association outside the jurisdiction of any local government that oversees road maintenance, parks, security guards, and other public goods normally produced by local government.

While contractual governments bear a general similarity to municipal governments, the specific characteristics of the public goods they provide are likely to differ. They have an advantage over municipal governments in developing constitutions that are more closely in line with the preferences of their citizens. They are instituted by entrepreneurs who sell shares in the government along with property that will be governed, with the intention that the existence of the contractual government will enhance the value of the property.

Contractual Governments and Constitutional Rules

The first factor that differentiates contractual from traditional governments is the incentive structure facing the governments' creators. Ideally, municipal governments are formed in response to the desires of their citizens for public goods such as roads, police protection, and so forth. Two important factors differentiate municipal governments from contractual governments, however. First, because residents are already in place when municipal governments are established, there is an inherent tendency for interest groups to form. Different locations, sizes, and costs of public goods will be preferred by different individuals, and it will be inevitable that interest-group politics will play a significant role in determining the characteristics of governmental activity even when there is general agreement on what the government should do. The second factor is that there is not a residual claimant to evaluate the desirability of various governmental alternatives.

A single owner who intends to subdivide property and sell individual parcels forms the typical contractual government. The owner's motivation is to increase the value of the parcels. As such, the creator of the contractual government has an incentive to create constitutional rules with the highest value. If a certain decision would enhance the value of one piece of property but lower the value of another, the entrepreneur has the incentive to choose the option with the highest net value, as opposed to having the issue determined through special-interest politics as in the case of a municipality.

The entrepreneur who forms a contractual government is a residual claimant whose income depends on the production of efficient constitutional rules. In municipal governments, by contrast, there is no residual claimant. Mayors, city managers, and town-council members may have some incentive for making efficient decisions, but not the direct incentive that they would have if they were able to capture the profit from efficient decisions directly, as is the case with contractual governments. Thus, a direct incentive exists to produce efficient constitutional rules under which a contractual government will operate, unlike the situation that exists with municipal governments.

The incentive structure is important, but as contractual governments become more common, there is also a market mechanism that reveals which constitutional rules are most valuable. By noting which rules provide the greatest enhancement to property values, entrepreneurs can emulate successful ones and abandon those that are unsuccessful, so that the quality of the constitutions of contractual governments should increase over time. The market determination of constitutional rules provides not only an incentive to produce efficient rules, therefore, but also a method for identifying efficient constitutions and weeding out inefficient ones. This type of mechanism is described by Jora R. Minasian (1964), who contrasts public and private television, and by David T. Beito (chap. 3 in this volume), who describes an actual process of constitutional competition in the "private places" of St. Louis in the late nineteenth and early twentieth centuries.

Land developers create contractual governments because they believe that their developments will be more valuable with such a government than without one. By using this method to enhance the value of their property, developers are actually in the business of producing and selling shares in constitutional rules. As Donald R. Stabile (2000) notes, contractual governments have an advantage over traditional governments because the bottom line of profits informs them about what provisions are successful. Enhancing a development with a contractual government prior to selling homes in the development is profitable because first, it sorts residents by the type of government they prefer before they buy property, much as in the Tiebout model; and second, it eliminates the political decision-making costs that would be involved if a large group of property owners tried to create a contractual government after lots had been subdivided and sold. As Evan McKenzie (1994) notes, people often choose to live in residences overseen by contractual governments because it enables them to control the types of neighbors they will have, but the result is oversight by what he calls a private government. The idea that homeowners' associations are private governments goes back for decades, however (Barton and Silverman 1994).

The role of decision-making costs in collective organizations is explored in Buchanan and Tullock 1962. The application of these concepts to the formation of contractual governments is developed further in Boudreaux and Holcombe 1989. The importance of reducing decision-making costs in drawing up a constitution cannot be overemphasized. The reader need only imagine how difficult it would be to assemble the residents of an area after they have taken title to their property and try to get them to agree to a set of constitutional rules that would determine what public goods would be provided, how these would be produced, how costs would be divided, and how the group would agree to make its future decisions. That existing neighborhoods so rarely produce such constitutions even though they have demonstrated value in new neighborhoods is an indication of the prohibitive nature of the decision-making and agreement costs at the constitutional stage. By drawing up a constitution ahead of time and selling the rules along with the property, the entrepreneur is able to receive payment for reducing this cost of securing agreement.

Consider the reduction in the cost of securing agreement in the following way. Because everyone under the government will have the same government, nobody is likely to get exactly the type of government he or she would most prefer. If everyone were to get together to bargain for the government's characteristics, they all would have to bargain and compromise to reach agreement. The fact that few contractual governments are established in this way suggests that the bargaining process would be prolonged and costly. By moving into the jurisdiction after the government has been formed, however, the entire compromise package of government characteristics has already been produced without the bargaining costs. Although the same is true of municipal governments, contractual governments have the advantage that the incentive structure leads them to offer more valuable constitutional rules.

Some Examples of Contractual Governments

Having developed a theoretical foundation for understanding the formation of contractual governments, we now look at the characteristics of three such governments in the United States.

Park West

Park West is a community of townhouses in Fairfax County, Virginia, near Washington, D.C. It is governed by the Park West Community Association. Information on Park West comes from a set of covenants totaling eighteen pages and bylaws of twelve pages. In the typical manner of contractual governments, a developer created the association and its constitution prior to the subdivision of the property. As individual lots are sold, each lot is entitled to one vote in the association. Presumably, each lot will be sold with a building constructed by the developer, although the constitution does not specify this feature. There is the possibility, therefore, that the subdivider could choose to sell undeveloped lots. Any construction, whether a new building, additions, or renovations, and even exterior color changes and fences must be approved by an architectural control committee appointed by the association's directors. This provides assurance about the visual aesthetics of the neighborhood regardless of who develops the individual lots.

While the constitution of Park West entitles each purchaser to one vote per lot, the developer retains the right to three votes per lot until either a purchaser or a renter occupies the property. Thus, the developer is able to retain a disproportionate amount of control until the community is completed. The developer also unilaterally has the right to annex into the community additional property, which becomes subject to the same constitutional rules. The developer's right to three votes per lot could make sense to the extent that it enables the developer to maintain continuity throughout the development process. It also opens the possibility that after most of the lots are sold, changes could be made that would favor undeveloped lots or lots in a particular area of the development if most of the undeveloped lots were clustered together. This risk is greater since the developer can annex property unilaterally.

Park West's constitution refers in general terms to common property. This includes some roads and common parking areas that it mentions specifically but also additional property called nothing more than "common grounds." The board of directors is responsible for overseeing the maintenance of the common property and for determining the amount of monthly assessments for each member of the association. Each lot, except unoccupied lots owned by the developer, pays an equal share. The developer's lots are assessed at 25 percent of the assessment rate of other lots; in exchange the developer has the responsibility for maintaining the common area until the development is completed.

The constitution also gives the board of directors the power to improve the common areas for the benefit of the association and to acquire additional property. It states this power generally enough to enable the board, for example, to purchase adjoining property and build a golf course without having to receive approval from the general membership of the association. The common area does contain a swimming pool even though the facility is not specifically referred to in the covenants. The board also has the power to determine the monthly assessment amounts and to levy special assessments if needed. The association can incur debt by mortgaging its common property, but this practice requires the approval of two-thirds of the members. The constitution can also be amended with two-thirds approval of the members.

The board of directors at Park West has tremendous discretion in determining the public goods to be provided and the taxes to be paid by Park West residents. The board is elected by majority vote, and the constitution specifies that from five to nine members will serve, each for three-year terms. The association also has a president, vice president, secretary, and treasurer, but the president and vice president (who have one-year terms) automatically become board members. Another important group is the three-member architectural control committee, appointed by the board. This committee must approve all exterior changes, including color changes, the construction of fences, and even the removal of trees more than six inches in diameter.

In the theoretical discussion at the beginning of this chapter, we suggest several reasons behind the formation of associations such as Park West. First, the optimal sharing group for the association's services is smaller than the constituency of the typical municipal government. While Park West is not within the bounds of a municipal government, it is not uncommon for such associations to be formed within an existing municipality. Second, the public goods provided by the association differ to some degree from traditional municipal public goods. One might question, for example, whether a municipality would have the right to specify the exterior color of one's home (although it might be able to prevent some colors that it deems nuisances or eyesores).

The association also provides more traditional public goods such as common grounds and roads. In addition, it has a one lot–one vote voting rule, which differs from the U.S. Constitution's provision of one person–one vote. The association was set up prior to selling any townhomes to owners to avoid the cost of agreement among eventual members regarding constitutional rules and retains a distinction from a conventional government in some of the ways that it operates after being turned over to its residents. The one lot–one vote rule is an example.

While specific constitutional provisions are interesting in a static sense, equally interesting are the dynamics by which the developer's rules lead to a contractual government. After creating the constitution, the developer retains disproportionate control over the development's rules until substantial completion of the community. While there are obvious reasons why the developer would prefer this constitutional rule, it also allows residents to avoid decision costs until major questions about the development process already have been answered. It also makes sense for the developer to retain disproportionate control because, as residual claimant, the developer has the incentive to maximize the value of the property.

Reston, Virginia

Like Park West, Reston is in Fairfax County, Virginia. But whereas Park West encompasses only a small neighborhood, Reston is a large planned community with a population of over forty thousand and is the place of employment for twenty-two thousand people.[2] The theoretical concepts underlying the formation of Reston and Park West are the same, however. In both cases, the developers believed that by producing a set of constitutional rules and physical amenities to be sold with their property, they would enhance the total value of the property. Although Reston is larger than many municipalities, it is not incorporated and remains governed by the Reston Association and, of course, by Fairfax County's government in Virginia.

Much of what distinguishes Reston from Park West has to do with their differing development plans. Reston's initial developer had a vision of a community containing a mix of apartments and detached homes, commercial and light-industrial businesses, schools and common areas such as lakes, trails, and golf courses. Despite their differences, Reston and Park West have much in common. Both were initially owned by a single developer who subdivided and sold parcels along with a set of constitutional rules governing the property's use, taxing it and using the revenue to produce public goods. Reston and Park West also developed remarkably similar forms of government and constitutional arrangements. Associations with boards of directors govern each community and provide for assessments, public goods, and other services. As in Park West, Reston has an architectural review board that must approve all exterior changes and make sure the property is maintained in good condition. The *Washington Post* reports that some Reston residents have been irritated at what they view as overzealous actions on the part of the review board.[3] It mandated, for example, that backboards on basketball goals must be painted "Reston brown." In both communities, the covenants specify that the subdivider retains a certain amount of voting power in the association as the community is being developed. The details differ, though. In Reston, the developer gets the larger of either the votes warranted by the property owned or one-third of the total votes, for a period of about nineteen years from the time the covenants were drawn up. After the nineteen-year period, the developer is entitled to votes based only on property still owned unless that exceeds 20 percent of the total votes, in which case the developer still is entitled to one-third of the votes.

The covenants at Reston specify that the assessments paid to the association are to be in proportion to the assessed value of the property as determined by Fairfax County. This is unlike many contractual governments, which assess each piece of property an equal amount. One difference is that property owners are relying on the county government rather than their own constitution to determine their share of the assessment. This might seem fair, because property will differ more in value in a larger, more heterogeneous community like Reston than in a more homogeneous community like Park West. Three factors weigh in favor of equal assessments, however.

First, the public goods residents enjoy are not likely to be very dependent on the value of the property they occupy. Second, because the assessments will be capitalized into the value of the property, equal assessments (relative to assessments in proportion to value) would have the effect of lowering the purchase price of inexpensive property and raising the purchase price of expensive property. There are no fairness implications regarding the magnitude of the assessments, because the tax structure becomes a part of the value of the property. If purchasers of less expensive property had less ready access to capital markets, there might be an additional efficiency argument for equal assessments. A lower price of inexpensive property lets individuals purchase property for less now in exchange for a higher present value of assessment payments. While purchasers of more expensive property would have to enter the capital market more heavily, they also should be able to do so more cheaply. Third, payments based on assessed value dampen the incentive to improve the value of the property. At Park West, for example, owners could improve their property without risking increased association fees; in Reston, improving their property could lead to a higher assessed value and higher fees.

There seem to be firm reasons for making assessments independent of property values, but it is interesting to note that Reston is not alone in this method of assessment. Columbia, Maryland, is another planned community in the Washington, D.C., area, and it also taxes its residents based on assessed value. The two communities were begun at about the same time, in the mid-1960s. Perhaps the differences between these larger planned communities and Park West are due to the ages of each community. Reston and Columbia are more than a decade older than Park West. Perhaps Reston's founders established the fee structure as an attempt to imitate local government without carefully looking at alternatives; perhaps they examined and rejected the equal-assessment option for some noneconomic reason. Perhaps there are good reasons for unequal assessments that this chapter does not consider. One would have good reason to think that the developers of such planned communities would have a better idea of optimal community rules than the two economists who wrote this chapter! On the other hand, one should not expect any constitution to be perfect, and Reston's assessment procedure may be an example of a constitutional rule that could be improved.

Another thing that sets Reston off from other contractual communities is its federal system of government. Within the Reston Association are cluster associations formed around neighborhoods. The cluster associations are similar to the overall association in that they are responsible for maintaining common areas within their clusters and have the power to tax their residents to do so. The Reston Association's covenants do not specify much about the cluster associations, thus enabling a variety of types of cluster associations to coexist within the community. The interesting aspect of the cluster associations is that they were created within a community smaller than many municipalities. Apparently, the developer believed that their existence would enhance the value of property in Reston.

While our thesis has been built around the ability of contractual governments to write constitutions superior to those of municipal governments, we also argue that they may be created because, following Buchanan's theory of clubs, the optimal sharing group for some public goods is smaller than an entire municipality. The existence of cluster associations within the Reston Association supports this latter hypothesis. If differently sized optimal-sharing groups did not exist for different public goods, then there would be less reason for Reston's developer to create smaller associations within the larger associations.

Sawgrass Players Club

The Sawgrass Players Club is a planned community in St. Johns County, Florida, near Jacksonville. The community is built around two golf courses and has some office and commercial locations in addition to a variety of residential areas, from single-family homes to apartments. As currently planned, Sawgrass will contain slightly under two thousand residential units. This does not include fifty-one acres for future residential development in the original plan nor the possibility that additional property could be annexed. Like the communities already discussed, Sawgrass owes its creation to a single developer.

The concepts described for the preceding two contractual governments carry over to Sawgrass.[4] In the process of development, the developer retains political control over the contractual government by creating separate classes of voters. Class A voters are owners of residential property, the developer is the only class B voter, and commercial-property owners are class C voters. Class A voters get one vote each, and class C voters get one vote per ten thousand square feet of commercial space, so the rule is one vote per unit of property rather than the one person–one vote rule granted in municipalities. Class B votes do not translate directly into a certain number of class A or class C votes. The value of the developer's vote arises because for some decisions all classes of voters must agree; the developer thus has veto power over these decisions. For example, the decision to annex noncontiguous property requires the approval of all classes of voters, meaning that such annexation cannot take place without the developer's approval (until the property is developed and the developer no longer has voting rights). The constitution gives the developer the right to annex contiguous property unilaterally, as well as to withdraw property from the association as long as it does not create noncontiguous property. As in the other contractual governments, the developer maintains control disproportionate to ownership share as long as the project is being developed.

As with Park West and Reston, an elected board of directors runs the contractual government. There are five elected directors, and while the property is being developed, the developer has the right to appoint three of the five directors. After sale of the lots, directors are elected exclusively by the residential and commercial-property owners.

The board determines the assessment level subject to an upper bound in the covenants; this upper bound is adjusted for inflation. In addition to the regular annual assessment, the covenants authorize the board to levy special assessments for such things as capital improvements to common facilities and additions to common areas, subject to the majority approval of voters in every class. Emergency assessments do not require approval.

Assessments pay for the types of public goods that municipal governments would provide, such as road maintenance, security, and maintenance of common grounds. Thus, it is noteworthy that Sawgrass's constitution bases assessments on the number of residential development units (RDUs) owned rather than the assessed value of property. While there are some complications, some property was sold before the approval of the covenants, and owners of this property are assessed less than owners of later-developed property. The covenants essentially count each residential unit as one RDU, each undeveloped lot as half an RDU, and every ten thousand feet of commercial space as one RDU. Thus, improvements to the property, with the exceptions of developing a vacant lot or adding commercial space, do not increase one's assessment. As discussed previously, this method of determining the assessments creates no disincentive for individuals to improve the value of their property.

Yoram Barzel and Tim R. Sass (1990) note that condominium associations commonly use equal assessments and a one unit–one vote rule to make collective decisions, but that larger and/or more heterogeneous condominiums are more likely to use assessed-value assessments or some other weighting scheme creating larger assessments for more valuable units and to have weighted voting schemes. Thus, it is interesting that Sawgrass, with a very heterogeneous mix of property, uses equal assessments and a one residential unit–one vote political decision rule. As noted earlier, both this assessment method and this voting rule offer advantages to homeowners.

The board of directors at Sawgrass must approve any exterior improvements, including such things as antennae, fences, and landscaping. Because the association owns the roads, the covenants give the board the right to exclude people who might create a nuisance and give the board the right (but not the obligation) to monitor traffic and assess fines for speeding.

Sawgrass is small by municipal standards, yet it is subdivided into subassociations containing from about fifty to just under two hundred residential units. The subassociations are governed by their own covenants, are responsible for maintaining public goods such as roads and common areas within the subassociation's jurisdiction, and have the power to tax to pay for these goods, as is done with the overall association. The constitution of each subassociation is much the same as that of the overall association. In addition to architectural review through the overall association, subassociations also can have architectural review committees. For the Cypress Creek subassociation, for example, the covenants are more detailed than for the overall association with respect to allowable architecture and include review and approval of exterior color, roof design, garage size, and driveway size and material. The covenants specifically allow the purchase of adjacent lots for recreational purposes (e.g., a swimming pool or tennis courts) but require both that recreational facilities be screened from public view and that the plans be approved by the review board. With this kind of flexibility, Sawgrass is not planned in as much detail as Reston, but there is considerable restriction on the type of construction that can be undertaken.

As is the case with Reston, the developer of Sawgrass designed it as a federal system of government, having smaller associations within the central association. The overall association provides public goods such as main roads and common areas and oversees architecture in a general way. The subassociations are responsible for roads and common areas within their smaller areas and have more detailed rules about allowable construction, architecture, and exterior appearance of buildings. The examples of Reston and Sawgrass suggest that the optimal size of the sharing group for some public goods is relatively small—much smaller than the typical municipality. If this were not the case, developers would see no advantage to creating subassociations within their overall associations.

Contractual Governments and Traditional Governments

We have already explored some of the fundamental differences between traditional governments and contractual governments in the beginning of the chapter, and the examples just described convey how these theoretical distinctions help explain actual contractual governments. While the earlier discussion focuses on differences in the formation of contractual versus traditional governments, however, the present section deals with differences after the governments have been established.

Differences between the two types of governments fall into two general categories: legal ones, which exist because the law views contractual governments and traditional governments as different types of entities; and theoretical ones, which arise independently of the way these governments are treated by the law. While there is a significant distinction between the formation of a contractual government and a traditional government, the distinctions are reduced after the two forms of government are in place.

In our theoretical framework, contractual governments are governments just as much as traditional governments are, but the law treats contractual governments as voluntary associations. One place where this is very evident is in the voting rules used by contractual governments. Whereas the U.S. Constitution requires institutions with the legal status of governments to allow each person of voting age one vote, contractual governments usually allow each property-owning unit one vote regardless of how many people of voting age live on the property. Even when this is not the case, voting rights are assigned based on the characteristics of the property rather than the number of adults living there. Because contractual governments commonly assign voting rights based on property ownership, this practice appears to be an optimal way to assign voting rights in such governments. Several interesting questions arise. Would this type of voting rule also be optimal with municipal governments? Would the optimal voting rule depend not only on the extent of government service but also on the way that the government had been established? In the United States, most states originally extended the right to vote only to property owners. Did this occur because it was much easier to become a property owner in the frontier United States, or was there a similarity with contractual governments? Would one expect to see voting rules change over time in contractual governments?

Contractual and traditional governments vary in other ways. Restrictive covenants are often much more severe than traditional zoning laws, sometimes specifying the minimum square footage for homes, allowable types and locations of fences, exterior house colors allowable, and even what types of vehicles can be parked outside of homes. Another common feature of contractual governments is an architectural review board that must approve any new building, including additions to existing homes. Would such arrangements also be desirable with municipal governments? This line of inquiry amounts to asking which differences between contractual and traditional governments can be traced to theoretical differences and which result from their different treatment under existing law. The *Washington Post* reports that some members of the Sequoyah condominium association in Fairfax County, Virginia, call their complex "little Russia" because they believe that the (elected) board of directors exerts too heavy a hand over the complex.[5] They complain of things ranging from the overzealous enforcement of rules to censorship of the *Sequoyan,* the association's newspaper. James L. Winokur (1994) notes that one general concern of contractual governments is that they create a mechanism whereby neighbors can impose their views on people's personal lives and private activities.

Further investigation of these issues is worthwhile not just from the standpoint of understanding more about the operation of contractual governments but also because it holds the promise of helping to suggest improvements to political institutions. In the past several decades, scholars such as Buchanan, Tullock, Robert Nozick, and John Rawls have examined the theoretical foundations of optimal legal and political structures. The study of contractual governments is complementary because it adds empirical content to the theoretical framework that is being developed.

Conclusion

Contractual governments have many of the characteristics of traditional governments but are created by private contract. Typically, a real-estate developer creates a contractual government to cover an area before the developer subdivides and sells lots to individual owners. Because the entrepreneurs who create these communities are able to sell the governed properties for a premium, the contractual government has demonstrated value to its citizens. The entrepreneur is able to profit from creating such a government because this enables the eventual owners of the property to receive the net benefits of the contractual government without having to incur the cost of agreeing with their neighbors about its characteristics. The contractual government's creator, then, is actually producing and selling constitutional rules.

While the study of contractual governments has value in its own right, it also adds a dimension to the theoretical study of optimal legal and political structures. The scholarly literature on the economics of constitutions has been growing over the past few decades, and contractual governments provide real-world examples that complement this theory. Far from being of interest just as a description of existing institutions, the study of contractual governments can help to improve governmental institutions in the future.

NOTES

The authors gratefully acknowledge helpful comments from David T. Beito, the late Katherine Boudreaux, Mark Flynn, Harold Leiendecker, John Metcalf, and Alexander Tabarrok.
    1. There are other limitations to the model in addition to those discussed here. See Buchanan and Goetz 1972 for a discussion. One practical limitation is

that individuals exercise locational choices for many reasons other than the discretionary offerings of local governments. These may severely limit the alternatives among governments that individuals actually have. The limitations discussed here would exist even if there were a wide array of choices of differentiated local governments.

2. Background information on Reston comes from Grubisich and McCandless 1985, unless otherwise noted.

3. *Washington Post* (February 2, 1989), section VA., 7.

4. Information on the Sawgrass Players Club comes from "The Declaration of Covenants for The Players Club at Sawgrass," "Articles of Incorporation of the Sawgrass Players Club Association, Inc.," "Bylaws of the Sawgrass Players Club Association, Inc.," and similar documents for Cypress Creek, a subdivision of the development, as well as documents for the hotel and commercial properties in the development.

5. *Washington Post* (November 22, 1988), section B, 1–2.

REFERENCES

Barton, S. E., and C. J. Silverman, eds. 1994. *Common Interest Communities: Private Governments and the Public Interest.* Berkeley: Institute of Governmental Studies Press.

Barzel, Y., and T. R. Sass. 1990. The Allocation of Resources by Voting. *Quarterly Journal of Economics* 105 (3): 745–71.

Beito, D. T., and B. Smith. 1990. The Formation of Urban Infrastructure Through Nongovernmental Planning: The Private Places of St. Louis, 1869–1920. *Journal of Urban History* 16 (May): 263–303.

Boudreaux, D. J., and R. G. Holcombe. 1989. Government by Contract. *Public Finance Quarterly* 17 (3): 264–80.

Buchanan, J. M. 1965. An Economic Theory of Clubs. *Economica* 33 (February): 1–14.

———. 1975. *The Limits of Liberty: Between Anarchy and Leviathan.* Chicago: University of Chicago Press.

Buchanan, J. M., and C. J. Goetz. 1972. Efficiency Limits of Fiscal Mobility: An Assessment of the Tiebout Model. *Journal of Public Economics* 1:25–43.

Buchanan, J. M., and G. Tullock. 1962. *The Calculus of Consent.* Ann Arbor: University of Michigan Press.

Epple, D., and A. Zelenitz. 1981. The Implications of Competition Among Jurisdictions: Does Tiebout Need Politics? *Journal of Political Economy* 89 (December): 1197–1217.

Grubisich, T., and P. McCandless. 1985. *Reston: The First Twenty Years.* Reston, Va.: Reston Publishing.

McKenzie, E. 1994. *Privatopia: Homeowner Associations and the Rise of Residential Private Government.* New Haven: Yale University Press.

Minasian, J. R. 1964. Television Pricing and the Theory of Public Goods. *Journal of Law and Economics* 7 (October): 71–80.

Nozick, R. 1974. *Anarchy, State, and Utopia.* New York: Basic Books.

Rawls, J. 1971. *A Theory of Justice.* Cambridge, Mass.: Belknap.

Stabile, D. R. 2000. *Community Associations: The Emergence and Acceptance of a Quiet Innovation in Housing.* Westport, Conn.: Greenwood Press.

Tiebout, C. M. 1956. A Pure Theory of Local Expenditure. *Journal of Political Economy* 64 (October): 416–24.

Tullock, G. 1970. *Private Wants, Public Means.* New York: Basic Books.

———. 1971. Public Decisions as Public Goods. *Journal of Political Economy* 79 (July/August): 913–18.

Winokur, J. L. 1994. Choice, Consent, and Citizenship in Common Interest Communities. In *Common Interest Communities: Private Governments and the Public Interest,* ed. S. E. Barton and C. J. Silverman. Berkeley: Institute of Governmental Studies Press.

13

Privatizing the Neighborhood

A Proposal to Replace Zoning with Private Collective Property Rights to Existing Neighborhoods

Robert H. Nelson

Two researchers recently announced a "quiet revolution in the structure of community organization, local government, land-use control, and neighbor relations" in the United States.[1] They were referring to the spread of homeowners' associations, condominium ownership of property, and other forms of collective private ownership of residential property. In describing these forms of ownership, different commentators have used terms such as "residential community association," "common interest community," "residential private government," "gated community," and others. Whatever term is best—and I will refer to such ownerships as "neighborhood associations" in this chapter, recognizing that some collective ownerships are smaller than the average neighborhood and others are larger—the spread of collective private ownership of residential property is a development of fundamental importance in the history of property rights in the United States.

Indeed, it may yet prove to have as much social significance as the spread of the corporate form of collective ownership of private business property in the second half of the nineteenth century. At that time, a new ease of transportation, economies of scale in mass production, improved management techniques of business coordination, and other business innovations led American industry to operate at a new scale, and corporate ownership proved financially and otherwise advantageous. Thus, although there were few business corporations before the Civil War, by 1900 corporations produced almost two-thirds of U.S. manufacturing output, a figure that reached 95 percent in the 1960s.[2] In 1932, Adolf Berle and Gardiner Means announced the transformation of the basic relationship between private ownership of property in the United States and managerial control over the means of production caused by the rise of corporate ownership.[3]

In the second half of the twentieth century, new economic forces wrought yet another transformation in private property ownership. These forces included: (1) higher densities of development; (2) the desire for precise control over neighborhood character; (3) more economical private provision of common neighborhood services; and (4) greater interest in common recreational and other facilities. They made private neighborhood associations the choice for millions of people for their residential property.[4] If private neighborhoods continue to spread at the pace of recent years, the long-run result may be collective ownership of most private property (residential and business) in the United States. Such a result would be a remarkable transition from the general expectation of individual ownership of property that has long prevailed in American political and economic thought.[5]

To date, almost all neighborhood associations have arisen as part of the development of a new neighborhood. The developer assembles the raw land and builds the neighborhood from its initial stages, including the establishment of the neighborhood association. Purchasers of new housing units must accept membership in the association as part of the original terms of ownership. However, in neighborhoods previously developed with individual ownership of the land and structures, there is little prospect for the formation of a neighborhood association. Forming such an association would require the individual members of the neighborhood to surrender voluntarily part of their individual rights and accept collective control over the use of the exterior parts of their property by their neighbors. Obtaining such voluntary consent from several hundred or more property owners is extremely time consuming and almost certainly would involve major problems with holdouts and other high transactions costs. Few existing neighborhoods have even considered making such an effort.

In this chapter, I propose enactment of legislation to facilitate the establishment of neighborhood associations in existing neighborhoods.[6] The establishment of a new legal mechanism for this purpose would allow existing neighborhoods to take advantage of collective control over the neighborhood's common environment and the private provision of common services, just as new neighborhoods are doing in such large numbers. Moreover, such an approach would facilitate the "deregulation" or "privatization" of zoning. Private neighborhood associations could administer the collective controls over neighborhood quality now exercised through land-use regulations at the municipal level. Compared with a private property-right regime, as described later, the governmental exercise of zoning powers has several major disadvantages.[7]

The Rise of the Neighborhood Association

As of 1998, in the United States there were about 205,000 neighborhood associations, in which almost forty-two million people lived, or about 15 percent of Americans.[8] In the fifty largest metropolitan areas, more than half of new housing is now built in neighborhood associations.[9] In the Los Angeles and San Diego metropolitan areas, this figure exceeds 60 percent.[10] California, Texas, and Florida have the greatest concentrations of neighborhood associations.[11] Other places where neighborhood associations are common include New York, Illinois, and the suburbs of Washington, D.C. In the D.C. area, about one-third of the residents in affluent Montgomery County live in neighborhood associations.[12]

The average neighborhood association serves a population of about two hundred people.[13] In 1990, about 42 percent of the units in neighborhood associations consisted of townhouses.[14] Single-family homes represented 18 percent of the units.[15] Most associations extended beyond individual buildings to include territorial responsibilities of some sort. The typical operating budget of a neighborhood association was $100,000 to $400,000 per year in 1990, but 5 percent of those associations belonging to the Community Associations Institute (CAI) had budgets in excess of $1.5 million per year.[16]

As recently as 1962, there were fewer than five hundred neighborhood associations in the United States.[17] By 1970, this number had risen sharply to ten thousand associations, but they still accounted for only 1 percent of U.S. housing units.[18] As of 1970, the terms of condominium ownership governed 12 percent of existing neighborhood associations.[19] The subsequent rapid spread of condominium ownership, reaching 42 percent of all neighborhood associations by 1990, was a key factor in the growth of collective ownership of American housing.[20]

Types of Ownership

Besides condominium ownership, the other main instrument for collectively owned residential property is the homeowners association in a planned unit development (PUD).[21] In a homeowners association, each person owns his or her residential unit individually, typically including the yard. The homeowners association, which every new homeowner must join, is a separate legal entity that holds title to the streets, parks, neighborhood common buildings, and other "common areas." The association also enforces the neighborhood covenants governing the allowable uses and modifications of individually owned units. In contrast, condominium owners have title to both their own personal units and, as a "tenant in common," a percentage interest in the "common elements."[22] These common elements include things like dividing walls, stairways, hallways, roofs, yards, parks, and other parts of the project outside the individually occupied units.[23]

As of 1998, PUDs accounted for 64 percent of housing units in neighborhood associations, and 31 percent of the units were in condominiums.[24] The other 5 percent were housing units in cooperatives, in which the collective ownership extended to all the land and buildings, including the interiors.[25] Cooperative ownership is most common for individual apartment buildings in New York and a few other large cities.[26] Under cooperative ownership, individual occupants have tenancy agreements with the cooperative that entitle them to the use of their own personal units.

The typical neighborhood association provides a range of services to residents such as garbage collection, street maintenance, snow removal, lawn mowing, gardening, and maintenance of recreational facilities and the common areas of the neighborhood. To cover the costs of these activities, the neighborhood association levies an assessment on each member. A typical fee is approximately $100 to $150 per month.[27] A member of the neighborhood association who fails to pay the assessment is subject to a lien on his or her property.

Neighborhood associations generally enforce covenants written by the developer to maintain the original character of the neighborhood.[28] Neighborhood covenants are typically much more detailed than zoning regulations, controlling not only types of land uses but also matters of aesthetics. Such matters can include the color of the house paint, the placement of trees and shrubbery, the size and location of fences, the construction of decks and other housing extensions, the parking of automobiles in streets and driveways, and the use and placement of television antennae, among other items.[29] In most neighborhood associations, the conditions, covenants, and restrictions (CC&Rs) regulate these matters, and an architectural review committee oversees enforcement. Neighborhood associations of senior citizens often require that at least one of the unit occupants be fifty-five years or older. Restrictions on possession of pets are another means by which associations often assert control over the neighborhood environment.

A board of directors elected by the full membership of the association governs the association.[30] Usually, only property owners may vote. The exclusion of renters from the franchise has resulted in considerable criticism that private neighborhoods are "undemocratic."[31] Nevertheless, renters can still participate in the political life of the neighborhood by coming to board meetings and serving on committees. The assignment of voting shares in neighborhood associations can be done according to a number of formulas, commonly one vote per residential housing unit (thus potentially giving the same person multiple votes if he or she owns more than one unit). Voting rights also may be allocated in proportion to measures (such as unit square feet) of shares of property value.

Private Governments

As Uriel Reichman wrote in an early article noting the rise of neighborhood associations, they "possess much of the power and trappings of local municipal government but arise out of private relationships."[32] Indeed, Reichman chose to describe them as "residential private governments."[33] From this perspective, the rise of neighborhood associations represents the most comprehensive privatization occurring in any sphere of government functioning in the United States today.

Initially the rise of private neighborhoods was not conceived in such broad terms.[34] Collective ownership of neighborhood property emerged as a matter of real-estate practice, designed to meet certain practical needs of land developers.[35] Enforcement of covenants to protect the quality of existing neighborhoods often proved unreliable, because no one entity was responsible for bringing the necessary legal actions. Collective private ownership provided the developer a way of overcoming the free-rider problem.

Collective ownership also allowed developers to provide common recreational and other facilities that new housing owners increasingly demanded. With higher densities of development, such as townhouses, maintenance of yards and other common areas became critical.

Finally, the fiscal crisis of many local governments in the 1970s and 1980s meant that these governments were unwilling to accept new responsibilities for building and maintaining streets, collecting garbage, and providing other services. Providing these services privately, through a neighborhood association, often became a condition of municipal approval for a new neighborhood.[36]

Although primarily economic forces drove the establishment of neighborhood associations, the government took several critical steps to promote their use. In 1961, the Federal Housing Administration (FHA) approved the provision of mortgage insurance for condominiums and in 1963 for residential units included in PUDs with homeowners associations.[37] Between 1961 and 1967, prompted in part by FHA actions, almost every state enacted a model condominium property act, thereby providing a firm legal foundation for condominium ownership.[38] Another key step was the approval in the mid-1970s by the Federal National Mortgage Association (FNMA) and the Federal Home Loan Mortgage Corporation (FHLMC) of purchases of condominiums and PUD-unit loans in the secondary mortgage-loan market.[39] With these steps, the ownership of housing units in neighborhood associations could offer the same forms of government support that had done so much to promote the spread of individual home ownership in the years following World War II.

A Proposal: A Five-Step Process

The volume of new development in neighborhood associations demonstrates their great appeal. Yet the advantages of private neighborhoods remain unavailable for people living in existing neighborhoods with individual ownership of the units. Many of these neighborhoods were built before the emergence of neighborhood associations. Today, even if most residents wanted to form a neighborhood association, the transaction costs of assembling unanimous neighborhood consent voluntarily would be prohibitive. Hence, as a solution, I propose that state governments enact a new legal mechanism, making collective ownership of residential property available to existing neighborhoods.

To offer the advantages of neighborhood associations to existing neighborhoods, state governments should enact a new law to allow self-governance in these neighborhoods, through new collective private ownerships. For purposes of discussion, I propose the following five-step process, recognizing that many variations are possible.

1. A group of individual property owners in an existing neighborhood could petition the state government to form a neighborhood association. The petition should describe: (a) the boundaries of the proposed private neighborhood; (b) the instruments of collective governance intended for it; (c) the services the neighborhood association would perform; and (d) the estimated monthly assessment. The petition should come from owners cumulatively possessing more than 60 percent of the total value of neighborhood property.

2. The state government would then certify that the proposed neighborhood met certain standards of reasonableness, including: (a) a contiguous area; (b) boundaries of a regular shape; (c) an appropriate relationship to major streets, streams, valleys, and other geographic features; and (d) other considerations. The state would also certify that the proposed private-governance instruments of the neighborhood association met state standards.

3. If the application met state requirements, the state would authorize a neighborhood committee to negotiate a service-transfer agreement with the appropriate municipal government. The agreement would specify the possible transfer of ownership of muncipal streets, parks, swimming pools, tennis courts, and other existing public lands and facilities located within the proposed newly private neighborhood (possibly including some compensation to the city). It would also specify the degree to which the neighborhood would assume responsibility for garbage collection, snow removal, policing, and fire protection. Finally, the transfer agreement would specify future tax arrangements, including any property or other tax credits that the members of the new neighborhood association might receive in compensation for assuming existing municipal burdens. Other matters of potential importance to the municipality and the neighborhood also would be addressed. The state government would serve as an overseer and mediator in this negotiation process.

4. Once the state had certified the neighborhood's proposed municipal-transfer agreement, the state would schedule a neighborhood election. The election would occur at least one year after the submission of a complete description of the neighborhood proposal, including the articles of neighborhood incorporation, the municipal-transfer agreement, estimates of assessment burdens, a comprehensive appraisal of individual neighborhood properties, and other relevant information. During the one-year waiting period, the state would supervise a process to inform property owners and residents of the neighborhood of the details of the proposal and to facilitate public discussion and debate.

5. The state would supervise the neighborhood election. Approval of the neighborhood association would require both of the following: (a) an affirmative vote of property owners cumulatively representing 90 percent or more of the total value of the proposed neighborhood; and (b) an affirmative vote by 75 percent or more of the individual unit owners in the neighborhood. If the election met these conditions, all property owners in the neighborhood would be required to join the neighborhood association and would be subject to the full terms and conditions of the neighborhood-association charter. The neighborhood association would have the right to collect assessments to fund its operation from each association member.

Advantages over Zoning

Municipal zoning already serves many of the functions of neighborhood associations.[40] Zoning protects the character of the neighborhood by excluding detrimental uses. Zoning regulates many of the details of housing design, such as the size of the lot, the amount of floor space, the setback from the street, and other such matters. Why, then, go to the trouble of devising a whole new property-right institution for neighborhoods and a new legal regime?

While zoning and neighborhood-association control over neighborhood environmental quality do overlap in a number of key respects, the private neighborhood has several major advantages. For example, except where a historic or other special district can be justified, zoning does not cover the fine details of neighborhood architecture, trees and shrubbery, yard maintenance, and other aesthetic matters that may have a major impact on the character of the neighborhood. Thus, neighborhood associations have a considerably greater degree of authority over actions potentially influencing the character of the neighborhood than zoning typically affords.

In addition, the administration of zoning takes place at the municipal level, where political considerations often include many people who are not residents of the neighborhood. But in matters such as the control of fine details of neighborhood architecture, there is no need or justification for broader municipal involvement. Indeed, under zoning the substantial influence on such matters by outsiders leaves the neighborhood exposed to regulatory actions that it does not want. This lack of secure control over the details of the administration of neighborhood zoning leads to neighborhoods' reluctance to accept more precise and comprehensive zoning controls over aesthetic matters.

Moreover, because zoning is a form of public regulation, the direct sale of zoning is not considered permissible (it would be "bribery"). However, if the exclusion of a use was an ordinary exercise of a private property right, neighborhoods could sell rights of entry (say for a new neighborhood convenience store) into the neighborhood, sell rights to make certain broader changes in land use within the neighborhood, or even sell all the neighborhood property in one package for comprehensive redevelopment. The private neighborhood's ability to put rights of entry into the neighborhood in the market would introduce greater flexibility in metropolitan land markets, significantly improving the efficiency of their operation.

Furthermore, the ability to sell zoning would allow the neighborhood to manage a transition to a different use of the neighborhood. Currently, because an entity outside the neighborhood controls changes in land uses under zoning and because these changes often do not bring financial gains to the neighborhood collectively (and may involve losses for some individuals), the residents of existing neighborhoods typically resist almost all land-use change.[41] Zoning serves many neighborhoods well as a protective instrument for maintaining the existing character of the neighborhood but fails wherever the objective is the transition from one type of use to another. Similarly, as described later in this chapter, the legal mechanism of private-neighborhood ownership could usefully be extended to "neighborhoods" of farmers owning large tracts of vacant land in transitional developing areas on the fringes of metropolitan regions.

Lastly, the advantages of neighborhood associations extend beyond improvements on zoning. Neighborhood associations can serve as vehicles to provide more efficient and effective garbage collection, recreational facility maintenance, and many other common services. Creating a neighborhood association can establish and sustain a strong spirit of community in the neighborhood, not usually found in neighborhoods without a formal institutional status. Private neighborhoods might also encourage residents' involvement in political affairs, both locally and at higher levels of government.

From Zoning to Neighborhood Associations

The proposal to create a new legal regime for the establishment of neighborhood associations in existing neighborhoods is more radical in form than in substance. Indeed, it would, in effect, formalize and extend existing arrangements that evolved under zoning.[42] In an existing neighborhood, the practical consequence of zoning is to provide a de facto collective private property right to the neighborhood environment.[43]

Origins of Zoning

A de facto property right was not the original intent of the founders of zoning. New York City adopted the first zoning ordinance in the United States in 1916.[44] During the 1920s, zoning spread rapidly across the United States.[45] In 1926, in a decision of great historic significance, the Supreme Court upheld the constitutionality of zoning, despite many doubters.[46] The Court accepted the arguments of zoning defenders that it met two essential needs. First, zoning extended and improved on nuisance law in that it provided advance notice that certain types of uses were incompatible with other uses in a particular district. Thus, zoning standardized the ad hoc procedures devised by individual judges ruling in individual nuisance cases. The nuisance justification was particularly important because zoning, like the enforcement of nuisance law, was considered an exercise of the local government's police power.[47]

The second argument for zoning, which also significantly influenced the Supreme Court, was that zoning was a necessary municipal-planning instrument.[48] This argument reflected the general philosophy of the Progressive movement, which believed that scientific management could be applied in all areas of American society and improve the efficiency and effectiveness of American institutions.[49] Applying scientific management methods to the municipal scene would allow comprehensive land-use planning. Thus, instead of the disorderly and haphazard patterns of land development of the past, American cities in the future would be planned according to a rational design. They would work much better economically and be visually more attractive—at least this was the great hope of Progressive municipal planners.[50]

Specifically, as envisioned by proponents, a city-planning staff would study housing, transportation, the job market, and other economic and social trends to project future housing needs. Planners would then allocate housing among parts of the city. Zoning would provide the practical legal instrument to enforce this design. Zoning would require that new housing be located and built according to the city's comprehensive plan.[51]

In practice, however, this grand land-use planning and regulatory scheme proved utopian.[52] Like the high hopes for socialist scientific planning in many fields, it presumed a predictability of economic events and capacity for central scientific understanding and management of human affairs that real planners never realized. Moreover, although Progressive theory prescribed that politicians should concede power to professionals in matters of scientific expertise, such as land use, the politicians had other ideas—especially when the scientific skills of the experts often seemed in doubt, as in city planning.[53] Indeed, as Dennis Coyle comments, "[B]eneath the arcane language and technicalities, disputes about property rights [to land] reveal fundamental clashes between opposing perspectives on the proper society"—matters that could hardly be left to technicians to resolve.[54]

Instead, land development occurred opportunistically, as housing or other facilities were proposed for particular locations.[55] The local municipality then decided whether it wanted that particular development at that particular time in that particular place. In making these decisions, municipalities often found that they could not rely on existing land-use plans to guide them. They had to do a new assessment and make a decision based on some other grounds. Approval of new development was not achieved by verifying consistency with an existing comprehensive plan, as legal theory prescribed. Rather, the municipality typically amended the zoning ordinance, granting specific approval for individual development. The process resembled a business negotiation between the municipality and the developer. The parties made or did not make a deal regarding a particular proposed development project according to the specific benefits to each party.[56]

As a result of these complications, formal plans often gathered dust on shelves while development proceeded through a process of finding projects mutually beneficial to individual builders and individual municipalities. Yet zoning required a comprehensive plan; therefore a new profession of land-use planners continued to turn out numerous costly planning documents. They acted out a fiction that had little bearing on land development but was required by the rituals of the law.[57]

The nuisance justification for zoning was equally a myth. In some cases, zoning did regulate true nuisances, for example, by excluding a noisy factory from a development of single-family homes. Yet far more often, zoning excluded uses that were never in any real sense nuisances. A typical zoning ordinance, for instance, might require that homes be built on lots of one acre or more. Although the neighborhood would prohibit half-acre lots, this exclusion could not be justified by any reasonable understanding of traditional nuisance standards. Zoning was in fact being used to address aesthetic matters and neighborhood environmental attractiveness generally, areas normally outside the scope of nuisance control.

A Property Right to the Neighborhood Environment

Maintaining the character of existing neighborhoods was thus the actual purpose of zoning.[58] A neighborhood of one-acre lots excluded half-acre lots because they were inconsistent with the "ambiance," the "prestige," and the "quality" of the neighborhood. Zoning ensured that only people of sufficient economic means—those able to afford at least a one-acre lot—could enter the neighborhood. In such respects, zoning conferred a collective property right to neighborhoods. If the defining feature of a property right is the power to exclude others, zoning gave neighborhoods precisely this legal ability. Zoning created a collective property right because it gave the entire neighborhood, exercising its political influence over the municipal administrators of zoning, the collective power to exclude unwanted uses.

As with any ordinary property right, an important social consequence of zoning was the segregation of residential neighborhoods according to economic means.[59] Although this kind of wide-ranging protective function for neighborhood quality was never part of the early official legal justifications for zoning, the actual purposes that zoning served were well understood by at least the 1960s.[60] In 1968, the National Commission on Urban Problems observed that "[z]oning . . . very effectively keeps the poor and those with low incomes out of suburban areas by stipulating lot sizes way beyond their economic reach. Many suburbs prohibit or severely limit the construction of apartments, townhouses, or planned unit developments which could accommodate more people in less space at potential savings."[61] The commission also observed that "zoning regulations still do their best job when they deal with the type of situation for which many of them were first intended; when the objective is to protect established character and when that established character is uniformly residential. It is in the 'nice' neighborhoods, where the regulatory job is easiest, that regulations do their best job."[62]

If the practical consequence of zoning was to provide a collective private property right, why not simply provide this property right directly through private means? As noted earlier, this is in fact what has happened since the 1960s, as the creation of neighborhood associations has become standard operating procedure for new development in many parts of the country. A neighborhood association provides privately the same legal authority afforded by zoning, namely, the establishment of detailed control over the use of property as it affects the character of the neighborhood. Because the neighborhood association is explicit about its exclusionary function, it can provide greater administrative discretion and flexibility for the neighborhood than public zoning controls.

Although neighborhood associations were just coming into prominence in the 1960s, the National Commission on Urban Problems recognized the similarity of function and the potential for substitution of private regulatory regimes for existing zoning. Indeed, for existing neighborhoods the commission report in 1968 suggested that:

> Another [reform] approach would be to create forms of land tenure which would recognize the interest of owners in what their neighbors do. Such tenure forms, which do not exist but which might resemble condominium tenure, might more effectively reconcile the conflicting interests of neighboring property owners than do conventional regulations. The objective of such tenure would be to leave the small scale relationships among neighbors for resolution entirely within the private sector, while public regulation would continue to apply to the neighborhood as a whole. In addition to giving neighborhood residents greater control over minor land-use changes within their neighborhood, such tenure could include provision for cooperative maintenance of properties where owners desire their services.[63]

An Exercise in Coercion

The commission did not follow up on this proposal with any specifics for implementation. Although new neighborhoods widely adopted the types of tenure proposed by the commission, few existing neighborhoods followed this course. Older neighborhoods continue to rely on zoning, essentially because the transaction costs of assembling a new land tenure are prohibitive. Zoning never faced this problem because, as a form of government regulation, it could be imposed by fiat.

In existing neighborhoods where zoning was first imposed, government simply used its police-power authority to redistribute coercively property rights in the neighborhood, canceling individual rights and imposing a collective-property-right regime. It was in a sense an exercise in eminent domain: the municipality took certain important rights from the neighborhood residents but then provided compensation by giving the residents other new and valued collective rights. In most cases, the compensation was sufficient as the majority of neighborhood residents considered themselves significantly better off in the end and thus supported the new zoning for the existing neighborhood.[64] Some objectors were inevitable.[65] Under zoning, the preferences of holdouts were simply overridden by government action in accord with the wishes of the majority.

Nothing in American legal and policy traditions justified such a coercive government redistribution of residential private property rights within neighborhoods.[66] The closest analogy might be the urban-renewal programs of the 1950s and 1960s, although in that case the government paid cash to owners of condemned property rather than compensation through an assignment of new rights in the overall project.[67] Given the legal climate of the 1920s, had zoning been described accurately, the Supreme Court might have held it to be unconstitutional. At a minimum, the Court would have required local governments to enact legislation spelling out the true purposes of the rights-assembly process provided by zoning and the way in which new rights were created to compensate for the rights being taken. Instead, zoning operated under the various myths and fictions noted earlier because it would have been politically difficult, if not impossible, to obtain acceptance for zoning if its real workings and purposes had been made explicit.

Thus, in retrospect, the nuisance law and planning justifications for zoning provided the necessary camouflage, as it were, to permit a fundamental land-law innovation that was much more radical than the early advocates of zoning cared to admit.[68] Zoning did nothing less than redistribute neighborhood property rights to create a new de facto private collective right to the neighborhood environment, decades before the collective rights that are more explicitly and formally created today as neighborhood associations spread across the landscape.[69]

Today, of course, zoning is entrenched in many thousands of American neighborhoods. Given this history, it would be a less radical step now to recognize formally the real workings of zoning by acting to privatize its functions in these neighborhoods. In short, the proposal to allow existing neighborhoods to establish neighborhood associations would in many ways formally recognize and improve upon a process that has existed informally for many years. It would be a logical extension of long-standing American zoning practice.[70]

How Property Rights Evolve

Such an evolution of zoning from a de facto collective right to a formal collective property right recognized in the law, moreover, would be consistent with long-standing patterns of property-right evolution.[71]

Except in times of revolutionary turmoil, legislatures seldom create new property rights from whole cloth.[72] Rather, property rights emerge gradually from informal practice, often at odds with the accepted economic and property-right theories of the day. As experience accumulates, however, the informal practice becomes better understood and the merits better appreciated. At a still later point, the informal practice may then gain full acceptance and perhaps codification.[73] The typical role of the legislature, in short, is not to create new rights but to ratify rights that evolve. This process can take decades or even centuries.[74]

For example, early settlers of the American West engaged in widespread illegal occupancy of the land.[75] Although the federal government regarded squatters as lawbreakers, it was without the power to stop their actions on a distant frontier. Eventually, political pressures drove the federal government to confirm the original squatter occupancy as a legal property right. When the Homestead Act passed in 1862, it was not a new idea but a final recognition by the federal government that squatting was a fact of frontier life. Rather than futile and ultimately harmful efforts to prevent it, the better course was accepting and regulating squatter actions, as the Homestead Act did.

Describing the long history of British land law, Sir Frederick Pollock wrote that "[t]he history of our land laws, it cannot be too often repeated, is a history of legal fictions and evasions, with which the Legislature vainly endeavoured to keep pace until their results . . . were perforce acquiesced in as a settled part of the law itself."[76] Although the substantive workings changed dramatically, the outward form of English land tenure varied little from the thirteenth to the nineteenth centuries. As Pollock described the manner of property-right evolution in Britain up to the late nineteenth century:

> [Over this period] the system underwent a series of grave modifications. Grave as these were, however, the main lines of the feudal theory were always ostensibly preserved. And to this day, though the really characteristic incidents of the feudal tenures have disappeared or left only the faintest of traces, the scheme of our land laws can, as to its form, be described only as a modified feudalism.[77]

In the twenty-first century, we like to think that the world is more rational; governments should do what they say they are doing. Whole professions, including the field of American public administration, depend upon the assumption that the true goals of society can be stated directly and realized by a process of rational selection among the alternatives. However, the history of zoning suggests otherwise. Zoning followed the traditional route of property-right development; it was yet another process of land-law making and of the evolution of rights under the guise of various legal myths and fictions that serve to obscure its real purposes.

The Property-Right School of Zoning

As the land law has evolved, there usually have been some people who have foreseen and advocated the later property-right outcome. As the evolving nature of the land laws is better understood and the merits of new ways of doing things better appreciated, their views might even prevail. In the short run, the mainstream has tended to dismiss their arguments as heretical and unacceptable because acceptance of these arguments would endanger the existing property-right regime, an outcome unacceptable to the broader society.

In the 1960s, Richard Babcock, a leading American zoning lawyer, took a dangerous step toward eroding the legitimacy of the system. Babcock provided an accurate depiction of zoning practice in the trenches, showing that there was little connection to the received legal theory.[78] By avoiding radical cures and proposing that the solution to zoning problems instead lay in reviving the original planning principles of zoning, however, Babcock largely preserved his mainstream status.

Instead, it was the members of a new property-right school of zoning who flirted with, if not fully entered into, the realm of zoning heresy.[79] Although the members of this school differ on a number of points, they have in common outright dismissal of the traditional rationales for zoning and instead analyze zoning as a redistribution of property rights with certain social and economic consequences.

Coasian Analysis

Ronald Coase's path-breaking 1960 article, "The Problem of Social Cost," revived scholarly interest in the institutional role of property rights, first among economists and then extending to legal scholars through the law and economics movement.[80] In the article, Coase highlights the notion that adequately defined property rights would obviate the need for government intervention in many perceived social problems. Instead, private negotiation could often resolve these problems.

An "externality," for example, did not necessarily require government regulation, as most economists had long supposed. Rather, a party negatively affected by the external impacts of some action could also stop it by paying for its cessation or modification. Or, if this party already had the legal right to stop the activity, payments could compensate the party for allowing continued activity. In either case, the most economically efficient outcome resulted. The social importance of well-defined property rights was that their clear specification up front might greatly reduce the transaction costs of such efficient bargaining.[81]

Since zoning attempts to deal with the pervasive externalities in the urban land market, the institution of zoning was an obvious candidate for the application of Coasian principles. Among the first to recognize this possibility was Dan Tarlock, who argued in 1972 that "contemporary zoning should be conceptualized as a system of joint ownership between the public entity and the regulated private owner. It is a form of joint ownership in which the owner of the fee [simple ownership] retains possession of the right to manage subject to a veto by a comanager, the public entity."[82] Although Tarlock does not say so directly, such a form of joint ownership is also characteristic of a condominium or other collective private property ownership.

For existing neighborhoods with separately owned properties, Tarlock found that high transaction costs of private actions to protect neighborhood quality often posed an insurmountable obstacle to collective private efforts.[83] Zoning was therefore a second-best choice; lacking a solution to the free-rider problem, government had to "intervene through a zoning ordinance to simulate the result that would have been accomplished had the initial landowners but for high transaction costs been able to impose a covenant scheme on surrounding landowners."[84] Zoning could thus be justified because by itself "private collective action fails to provide sufficient quantities of a desired public good, in this case [neighborhood] amenity levels."[85]

However, Tarlock recognizes a problem: municipalities tended to rigidly administer their new zoning authority. Unlike an ordinary private-property owner, the municipality could not profit monetarily (legally, that is) from the transfer of the zoning rights to someone else. To address this problem and thereby improve the efficiency of land-market operations, Tarlock suggests it would be helpful "if existing [neighborhood] users took some sort of collective action to bind themselves to a bargain such as a voting procedure or the creation of a board to act for them."[86] With this collective organization they could bargain with potential entrants into the neighborhood. As Tarlock elaborates:

> Under the existing zoning system subsequent users who wish to deviate from the surrounding land-use pattern must "buy" their way in through the political process. Majority approval from an appointed commission or elected local legislative body is required. The process, I have argued, is very costly and produces doubtful efficiency gains. Arguably the costs of administering a zoning system would be decreased and efficiency gains more certain if entrants had to bargain directly with surrounding landowners. The function of the government would be to impose an initial covenant scheme and then let the market or a close proxy determine subsequent reallocations of land.[87]

In other words, as Tarlock suggests, the neighborhood should possess the property rights to neighborhood entry, with the option to sell these rights. This approach would open the land market to greater and easier entry for new uses that might be socially desirable. Robert Ellickson developed a related proposal, if in considerably more detail, for the application of Coasian principles to land-use regulation.[88] Nuisance law and zoning, Ellickson observed, ignored important options that might promote a more efficient use of the land.[89] If the courts declared an activity a nuisance, under current law they would simply issue an injunction to halt it or use zoning to keep it out in the first place.

Compensation for Regulatory Changes

A more economically efficient result, however, might be for the objectionable activity to locate where it wished but to pay nearby property owners compensation for any damages. For example, if a high-tech company had a strong incentive to move into a particular neighborhood (perhaps its most valued employees lived there), it might be better to allow the company to negotiate with the neighbors living nearby rather than to issue an absolute prohibition on nuisance or zoning grounds. In effect, following a Coasian scheme, this approach emphasizes property-right negotiation rather than public regulation of a perceived unacceptable harm through nuisance or zoning law.

In 1977 Ellickson extended this analysis to broader aspects of land-use law.[90] He argued that there should be a "normal" standard of zoning restriction defined for undeveloped land in the specific circumstances of each suburban community. If the municipality wanted to impose tighter restrictions on a particular parcel, say to preserve open space, it would have to adequately compensate the landowner for the loss of land value. In effect, establishment of a "normal" standard of development would create a legal criterion that would allow division of the development rights at any given site between the municipality and the landowner. The landowner would possess some "sticks" in the overall bundle of land rights outright, while the municipality shared the remaining development rights. Unlike several others in the property-right school, for fairness and other reasons Ellickson does not propose allowing the municipality to sell its zoning rights for general municipal revenues or other types of broad benefit.[91] Thus, the municipality would not possess the full benefits of ownership of its portion of the development rights. (And in this respect, partly depending on how well "normal" development was defined, there could remain a legal obstacle to the efficient use of the land.)

The basic thrust of the Tarlock and Ellickson arguments is that, in essence, zoning constitutes a redistribution of property rights and that there are significant advantages to more formally recognizing and dealing with it as such. Another law professor, Bernard Siegan, also viewed zoning as a matter of a redistribution of property rights but came to a much different policy conclusion.[92] The nuisance and planning justifications for zoning, he agreed, are patently false. Indeed, in Siegan's view there is no justification—either in legal thought or in social or economic theory—for the coercive redistribution of property rights between municipalities and landowners that zoning accomplishes.[93] The whole scheme is a fraud of sorts.[94] Once municipalities took possession of their new zoning rights, municipal politicians found it impossible to resist the temptation to exercise these rights promiscuously. Zoning ultimately serves the political interests of the most powerful elements of the municipality rather than any public interest. This result is unnecessary. As Siegan contends, and sought to demonstrate by his study of Houston, covenants and other private solutions achieve valid zoning purposes just as well.[95] The solution to all this, as Siegan argues, is straightforward: zoning must be abolished.

In 1977, I made the redistribution of property rights accomplished by zoning in existing neighborhoods still more explicit.[96] On the whole, while the legal profession did not get high marks for intellectual forthrightness or integrity, the scheme seemed to work in such neighborhoods. Creating new collective property rights for neighborhoods had the same beneficial incentive and other effects as any other system of property rights would have in other areas of economic activity. Property rights in neighborhood environmental quality created the necessary incentives to build and maintain high-quality neighborhood environments. Similarly, the private rights to the profits of a business created the necessary incentives to form new businesses; the private rights to the future use of one's personal property created the incentive to purchase and then maintain this property.

In undeveloped areas, however, I argued that the policy considerations relating to zoning were fundamentally different than in existing neighborhoods.[97] On farms and other vacant land on metropolitan fringes—land facing the prospect of new housing development—zoning effectively redistributed the property rights from the original landowners to others in the municipality. Recent entrants, arriving at higher densities of housing development and with the voting strength to take political control in the municipality, typically benefited from this redistribution. In existing neighborhoods zoning met a key test, as described by Richard Epstein, of an acceptable government regulation.[98] Although the existing neighborhood residents lost some rights, they gained sufficient other rights in return that, in most cases, they were adequately compensated. In an undeveloped area, however, farmers or other original landowners lost the development rights but did not receive any significant rights or other compensation in return. In effect, zoning resulted in an outright confiscation of development rights by the municipal government.

Buying and Selling Zoning

One solution, following Siegan, would be to abolish zoning for undeveloped land as an unconstitutional taking of private property. However, given the great political uproar that would follow any such step and the inevitable hesitation of the courts to provoke such intense public anger, I suggest what might be a politically more promising possibility.[99] Municipalities should be allowed to sell zoning directly. This approach recognizes the urgent social need to make more land-development rights available in the market and the fact that the municipalities effectively possess these rights.

The sale of zoning might be ethically questionable because it would reward municipalities for an unjustified initial confiscation of property rights. Nevertheless, in many cases the courts' failure to put any real limits on government zoning actions occurred decades ago; the resulting taking is an accomplished fact of life. There may be no way to compensate the original losers; subsequent purchasers of the land did not suffer any loss, because they had paid a lower price, reflecting the restricted development rights that went with the land. Indeed, giving later purchasers new development rights would bestow an unexpected windfall on this group.

Professor of economics William Fischel, in a series of writings beginning in 1978, focused his attention on the problem of zoning undeveloped land.[100] Like others in the property-right school, Fischel argued that zoning transferred key development rights from owners of vacant land to the municipality. In his view, the problem was that the justifications for zoning also made the municipal sale of zoning difficult or impossible. Governments are not supposed to sell relief from their regulations; that would be regarded as bribery.[101]

In practice, municipalities routinely sold zoning.[102] One commentator said in the mid-1960s that by the very nature of its workings, zoning posed an almost irresistible "invitation to bribery."[103] In 1966, observing the widespread corruption in zoning decisions, Marion Clawson proposed that it would be simpler and better to dispense with the fictions and to have "open, competitive sale of zoning and zoning classifications."[104] In essence, Clawson was saying, "Let's call it a property right and put it back into the marketplace like any other property right." In 1979, Fischel made a similar proposal, suggesting adoption of a new system in which "any existing zoning restriction may be sold by the community."[105] The payments received "should be made to the general municipal treasury, to be dispersed as decided upon by community rules."[106]

Zoning under Attack

By the early 1980s, the critique of zoning as developed by the property-right school achieved wider recognition. New influential articles portrayed zoning as a redistribution of property rights with perhaps some practical benefits but also many harmful consequences. A succession of law-journal articles appeared with titles such as "Abolish Zoning"; "California's Land Planning Requirements: The Case for Deregulation"; "Deregulating Land Use: An Alternative Free Enterprise Development System"; "Brandeis Brief for Decontrol of Land Use: A Plea for Constitutional Reform"; and "Local Land Use Controls: An Idea Whose Time Has Passed."[107] By 1983, Douglas Porter asked, "Who likes zoning? Hardly anyone, if you listen to recent criticisms of zoning standards, zoning procedures, and the whole zoning concept. Bemoaning zoning seems to be a major sport these days."[108]

The critics' common theme was that the hopes for expert management of urban land use through comprehensive land planning had failed. Critics argued that a narrow group captured zoning benefits; that zoning restrictions kept valuable suburban land bottled up in less productive uses; and that, in general, the broader public interest in a fair and efficient land market suffered as a result.[109] The biggest beneficiaries were the groups already well off in American society, while the losers were those whose income level precluded them from finding good land at acceptable prices for homes. Lower- and moderate-income groups remained clustered in older housing in existing cities, the only places that they could afford.

The *Report of the President's Commission on Housing* in 1982 carried these arguments from the law journals to the public policy arena. The commission found that "[e]xcessive restrictions on housing production have driven up the price of housing generally," creating concern for "the plight of millions of Americans of average and lesser income who cannot now afford homes or apartments."[110] To redress this unacceptable outcome, the commission offered recommendations for a detailed "program of land use deregulation."[111]

1980s Trends

The old zoning warrior and practitioner, Richard Babcock, regarded these attacks on zoning as the lamentations of yet another group of academics removed from the real world. Babcock declared that whatever the legal and economic scholars were saying, "people love zoning" and that therefore it is "alive and well . . . in every urban and suburban neighborhood" and would remain so for a long time to come.[112] Zoning was going its merry way, independent of all the scholarly fussing and fuming.[113] Rather than theorizing about an end to zoning, Babcock characteristically thought it more important to see what was really happening on the ground. Here, he discerned two basic trends in the 1980s in zoning practice. One was an increasing insistence by municipalities that they be compensated for zoning changes.[114] As Babcock wrote:

> Governments simply are not playing the game unless they demand exactions. In one of the last cases in which I was involved, a city asked the developer of a particular project to build a $750,000 swimming pool—on the other side of town from the project. What did the developer do? After figuring out the cost of litigation, the time it would take, and the interest on the construction loan he was

paying the bank, he agreed to build the swimming pool—even
though it had nothing to do with his development.[115]

In Washington, D.C., the Department of Housing and Community
Development wanted its compensation in cash, rather than an in-kind
payment like a swimming pool. For example, in 1987 the *Washington
Post* reported that the Hadid Development Company proposed building a large office building near the D.C. Convention Center. In
exchange for development permission, Hadid offered to donate $1.4
million to a general-purpose low-income housing fund, but the D.C.
government wanted $4.6 million. The *Post* reported that "the zoning
commission sent the entire Hadid case to the housing agency to determine if the cash offer was appropriate."[116]

The second important trend Babcock noted was the rise of "special
districts" by municipalities. Cities exercised tighter control over new
development in these districts. They also often imposed detailed
requirements for development permission. For instance, New York
City effectively required that new office towers and hotel buildings provide a Broadway theater on the lower floors in the Times Square special
district.[117]

As usual, Babcock was an accurate and insightful reporter on
recent zoning practices. However, his analysis in some ways misses the
forest for the trees. The key fact that Babcock fails to note is that these
trends are consistent with the predictions and recommendations of the
property-right school of zoning. By 1990, Babcock observed that the
"bargaining for zoning—the let's make a deal mentality—became the
common denominator of zoning in the 1980s. . . . Cynical observers
suggested that the system of bargains and exactions was little more
than 'zoning for sale.'"[118]

In other words, the earlier recommendations of Tarlock, Fischel,
and others that municipalities sell zoning were in a real sense being followed; cities and suburban municipalities alike routinely marketed zoning and other regulatory permissions. Marketable zoning also had the
predicted salutory effect of opening up space for socially desirable new
uses of land. Ironically perhaps this marketing reduced the pressures
for more direct zoning reforms. But true to the history of land-law evolution, this shift took place in indirect and informal ways, often at odds
with the received theory of zoning. Babcock, for example, rather than
welcoming it as a necessary corrective to fundamental problems in the
basic workings of zoning, expressed his dismay and disgust with the
widespread, thinly disguised sale of zoning. His criticisms notwith-

standing, Babcock offered no practical proposal of his own to open up more land for development.[119]

A similar observation applies to special zoning districts.[120] Special districts were most common in larger cities. One effect of the special district was to shift the focus of zoning administration from the municipal to the neighborhood level. Rather than citywide administration of zoning, each neighborhood had its own special zoning arrangements. Indeed, special districts often had much more detailed rules than ordinary zoning districts, covering matters of architectural style and other aesthetic concerns. When combined with a "business improvement district," special districts can assess property owners within the district for security, street cleanup, and other district services.[121] In short, the new special district was virtually a private neighborhood association, except that it was created in an existing city neighborhood rather than by the developer of a brand-new neighborhood in the suburbs. Special districts also often actively entered into the ongoing bargaining processes for zoning sales as districts granted development permission in return for other general benefits provided by the developer.

The Origins of Private Neighborhoods

On the whole, the members of the property-right school tended to focus on the need to recognize zoning as a basic new property-right institution and on the importance of allowing the freedom to buy and sell newly created rights in the market. There has been much less attention among the members of this school to the need to develop intermediate institutions such as the neighborhood association as a means of facilitating such market transactions.[122] Zoning theorists also pay less attention to the nonzoning benefits of private neighborhoods, such as the provision of neighborhood services or the encouragement of a stronger sense of neighborhood identity and community spirit.[123]

Yet there is a rich history here. While the explosion of neighborhood associations occurred after the 1960s, neighborhood associations have been around in the United States since the nineteenth century, although used on only a limited scale.

Early Neighborhood Associations

The first neighborhood association in the United States was formed in 1831 to supervise the use of Gramercy Park in New York City.[124] A land developer, Samuel Ruggles, set aside and fenced in a common area for the mutual enjoyment of sixty-six surrounding residential-lot owners. Ruggles then deeded over ownership of the central area to trustees, with the lot owners collectively as the beneficiaries. The first true homeowners association was established to provide for the upkeep of Louisburg Square in Boston. Built in 1826, the development included a central common area, but there was no special provision for its maintenance. In 1844, the twenty-eight nearby lot owners signed a mutual agreement establishing the Committee of the Proprietors of Louisburg Square, binding themselves and their successors to care for the park. This agreement was a rare instance in which a neighborhood association formed after the fact of development in individual home ownership.

Beginning in the 1890s, housing developers in the United States began building an increasing number of large planned private communities. To protect the character of the community environment, developers included extensive private covenants in the deeds binding both initial purchasers and subsequent owners. Enforcement in many cases depended on some individual pursuing the necessary legal actions. Since enforcement was uncertain, dependent on a volunteer willing to shoulder the costs, developers conceived the idea of a mandatory association to enforce the covenants and provide certain other common services. In 1914, a leading American community builder, James Nichols, established the first such association at the Mission Hills development near Kansas City, Missouri.[125]

By the 1920s, similar land-development projects had spread across the United States. The famous new town of Radburn, in New Jersey, designed in the 1920s by Progressive reformers seeking to demonstrate the advantages of comprehensive social and physical planning, included an association that enforced an extensive set of covenants.[126] The growing use of covenants and homeowner associations was, interestingly enough, almost coincident with the rapid spread of zoning. Both new property-right institutions met similar needs, but as noted earlier, in most cases only zoning was feasible in existing neighborhoods of individually owned homes. Where collective property rights could be established before the fact, it was possible to maintain a much tighter degree of control over neighborhood quality, as well as to employ the neighborhood association for various other common purposes. Another factor motivating the use of covenants was that the Supreme Court declared racial zoning unconstitutional in 1917, whereas it did not declare racially exclusive private covenants unconstitutional until 1948.[127] A formal policy of racial segregation was an unfortunate feature of many large housing developments in both the North and South in the period between the wars.

Following World War II, individual home ownership soared in the United States. The Urban Land Institute (formed in 1936) and other builder organizations promoted the mandatory homeowner association to take care of parks, tennis courts, and other common property in large developments.[128] Many developers employed this device although, as noted earlier, it is estimated that fewer than five hundred neighborhood associations existed in the United States in 1962.[129] By 1973, the creation in that year of the Community Associations Institute (CAI) reflected the fact that neighborhood associations were now a routine part of the American land-development process.[130]

Theorizing about Private Neighborhoods

Neighborhood associations were largely the response of land developers to practical real-estate needs. However, although their work received little public attention and had little impact on real-world events, a few theorists wrote about private neighborhoods as early as the 1930s.[131] In a recent book, Fred E. Foldvary provides a useful survey of this early literature, introducing some of this insightful body of writings to a wider audience.[132]

Privatization of Local Governance

In 1936, Spencer Heath proposed substituting private neighborhoods for local governments.[133] Heath's concept was that "the proprietary department eventually will take on and exercise its full administrative functions over all the public services."[134] Private proprietors would provide services to neighborhood residents (including enforcement of land-use restrictions), charge land rent for the services, and keep any residual as the profit for their entrepreneurial role. Heath used the hotel as a model. The hotel represented "an organized community with such services in common as policing, water, drainage, heat, light and power, communications and transportation, even education facilities such as libraries, musical and literary entertainment, swimming pools, garden and golf courses, with courteous service by the community officers and employees."[135] In the future, whole neighborhoods of many homes and other types of properties, Heath suggested, should be organized and managed on the model of the private hotel.

Heath's grandson, Spencer Heath MacCallum, took up the cause. MacCallum observed in a 1965 article that a new species of private property had emerged in the United States after World War II.[136] The private shopping center, for example, built and operated by private entrepreneurs, was supplanting the strip highway development of the past. Other new forms of land development included industrial parks, professional and research centers, marinas, mobile-home parks, medical centers, and many types of multifunctional building complexes. In these new forms of property, one found "all of the functional requirements of municipalities."[137] Indeed, MacCallum argued that "there are no longer any political functions being performed at the muncipal level and upward in our society that differ substantially from those that we can observe being performed on a smaller scale entirely within the context of normal property relations."[138]

In 1970, MacCallum observed further that in private ownerships "the manner of the relationship of each toward the others is specified in the terms of the individual contracts, the sum of which at any time is the social charter or constitution of the community."[139] Hence, constitutions were not limited to nations, states, or other sovereign entities. A private organization, like a neighborhood association, could have a constitution of sorts as well, setting well-defined and difficult-to-change rules governing future relations among those who lived within its boundaries.[140]

Municipal governments also had charters or other founding documents that represented yet another constitutional form. However, private territorial associations had an advantage in that their private status offered flexibility in constitutional design typically denied to public bodies. For example, as required by the Supreme Court, the rule of one person–one vote applied necessarily to a public entity, but private associations could experiment freely in this regard.[141] Private associations could engage in various profit-making activities generally considered inappropriate for a municipal agency. They might, for example, operate a drug store, bank, or insurance office. As mentioned earlier, they might also decide to enter the business of selling entry into a neighborhood, while a municipality could not similarly sell the zoning (or at least could not do so legally, in a manner that could be formally authorized by its constitution).

Another advantage of the private neighborhood association is its greater insulation from unilateral governmental alteration of the initial constitutional terms. For example, if the government attempted to regulate a private association, such regulation might be declared a taking of private property, requiring that the state either desist or pay compensation for its impositions on the neighborhood. Certainly, new judicial decisions and legislation can override the provisions of a neighborhood association's founding documents, such as a new law banning age or handicapped discrimination in any private actions, including those of a neighborhood association. However, municipal governments are the creatures of state governments, and the full terms of their municipal founding documents are potentially subject to state revision. The security of municipal constitutional forms, thus, may be less than that of private associations.

The private developers of new neighborhoods, MacCallum observes, seek "to optimize the total environment of each site within a system of sites to maximize the combined rents they will command."[142] MacCallum notes that in shopping centers and other large business properties, the ownership is typically retained by the developer, who then rents out space to the business tenants. In residential private neighborhoods, however, ownership typically transfers directly to the residents themselves through collective-ownership vehicles such as a condominium or a homeowners association. MacCallum, who strongly favors the shopping-center model of a single private owner renting to individual tenants, attributes the prevalence of individual resident ownership of one's own unit to the greater federal tax advantages afforded by owning a residence, as compared with renting.[143] Foldvary suggests that the scarcity of rental arrangements may be due as well to the "economic and cultural values of living in a democratically run community."[144] There may also be significant psychological benefits to owning property.[145]

Another possible explanation is that the "principal-agent" problem may take a different form in business and residential common properties. Many tenants of shopping centers typically have time horizons of five years or less, while purchasers of homes and other residential units commonly plan to stay for twenty years or more. It may be easier to move out of a shopping center that proves to have incompetent management than to leave a residential community. The determinants of neighborhood quality may involve greater elements of subjective judgment in the case of residential property, thus making it more difficult to specify in a contract the standards of quality to be maintained over a long period of time. As a result, residents of neighborhoods may prefer to take collective ownership of their own neighborhood, while control of business "neighborhoods," like shopping centers, is left more easily in the hands of the developer under a rental agreement with the tenants.

Drawing on the writings of Heath, MacCallum, and others, Fold-vary proposes that the advantages of private neighborhoods are so great that the place of municipal governments in American life should be greatly circumscribed. As Foldvary explains:

> To sum up, the theory of contractual community thus has these elements. The private ownership of space permits the collection of the rents generated by the civic services which induce the rents. Communities such as hotels, shopping centers, industrial parks and estates, and ships are examples of the [private] proprietary provision of civic goods. Residential community associations are another form of contractual governance, many of which implement Ebenezer Howard's conception of city services financed by site leases. Their constitutions are typically provided for by the developers, enhancing the value of the property with constraints against future exploitation by the association governance. Civic entrepreneurs also foster community spirit, sympathy with the community, which enables non-excludable civic goods to be produced in addition to funding by rental assessments. Finally, a theory of public goods needs to recognize that society is always in community, and that the realistic choice in the provision of civic goods is not market versus governance, but whether the governance that provides the goods is imposed or voluntary.[146]

The Liebmann Concept

Another recent advocate of private neighborhoods is George Liebmann, who in a 1993 article calls for substantial "devolution of power to [private] community and block associations."[147] Private associations, he argued, could assume a much greater role in functions such as day care, traffic regulation, zoning adjustments, schooling, and law enforcement. Liebmann proposes that state governments enact enabling legislation to allow existing neighborhoods to form a neighborhood association. In order to establish a new association, he suggests a requirement that two-thirds of the neighborhood residents approve it.[148]

Neighborhood associations would have the authority to provide services in the neighborhood and would have much greater flexibility than existing zoning in administering controls over the entry of new uses into the neighborhood. Specific responsibilities suggested by Liebmann for neighborhood associations include, among others:

1. Operating or permitting the operation of family day care centers;
2. Operating or permitting the operation of convenience stores of not more than one thousand square feet in area, whose signage is not visible from a public road;
3. Permitting the creation of accessory apartments where a principal residence continues to be owner occupied;
4. Cooperatively acquiring building materials and services for the benefit of its members;
5. Partially closing roads and streets, imposing right-of-way regulations, and enhancing safety barriers, except where local government finds that the closure, regulation, or obstruction interferes with a street necessary to through traffic;
6. Petitioning local government for imposition of a juvenile curfew on association property;
7. Contracting with local government to assume responsibility for street paving, trash collection, street lighting, snow removal, and other services;
8. Acquiring from local government contiguous or nearby public lands;
9. Petitioning local government for realignment of election-precinct and voting-district boundaries to conform to association boundaries;
10. Maintaining an unarmed security force and appropriate communications facilities;
11. Issuing newsletters, which may contain paid advertising; and
12. Operating a credit union, to the extent otherwise permissible under state or federal law.[149]

The flexibility of the neighborhood association, as seen by Liebmann, would thus promote a happier blend of functions traditionally divided artificially into public and private domains.

Cities as Private Businesses

If municipal governments are today constitutionally restricted, in comparison to private neighborhood associations, an alternative reform would be to loosen the restrictions on the municipality. Indeed, in a 1980 article, Gerald Frug demonstrates that the constricted range of current municipal functions is an historical artifact of the past 150 years.[150] As Frug observes, "before the nineteenth century, there was no distinction in England or America between public and private corporations, between businesses and cities."[151]

By the late nineteenth century, however, leading economic and legal theorists came to see the neighborhood and the city as parochial entities that presented an obstacle to the political and economic rationalization of society.[152] As a result, there was a concerted "attack on city power" that was "but an example of the more general liberal hostility towards all entities intermediate between the state and the individual, and thus all forms of decentralized power."[153] Instead, as the new professional classes in the social sciences and other expert fields saw matters, power should be concentrated in the marketplace, on the one hand, and in government at the national level, on the other hand. The market worked to advance national (and even international) economic efficiency; if automobiles could be manufactured more cheaply in Detroit than in other places, then the workings of markets meant that Detroit would supply the automotive needs of the whole nation. Similarly, as Frug wrote, at the national level "a rational, bureaucratic government of experts" would be entrusted with "wielding power in the public interest" for the benefit of the entire United States.[154]

Frug believes that the Progressive era claims of scientific rationality and management that justified the subsequent centralization of governing authority are no longer credible. Governing is about choices of values at least as much as about expert decisions, and these choices can only be made through the political process, preferably at the local level.[155] The current need, therefore, is for "a genuine transfer of power to the decentralized units" of American society.[156] In this category, Frug mentions regions, cities, and neighborhoods. Yet such a transfer would be no small task, because "real decentralization requires rethinking and, ultimately, restructuring American society itself," including putting an end to "the current powerlessness" of American neighborhoods and cities.[157] The objective should be to create a new "ability of a group of people, working together, to control actively the basic social decisions that affect their lives."[158]

Frug says that this shift would require, as one element, "recognizing the rights of the city [and neighborhood] as an exercise of freedom of association."[159] It would involve a turn back to an earlier era when cities acted as corporations and "there was no difference between a corporation's property rights and its rights of group self-government."[160] Under the old model, Frug comments, the city (or neighborhood) could be "an association promoted by a powerful sense of community and an identification with the defense of property."[161] Regrettably, neighborhoods and cities today have "lost the elements of association and economic strength that formerly enabled them to have an important part to play in the development of Western society."[162]

Business corporations and cities represent alternative forms of decentralized association of people. Corporations are based on people coming together for the purposes of economic production; cities are based on a territorial kind of association. Frug suggests that the present private status of business gives it a large and unfair advantage in meeting the needs for communal association of Americans. To help equalize the competition, he proposes authorizing cities to operate their own private banks, credit unions, insurance companies, and retail food outlets, among other business possibilities. The city must have powers more like those of a private business corporation because territorial association presents a fertile ground for reinjecting into American life the elements of community lost in the headlong rush to modernization and economic rationalization:

> A territorial association . . . can readily include every individual in the geographic area, thereby presenting the greatest opportunity for widespread participation in its decisions. Because of this inclusiveness, it can further a broad range of possibilities for human association. It can also further stable expectations, since once formed, it cannot simply pack up its economic assets and leave town. On the other hand, a territorial association seems to present a visible threat to its participating members. Once a decision is made, members must choose to accept the decision, leave the association, or face the consequences of being dissenters. Being tied to a geographic area is in this sense a restriction of freedom.[163]

Privatization by Neighborhood Association

It is remarkable that, writing in 1980, Frug did not comment on the obvious parallels between his proposal for enhanced power for neighborhoods and cities and the rise of private collective ownership of property. It was Robert Ellickson, responding in part to Frug's article, who made the connection. In 1982, Ellickson commented that "the private homeowner association . . . not the business corporation, is the obvious private alternative to the [public] city."[164]

Ellickson observes that the judiciary tended to treat municipalities and homeowners associations differently, sometimes to the advantage of the former and sometimes the latter. This different treatment reflected a view in the public mind that a definite distinction could be made between "public" and "private," a distinction that Frug rejects. Also finding this distinction tenuous, Ellickson suggests that perhaps the absence or presence of "involuntary members" could serve as an adequate basis of distinction. Ellickson suggests that membership in a homeowners association is entirely voluntary, therefore making this a private activity and justifying a freedom from many constitutional restrictions normally applied to governmental activities. However, cities contain at least some residents whose presence is involuntary, thus making them public entities.[165]

On reflection, however, this distinction may be difficult to sustain. The initial move into a small municipality seems just as voluntary as the initial move into a homeowners association. Thus, at some point, everyone (or at least their parents or some other ancestor) voluntarily chose to live in the municipality. It is true that among the members of a neighborhood association, most are likely to have entered more recently, thus making their grant of consent to its founding documents seem more clear. However, this greater element of voluntariness is a product of the relative youthfulness of the average neighborhood association and does not provide a long-run basis for making any fundamental distinctions between the two forms of territorial association.

Rather, as suggested earlier, perhaps the best explanation for the difference between "public" and "private" is that these terms today create different legal and cultural expectations with respect to the permissible elements of a local constitution and the allowable procedures for a constitutional amendment.[166] Indeed, as Ellickson points out, the original governing documents of a private neighborhood association "are a true social contract" amounting to "a private 'constitution.'"[167] Ellickson also observes that private governments have a range of constitional options open to them in structuring democratic rules for decision-making, while cities are bound by the one person–one vote rulings of the Supreme Court. In a surprising twist, agreeing with Frug's basic viewpoint that cities are unduly restricted, Ellickson proposes that the constitutional possibilities for cities might be expanded by means of a new Supreme Court decision that would "overrule *Avery* (and related decisions) to eliminate the current federal constitutional requirement that local elections be conducted on a one-resident/one-vote basis."[168] Municipalities might then be free to adopt, for example, "some system that weighted votes by acreage or property value," as was the case in local elections in the early history of the United States.[169]

The exchange between Frug and Ellickson shows that the current concepts of the private neighborhood association and the small local municipality are the product of one time and place in American history and culture. At least for the purposes of discussion, there is room for exploring many new constitutional options for both types of institutions. Frug himself advocates steps to "privatize" local government, not by turning to private neighborhoods, as suggested in this chapter, but by rethinking the basic concept of the municipality to make it comparable in property status to the private business corporation.[170] Although they do so in different ways, what is most important and interesting in the exchange between Frug and Ellickson is that both, representing two very different outlooks on the law, come to a similar conclusion: that local government in the United States, presumably including its land-use regulatory functions, should have a more "private" activity status.[171]

A Monster Let Loose?

By some estimates, neighborhood associations will house more than fifty million Americans, or about 20 percent of the population, by the year 2002.[172] This remaking of the face of property ownership in suburban America occurred in a few decades without much critical scrutiny. Academic researchers and theorists recognized this trend only slowly; in the beginning, they had almost no role in initiating these property-right developments.

Eventually, however, this was bound to change. A key event was a conference in 1988 sponsored by the Advisory Commission on Intergovernmental Relations (ACIR) entitled "Residential Community Associations: Private Governments in the Intergovernmental System?" The subsequent ACIR report stated that "traditionally the intergovernmental system has been thought to include the national government, state governments, and local governments of all kinds."[173] Such thinking now had to be modified to recognize that "the concept of intergovernmental relations should be adapted to contemporary developments so as to take account of territorial community associations that display many, if not all, of the characteristics of traditional local government."[174] Given the explosive growth of such associations, by which "private organizations substitute for local government service provision," it would be important to devote much greater critical attention to this new social phenomenon.[175]

Perhaps encouraged by the ACIR and the ever-increasing number of Americans living in neighborhood associations, the literature on private neighborhoods is now growing rapidly.[176] On the whole, the more recent writings tend to have a less sympathetic outlook than earlier commentators. Indeed, some of the newer commentators are harsh critics, going so far as to suggest the unleashing of a new private monster in the land.[177] Although they recognize the great political obstacles at this point, rather than expand the realm of private neighborhoods further, some critics even suggest that it might be desirable to curtail sharply, or even conceivably eliminate, the role of the private neighborhood association in the land-use scene.[178]

Evan McKenzie, for one, rues the "astonishing nationwide growth" in neighborhood associations.[179] One consequence of the growth is that those who are wealthy enough to afford a private neighborhood and government will become "increasingly segregated from the rest of society."[180] Even the people who live in these private neighborhoods may become disenchanted.[181] For Americans used to democratic procedures, private associations are "illiberal and undemocratic."[182] For example, they disenfranchise renters, putting all the political power in the hands of the property owners. McKenzie argues that the proponents of private neighborhoods are the captives of a "utopian faith." Like the advocates of other utopian communal movements, they believe that "the route to community is through joint ownership of private property by an exclusive group living according to its own rules."[183]

McKenzie quotes approvingly the characterization of Robert Reich, former Secretary of Labor, that neighborhood associations represent the "secession of the successful" from society.[184] Reich contends that:

> condominiums and the omnipresent residential communities dun their members to undertake work that financially strapped local governments can no longer afford to do well—maintaining roads, mending sidewalks, pruning trees, repairing street lights, cleaning swimming pools, paying for lifeguards, and, notably, hiring security guards to protect life and property. (The number of private security guards in the United States now exceeds the number of public police officers.)[185]

Among a certain circle of American intellectuals, the private neighborhood association represents the epitome of a long-lamented, indeed potentially disastrous, trend—the balkanization of American life attendant to the suburbanization of the nation.[186] One critic writes that "the suburb is the last word in privatization, perhaps even its lethal consummation, and it spells the end of authentic civic life."[187] More moderately, political commentator William Schneider observes that "[t]o move to the suburbs is to express a preference for the private over the public. . . . Suburbanites' preference for the private applies to government as well."[188]

For many critics, the ultimate symbol of the private neighborhood is the gated community. According to some estimates there are now thirty thousand gated communities in the United States with nearly four million residents.[189] As many as one million Californians are believed to be living in what Edward Blakely and Mary Snyder characterize as "walled security compounds."[190] In a report for the Lincoln Institute of Land Policy, Blakely and Snyder see all this in dire terms:

> The forting up phenomenon also has enormous policy consequences. By allowing some citizens to internalize and to exclude others from sharing in their economic privilege, it aims directly at the conceptual base of community and citizenship in America. The old notions of community mobility are torn apart by these changes in commmunity patterns. What is the measure of nationhood when the divisions between neighborhoods require armed patrols and electric fencing to keep out other citizens? When public services and even local government are privatized, when the community of responsibility stops at the subdivision gates, what happens to the function and the very idea of democracy? In short, can this nation fulfill its social contract in the absence of social contact?[191]

It was inevitable, given the rapidly increasing social importance of private neighborhoods, that a public debate would arise concerning their social consequences. Thus far, however, it has been a more heated than insightful discussion. The critics often make points that apply to any system of private property rights.[192] As long ago as Plato, private property was condemned as socially divisive and an encouragement to base motives of self-interest. It is no great contribution to public discussion to repackage these utopian themes for a new form of contemporary private property.

Neighborhood Associations in Inner-City Areas

The criticisms of private neighborhoods, although now heard with growing frequency, may have matters almost exactly backward. The real inequality may not be in the social divisions resulting from economically and socially segregated patterns of living in the suburbs. The fact that so many people, including people with many options, choose this style of private living is strong evidence that it has much to offer. Rather, the greatest inequality may be in the denial of a similar private opportunity to people in the inner city. Many inner-city residents would like to exclude criminals, hoodlums, drug dealers, truants, and others who often undermine the possibilities for a peaceful and vital neighborhood existence there.[193]

Politically, rather than join the suburbs, civil-rights groups and other organized supporters of inner-city residents often seek to undermine suburban powers of exclusion.[194] A wiser approach, could they overcome their ideological straitjackets, might be to bring suburban powers of exclusion—the rights of private property, if now in a collective form—into the inner city. This strategic redirection would require strong inner-city neighborhoods, free from the meddling of city hall and able to choose who will live in and who will be excluded from the neighborhood. Inner-city private neighborhoods could then exercise authority over their own police, garbage, street cleaning, snow removal, recreational facilities, and other services. They could have the ability to enforce aesthetic controls over the uses of and alterations in neighborhood properties, thus ensuring the maintenance of an attractive exterior environmental appearance.[195] In short, what inner-city neighborhoods really need is some form of private neighborhood association.

The single greatest problem for many neighborhoods in the inner city is the general lack of personal security for residents. Few things would do more to improve the overall quality of inner-city life than a significant reduction in crime. Urban scholar John Dilulio has recently argued that declining crime rates in the United States in part reflect the spread of private neighborhoods in the suburbs. As he puts it, "potential victims are making it more difficult for criminals to prey on them," partly by moving into a "common interest development." Private neighborhoods "virtually guarantee . . . greater safety from crime: No criminals need apply, strangers are stopped before entering, and troublemakers are easily evicted."[196]

There is no physical or other practical reason why an inner-city neighborhood could not become a gated neighborhood.[197] The potential benefits to the residents in reduced crime and general control over the character of the neighborhood environment are significant. That there are almost no such neighborhoods in inner cities shows that ideas do matter; too many people are appalled at the idea of dividing the city into a web of walled neighborhoods.[198] Yet it is the poor who pay a great price in the name of preserving an abstract ideal of an America undivided by racial, class, or other lines. The rich in the suburbs, given wider choices, refuse to make a similar sacrifice.

Hence, the proposed procedures described earlier for the creation of neighborhood associations should be available in inner cities as well. Indeed, this may be their most important application. Inner-city neighborhoods should have the right to establish land-use and other controls, including building neighborhood walls, if necessary, to maintain neighborhood quality. Just as businesses have been creating "business improvement districts" (BIDs) to improve the surrounding environment in cities across the United States, the residents of cities should be able to create what might be called "residential improvement districts" (RIDs).[199]

One American city has such a policy on a limited scale. Since the nineteenth century, St. Louis has allowed the privatization of municipal residential streets, an authority that remains in force.[200] In the past, a number of St. Louis neighborhoods have used this authority to take over ownership of their streets, including closing off streets to traffic and creating a neighborhood association to manage the street area. According to community planner Oscar Newman, the "residents claim that the physical closure of streets and their legal association together act to create social cohesion, stability and security."[201] Newman summarizes the findings from his study of this St. Louis experiment as follows:

> For many students of the dilemma of American cities, the decline of St. Louis, Missouri, has come to epitomize the impotence of federal, state, and local resources in coping with the consequences of large-scale population change. Yet buried within those very areas of St. Louis which have been experiencing the most rapid turnover of population are a series of streets where residents have adopted a program to stabilize their communities, to deter crime, and to guarantee the necessities of a middle-class lifestyle. These residents have been able to create and maintain for themselves what their city was no longer able to provide: low crime rates, stable property values, and a sense of community. Even though the areas surrounding them are experiencing significant socio-economic change, high crime rates, physical deterioration, and abandonment, these streets are still characterized by middle-class ownership—both black and white. The distinguishing characteristic of these streets is that they have been deeded back from the city to the residents and are now legally owned and maintained by the residents themselves.[202]

New institutions that facilitate the much wider privatization of inner-city neighborhoods could offer similar benefits in cities across the United States. After decades of urban renewal, public housing, and other government efforts to improve the quality of life in inner-city neighborhoods, the time has come to try a private-property approach, empowering local residents to help themselves and rely on market incentives.

Landowner Associations in Newly Developing Areas

Under the original zoning concept, municipalities determined in advance what housing would be located in which neighborhoods and then established zoning districts accordingly. The net effect of the zoning was the imposition of a kind of rationing scheme on the supply of undeveloped land in the municipality. So many acres were available for townhouses, so many for certain types of homes on one-acre lots, so many for homes on three-acre lots, and so forth. With similar actions occurring throughout a metropolitan area, the cumulative rationing scheme among all municipalities controlled the total supply of each kind of undeveloped land throughout the region.

Yet among other problems, metropolitan land-use planners had no economic or other models to project future housing needs with sufficient accuracy to meet the information requirements of this land-allocation system. Moreover, in practice, zoning actions by one municipality were seldom closely coordinated with zoning actions of other municipalities. If the zoning districts remained fixed in place, as early zoning advocates urged, the overall effect inevitably would be to create systematic mismatches between available land supplies and the demands for different types of housing.

In practice, municipalities typically resolve this problem in part by refusing to zone in advance for a final lot size and type of housing. Instead, they zone undeveloped land for a highly restrictive category that prohibits virtually all new housing development. In order to develop, a rezoning is necessary—effectively transferring the development rights from the municipality to the developer. Then, as discussed earlier, municipalities negotiate the terms of rezonings with developers, typically exacting some kind of compensation for the transfer of rights. In the more extreme cases, municipal practices verge on the outright sale of the zoning changes.

While such municipal flexibility in zoning administration introduced a necessary element of realism into the system, averting some of the worst potential problems, it still falls well short of resolving the problem of an adequate supply of undeveloped land for many kinds of new housing.[203] California courts have been particularly tolerant of municipal restrictions, essentially giving municipalities the latitude to do almost anything they want with their zoning (or other types of growth controls). According to one study, the California Supreme Court has been "more hostile to development than any other high court in the nation."[204] Combined with the strong preference for open spaces and environmental amenities of many California residents, the result has been a severe restriction on the amount of land available for new housing in most metropolitan regions.

The net effect of this restriction is significant: it drives up the price of developable land in California and thus raises the price of housing. One study found housing in communities with growth controls selling at prices 17 to 38 percent higher than in communities without such controls.[205] In 1970, even before the growth-control enthusiasm spread to municipalities throughout the state, the price of California housing on average was 35 percent higher than in the rest of the nation.[206] By 1980, the cost of California housing was 79 percent higher than the national average, and by 1990 it was 147 percent higher.[207] Adjusted for quality, one estimate in 1978 showed that the cost of California housing was 57 percent higher than in other parts of the United States.[208]

Not all Californians wanted strict limits on new development. Many owners of undeveloped land would have preferred fewer restrictions and higher land prices. To understand why planners ignored the preferences of such landowners, it is necessary to examine the typical political dynamics of municipalities that lie in the path of metropolitan development.

Suburbanites versus Farmers

Consider a hypothetical municipality consisting initially almost entirely of farmers. Due to growth of the metropolitan area, development approaches this municipality and the price of land rises. However, to preserve farming and control the pace of development, the municipality imposes a ten-acre requirement for homes, effectively excluding almost all development. At some point, however, the rising land prices will cause some farmers to sell. Their fellow farmers have no incentive to block such sales, partly because they may expect to follow suit at some point in the future. Hence, the municipality will probably change the zoning to allow development, perhaps granting approval for homes on lots one or two acres in size. Such rezonings are likely to occur piecemeal, as developers propose new subdivisions and the municipality responds to some of the proposals favorably.

At some point, as development of the municipality proceeds, the incoming newer residents will begin to outnumber the farmers. At some further point, they will very likely obtain the political power to determine future municipal zoning decisions. Now, a new set of incentives comes into play. Unlike the remaining farmers, who stand to make a large profit from sale of their land, the incentive for the new residents is to limit further housing development as much as possible, to preserve open space and environmental amenities for their own enjoyment. If the courts allow them to exclude most prospective development, as has been the case in California and a number of other states, and if the new residents are indifferent to the fate of the farmers, the politically dominant majority of newer residents will simply refuse any further rezonings. The overall effect across many municipalities in similar circumstances will be to remove a large area of undeveloped metropolitan land from the market.[209]

While this example is hypothetical and the typical circumstance in the real world involves a larger number of players and a more complex set of motivations, this basic scenario has repeated itself many thousands of times over the years in metropolitan areas across the United States.[210] Over the past few decades the "doorslammer" or "last-to-get-in" phenomenon has been a common practice. Large areas of metropolitan land in the United States have been held out of development, at large cost to the society as a whole but providing substantial environmental benefits to the locally dominant political groups of homeowners. As Fischel has explained:

> [Through zoning] communities can have a substantial impact on the overall density of population. The major reason is that courts of law are willing to sustain zoning laws (or, more frequently, amendments to zoning laws) that substantially reduce the value of undeveloped land. This allows the community to reap the benefits of restrictive zoning (to current homeowners and other voters) without having to confront the cost that these regulations impose on developers and prospective residents. . . . Communities do not have to do anything approximating benefit-cost analysis before imposing land use regulation. This leads to overregulation and residential densities that are too low.[211]

Much of the policy literature of zoning seeks a solution to this problem. A common, though politically naive, policy proposal is that municipalities should take full account of broader metropolitan needs in their planning and then actually follow their plans.[212] Others propose that state governments exercise greater oversight over municipal land-use regulatory actions, ensuring the protection of statewide interests.[213] Still other observers suggest that the courts should more aggressively overturn unduly restrictive zoning practices.[214] The Supreme Court of New Jersey has prominently pursued this course.[215]

As discussed earlier, a much different policy alternative would allow the sale of zoning, giving municipalities a significant financial incentive to relax zoning. Through "impact fees" and other exactions, commitments to build recreational facilities for the benefit of all the municipal residents, and in other ways, developers possess a number of indirect ways of paying municipalities for valuable rezonings. Yet while this strategy can work in practice, it requires that the courts look the other way in terms of ignoring the large departure from received legal theory.

The courts are not always willing to do this. Indeed, the Supreme Court in *Nollan v. California Coastal Commission* and in *Dolan v. City of Tigard* posed significant new obstacles that potentially impede the ability of municipalities to go much further in selling zoning.[216] In each case, the Court said that municipalities could establish conditions for rezonings only when they are closely related to the actual impacts of the specific project.[217] Such well-intentioned interventions by the Court are economically harmful and in that respect misguided. If carried to their logical conclusion, judicial interventions would upset many of the existing practices by which developers are now able to pay off municipalities to obtain socially desirable rezonings. If enforced fully and uniformly across the United States, the Court's insistence that future rezonings be in full accord with received zoning theory could bring the whole land-development process to a virtual standstill.

A Proposed Solution

The proposed procedures described earlier in this chapter for the creation of new neighborhood associations offer an effective and practical solution to the problem of insufficient land supplies for new development in suburban areas. Finding a solution starts with a recognition that the voting rules for private neighborhoods and municipalities serve to protect landowners from later confiscations of their development rights.

Consider the same example described earlier. Assume that everything is unchanged, except that instead of a municipality, the farmers formed a neighborhood association to hold their rights in collective ownership and took control over land development in their area. Also assume that the municipality, now redundant, abolished its zoning restrictions over the area covered by the neighborhood association. Politically, this would be possible because the farmers would still have firm political control over the municipality.

In almost every large private development project over the past three decades, it has been understood from the start that there will be many potential conflicts of interest between the developer and the early residents of the project. It is well established and accepted among all the parties that the developer must have firm legal protection from the early residents of the project taking premature political control over later land-development decisions.[218] Developers will not commit large amounts of capital if they face the risk that their development plans will later be overturned. Without such protection, the incoming residents of a project might, for example, block the developer from completing a key portion of the overall private project plan or revise the plan significantly and thereby deny the developer much of the total profit expected. The incoming residents would benefit, however, from more green space than the original plan contained.

Protection for the developer from such outcomes is found in the voting rules generally adopted by neighborhood associations. In most new associations, the developer retains the majority of the votes until the late stages of project development, when he or she is no longer exposed to the risk of subsequently imposed restrictions. In the interim, the developer may transfer control over certain day-to-day aspects of project management to the residents but retain control over the implementation of the overall development design for the project. In a typical arrangement, the developer retains three votes for every one assigned to new resident owners, until the overall development project is at least 75 percent complete.

Accordingly, if the farmers in the example discussed earlier formed a neighborhood association, such a set of private voting rules would apply. The farmers would then retain political control over new uses of land, denying the incoming residents full voting power until the entire plan for sale of their farmland and its development had neared completion. Unlike current political arrangements under zoning, the new residents in a private regime would not be able to change the planned future land uses or to impose other unreasonable restrictions on the sale of developable land in the area.

In concept, a municipal government could adopt the same voting procedure, disenfranchising recent residents in land-development matters. In fact, Ellickson hints at such a solution in his proposal noted earlier—that the Supreme Court should abandon its one person–one vote rulings and instead allow municipal voting rules based on considerations such as ownership of land and property.[219] However, short of a surprising reversal of the Court's earlier constitutional interpretations in this area, this approach is not available. Under the Court's current jurisprudence and the cultural attitudes toward "public" and "private" that prevail in the United States today, it is simply a fact of life that private neighborhood associations will have considerably greater constitutional flexibility than municipalities in designing their internal voting rules.[220]

Hence, I propose that in a municipality containing mostly farmers and other owners of undeveloped land, the owners should have the legal option of following the five-step process laid out earlier in this chapter to create a new neighborhood association with collective ownership of the local development rights. If approved in an election along the lines proposed, the resulting private "neighborhood" of farmers, by law, would retain the right to regulate land use until the entire municipality reached an advanced stage of land development. Until then, the incoming owners of residential property in the area encompassed by the farmers' "neighborhood association" would have only a minority vote in basic land-use matters. Upon completion of development (a process that could last as long as five or ten years), the majority of municipal residents would be free to regulate land development however they wished, whether by continuation of the private association or through newly established municipal zoning powers.

In current political jurisdictions, with a mixture of some existing densely developed residential areas along with substantial vacant farmland, the state government might have to mandate a similar process to establish one or more farmer land-development associations. States should limit the zoning powers of such municipalities to the land areas already developed and occupied by recent (suburban residential) arrivals at higher densities.

Secession, Voting Rules, and Provision of Public Services

Critics of neighborhood associations sometimes argue that they represent a form of secession from the municipality. As McKenzie comments, "some feel this division is reaching the point at which many CID [common interest development] residents may develop an attenuated sense of loyalty and commitment to the public communities in which their CIDs are located, even to the point of virtual or actual secession."[221]

Indeed, a few proponents of neighborhood associations would like to see their independence from existing municipal authority extended to the point of a true secession. Foldvary suggests that in an ideal world "any person or organization having a title to land [could] withdraw the site from any government jurisdiction and create its own governance."[222] In such a regime of "legalized geographic exit," it would be possible for people collectively to "withdraw from a dysfunctional process as an alternative to [attempting] an infeasible reform of the system."[223] Neighborhood groups choosing to withdraw from an existing municipality could do so at their option, as in a no-fault divorce from a marriage, and thus would not be required to provide "any substantive grounds to justify the secession."[224]

Despite some suggestions to the contrary, neighborhood associations do not represent true secessions from the municipality.[225] First, the members of neighborhood associations commonly continue to pay their full share of municipal taxes. Second, the municipality continues to provide some services, such as schools. And third, members of neighborhood associations have full voting rights in municipal elections.

In some cases, however, there have been steps toward secession. In Montgomery County, Maryland, and some other jurisdictions, the local government gives a property-tax rebate to compensate for the costs of public-service burdens that the neighborhood associations assume.[226] If this approach were carried to its ultimate logical conclusion, the neighborhood association could provide all the services and get a complete tax rebate. In that case, one might also argue that members should not vote in municipal elections, since the most important municipal decisions involve matters of public services. It would all amount to, as a practical matter, a true secession of the neighborhood from the municipality.

Whether it would be a good thing to provide a full-secession option for appropriate groupings of neighborhood residents of a municipality raises a number of complex issues.[227] Secession from an existing local government to incorporate as a new municipality is possible under existing laws of municipal incorporation for appropriate geographic groupings. Thus, the significance of a neighborhood association is not that it creates a secession option where none existed before. Rather, creating a private neighborhood allows a new form of secession as compared with incorporating a new public entity under current law. This potentially greater ease of exit is yet another example of how private neighborhoods provide greater constitutional flexibility. This flexibility creates institutional alternatives that would not otherwise be available.

Albert Hirschman provides a general analysis for all kinds of social issues of the secession option versus staying put and improving the existing system.[228] If a municipality is in the business of providing certain services, secession simply means taking your business elsewhere, just as someone might decide to buy a Chevrolet after driving a Ford for ten years. As the current debate over school vouchers and charter schools illustrates, there are many advantages to expanding the field of choices and the resulting enhancement of competition within the public sector.

The provision by a neighborhood association of some important public services but reliance on the municipality for others can create significant complications for municipal governance. First, the members of the neighborhood association then have an interest in minimizing municipal spending for the services they obtain through their own private association and potentially the voting power to express this preference effectively in municipal elections. On the other hand, other residents of the municipality (those not living in a neighborhood association) have an interest in providing a higher level of the same municipal services. They factor into their calculations the fact that the members of the neighborhood association will contribute significant taxes but not get any service benefits in return, thus significantly reducing the average cost per resident of those who continue to be publicly served.

There are possible ways of resolving these problems, although they are likely to be cumbersome to implement and may not work well in practice, depending on the specific local circumstances. Let us say a municipality provides a public service such as a school. Let us also say that the neighborhood association then decides to build and operate its own private elementary school to educate the children living in the private neighborhood. Although seldom the case today in education, one can imagine that in the future, municipalities might even pressure developers to build and operate neighborhood schools, because provision of new schools is potentially costly to the municipality.

Then, a possible method of resolving the problems noted earlier would be as follows. For each student at the neighborhood school, the municipality would rebate the neighborhood the average public cost per elementary-school student (amounting to an indirect voucher scheme). In turn, in any municipal election on new taxes for public schools, the residents of the neighborhood association would be ineligible to vote. If school matters came before the municipal council for a vote, the representatives from the district(s) with private neighborhoods would withdraw from the vote (as they might if they had any other type of conflict of interest). For this scheme to work, city-council districts would have to match closely the boundaries of neighborhood associations.

Admittedly, a perfect system of municipal taxing, service provision, and voting rules will never be possible. The difficulties posed in these regards by private neighborhoods are not fundamentally different from similar problems that already exist today, especially in larger local jurisdictions with a wide mixture of residents from different backgrounds and with different public-service preferences.[229] For example, residents who currently send their children to private schools have an incentive to vote to minimize public-school funding. In some municipalities where many children attend Catholic schools, this issue has long been divisive.[230] Some people will always be heavier users than others of particular municipal services, creating diverse incentives within the municipality.

Dismantling a Progressive Legacy

Alexis de Tocqueville found the prominent role of associations to be one of the distinguishing features of American life.[231] As he commented, "nothing, in my view, deserves more attention than the intellectual and moral associations in America."[232] Americans were devoted to achieving "equality of conditions," but it was equally important that "the art of association must develop and improve among them at the same speed."[233] In his travels, he found that this requirement was being met amply:

> Americans of all ages, all stations in life, and all types of disposition are forever forming associations. There are not only commercial and industrial associations in which all take part, but others of a thousand different types—religious, moral, serious, futile, very general and very limited, immensely large and very minute. Americans combine to give fetes, found seminaries, build churches, distribute books, and send missionaries to the antipodes. Hospitals, prisons, and schools take shape in that way. Finally, if they want to proclaim a truth or propagate some feeling by the encouragement of a great example, they form an association.[234]

However, the nineteenth-century American tradition of forming associations was, in significant part, lost in the twentieth century. Frequently, government assumes the social roles formerly played by private associations. Where churches and other private charitable organizations provided support for the poor in the nineteenth century, in the twentieth century government welfare programs provided poverty relief. This movement away from associations was part of the shift to the "scientific management" of American society, the guiding political ideal since the Progressive era early in the twentieth century.[235]

Scientific management was by its nature a centralizing undertaking.[236] The national government had the resources to find and attract the best scientists and to distribute the findings throughout the nation. The national government had the necessary scope of authority to implement comprehensive plans and coordinate economic activities throughout the United States. The assumption was that government decisions made on a scientific basis would provide the best answers in most circumstances. Because government was best equipped to discover such answers, the federal government could reasonably claim the authority and legitimacy to make the ultimate social decisions for every part of the nation.[237]

In the last decades of the twentieth century, there was a growing body of criticism contending that the Progressive design did not serve the nation well.[238] In many cases, central scientific management means bureaucratic management. The methods of science, as applied in social and administrative realms, have been much less powerful than the earlier high Progressive hopes. Government has been driven by interest-group bargaining rather than expert determinations. Political meddling has not been separated from the day-to-day management of the government; and the transfer of major governing responsibilities to the national level all too often yields partisan conflict and gridlock.

Indeed, an emerging conviction is that a revival of American democracy and of American civic life may require a turn away from traditional Progressive precepts.[239] This could involve a rediscovery of the habits of small-scale association of the nineteenth century. Robert Wiebe reports that in the nineteenth century there was a "vision of an all-inclusive People" that helped to hold American democracy together.[240] This vision found powerful symbolic expression in the rituals of national presidential elections, a time when the feeling of being part of a broad community of all Americans reached its height. The greater sense of community was one reason voter participation rates in national (and local) elections were much higher in the nineteenth century than they are today. If American democracy in that era was a rough and tumble affair, it also possessed a degree of vitality and energy now missing.

As Wiebe finds, beneath the "universalistic covering" of nineteenth-century American democracy "lay a multitude of particularistic groupings whose values set boundaries and whose behavior policed them. The meaning of democracy flowed as much from these everyday urges toward exclusiveness as it did from an overarching spirit of inclusiveness, and the results, scarcely a celebration of universalism, showed it."[241] Government in the United States was characterized by "a persisting decentralization, even after the Civil War, [that] ensured an unevenness, an uncertainty to decisions about inclusion and exclusion."[242] Some groups were able to hold their own within "lodge democracies' roughly egalitarian competition," while others were excluded from active participation.[243] Yet even here, the struggles between "insiders and outsiders," involving a "procession of claimants" to full political inclusion, stimulated political activity and the sense of being part of a common national process of representative democracy.[244] The "tension between these assertions [of the various groupings] and the resistance to them became in its own right a defining component of democratic life" in the United States.[245]

Like many others, Wiebe also faults the Progressive era as the point at which a basic loss of civic energy occurred in American life.[246] It was perhaps an inevitable result of a governing vision that saw the political process as dominated by the discovery of expert solutions to well-defined technical problems of management, hardly a vision designed to inspire the involvement of the citizenry. A turn away from the Progressive vision could include a revival of the role of neighborhoods in American life. However, if neighborhoods are to become more important, new legal mechanisms are necessary to provide the requisite institutional support and foundation.

Neighborhood associations in new neighborhoods have already significantly displaced the role of one of the most important regulatory innovations of the Progressive era, zoning control over the use of private land. The creation by state governments of a new and practical legal mechanism by which existing neighborhoods can also form their own private neighborhood associations, thereby rendering municipal zoning superfluous in these neighborhoods as well, would represent a large step toward the full dismantling of the failed zoning legacy of the Progressive era.

Conclusion

As proposed in this chapter, state governments should enact legislation enabling the creation of new private neighborhood associations to own and manage the common elements in existing neighborhoods. Citizens in an existing neighborhood could petition the state government, triggering procedures that could lead to the formation of this new instrument of private neighborhood ownership and governance. The full details of each collective-ownership arrangement for each neighborhood, a kind of private constitution that could be tailored to the needs of each individual neighborhood, would have to be negotiated and presented to all the residents of the neighborhood. In order to create a new private neighborhood, a positive vote of (some kind of) supermajority of the neighborhood would have to occur.

New legal procedures for the creation of private neighborhoods would go far toward solving two urgent social problems. In inner-city areas, creation of new private neighborhood associations would help greatly to improve the quality—including reducing the rate of crime—in these often deteriorated environments. In rural areas that will soon face development, new collective-ownership instruments for groups of farmers (farmer "neighborhoods"), including voting rules to protect the original farmer-developers, could open large areas of land for lower- and moderate-income housing. Generally, the establishment of private neighborhoods throughout urban and suburban areas would offer major social and economic advantages over the existing zoning and public-service delivery system. In the twenty-first century, the general adoption of collective private ownership of residential property could offer social benefits as great as those experienced in the twentieth century as a result of widespread private corporate ownership of business property. There seems to be an inexorable process of collectivism in the ownership of private property—first business and now residential property—taking place in response to the institutional imperatives of modern life. State governments should facilitate this evolution rather than obstruct it.

NOTES

This article is based upon a paper presented at the Donner Conference on Freedom of Contract in Property Law, sponsored by the Law and Economics Center, George Mason University School of Law, December 1997. It first appeared in *George Mason Law Review* 7, no. 4 (1999): 827–880. Reprinted with permission.
    1. Barton and Silverman 1994b, xi.

2. Means 1964, 12, 15.

3. Berle and Means 1932.

4. U.S. Advisory Commission on Intergovernmental Relations 1989; Dilger 1992; McKenzie 1994.

5. Harris 1996. Of course, the spread of individual ownership was itself a development only a few centuries old. It was part of the evolution of property-rights institutions by which capitalism supplanted feudalism as the dominant social form.

6. The growing importance of private neighborhoods and a proposal for new legal mechanisms of collective private ownership in existing neighborhoods are also explored in Nelson (1999).

7. For reviews of this literature, see Fischel 1985 and Fischel 1995.

8. Treese 1999, 3.

9. Treese 1999, 19.

10. Barton and Silverman 1994b, 12.

11. Barton and Silverman 1994b, 11.

12. McKenzie 1994, 120.

13. Treese 1993, 13.

14. Treese 1993, 17.

15. Treese 1993, 17.

16. Treese 1993, 22.

17. Dowden 1989, 27.

18. Treese 1993, 13.

19. Treese 1993, 13.

20. Treese 1993, 13.

21. Treese 1993, 9.

22. Treese 1993, 1.

23. W. Hyatt 1975.

24. Treese 1999, 3.

25. Treese 1999, 3.

26. Clurman, Jackson, and Hebard, 1984.

27. Treese 1999, 13.

28. A. Hyatt 1996.

29. For a description of one planned community, Celebration, Florida, created by the Disney Corporation in the vicinity of Disney World, see Pollan 1997, 56.

30. Calmes 1997.

31. Foer 1969, 379, 397–98. See also Garreau 1991, 200–201.

32. Reichman 1976, 253.

33. Reichman 1976, 253.

34. For a history of the development of condominium forms of land tenure outside the United States, see Natelson 1987.

35. McKenzie 1994, 29–55; Weiss and Watts 1989, 95–103.

36. Dowden 1989.

37. Treese 1993, 11; Barton and Silverman 1994a, 10.

38. McKenzie 1994, 95–96.

39. Treese 1993, 12.

40. Delafons 1969; Popper 1981; Coyle 1993.
41. See Eagle 1996, 347.
42. Nelson 1989a, 45–51.
43. Nelson 1977, 22–51; Nelson 1979, 713.
44. Toll 1969, 172–87.
45. Bassett 1936.
46. See *Village of Euclid v. Ambler Realty Co.,* 272 U.S. 365, 394 (1926).
47. R. A. Williams 1989, 278–80.
48. Tarlock 1982.
49. Lee 1995; Waldo 1984.
50. Advisory Committee on Zoning 1928.
51. Haar 1955.
52. Huffman and Plantico 1979; Kaplan 1973.
53. Linowes and Allensworth 1973, 23–24; Linowes and Allensworth 1976.
54. Coyle 1993, 18.
55. Babcock 1966.
56. Lassar 1990; Altshuler and Gomez-Ibanez 1993.
57. Altshuler 1965, 392–405; Frieden 1979, 157–83.
58. Eagle 1996, 347.
59. Eagle 1996, 349–50.
60. Toll 1969, 266; Babcock 1966, 116.
61. National Commission of Urban Problems 1969, 7.
62. National Commission of Urban Problems 1969, 16.
63. National Commission of Urban Problems 1969, 248.
64. Otherwise, politically, the zoning would not have happened.
65. Babcock 1966, 140.
66. Babcock 1966, 115.
67. In other countries, there have been "land pooling" programs whereby the government condemns property in an area expected to be redeveloped for a new use and then pays the original property owners by assigning them new rights in the overall collective landholding resulting from the pooling effort. See Doebele 1982.
68. Babcock 1966, 115–16.
69. The growing popularity of historic districts in recent years reflects the fact that they accomplish much the same purposes as a full-fledged neighborhood association and, like zoning, can be created by government fiat over the wishes of neighborhood holdouts. See Rose 1981, 473.
70. Nelson 1977, 7–21.
71. Nelson 1986, 361.
72. Rose 1985, 73.
73. Holmes 1963.
74. The law of usury, for example, evolved in this manner. Usury was at first prohibited formally, but the charging of interest was widely practiced through a host of indirect devices that had the same practical effect. Eventually, although it took many centuries, the direct charging of interest became routine and legally permissible. See Noonan 1957.
75. See Gates 1968; Nelson 1995, chapter 1; Nelson 2000.
76. Pollack 1979, 64–65.

77. Pollack 1979, 53.

78. Babcock 1966, 55.

79. Nelson 1989b, 299, 306.

80. Coase 1960. This article was the most important reason for Coase's receipt of the Nobel Prize in economics in 1991.

81. There was also a significant effect on the distributional outcome.

82. Tarlock 1972, 141.

83. Tarlock 1972, 146.

84. Tarlock 1972, 146.

85. Tarlock 1972, 145.

86. Tarlock 1972, 146.

87. Tarlock 1972, 147.

88. Ellickson 1973; Ellickson 1977.

89. Ellickson 1973.

90. Ellickson 1977.

91. Ellickson 1977.

92. Siegan 1972. See also Siegan 1998 and Siegan 1976.

93. Siegan 1972, 231.

94. Siegan 1972, 75–76.

95. Houston is the only major city in the United States without zoning. Siegan 1972, 92.

96. Nelson 1977, 43.

97. Nelson 1977, 22–51.

98. Epstein 1985, 195–96.

99. Nelson 1985, 3.

100. Fischel 1985. See also Fischel 1980; Fischel 1979; Fischel 1978.

101. Noonan 1984.

102. Babcock and Larsen 1990, 1–2. See also Altshuler and Gomez-Ibanez 1993.

103. Balk 1966, 18.

104. Clawson 1966–67, 9.

105. Fischel 1979, 322.

106. Fischel 1979, 322.

107. Krasnowiecki 1980, 719; Lefcoe 1981, 447; Kmiec 1981, 28; Pulliam 1983, 435; Delogu 1984, 261.

108. Porter 1983, 34; see also Nelson 1983b, 36.

109. Johnson 1982.

110. *Report of the President's Commission on Housing* 1982, 199.

111. *Report of the President's Commission on Housing* 1982, 199.

112. Babcock 1984, 34.

113. Babcock and Siemon 1985.

114. Babcock 1990, 56.

115. Babcock 1984, 34.

116. Precious 1987, 1.

117. Babcock and Larsen 1990, 32.

118. Babcock and Larsen 1990, 1–2.

119. For a more ambitious set of proposals, see Downs 1994.

120. Babcock and Larsen 1990, 103.
121. Briffault 1999; see also Houston 1997.
122. One partial exception is Nelson 1984. The concept developed in this chapter is briefly sketched in an earlier publication as follows:

> Current trends toward greater collective possession of important neighborhood property rights could be significantly stimulated by the creation of a new, more satisfactory neighborhood tenure. Protection of neighborhood quality ought to be provided under private tenures. A new private tenure instrument—the neighborhood association—is proposed here for that purpose. The legal status of the neighborhood association would resemble in certain respects each of the already existing forms of collective property ownership. . . .
>
> Under zoning, the local government effectively holds the rights to control new uses and major changes in property in a neighborhood. Under the tenure proposed, the zoning rights would instead be held directly by the neighborhood association. Hence, where a neighborhood association was formed, the first step would be to transfer to it the existing zoning rights now held by the local government. (Nelson 1977, 207–8)

123. Other writers have, however, addressed these potential benefits of neighborhood revitalization. See Boyte 1980; Wireman 1984; Morris and Hess 1975; National Commission on Neighborhoods 1979.
124. This history draws heavily on McKenzie 1994, 29–78.
125. McKenzie 1994, 40; see also Weiss 1987.
126. Weiss and Watts 1989, 99.
127. McKenzie 1994, 74–76.
128. McKenzie 1994, 39.
129. Dowden 1989, 27.
130. McKenzie 1994, 27.
131. Foldvary 1994.
132. Foldvary 1994, 86–113.
133. Heath 1936b.
134. Heath 1936a, 65–66.
135. Heath 1957, 82.
136. MacCallum 1964–65, 58; see also MacCallum 1972.
137. MacCallum 1964–65, 58.
138. MacCallum 1964–65, 58.
139. MacCallum 1970, 5.
140. French 1992; Epstein 1988.
141. See *Baker v. Carr,* 369 U.S. 186 (1962).
142. MacCallum 1970, 50.
143. Hansmann 1991.
144. Foldvary 1994, 97.
145. Frazier 1980.
146. Foldvary 1994, 111.
147. Liebmann 1993; see also Liebmann 1994 and Liebmann 1991.
148. Liebmann 1993, 382–83.

149. Liebmann 1993, 381–82.
150. Frug 1980, 1059.
151. Frug 1980, 1082.
152. Wiebe 1995, 138–61.
153. Frug 1980, 1080.
154. Ellickson 1998, 75.
155. Frug 1980, 1070.
156. Frug 1980, 1070.
157. Frug 1980, 1122.
158. Frug 1980, 1122.
159. Frug 1980, 1106.
160. Frug 1980, 1107.
161. Frug 1980, 1119.
162. Frug 1980, 1119–20.
163. Frug 1980, 1145.
164. Ellickson 1982, 1519.
165. Ellickson 1982, 1523.
166. Rose 1994.
167. Ellickson 1982, 1527.
168. Ellickson 1982, 1558.
169. Ellickson 1982, 1560–61; Steinfeld 1989, 335.
170. Frug 1980, 155.
171. Frug wrote as a member of the critical legal studies movement, Ellickson as a member of the law and economics movement. Norman Macrae (1984, 124) prophesies that in the future the dominant form of local governance may consist of "profit-making local governments run by private-enterprise performance contractors."
172. Dilger 1992, 145.
173. U.S. Advisory Commission on Intergovernmental Relations 1989, ii.
174. U.S. Advisory Commission on Intergovernmental Relations 1989, ii.
175. U.S. Advisory Commission on Intergovernmental Relations 1989, ii–iii.
176. Barton and Silverman 1994c; Dilger 1992; Korngold 1995; McKenzie 1994; Natelson 1990, 41.
177. Garreau 1991, 183–93.
178. Alexander 1989; see also Alexander 1994.
179. McKenzie 1994, 11.
180. McKenzie 1994, 22.
181. For complaints about oppressive local controls in historic districts and other contexts, see Bolick 1995; see also Bolick 1993.
182. McKenzie 1994, 21.
183. McKenzie 1994, 24.
184. Reich 1991, 16.
185. Reich 1991, 42.
186. Burns 1994.
187. Andres Duany and Elizabeth Plater-Zyberk, quoted in Schneider 1992, 37.
188. Schneider 1992, 37.

189. Blakely and Snyder 1997.

190. Blakely and Snyder 1997, 1.

191. Blakely and Snyder 1997, 2.

192. Blakely and Snyder 1997, 81.

193. Wilson and Kelling 1982, 29.

194. Haar 1996; see also Danielson 1976.

195. For a study of the important role of neighborhoods in the city of Baltimore, suggesting an even greater potential with the proper institutional supports, see Crenson 1983.

196. Dilulio 1997, 14.

197. There are, however, ideological obstacles.

198. Louv 1985, 127–46.

199. Ellickson 1998, 75.

200. Beito, chap. 3 in this volume; Beito and Smith 1990, 263; see also Beito and Smith 1989; Oakerson 1989, 55.

201. Newman 1980, 126.

202. Newman 1980, 124.

203. Plotkin 1987.

204. DiMento et al. 1980, 872.

205. Fischel 1995, 223.

206. Fischel 1995, 223.

207. Fischel 1995, 223.

208. Rosen describes an "affordability crisis" for California housing in which many current home buyers could not afford to buy the house the currently live in. See Rosen 1984, 45.

209. Bobo et al. 1975; see also Downs 1994, 9–11.

210. President's Committee on Urban Housing 1968; see also Advisory Commission on Regulatory Barriers to Affordable Housing 1990; Eagle 1996, 346–351.

211. Fischel 1985, 65.

212. Anderson 1968; N. Williams 1974.

213. Reilly 1973; see also *Model Land Development Code* 1976; Degrove 1992; Abbott, Howe, and Adler 1994.

214. Sager 1969, 767; Danielson 1976, 325; Fischel 1995, 329. Hagman argues that courts should instead require the payment of compensation for unreasonable regulations (1978, 292–93).

215. *Southern Burlington County NAACP v. Township of Mt. Laurel,* 336 A.2d 713 (N.J. 1975); *Southern Burlington County NAACP v. Township of Mt. Laurel,* 456 A.2d 390 (N.J. 1983). See also Haar 1996.

216. *Nollan v. California Coastal Commission,* 483 U.S. 825 (1987); *Dolan v. City of Tigard,* 512 U.S. 374 (1994).

217. Eagle 1996, 255–57, 75.

218. A. Hyatt 1996, 17–26.

219. Rose 1994; Ellickson 1982.

220. See Ellickson 1998 for a discussion of innovative voting rules based on property.

221. McKenzie 1994, 186.

222. Foldvary 1994, 206.

223. Foldvary 1994, 206.

224. Foldvary 1994, 206.

225. In recent years, some local areas have actively attempted to secede from their existing jurisdictions. Two such efforts with high national visibility have been the attempts of Staten Island to secede from the city of New York and, most recently, of the San Fernando Valley area to secede from the city of Los Angeles.

226. U.S. Advisory Commission on Intergovernmental Relations 1989, 20.

227. Buchanen 1991; Sunstein 1991; Gauthier 1994.

228. Hirschman 1970.

229. Fischel 1995, 253–88.

230. For a discussion of the effects of various fiscal incentives, see Ladd and Yinger 1989.

231. Tocqueville 1969, 517.

232. Tocqueville 1969, 517.

233. Tocqueville 1969, 517.

234. Tocqueville 1969, 513.

235. Nelson 1991, chapter 5; Waldo 1984.

236. Lee 1995, 544.

237. Progressive ideas of scientific management justified, for example, the retention of management responsibility for federal lands (almost 30 percent of the U.S. land area) at the federal level. See Nelson 1991, 47–51; Nelson 1983a, 15–22; Tarlock 1985, 349.

238. This literature is voluminous. For a few examples, see Epstein 1985; Friedman 1962; Coase 1988; and Niskanen 1998.

239. An early prominent example of this body of writings is Berger and Neuhaus 1977. More recently, Rivlin 1992 has called for a reversal of centralizing trends in American government.

240. Wiebe 1995, 110.

241. Wiebe 1995, 110.

242. Wiebe 1995, 86.

243. Wiebe 1995, 86.

244. Wiebe 1995, 86.

245. Wiebe 1995, 86.

246. Wiebe 1995, 113.

REFERENCES

Abbott, C., D. Howe, and S. Adler. 1994. *Planning the Oregon Way: A Twenty-Year Evaluation.* Corvallis Oreg.: Oregon State University Press.

Advisory Commission on Regulatory Barriers to Affordable Housing. 1990. *Not in My Backyard.* Washington, D.C.: U.S. Department of Housing and Urban Development.

Advisory Committee on Zoning. 1928. *A City Planning Primer.* Washington, D.C.: U.S. Department of Commerce.

Alexander, G. 1989. Dilemmas of Group Autonomy: Residential Associations and Community. *Cornell Law Review* 75: 1–61.

————. 1994. Conditions of "Voice": Passivity, Disappointment, and Democracy in Homeowner Associations. In *Common Interest Communities: Private Governments and the Public Interest,* ed. S. Barton and C. Silverman. Berkeley: Institute of Governmental Studies Press.

Altshuler, A. 1965. *The City Planning Process.* Ithaca, N.Y.: Cornell University Press.

Altshuler, A., and J. Gomez-Ibanez. 1993. *Regulation for Revenue: The Political Economy of Land Use Exactions.* Washington, D.C.: Brookings Instutution.

Anderson, R. 1968. *American Law of Zoning.* Rochester, N.Y.: Lawyers Co-operative.

Babcock, R. 1966. *The Zoning Game: Municipal Practices and Policies.* Madison: University of Wisconsin Press.

————. 1984. The Outlook for Zoning. *Urban Land* (November): 34–35.

————. 1990. The City as Entrepreneur: Fiscal Wisdom or Regulatory Folly. In *City Deal Making,* ed. T. Lassar. Washington, D.C.: Urban Land Instutute.

Babcock, R., and W. Larsen. 1990. *Special Districts.* Cambridge, Mass.: Lincoln Institute of Land Policy.

Babcock, R., and C. Siemon. 1985. *The Zoning Game Revisited.* Boston, Mass.: Oelgeschlager, Gunn, and Hain.

Balk, A. 1966. Invitation to Bribery. *Harper's Magazine* (October): 18–24.

Barton, S., and C. Silverman. 1994a. History and Structure of the Common Interest Community. In *Common Interest Communities: Private Governments and the Public Interest,* ed. S. Barton and C. Silverman. Berkeley: Institute of Governmental Studies Press.

————. 1994b. Preface to *Common Interest Communities: Private Governments and the Public Interest,* ed. S. Barton and C. Silverman. Berkeley: Institute of Governmental Studies Press.

————, eds. 1994c. *Common Interest Communities: Private Governments and the Public Interest.* Berkeley: Institute of Governmental Studies Press.

Bassett, E. 1936. *Zoning.* New York: Russell Sage Foundation.

Beito, D. T., and B. Smith. 1989. Owning the "Commanding Heights": Historical Perspectives on Private Streets. Chicago, Ill.: Public Works Historical Society. December: 1–47.

————. 1990. The Formation of Urban Infrastructure Through Nongovernmental Planning: The Private Places of St. Louis, 1869–1920. *Journal of Urban History* 16 (May): 263–303.

Berger, P., and R. Neuhaus. 1977. *To Empower People.* Washington, D.C.: American Enterprise Institute for Public Policy Research.

Berle, A., and G. Means. 1932. *The Modern Corporation and Private Property.* New York: Commerce Clearing House.

Blakely, E., and M. Snyder. 1997. *Fortress America.* Washington, D.C.: Brookings Institution Press.

Bobo, B., et al. 1975. *No Land Is an Island: Individual Rights and the Control of Land Use.* San Francisco: Institute for Contemporary Studies.

Bolick, C. 1993. *Grassroots Tyranny.* Washington D.C.: Cato Institute.

————. 1995. Leviathan in the Suburbs. *Weekly Standard* (December 18): 25–28.

Boyte, H. 1980. *The Backyard Revolution.* Philadelphia: Temple University Press.

Briffault, R. 1999. A Government for our Time?: Business Improvement Districts and Urban Governance. *Columbia Law Review* 99: 365–477.

Buchanen, A. 1991. *Secession.* Boulder: Westview Press.

Buckley, F., ed. 1999. *The Rise and Fall of Freedom of Contract.* Durham, N.C.: Duke University Press.

Burns, N. 1994. *The Formation of American Local Governments.* New York: Oxford University Press.

Calmes, A., ed. 1997. *Community Association Leadership: A Guide for Volunteers.* Alexandria, Va.: Community Association Institute.

Clawson, M. 1966–67. Why Not Sell Zoning and Rezoning (Legally, That Is). *Cry California* (winter).

Clurman, D., F. S. Jackson, and E. L. Hebard. 1984. *Condominiums and Cooperatives.* New York: Wiley.

Coase, R. 1960. The Problem of Social Cost. *Journal of Law and Economics* 3:1–31.

———. 1988. *The Firm, the Market, and the Law.* Chicago: University of Chicago Press.

Coyle, D. 1993. *Property Rights and the Constitution.* Albany: State University of New York Press.

Crenson, M. 1983. *Neighborhood Politics.* Cambridge, Mass.: Harvard University Press.

Danielson, M. 1976. *The Politics of Exclusion.* New York: Columbia University Press.

Degrove, J. 1992. *Planning and Growth Management in the States.* Cambridge, Mass.: Lincoln Institute of Land Policy.

Delafons, J. 1969. *Land-Use Controls in the United States.* Cambridge, Mass.: MIT Press.

Delogu, O. 1984. Local Land Use Controls: An Idea Whose Time Has Passed. *Maine Law Review* 36:261–310.

Dilger, R. 1992. *Neighborhood Politics.* New York: New York University Press.

Dilulio, J., Jr. 1997. A More Gated Union. *Weekly Standard* (July 7): 13–15.

DiMento, J., M. D. Dozier, S. L. Emmons, D. G. Hagman, C. Kim, K. Greenfeld-Sanders and J. A. Wodacott. 1980. Land Development and Environmental Control in the California Supreme Court: The Deferential, the Preservationist, and the Preservationist-Erratic Eras. *UCLA Law Review* 27:859–1066.

Doebele, W., ed. 1982. *Land Readjustment: A Different Approach to Financing Urbanization.* Lexington, Mass.: Lexington Books.

Dowden, C. 1989. Community Associations and Local Governments: The Need for Recognition and Reassessment. In *Residential Community Associations: Private Governments in the Intergovernmental System?* Washington, D.C. Advisory Commission on Intergovernmental Relations.

Downs, A. 1994. *New Visions for Metropolitan America.* Washington, D.C.: Brookings Institution.

Eagle, S. 1996. *Regulatory Takings.* Charlottesville, Va.: Michie Law Publishers.

Ellickson, R. 1973. Alternatives to Zoning: Covenants, Nuisance Rules and Fines as Land Use Controls. *University of Chicago Law Review* 40:681–781.

———. 1977. Suburban Growth Controls: An Economic and Legal Analysis. *Yale Law Journal* 86:385–511

————. 1982. Cities and Homeowners Associations. *University of Pennsylvania Law Review* 130:1519–80.

————. 1998. New Institutions for Old Neighborhoods. *Duke Law Journal* 48:75–110.

Epstein, R. 1985. *Takings: Private Property and the Power of Eminent Domain.* Cambridge: Harvard University Press.

————. 1988. Covenants and Constitutions. *Cornell Law Review* 73:906–927.

Fischel, W. 1978. A Property Rights Approach to Municipal Zoning. *Land Economics* 54:64–81.

————. 1979. Equity and Efficiency Aspects of Zoning Reform. *Public Policy* 27:301–331.

————. 1980. Zoning and Land Use Reform: A Property Rights Perspective. *Virginia Journal of Natural Resource Law* 1:69–98.

————. 1985. *The Economics of Zoning Laws.* Baltimore: Johns Hopkins University Press.

————. 1995. *Regulatory Takings.* Cambridge: Harvard University Press.

Foer, A. 1969. Comment, Democracy in New Towns: The Limits of Government. *University of Chicago Law Review* 36:379–412.

Foldvary, F. 1994. *Public Goods and Private Communities.* Aldershot, U.K.: Edward Elgar Publishing.

Frazier, M. 1980. Privatizing the City. *Policy Review* 12 (spring): 91–108.

French, S. 1992. The Constitution of a Private Residential Association Should Include a Bill of Rights. *Wake Forest Law Review* 27:345–95.

Frieden, B. 1979. *The Environmental Protection Hustle.* Cambridge MIT Press.

Friedman, M. 1962. *Capitalism and Freedom.* Chicago: University of Chicago Press.

Frug, G. 1980. The City as a Legal Concept. *Harvard Law Review* 93:1059–1154.

Garreau, J. 1991. *Edge City.* New York: Doubleday.

Gates, P. 1968. *A History of Public Land Law Development.* Washington, D.C.: Government Printing Office.

Gauthier, D. 1994. Breaking Up: An Essay on Secession. *Canadian Journal of Philosophy* 24(3):357–72.

Geisler C., and F. Popper, eds. 1984. *Land Reform, American Style.* Totowa, N.J.: Rowman and Allanheld.

Haar, C. 1955. In Accordance with a Comprehensive Plan. *Harvard Law Review* 68:1154.

————. 1996. *Suburbs Under Siege.* Princeton, N.J.: Princeton University Press.

Haar, C., and J. Kayden. 1989. *Zoning and the American Dream.* Chicago: Planners Press, American Planning Association.

Hagman, D. 1978. Compensable Regulation. In *Windfalls for Wipeouts: Land Value Capture and Compensation,* ed. D. Hagman and D. Misczynski. Chicago: Planners Press, American Planning Association.

Hagman, D., and D. Misczynski, eds. 1978. *Windfalls for Wipeouts: Land Value Capture and Compensation.* Chicago: Planners Press, American Planning Association.

Hansmann, H. 1991. Condominium and Cooperative Housing: Transactional Efficiency, Tax Subsidies, and Tenure Choice. *Journal of Legal Studies* 20:25–71.

Harris, J. W. 1996. *Property and Justice.* New York: Oxford University Press.

Heath, S. 1936a. Outline on the Economic, Political, and Proprietary Departments of Society. N.p. Manuscript in possession of author.

———. 1936b. Politics Versus Proprietorship. N.p. Manuscript in possession of author.

———. 1957. *Citadel, Market and Altar.* Baltimore: Science of Society Foundation.

Hirschman, A. 1970. *Exit, Voice and Loyalty.* Cambridge: Harvard University Press.

Holmes, O. [1881] 1963. *The Common Law.* Ed. M. Howe. Cambridge: Harvard University Press.

Houstoun, L., Jr. 1997. *Business Improvement Districts.* Washington, D.C.: Urban Land Institute.

Huffman, J., and R. Plantico. 1979. Toward a Theory of Land Use Planning: Lessons from Oregon. *Land and Water Law Review* 14:1–74.

Hyatt, A. 1996. *Transition from Developer Control.* Alexandria, Va.: Community Associations Institute.

Hyatt, W. 1975. Condominium and Home Owner Associations: Formation and Development. *Emory Law Journal* 24:977–1008.

Johnson, M. B., ed. 1982. *Resolving the Housing Crisis: Government Policy, Decontrol and the Public Interest.* Cambridge, Mass.: Ballinger.

Kaplan, M. 1973. *Urban Planning in the 1960s.* Cambridge: MIT Press.

Kmiec, D. 1981. Deregulating Land Use: An Alternative Free Enterprise Development System. *University of Pennsylvania Law Review.* 130:28–130.

Korngold, G. 1995. *Private Land Use Controls: Balancing Private Initiative and the Public Interest in the Homeowner Association Context.* Cambridge, Mass.: Lincoln Institute of Land Policy.

Krasnowiecki, J. 1980. Abolish Zoning. *Syracuse Law Review* 31:719–53.

Ladd, H., and J. Yinger. 1989. *America's Ailing Cities.* Baltimore: Johns Hopkins University Press.

Lassar, T., ed. 1990. *City Deal Making.* Washington, D.C.: Urban Land Institute.

Lee, E. 1995. Political Science, Public Administration and the Rise of the American Administrative State. *Public Administration Review* 55:538–46.

Lefcoe, G. 1981. California's Land Planning Requirements: The Case for Deregulation. *Southern California Law Review* 54:447–501.

Liebmann, G. 1991. Modernization of Zoning: Enabling Act Revision as a Means to Reform. *Urban Law* 23:1.

———. 1993. Devolution of Power to Community and Block Associations. *Urban Law* 25:335–83.

———. 1994. *The Little Platoons.* Westport, Conn.: Praeger.

Linowes, R., and D. Allensworth. 1973. *The Politics of Land Use.* New York: Praeger.

———. 1976. *The Politics of Land Use Law.* New York: Praeger.

Louv, R. 1985. *America II.* New York: Penguin Books.

MacCallum, S. 1964–65. The Social Nature of Ownership. *Modern Age* 9 (winter): 49–61.

———. 1970. *The Art of Community.* Menlo Park, Calif.: Institute for Humane Studies.

———. 1972. Associated Individualism: A Victorian Dream of Freedom. *Reason* 4 (April): 17–24.

Macrae, N. 1984. *The 2025 Report.* New York: Macmillan.

McKenzie, E. 1994. *Privatopia: Homeowner Associations and the Rise of Residential Private Government.* New Haven: Yale University Press.

Means, G. 1964. Economic Concentration, Part I—Overall and Conglomerate Services. *Hearings before the Subcommittee on Antitrust and Monopoly of the Senate Committee on the Judiciary.* 88th Congress, 12, 15.

Model Land Development Code. 1976. Philadelphia: American Law Institute.

Morris, D., and K. Hess. 1975. *Neighborhood Power.* Boston: Beacon Press.

Natelson, R. 1987. Comments on The Historiography of Condominium: The Myth of Roman Origin. *Oklahoma City University Law Review* 12:17–58.

Natelson, R. 1990. Consent, Coercion and "Reasonableness" in Private Law: The Special Case of the Property Owners Association. *Ohio State Law Journal* 51:41–88.

National Commission on Neighborhoods. 1979. *People Building Neighborhoods.* Washington, D.C.: Government Printing Office.

National Commission of Urban Problems. 1969. *Building the American City.* New York: Praeger.

Nelson, R. 1977. *Zoning and Property Rights.* Cambridge, Mass.: MIT Press.

———. 1979. A Property Right Theory of Zoning. *Urban Law* 11:713–32.

———. 1983a. *The Making of Federal Coal Policy.* Durham, N.C.: Duke University Press.

———. 1983b. Rethinking Zoning. *Urban Land* (July): 36–37.

———. 1984. Private Neighborhoods: A New Direction for the Neighborhood Movement. In *Land Reform, American Style,* ed. C. Geisler and F. Popper. Totowa, N.J.: Rowman and Allanheld.

———. 1985. Marketable Zoning: A Cure for the Zoning System. *Land Use Law and Zoning Digest* (November): 3–8.

———. 1986. Private Rights to Government Actions: How Modern Property Rights Evolve. *University of Illinois Law Review* 361–386.

———. 1989a. The Privatization of Local Government: From Zoning to RCAs. In *Residential Community Associations: Private Governments in the Intergovernmental System?* Washington, D.C. Advisory Commission on Intergovernmental Relations.

———. 1989b. Zoning Myth and Practice: From Euclid into the Future. In *Zoning and the American Dream,* ed. C. Haar and J. Kayden. Chicago: Planners Press, American Planning Association.

———. 1991. *Reaching for Heaven on Earth.* Lanham, Md.: Rowman and Littlefield.

———. 1995. *Public Lands and Private Rights.* Lanham, Md.: Rowman and Littlefield.

———. 1999. Contracting for Land Use Law: Zoning by Private Contract. In *The Rise and Fall of Freedom of Contract,* ed. F. Buckley. Durham, N.C.: Duke University Press.

———. 2000. *A Burning Issue: A Case for Abolishers to U.S. Forest Service.* Lanham, Md.: Rowman and Littlefield.

Newman, O. 1980. *Community of Interest.* New York: Anchor Press/Doubleday.

Niskanen, W. 1998. *Policy Analysis and Public Choice.* Northhampton, Mass.: Edward Elgar.

Noonan, J. 1957. *The Scholastic Analysis of Usury.* Cambridge: Harvard University Press.

———. 1984. *Bribes: The Intellectual History of a Moral Idea.* New York: Macmillan.

Oakerson, R. 1989. Private Street Associations in St. Louis County: Subdivisions as Service Providers. In *Residential Community Associations: Private Governments in the Intergovernmental System?* Washington, D.C. Advisory Commission on Intergovernmental Relations.

Plotkin, S. 1987. *Keep Out: The Struggle for Land Use Control.* Berkeley: University of California Press.

Pollack, F. [1883] 1979. *The Land Laws.* 3d ed. Littleton: Co.; Fred B. Rothman and Co.

Pollan, M. 1997. Town-Building is No Mickey Mouse Operation. *New York Times Magazine* (December 14).

Popper, F. 1981. *The Politics of Land-Use Reform.* Madison: University of Wisconsin Press.

Porter, D. 1983. On Bemoaning Zoning. *Urban Land* (March): 34–35.

Precious, T. 1987. D.C. Seeks to Raise Hadid "Linkage" Fee. *Washington Post* (November 14), section E, 1.

President's Committee on Urban Housing. 1968. *A Decent Home.* Washington, D.C.

Pulliam, M. 1983. Brandeis Brief for Decontrol of Land Use: A Plea for Constitutional Reform. *Southwestern University Law Review.* 13:435–76.

Reich, R. 1991. Secession of the Successful. *New York Times Magazine* (January 20).

Reichman, U. 1976. Residential Private Governments: An Introductory Survey. *University of Chicago Law Review* 43:253–306.

Reilly, W., ed. 1973. *The Use of Land.* Task Force on Land Use and Urban Growth. New York: Crowell.

Report of the President's Commission on Housing. 1982. Washington, D.C.

Rivlin, A. 1992. *Reviving the American Dream.* Washington, D.C.: Brookings Institution.

Rose, C. 1981. Preservation and Community: New Directions in the Law of Historic Preservation. *Stanford Law Review* 33:473–534.

———. 1985. Possession as the Origin of Property. *University of Chicago Law Review* 52:73–88.

———. 1994. *Property and Persuasion.* Boulder, Co.: Westview Press.

Rosen, K. T. 1984. *California Housing Markets in the 1980s.* Cambridge, Mass.: Oelgeschlar, Gunn and Hain.

Sager, L. G. 1969. Tight Little Islands: Exclusionary Zoning, Equal Protection, and the Indigent. *Stanford Law Review* 21:767:800.

Schneider, W. 1992. The Suburban Century Begins. *Atlantic Monthly* (July).

Siegan, B. 1972. *Land Use without Zoning.* Lexington, Mass.: Lexington Books.

———. 1976. *Other People's Property.* Lexington, Mass.: Lexington Books.

———. 1998. *Property and Freedom.* New Brunswick, N.J.: Transaction Publishers.

Spink, F., ed. 1999. *Community Association Factbook* 3. Alexandria, Va.: Community Associations Institute.

Steinfeld, R. 1989. Property and Suffrage in the Early American Republic. *Stanford University Law Review* 41:335–76.

Sunstein, C. 1991. Constitutionalism and Secession. *University of Chicago Law Review* 58:663–70.

Tarlock, A. D. 1972. Toward a Revised Theory of Zoning. In *Land Use Controls Annual* ed. F. Bangs, Jr., 141–52.

———. 1982. Euclid Revisited. *Land Use Law* 34:4–8.

———. 1985. The Making of Federal Coal Policy: Lessons for Public Land Management From a Failed Program, an Essay and Review. *Natural Resources Journal* 25(2):349–74.

Tocqueville, A. de [1835] 1969. *Democracy in America,* ed. by J. Mayer. Garden City, N.Y.: Doubleday.

Toll, S. 1969. *Zoned American.* New York: Grossman Publishers.

Treese, C. 1993. *Community Associations Factbook* 13. Alexandria, Va.: Community Associations Institute.

———. 1999. *Community Associations Factbook* 3. Ed. F. Spink. Alexandria, Va.: Community Associations Institute.

U.S. Advisory Commission on Intergovernmental Relations. 1989. *Residential Community Associations: Private Governments in the Intergovernmental System?* Washington, D.C. Advisory Commission on Intergovernmental Relations.

Waldo, D. [1948] 1984. *The Administrative State.* New York: Holmes and Meier Publishers.

Weiss, M. 1987. *The Rise of the Community Builders: The American Real Estate Industry and Urban Land Planning.* New York: Columbia University Press.

Weiss, M., and J. Watts. 1989. Community Builders and Community Associations: The Role of Real Estate Developers in Private Residential Governance. In *Residential Community Associations: Private Governments in the Intergovernmental System?* U.S. Advisory Commission on Intergovernmental Relations. Washington, D.C. Advisory Commission on Intergovernmental Relations.

Wiebe, R. 1995. *Self-Rule: A Cultural History of American Democracy.* Chicago: University of Chicago Press.

Williams, N. 1974. *American Planning Law.* Chicago: Callaghan.

Williams, R. A. 1989. Euclid's Lochnerian Legacy. In *Zoning and the American Dream,* ed. C. Haar and J. Kayden. Chicago: Planners Press, American Planning Association.

Wilson, J. Q., and G. L. Kelling. 1982. Broken Windows: The Police and Neighborhood Safety. *Atlantic Monthly* (March).

Wireman, P. 1984. *Urban Neighborhoods, Networks, and Families.* Lexington, Mass.: Lexington Books.

14

The Case for Land Lease versus Subdivision

Homeowners' Associations Reconsidered

Spencer Heath MacCallum

The last third of the twentieth century witnessed a profound revolution in local government in the United States, namely the addition of a new level of formal government below that of the municipality. The rise of formal neighborhood government came about through the growth of "common interest developments" (CIDs) in residential housing. Residents of virtually all newer subdivisions, including condominiums, today enjoy a "common interest" not only in the streets and other common areas of their neighborhood but in the lifestyle of their neighbors so far as that might be construed as affecting the resale value of their home. The instrument for regulating lifestyle and policing that common interest is the governing board of a mandatory-membership homeowners' association set up by the developer in the original design of the project and subsequently "running with the land," which is to say, perpetuated in the property deeds.

These neighborhood governments evolved slowly from the early 1900s, gradually acquiring legal standing to exercise police and tax powers. From the mid 1960s they spread rapidly, growing from fewer than 500 in 1965 to more than 230,000 throughout the United States today, with jurisdiction over more than 47 million Americans. Virtually all new residential housing in major metropolitan areas is now organized as CIDs.[1]

Despite this rapid growth, which would seem to imply a broad market acceptance, the quality of life residents tend to expect on entering a new subdivision under CID government has not always been realized. Exceptions notwithstanding, judging from the numbers of complaints and litigation, these neighborhood governments are often arbitrary, unresponsive, and dictatorial. The uniform response has been to call for municipal, state, and federal legislation and oversight to bring neighborhood government into conformity with government at those levels. There has been little sociological or organizational study of homeowners' associations, and nowhere in the media, in the trade literature, or in academic journals has anyone suggested that there might be any other basis for residential neighborhood organization.

In this chapter, fearing that some of the most attractive features of the traditional American lifestyle, such as tolerance, neighborliness, and freedom to enjoy the use of one's property, are being lost, I will urge consideration of a neighborhood organizing principle alternative to the CID formula of subdivision under a homeowners' association. I will urge consideration of land-leasing, a *nonpolitical* approach to neighborhood organization long employed in commercial real estate that, if federal policy allowed it to compete on an equal footing with CIDs, presumably would bring innovation and variety to the housing field, providing consumers attractive lifestyle options they do not now have.

Under the land-lease approach, the land underlying a neighborhood of individually owned improvements on leased sites is retained in single ownership and administered as a long-term investment property for income. This option is now largely foreclosed by federal tax policy, which penalizes leasing ground for residential use, as well as by federal subsidies of subdivision housing. Even apart from these formidable political obstacles, land-leasing might strike the reader as an unlikely suggestion for residential development, considering our long-standing American tradition of freehold land tenure. But important insights can be gained from looking at the unexpected.

Because of its many advantages as a principle of social organization, advantages that I will endeavor to explain, land-leasing has been employed increasingly and with great success in commercial real estate. Its history is so distinct from that of subdivision that a brief overview of the background of each is in order before comparing and contrasting what each has to offer with respect to enhanced lifestyle and community.

Managing the American Subdivision

Subdivision, whether large and systematic or casual, has been the characteristic pattern of American settlement from earliest colonial times.

While it is commonly thought of today as a recent suburban phenomenon, a moment's reflection tells us that all American cities and towns are subdivisions. The few land-lease experiments under the colonial proprietary governments were short-lived, and federal land policy for as long as there has been any has favored single-family homes on subdivision lots.

The prevailing form of government in early American subdivisions was by vote of landowners. Only landowners participated in local politics. A property qualification for voting in American towns and cities lasted until well into the nineteenth century, eventually giving way everywhere under the advance of egalitarian and democratic ideology.

As the outward suburban push began in the United States early in the twentieth century, pioneering large developer/builders such as Edward H. Bouton of Baltimore and the legendary Jesse Clyde Nichols of Kansas City began the now-standard practice of inserting restrictive covenants in the deeds to help ensure that the lots and houses they sold would maintain their sales value. Initially this helped the developer by assuring that inventory would not decline in value before the last lot was sold, but it also conveyed an aura of exclusivity that at once became a selling point for prospective residents. The weakness of restrictive covenants was that once a subdivision was sold out and the developer gone, the new property owners were left on their own to police a vanished interest, and enforcement of deed restrictions among neighbors is not easy. Consequently, to make enforcement more practical and thereby to be better able to represent the notion that home ownership was a safe investment that would hold its value, developers began to provide in the deeds for homeowners' associations that would maintain the common areas and help enforce the deed restrictions. At first they provided for voluntary and then later for mandatory membership.

From the early 1960s onward, these associations vastly multiplied as condominiums, a specialized form of subdivision, joined planned-unit developments on the building scene. The Federal Housing Administration in 1963 authorized federal home mortgage insurance exclusively for condominiums or for homes in subdivisions where there was a qualifying homeowners' association.[2] The rationale for this bonanza for subdivision builders was that homes in tracts where there was a homeowners' association would be more likely to maintain their value. What it did, however, was divert investment from multifamily housing and home construction or renovation in the inner cities, speeding the middle-class exodus to the suburbs and into common-interest housing. The federal highways program facilitated the process.

A growing scarcity of suitable land for development in the suburbs began to be felt by the early and mid-1970s, with the result that land costs escalated. In order to continue to make a profit, developers found they had to increase the density of homes on the land. They did this while still retaining a suburban look by clustering homes around green open areas. Open areas require management, however, and associations were promoted to the buying public as a satisfactory solution.

As this was happening federal aid to cities began to dry up and developers found it increasingly necessary to provide services that formerly had been provided by municipalities and paid for from public funds. This enabled financially strapped cities to cut down on their expenditures at the same time that more homes were being built, increasing the property-tax base. Municipal governments were anxious, therefore, to promote subdivision development. These factors and others, in concert with the population boom, contributed to the exploding number of homeowners' associations.

To qualify their product for federal insurance and thus to be able to compete in the industry, subdivider/builders routinely included a boilerplate homeowners' association in each development. Today, although technically called "voluntary associations" since to call them "governments" would subject them to the same constitutional review as municipal governments, homeowners' associations have become in point of fact a new layer of political government.

Throughout their formative years, though not recently because of the threat of constitutional restraints, advocates had clearly and explicitly recognized the homeowners' association as a new type of local government patterned on the Progressive era council/manager plan and perfected in 1928 for the town of Radburn, New Jersey. Besides doing the common-area maintenance, these neighborhood governments now regularly tax, regulate, and police. In the event of noncompliance with rules or nonpayment of assessments, the governing boards of associations have the power to place liens on residents' homes. Regulations can be amended or new ones adopted by vote of the property owners. The pattern of early American subdivisions has come full circle.

In the democratic Western world, at least, it may be stated as a principle that if voting behavior is not already present, any extensive subdivision of lands will give rise to it. So predictable is this that it permits the classification of subdivisions into one of two categories, depending on whether voting is per capita or by property qualification. That is one of the chief distinctions between municipalities and CIDs. The latter differ in that the franchise has a property qualification attached; board members are elected by the landowners. Otherwise the governing board operates much as a traditional political government although, being exempt from state and federal constitutional review, with a wider latitude of powers.

The property qualification assumes enough importance in the minds of some classical-liberal commentators that several have adopted the name "proprietary community" as a descriptive term for CIDs.[3] They speak approvingly of the governing boards of homeowners' associations as "contractual," "private-enterprise," "voluntary," or simply "private" governments. They feel these governments differ significantly from municipal governments for having been established by private contract, their powers deriving from the covenants originally placed on the land by the developer and the membership being conditioned in the property deed each unit owner signed when buying a lot. (e.g., see Boudreaux and Holcombe in this volume)

This argument does not take into account, however, that once established, any distinction in principle between the governing boards of associations and conventional political governments vanishes. The argument that they are more voluntary because homeowners know what they are agreeing to when they buy into the subdivision and are free at any time to sell and leave does not hold up, since the same can be said of any municipality; people are free to move into or out of any community, always knowing that while they are there, they will be subject to the jurisdiction of the local political government.

In point of fact, CID boards tend to be far more restrictive of the individual's freedom of behavior and use of property than municipal governments. The Community Association Institute (CAI), the trade organ of CID managers and associated professionals, prepared a document in 1985 entitled, *Community Association Members' and Residents' Bill of Rights.* A lawyer who has represented CIDs evaluates this supposed "Bill of Rights" as follows:

> The . . . document is a listing of procedural matters, largely parliamentary, that are the "rights" reserved for the owners—all of which are "subject to the community association's duty to fulfill its purposes, and subject to the need for timely response to emergencies." The document does not really place any part of the individual's life beyond the reach of private government because the rights are surrounded by such words as "reasonable," "as appropriate," and "in light of needs and circumstances." For example, the right to privacy merely provides that the association shall "minimize intrusion into the privacy of individual units, individual affairs and personal records."

This "bill of rights" does not include any right to an independent judiciary, leaving the association board with the power to make the rules, charge people with violating them, and try the violators. The accused has merely the right to "notice and an opportunity to be heard," but the association board has the power to levy fines, including "imposition of special charges or fees for misconduct," which seems to suggest almost a quasi-criminal jurisdiction.[4]

The arbitrariness of many association boards and the friction caused by association politics have attracted the attention of the media. For example, the following is from a column in the *Las Vegas Sun:*

The trouble with homeowner associations is that deep down Americans don't believe in them. They're not founded on liberty and justice for all. They're not founded on the proposition that all men are created equal. And they're definitely not founded to ensure domestic tranquility. . . .

. . . [I]n the process, many fundamental rights that Americans hold dear . . . are signed away. Little things like private property rights, due process and access to government. Because, let's face it, these associations are mini-governments, dictating a whole range of lifestyle restrictions that public agencies can't even look at.

First, the rules aren't written by a duly elected body. . . .

Second, the government is elected by the property owners. Renters are disenfranchised in this democracy.

Third, the board not only levies the fines for breaking the rules, but it also functions as the judge and jury for appeals. This doesn't sound like due process to most folks who have been through it. . . .

So long as boards operate as . . . oligarchies in a land dedicated to life, liberty and the pursuit of happiness, the horror stories, ugly confrontations and lawsuits will continue. If association boards and members want to live in harmony, they . . . had better figure out how to do it the American way.[5]

It would seem but a matter of time before residents sue for federal protection of the freedoms of assembly, speech, religion, and voting, not to mention guarantee of due process, to which they may suppose themselves to be entitled as United States citizens. Moreover, those disenfranchised by the one-vote-per-unit rule—in other words, renters, spouses, and other adult unit occupants—normally constitute a majority of the residents.[6] This majority might well become restless under the governing board's undemocratic regime (especially since developers themselves often cast three votes for each unsold home) and sue for a voice in their local government. Lawyers then would argue in court that since associations are in plain fact governments, federal and state constitutions entitle their clients to the right to vote.

Should efforts to extend the franchise to all residents succeed, this would merely recapitulate the process by which, historically, American municipalities founded as subdivisions under proprietary government broadened their voting base and became democratic. In the light of American history, it would seem premature to name CIDs "proprietary communities."

"Catch-22"

The exemption of CID boards from state or federal constitutional review derives from the fact that the common areas in a CID are (collective) private property, and historically, what anyone does on private property has been for the most part independent of constitutional review. All it would take for that to change would be for the courts to call homeowners' associations "governments"—as they were called by their original promoters. Are homeowners' associations thus a Trojan horse within the walls, destined to open private property to state and federal regulation greater by orders of magnitude than at present?

On the other hand, if the courts continue to construe homeowners' associations as voluntary associations and not as governments and therefore not subject to constitutional review, much the same will result. For then it will be up to traditional governments to regulate homeowners' associations. Already a rising tide of legislative regulation is in evidence. Since homeowners' associations are created by private contracts, these regulatory currents threaten to undermine traditional freedom of contract. Freedom of contract will be compromised and the terms and conditions of association progressively regulated by statute.

CIDs have been promoted by large corporate developers in concert with the federal government to the point that they are virtually the only housing available. With government backing, they have monopolized the housing market. The public is thereby being denied alternative housing choices, not the least of which might well be housing options that, given equal access to the market, land-lease developers might have provided. Certainly it is unsound to assume that the widespread development of CIDs reflects an overwhelming consumer demand for subdivision. It may reflect instead a market distortion. Anthropologist Erna Gunther once asked a woman weaver of one of the Northwest tribes why they used harsh aniline colors rather than softer ones that more closely resemble natural plant dyes. The woman replied that these colors were the ones available at the trading post. Later Gunther asked the trader why he did not carry a wider selection of colors. "Because," he answered, "these are the colors they buy."[7]

It is even less self-evident that the rapid spread of CIDs is indicative of an advance in the art of neighborhood governance.

Ebenezer Howard

Most of the physical planning innovations in American subdivision, such as functional zoning, density control, design control, and greenbelt, stem from the work of Ebenezer Howard, who in turn-of-the-century England built on rural land outside of London, as a grand social experiment, the "Garden Cities" of Letchworth and Welwyn. Radburn, New Jersey, was a self-conscious effort to transplant the Garden City idea to this side of the Atlantic. But curiously, half of Howard's legacy, and to his mind almost certainly the greater half, did not survive the ocean crossing. For Howard's Garden Cities were not conceived or built as subdivisions. His genius was to propose and build his cities on the land-lease principle—that of a hotel opened out and on a large scale. There would be no need for taxation or levies because the revenue from the land would finance the town administration.

A follower of Howard, wondering how such an innovation could have been lost sight of, plaintively wrote:

> Howard and his associates made one propagandist mistake in siting Letchworth and Welwyn—building them in England within an hour's journey of London. One should have been built on some remote island like Mauritius, and the other in the Soviet Republic of Uzbuzchakistan. Planners and journalists would then have visited them and written them up, and we should have had lots of illuminating books on them. Also we should have been excited about them as wonderful achievements, and be wanting to know why we can't have new towns of the same type in Dear Old Stick-in-the-Mud England.[8]

Subdividing its land leaves a new community after the developer's departure without either a source of public revenue or a means of administration. (Imagine the management problems that would ensue if, upon its completion, a hotel were subdivided.) To fill that void, the developers of Radburn, in a conscious application of Progressive era political science, perfected and honed the homeowners' association that American subdivider/builders had been experimenting with. For the wholly contractual and voluntary administration of a community that was Howard's ideal, they substituted a form of quasidemocratic, compulsory-membership government endowed with whatever regulatory and taxing power it requires.

In one sense, therefore, this chapter picks up the other half of the Garden City legacy, joining many who find inspiration in the English Garden City movement. But it does this more by way of acknowledgment than by attempting to transplant a European idea. For the main source of its inspiration is a parallel but independent, altogether native tradition of land lease in America. I refer to the ubiquitous development of multiple-tenant income properties, of which the shopping mall and the hotel are examples.

Multiple-Tenant Income Properties (MTIPs)

Conservative commentators who refer to CIDs as "proprietary communities" may be unaware that proprietary communities can take another form that, if anything, is even more deserving of the name. Not only is this other form, like the CID, wholly governed by its proprietors, but land within the community is not taxed, nor is its use circumscribed by the nonproprietary process of voting. This alternative form of proprietary community is not a subdivision at all. Title to the underlying ground (as distinct from improvements on it) is not subdivided upon completion of the development but is kept intact, and parceling into sites is accomplished by leasehold. This is the multiple-tenant income property (MTIP), which English speakers in most parts of the world outside the United States call an "estate."

In agrarian society throughout much of the world, under the broad rubric of "manorialism," parceling by means of leasehold rather than subdivision has a long and respected history. Today it is no longer, as in ages past, chiefly identified with agriculture, but has become a land tenure of choice in many urban contexts. This is especially true in the

United States, where land-leasing has come to be applied across a wide range of predominantly commercial land uses. Indeed, the history of MTIPs has been one of the more dramatic and least remarked developments in American land usage. If the rise of CIDs has had little academic attention, the rise of MTIPs has had almost none at all.

Precursors of many forms of MTIP were not strangers to the ancient and medieval world, but the differences between them and their modern counterparts, operating in and integral with a competitive global market economy, were often profound.[9] In the United States, the earliest distinctly modern manifestation was the hotel, acknowledged by the hotel industry as having begun with the Tremont House in Boston in 1829. Later in that century office buildings and apartment houses made their debut. But the dramatic growth of MTIPs, like that of CIDs in residential housing, followed on the heels of World War II, when they proliferated in form, function, and number. While proliferating, they were also growing in size and in complexity, the latter by combining, as atoms of different kinds will combine to form more complex molecules.

Conspicuous in that postwar growth was the shopping center, which arrived barely in time to save the United States from inundation with an unholy snarl and sprawl of commercial strip development—as any who lived at that time will remember. Shopping centers numbered less than a dozen at the close of the war, and those were experimental—small convenience centers called "park-and-shops." Now approaching fifty thousand in the United States alone, they include vast shopping malls that accommodate hundreds of stores and other kinds of businesses together with a broad spectrum of cultural activities and draw patronage from an entire geographic region.

Other forms of MTIP besides hotels and shopping centers include land-lease manufactured-home communities, marinas, mobile-home parks, apartment complexes, medical clinics, research parks, office parks, and combinations of these and other types. Even passenger ships, trains, and planes satisfy the criteria of the definition and fall within the category. These latter have the highest frequency of turnover, and they offer a unique public good, namely variable location.[10]

A prominent aspect of this growth of MTIPs has been a trend in all categories not only toward greater size (many hotel enterprises today accommodate daily populations in the tens of thousands) but away from narrow specialization toward ever greater complexity in mixed-use developments that are more heterogeneous, more generalized.[11] These trends suggest to the imagination that the entrepreneurial approach to community management might one day offer public services on a competitive, free-market basis over wide areas in lieu of local governments as we know them. In fact, Ebenezer Howard's Garden Cities of Letchworth and Welwyn, in England, with a combined population of some eighty thousand people, operated on very nearly this principle for nearly half a century until they were nationalized by the Labor government after World War II. During that time they offered outstanding public services and had no occasion to levy a tax on their residents.[12]

This entrepreneurial form of land administration, which is proliferating so vigorously in commercial real estate, has seriously lagged in the market for residential housing. Besides the immediate explanations of discriminatory taxing policy and federal subsidy, there is also the consideration that innovations often appear first in the commercial and luxury markets and only then spread to the general population. Whatever the full explanation, entrepreneurial land-leasing represents a principle of neighborhood organization altogether distinct from subdivision and one that promises significant advantages with respect to quality of life enjoyed by residents. But for the political problem of equal access to the housing market, it would appear to hold the seeds of far-reaching entrepreneurial opportunity with commensurately broadened consumer choice.

Advantages over Subdivision

Opening Caveat

The following discussion contrasts CIDs and MTIPs, or land-lease communities, in ten different areas, showing in all cases the advantage of the latter. In fairness, this is an idealized construct, designed to point out sharply the behavioral differences resulting from two very different incentive structures. To do this, the discussion assumes that all else will be equal. In real life, however, "other things" are seldom equal or even approximately so. Particular factors come into play, as a result of which we may find excellently governed subdivisions and badly governed MTIPs. Personality mix is probably the most important single factor. In a subdivision, for example, strong personal leadership can overcome almost any structural deficiency, reminding us of the truth in Alexander Pope's aphorism, "For forms of government let fools contest; what is best administered is best." Numerous other factors include size, which may hamper the performance of an MTIP too small to warrant professional or on-site management. Lack of effective competition due to restrictive zoning is a factor of long standing in the case of manufactured-home communities.

Despite these and other offsetting factors affecting both MTIPs and subdivisions, the incentive structure in the one inclines it toward optimization of resident satisfactions whereas in the other it does not. That is the premise of the land-lease community, which is in business to succeed in a competitive market environment. The subdivision, on the other hand, is not a business. It is altogether a matter of consumption. There is no new wealth being produced there. The incentive to provide effective, service-oriented administration in a subdivision is weak and more readily overwhelmed by conflicting interests, personal agendas, and inertia.

Informed Decision-Making

The first advantage of the multiple tenant income property is that it is entrepreneurial. That means that there is someone to make decisions and that those decisions are not made in a void; they are informed. In fact the entrepreneur in any matter requiring a policy decision has the strongest possible incentive to seek the optimal decision for the overall benefit of the community. The entrepreneur is in an ideal position to serve in a leadership capacity, being at once interested and disinterested, which is to say both motivated and nonpartisan. He or she is actively concerned for the success of the community *qua community.* While this can be seen at its best in the management of an active land-lease community such as a shopping mall—which is a community of landlord and merchant tenants with many thousands of visitors—it applies to all.

Subdivision residents, on the other hand, have no champion. Consequently they must resort to voting, a process in which there must always be losers, for if there were no dissenting minorities to be overridden, there would be no voting. Because of fragmented titles and interests, there is no other way in the Anglo-American tradition to manage a subdivision. Moreover, the issues submitted to vote and the resulting policies tend to be reactive and restrictive rather than proactive and facilitative precisely because of the lack of a concentrated entrepreneurial interest in the whole. The lowest-common-denominator interest among the residents is self-protective—to maintain the status quo and prevent property values from deteriorating. Anything more creative is likely to die on the barricades of conflicted interests. Fortunate is the community where volunteer leadership, blessed with an uncommon degree of charisma, vision, and common sense, can inspire a reduction or opening of the barricades and produce creative common action.

Voting, widely held to be democratic, serves as the great legitimizer of the political process.[13] But the fact is that like the political process itself, it is a makeshift, like a coin toss, that people fall back upon in the absence of any better alternative. While it is good to have a fallback, we must never lose sight of the fact that voting is not a proprietary process. It is a recourse where property relations are lacking or little developed. Jonathan Swift supposedly quipped that "some people have no better idea of determining right from wrong than by counting noses." Voting is not a procedure for discovering truth or for making informed decisions. It is an agreed-upon method for people to gang up on one another without overt violence, an example of what anthropologists call in exotic societies "ritual combat." In Western democracies, rather than resorting to violence, combatants "count noses," each faction by lobbying and confrontational tactics marshaling numbers to its cause. Then they let the tally symbolize victory for one or another, the primitive idea presumably being that the combatant that marshals the most bodies would come out the winner in combat if it had to come to that. Instead of navigating toward a win-win situation, voting is a method of breaking resistance to a course of action while ignoring the differences underlying the resistance. Its zero-sum nature is starkly dramatized in that wonderful vignette, attributed to Mencken, of two wolves and a lamb voting on the question of what to have for dinner.

Concert of Interests

Voting is closely associated with subdivision, the reason being that while every community has its owner or owners, the owners of a community that is subdivided find themselves with conflicting interests built into the situation. The particular interest of each owner is identified with a separate location having its unique attributes, so that when it comes to actions affecting the whole community, the outlook of each frequently conflicts to a greater or less degree with that of every other. The generic illustration is the plight of a hypothetical 1950s downtown business district laid out a century earlier for horse-drawn vehicular traffic. Main Street has become gridlocked. All of the property owners agree that the street needs to be widened and off-street parking provided. However, when it comes to executing these improvements that all endorse, each site owner, no matter how well intentioned, has no choice but to insist the widening take place on the other side of the street from his or her property while the proposed new parking be on his or her side and as close to his or her property as possible—without, of course, taking any. By voting in this scenario, no one wins except at another's expense.

The MTIP, by contrast, may have many times more owners than a subdivision of comparable size. But because their ownership takes the form of undivided shares in the whole, their interests are aligned. To attain consensus, they need only agree on whether a policy will benefit the community as a whole and not some particular parcel. An exception might be where one of the owners is also a tenant, but this does not affect the principle.

Flexible Land Usage

Land-leasing permits flexibility in land usage, since changes can be effected gradually over time as leases run out and come up for renewal. This flexibility extends even to the basic layout of streets and common areas, an important consideration in times of rapid technological change like the present.

In the subdivision, by contrast, once the developer has disposed of the last parcel or even a significant number of them, the layout is frozen. This is the situation with virtually all American towns and cities. As obsolescence becomes more pronounced, pressure mounts for a government agency to intervene and break up the ownerships by eminent domain. The alternative is to wait until obsolescence is so far advanced and land values correspondingly so low that it is economic to privately reassemble the titles for redevelopment. This may take many years, during which time the land is being used suboptimally, a condition we know as blight.

Financially Self-Sustaining

Under a land-lease approach there is no occasion for taxation. Ground rents finance the community administration. Rather than operating at a chronic deficit to be made up by tax levies, as every subdivided community must do, the public administration when carried out competently by the owners of an MTIP yields a revenue, making the community a self-sustaining enterprise.

The weakness of the subdivision is that it lacks any entrepreneurial opportunity with respect to building value in the community as a whole. Once the land title is subdivided and the parcels are sold, the developer's interest, which permitted the creation of an integrated development in the first place, vanishes and so does the developer, there being no opportunity left for him or her there. But where title to the underlying real estate remains intact (and we are always talking about the ground and not the buildings, which can be owned separately), then the business opportunity and the challenge for the community entrepreneur are to create such an optimal environment in that location that everyone will want to live and/or work there in preference to whatever other options may be available. So far as the developer succeeds, land values measured by revenue flow will be bid up, more than compensating for the cost of the public services. The result is a community that might be termed "entrepreneurial"—as opposed to "political."

Effective Planning

The successful community entrepreneur is *responsible* in his or her decision-making in the sense of being *responsive* to the wants and desires of the public the entrepreneur wishes to attract, which is to say, his or her special market niche. The entrepreneur's success is measured by the land revenue, which affords *quantitative feedback*. It is interesting to consider that under political auspices community planning never developed as a science, not for want of incentive alone (indeed, there was frequently disincentive) but because it lacked feedback or even any unit of measure. It had no means of measuring past performance or of estimating the worth to the community of plans under consideration. Under proprietary auspices, on the other hand, there is such a measure. Consequently planning in land-lease communities—some of the larger hotels and regional malls, for example—has reached a level of sophistication that has never been approached by traditional city planners. It is clear that the future of town or city planning as a science lies with the land-lease community and not with the subdivision, where most efforts at planning—probably better termed "monument building"—have been made in the past.

Predictability

Predictability as to how a person can use private property is the essence of ownership. In the CID, because everything is subject to the voting of neighbors, uncertain probabilities take its place. Because the outcome of a vote cannot be known in advance and because there is nothing in the covenants, conditions, and restrictions (CC&Rs) that cannot be changed by the vote of the neighborhood, what a person actually agrees to in buying into the development is total uncertainty. In many cases this may be acceptable to all concerned; they may feel such rules as the one at the Double Diamond subdivision, in Reno, Nevada, prohibiting garage doors being in an up position more than three hours a day are only a minor annoyance, a small price to pay for living in the community. But should the behavior of the board become tyrannical or insufferable, the only recourse would be to appeal to higher levels of government, for relief from the courts in particular situations, or for new legislation to regulate board behavior. But for that possible recourse, itself hardly certain, control over lifestyle and permitted uses of property is subject to the fortunes of the vote of the neighborhood. This finds its justification in the philosophy of New Urbanism, which, as Todd W. Bressi approvingly notes in his essay entitled "Planning the American Dream," is based on one simple principle: "Community planning and design must assert the importance of public over private values."[14]

Though philosophically attractive to some, the practical downside of CIDs legislating rules or laying them aside, changing the restrictive covenants, and levying fines and taxes, all solely by vote of the neighborhood, is that it gives residents no control or ability to predict, from day to day or from one year to the next, how they will be allowed to enjoy their property. Individual autonomy, which is nothing if not control of one's person and property, is for all intents and purposes negated. While such unpredictability may be of less concern in residential areas, where no business is transacted, it becomes serious in commercial properties, where businesspeople every day have to be able to commit to contracts extending into the future. This may in some measure account for the dramatic spread of land-leasing in commercial real estate, for in an MTIP, all of the rules that will ever apply are stipulated not by faceless others through periodic votes of the community or an elected board but by the private parties to the lease and no one else. For the term of the lease, however short or long, barring only government intervention, these contracting parties know where they stand. Though the lease be written for 999 years, a not-uncommon practice in English common law, the terms are fixed and dependable unless amended by mutual agreement. The stability that can be found in such contractual arrangements was attested to recently by a news item that a 999-year lease had run its course in England.

Continuing Involvement: The Long-Term View

The MTIP is a long-term contractual undertaking. While a CID is sometimes called a "contractual community," a home buyer's contracting partner (party of the first part) typically disappears after consummation of the property sale. This partner's counterpart in the land-lease community, on the other hand, remains very much in the picture and continues to be responsible for what he or she represents and sells. The land-lease community being an income property, the community entrepreneur (so far as tax policy and political regulations allow) is motivated to take a long-term view. By contrast, it is sufficient for the subdivider/builder that he or she create a saleable product. While subdivider/builders will be concerned for their reputation as businesspeople, they need not take a very much longer-term view of the community than the customer, who is usually inexpert, is likely to take. This may have been a contributing factor in the rash of quality-control problems encountered in the construction of subdivision housing from the late 1970s through the 1990 recession, problems that have become the subject of extensive litigation.[15]

Service-Oriented Personnel

The difference between subdivisions and MTIPs is sometimes reflected in the attitudes of their respective personnel. The governing board of the association, beyond its responsibility for the operation and maintenance of the common areas, is largely an enforcement body to prevent behavior in the subdivision that might negatively affect the resale value of houses in the project. Its mandate to enforce the CC&Rs requires treating all cases alike rather than judging each on its merit, not only to avoid charges of favoritism come election time but to avoid the appearance of relaxing the rules in some cases and not in others and so weakening the rules overall. A policy of treating all alike is further required by the fact that the board is operating not with its own funds but with community funds, which creates a fiduciary relationship and circumscribes its options. Board members and professional managers have a further incentive to enforce the CC&Rs aggressively and inflexibly—in order to protect themselves from personal liability for error under the "good business judgment rule." Finally, indulging in rigid or arbitrary behavior that might be needlessly offensive to residents costs a board member little, since his or her proprietary interest in the subdivision is so attenuated as to be practically nonexistent; only if residents began to sell their homes and move out in droves would it begin to affect the board member's investment in his or her home. The resulting psychology is that residents come to be regarded as *subjects,* that is, as persons *subject to* the jurisdiction of the board. Compliant residents are good residents, while insubordinates must be made examples of. Sadly, the following stories are not atypical.

[In Rancho Bernardo, California, the Bernardo Home Owners Corporation] cited . . . a homeowner for violating the rule against television antennas by installing a satellite dish, which he had concealed from view inside a structure. The point, members of the BHOC [Bernardo Home Owners Corporation] argued, was that a satellite dish is an antenna. The fact that in this case it neither looked like an antenna (in fact, it was not visible to anyone) nor sat atop the roof was deemed irrelevant by the board.

In Delaware County, Pennsylvania, a man put up a four-foot-high fence of black fabric in his back yard to keep his young son from falling off a four-hundred-foot cliff. His homeowner association took him to court, contending that he had violated a rule against fences, but a judge ruled in his favor.

In Monroe, New Jersey, a homeowner association took a married couple to court because the wife, at age forty-five, was three years younger than the association's age minimum for residency. The association won in court, and the judge ordered the sixty-year-old husband to sell, rent the unit, or live without his wife.

Near Philadelphia is a development of $225,000 homes called Courtly. Construction of the homes began in the late 1980s. A married couple bought one in 1989 and brought their son's metal swing set with them when they moved in. One year later the association told them to take the swing set down, even though there were as yet no written rules regarding swing sets. When the rules finally appeared, they prescribed that all swing sets must be made of wood. Why? "It has to do with what the overall community should look like," said an attorney for the association. The couple then submitted a petition in support of the swing set that was signed by three-fourths of the homeowners, along with Environmental Protection Agency warnings about the dangers to children (in this case, aged two and four) posed by the poisonous chemicals used in pres-

sure-treated wood—the type needed for swing sets. The association's response was to impose a daily fine of ten dollars until the set
was removed and to refuse offers to compromise, which included
painting the swing set in earth tones. The association passed rules
governing the placement of firewood, rabbit hutches, and trash cans
on the curb. It also banned "offensive conduct," which it defined as
"activity which in the judgment of the Board of Directors is noxious or offensive to other home lot owners."[16]

Compare all of these examples with the attitude of the manager of
a land-lease development. Being in business to make a profit, he or she
has a strong disincentive for arbitrary behavior. The competitive nature
of business makes it clear to the manager that tenants are customers
rather than subjects, and he or she understands that the manager's role
is to assist customers in optimizing the satisfactions of community life.
The management objective is not to keep values from depreciating by
enforcing uniform compliance with rules, which is merely a staying
action, a matter of maintaining the status quo while protecting the
manager from liability, but through proactive management to build
land value, which is the market measure of overall community desirability.

An early study of trouble situations that arise in mobile-home
parks and shopping centers noted the flexibility that is possible in the
management of MTIPs as contrasted with CIDs.[17] It cites the case of
an elderly woman in a mobile-home community who had saved the life
of a kitten and, in violation of a no-pets rule, given it a home. Worse,
she let it wander. The manager spoke to her one or two times but did
nothing until some neighbors complained. When the elderly woman
next made a visit to the office to pick up her mail, the manager asked
her to sit down and spoke with her. She told her she would have to
move out of the park if her kitten continued to wander. The woman
cried. Afterward, the manager called the neighbors who had complained to the office and told them what she had said to the woman,
adding, "Do you want her to leave—and take your chances on a new
neighbor whom you don't know?" The upshot was that the kitten continued to wander and that there were no further complaints. The neighbors felt they had been listened to. "Kitty is on probation" is how the
manager summed it up. The manager of a different mobile-home community disclosed the presence of both children and animals in violation
of the rules, adding, "They're all on probation."

The policy of these managers was that a rule need not be enforced in the absence of complaints. The manager of yet another mobile-home community never issued printed rules at all, saying that he relied on new tenants learning from others in the course of living in the park what the customary behavior was.

A further illustration concerns a mall merchant who had broken a leg in a weekend skiing accident and had been fitted with a walking cast. On Monday morning, he parked his car near his store instead of in the designated area for tenant and employee parking. A rule strictly enforced in all malls is that spaces near the stores are reserved for customer use. He received a warning from a security guard and another on Tuesday. The manager found out the circumstances and informed the guards. No further notices were issued. Later the merchant resumed parking in the designated area. The manager was quoted as saying, "There are mitigating circumstances you must take into consideration. You have to use your head and be reasonable." The outcome in another case was entirely different. When a nurse employed in the mall openly flouted the parking rule not once but several times, the doctor who employed her was given the choice of firing her or leaving the mall.

The fact that the manager of an MTIP has more discretion in decision-making than the board members of a homeowners' association is no guarantee against the manager's making bad decisions. The point is that the manager/owner is more likely to arrive at an optimal decision than popularly elected board members in a subdivision who, being relatively insulated from the consequences of their actions, have a greater likelihood of indulging their private agendas. A proprietor acting in proper self-interest and disciplined by the competition of the marketplace is more apt to practice effective leadership than are elected officeholders.

Effective Dispute Management

CIDs are notorious for their litigiousness. An attorney experienced in representing homeowners associations in California writes:

> Covenant enforcement litigation has become a profitable legal specialization for attorneys in states with many CIDs, as has its corollary: suit, or countersuit, by members against their boards for negligence, breach of their fiduciary duty to the members, abuse of authority, and suit under some theory of quasi-governmental liability, such as alleged violations of constitutional rights. . . . To alleviate the oppressive burden of lawsuits arising from CIDs, several

states have considered or enacted special provisions for alternative dispute resolution.[18]

Because of the number of association directors being harassed or threatened with lawsuit (44 percent during one year according to a study), the California legislature in 1992 established tort immunity for board members, giving them protections not unlike those of municipal officials. However, "in making the job of volunteer director less hazardous, this immunity reduced the incentive for board members to be consistently cognizant of the consequences their actions might have, for residents and others."[19]

MTIPs offer a remarkable contrast. As can easily be imagined, highly competitive businesspeople in a mall setting are not immune to differences. Yet in the study of dispute cases referred to earlier, of forty-one cases collected, only one involved a lawyer, and his only action had been to write a letter to the mall manager.

It is critical that mall merchants work as a team. But need alone will not make it happen. Teams need coaching. Disputes among merchants typically are resolved internally, sometimes through the offices of an ad hoc merchant delegation but most frequently through the manager, who represents the unifying landowning interest. The manager exercises a leadership role with a peacekeeping function little different, if at all, from that of the headman of an African village. A manager will allot time each day for walking casually on the mall, talking with his or her tenants. In the course of these contacts the manager hears of difficulties and complaints, usually from other merchants than those directly involved. One manager remarked that about 90 percent of the complaints he got were indirect: "Somebody says, 'So-and-so's been beefing about that.'" A manager will make it a point to learn about problems before they become serious, hear the stories of the offended parties, go back and forth between them both personally and by phone, and mediate a solution, being careful, as one said, not to act precipitately but to give each party "time to cool off." Recounting some of the ways he keeps in constant touch with his tenants, one manager reported a Rotary Club organized entirely within the center for which fifty-two merchants met together every week: "We're very close here; it's just like a little town. Now at lunch today, I talked to seven of my tenants."

Quality of Community Life

A frequent lament of commentators is that something about the quality of life in contemporary suburbia seems lacking. Of doubtless many

392   The Voluntary City

contributing causes, one is all too often overlooked. The subdivision formula has built-in incentives that work against the development of "community" in the sense of supportive and stimulating interpersonal relations. By its nature, subdivision prompts residents to want to coerce the behavior and lifestyle of their neighbors. What is the logic of this? Because in our highly mobile society few people anticipate spending a lifetime in one place, we attach particular importance to liquidity and safety in a real-estate investment. Now imagine a couple who have bought their new home in a subdivision. It is perhaps the largest single investment they will make in their lifetime. It is not necessarily the best investment they could have made, but since virtually all new housing today is CID housing, which is premised on the purchase of a house and lot, other options are effectively closed. However that may be, they are concerned that it hold its value. But note especially that theirs is not a productive investment but a speculative one. It is a consumer expenditure—a residence. There is no capital employed on the site, no business to generate value apart from the site value. The value, therefore, is locational, rising and falling with the fortunes of the neighborhood. It is speculative because its value depends upon factors beyond the control of the couple. If they want to make their investment less speculative, their recourse is to try to control some of those locational, or neighborhood, factors influencing the value and liquidity of their individual site. In plain words, that means controlling who their neighbors are and how their neighbors live. The effect of this conflict between resale value and enjoyment of "community" is frequently a sterile neighborhood.

The land-lease community mitigates this problem in two ways. First, the site being leased reduces the size of the investment by the capitalized value of the land. But more significant, the speculative element is eliminated or substantially reduced by the fact that there is someone in the picture—the community entrepreneur—who is solely dedicated to building land value in the development. The investment in the home is actively protected by a responsible business enterprise dedicated to making the neighborhood successful and commanding the resources and skills to do so.

Objections to the Land-Lease Community Idea

The suggestion that land-leasing would be appropriate for residential housing communities may raise an objectionable image of "company towns."[20] Would anyone want to live in a community where all the land was owned by a private company? What would stop the landlord from becoming exploitive? The objection is answered in part by pointing out the successful examples of land-lease communities that do exist. One of the most interesting examples is the already mentioned Garden Cities of Letchworth and Welwyn, in England. In the United States, a small amount of land-leasing is practiced in residential housing by RV campgrounds and by the more recent land-lease manufactured-home communities.

A more fundamental response, however, has to do with the effects of advancing technology. The theoretical argument against a single-owner town is that once a family moves in, invests in a home, puts down roots, makes friends, and settles into jobs and school, it is difficult and costly for them to pick up and move again even if they could know in advance whether anyplace else would be preferable. Knowing this, the landlord can raise rents above market, exploit them in other ways, or let management deteriorate, and what can the family do?

A full answer would discuss the inbuilt incentives for the entrepreneurial landlord in an MTIP, but these have already been touched upon. An area not touched upon is that of technology, which is in the process of making land-lease towns more feasible than they ever have been before. Technological advances in transportation, information processing, and communications are lowering the psychological and economic costs and simplifying the physical task of moving, enabling people to keep in touch with their personal network by visiting more readily or at other times maintaining communication regardless of physical location, exploring alternative places to live and everything about them such as employment conditions, quality of schools, and satisfaction of other residents, even interviewing prospective landlords, all via the internet in the privacy of home. Brokers and other intermediaries are having to modify their role or leave the field, since prospective tenants are increasingly able to do their own research. Technological advancement is drastically reducing transaction costs, erasing the traditional distinction between real estate and other kinds of goods and services in the market. It is radically increasing competition, making the tenant, as customer, king to a degree that he or she has never been before—and there is no end in sight to this trend.[21]

A different kind of objection to MTIPs has to do with the cultural bias against "tenancy" that has been a part of the American heritage since colonial times, when Europeans sought escape from feudal conditions in much of Europe and each wanted to own freely a piece of land on which to be a king, as it were, on a private domain. Even today, although doubtless in large part because of public policy discouraging development of attractive options in residential land lease, tenants are looked down upon and homeowners given preference. Could it be that, given a level playing field, no one would show up for the game? That people intrinsically dislike leasehold? Despite the fact that home ownership for most people is only a technicality, with the mortgage lender standing close behind the curtain, many people nevertheless like the appearance of ownership—which they do have in CIDs. How difficult might it be to overcome this bias?

Such cultural discrimination can change quickly, given the need—and this chapter argues for a need on many levels for a satisfactory alternative to homeowners' associations. How quickly and easily cultural attitudes can change is evident in the rapid change from single-family housing to apartment living in New York City in the mid-nineteenth century. By the 1860s, rising land values on Manhattan Island had made detached, single-family homes prohibitively expensive even for the well-to-do. Apartment houses, then called "tenements," were not an option. They were wholly unacceptable socially. At this point a society matron, recently returned from a tour on the Continent, wrote some glowing articles for the newspaper about the luxurious apartment buildings of Paris. Almost within the year, construction was underway on New York's famed luxury high-rise apartments. Apartment living in New York City was suddenly fashionable and continues so to this day.

Collectivism and Private Local Government

Many classical liberals defend CIDs because they see attempts to regulate them by statute as an attack on freedom to make contracts. That is a true observation. What they miss is that CIDs in their present form, vested with public powers, are no longer purely a market phenomenon. The pioneers of CIDs—including the great subdivider/builders such as Edward H. Bouton and Jesse Clyde Nichols, allied with Charles S. Ascher, Clarence Stein, Louis Brownlow, and other Progressive era lawyers, political scientists, architects, planners, and public-administration experts—set up, even if in full innocence, another of humankind's questionable experiments in compulsory collectivism.[22] Had CIDs not been given blanket enforcement powers by the courts and been aggressively marketed with public backing and public funding, the experiment would not have come to monopolize the housing field as it has. When homeowners' associations, instead of continuing as voluntary associations, were given powers of traditional governments in a series of court decisions from the 1920s, especially in the New York Supreme Court's *Neponsit* decision of 1938 and cases following it, they left the sunlit field of private property and freedom of contract for the shadowy realm of politics.[23] Ironically, the successes of voluntary homeowners' associations in St. Louis shows that they could have continued to serve a useful function without taking on powers of government.[24]

Many of the same commentators applaud the rise of CIDs as privatization of local government.[25] They are looking in the wrong place. The point cannot be made too strongly that it is land-lease communities, and not CIDs, that represent authentic privatization of government. The reason is that CIDs still involve *taxation* of the residents and *voting* by the residents, which is political government as usual. Evan McKenzie concludes from an exhaustive historical study of common interest developments that "[t]here is no reason to believe that CID housing . . . offers a superior form of social organization to the municipality."[26] Land lease, on the other hand, does exactly that. The director of a mall merchants' association once told the author, "If something has to come to a vote, we don't want it."

Land-lease communities are nothing like municipalities in the powers they exercise. They are purely business arrangements among consenting individuals, subject to the free play of market competition. Their history bears this out. Unlike CIDs, which are the offspring of a marriage between large corporate developers and the federal government, the various manifestations of land-lease communities have grown up spontaneously and independently with the hardiness of uncultivated weeds. Their relatedness as a class has scarcely been remarked in any literature to this day. Yet within their limited but expanding spheres they are performing effectively and quietly—and profitably—the same kinds of essential community functions traditionally performed by municipal governments.

Conclusion

A final observation is appropriate to close this comparison and contrast of the CID and the MTIP. Unlike the former, which establishes another layer of local political government below that of municipalities, the land-lease community interposes between the individual *and all layers of political government* an effective buffering organization that is wholly proprietary and nonpolitical. A mall manager volunteered to the author that an important part of his role as he conceived it was to facilitate the interface between his merchant tenants and the local governing establishment in order to free his tenants to devote their time more productively to their business. This was good for his tenants, and it was good for the mall. In order to do this, he said, he made it a point to cultivate friendly relations with the local authorities. He said he participated widely in civic organizations in the community to make friends for the center and consequently knew "the right people to go to to get something done, as long as it's fair." He cited cooperation with civic clubs, the Boy Scouts, and the schools and said he counted among his friends in the town the mayor, city manager, chief of police, and fire chief.

The late Robert Nisbet acknowledged MTIPs to be an important class of the "intermediate associations" described in his major work, *The Quest for Community.*[27] Because of their low profile in the days immediately following World War II, when he was writing on the decline of intermediate associations in contemporary society, multiple-tenant land-lease arrangements had escaped his attention. As a class, they had barely emerged at that time. Their dramatic growth since, however, constitutes a countervailing trend to the one that he so poignantly documented. As such, they may afford grounds for cautious optimism regarding prospects for a humane society of the future.

I say *cautious* optimism because the land-lease approach, which has enjoyed spectacular success in commercial real estate, is virtually precluded by government policy from competing with subdivision in residential housing. If public-policy discrimination were to cease, the entrepreneurial vitality inherent in the approach might bring to an end the sterile planning of so much of the contemporary housing landscape. Given a level playing field, land-leasing might compete successfully with subdivision, providing consumers with many attractive and innovative housing options. Undoubtedly even CIDs would benefit from the competition. If we allow ourselves to dream a bit, here may lie the seed of truly voluntary cities.

NOTES

1. Statistics courtesy of Mary Shoman, Director of Media and Public Relations, Community Associations Institute, Alexandria, Virginia, January 30, 2001.
2. Federal Housing Administration 1964, 52.
3. More than a half-century ago Spencer Heath coined the phrase "propri-

etary community" exclusively for land-lease communities as opposed to subdivisions (see Item 1143, August 21, 1947, Spencer Heath Archives, Heather Foundation, Box 180, Tonopah, Nevada 89049). He first developed the rationale for "proprietary public administration" as a profit-seeking enterprise through land-leasing in a 1934 article, "The Capitalist System," written for *Atlantic Monthly* but never published. A comprehensive discussion of the idea can be found in his major work, *Citadel, Market and Altar* (1957). Because "proprietary community" no longer means exclusively multiple-tenant properties, I have adopted "land-lease community" as the general term of reference for these. It should be noted that within this class there is one form that falls outside this discussion. In the cooperative, which has its own separate history, the land is intact and the private areas leased, but the fact that it is nonprofit and ownership is tied to occupancy causes it to function more as a CID.

4. McKenzie 1994, 226. The document was adopted by the board of trustees of the CAI on March 29, 1985, and then amended and once more approved on October 10, 1993. The parts quoted by McKenzie are unchanged in the amended version.

5. McCall 1997.

6. "In California, a median of 20 percent of the CID units are rented; in 14 percent of the developments the majority of units are rented" (McKenzie 1994, 128, citing Barton and Silverman 1987).

7. Personal communication, 1959.

8. Osborn 1946, 36.

9. See, for example, a discussion of differences between the medieval and ancient inn and their modern counterpart, the hotel, in MacCallum 1970, 7–10.

10. Interestingly, land-lease manufactured-home communities have a notably low rate of turnover. In a personal communication to the author, George Allen, publisher of the *Allen Report,* which surveyed five hundred major owners of this type of real estate, said that the national turnover rate averages 10 percent per annum for homeowners, who become all but permanent residents of the leasehold property and sell their homes when they relocate. This compares with a turnover rate of 16 percent for families nationwide in housing of all types (*Statistical Abstracts of the United States* 1998, 32).

11. The two largest hotels in the world, the Ambassador Jomtien Hotel in Thailand and the MGM Grand in Las Vegas, each exceed five thousand rooms. According to statistics provided on January 20, 1998, by Michelle Tell, publicity director for the MGM Grand, the population of the Grand, exclusive of the theme park but including staff, room guests, and visitors, ranges from 35,000 to 70,000 daily. The theme park averages an additional 9,000 visitors. To put this in perspective, on any given day the constituency of the MGM Grand is two to four times greater than that of the city of Boston at the time of independence from England. (According to information provided by the Boston Public Library reference desk, Boston in 1765 had 15,520 inhabitants. By the United States Census of 1790, this had grown to 18,038—freemen only.)

12. MacCallum 1972, 17–24. In financing their public administration entirely from ground rents in lieu of taxes, Letchworth and Welwyn anticipated modern land-lease communities. They differed only in being established as a nonprofit trust

whose members were elected by the townspeople. C. B. Purdom, accountant for Letchworth, observed that "[t]he absence of any equity interest was to prove well-nigh fatal to the company" (Purdom 1949, 14). Despite this defect, which contributed to considerable weakness of management, both ventures were financially solvent, vindicating Howard's ideal of financing local government entirely from private ground rents without recourse to taxation. Regrettably both towns were nationalized when the British Labor government came into power.

13. For an insightful analysis of the political functions of voting, see Weissberg 1996, 11–13.

14. Bressi 1994, quoted by Peyser 2000, 34.

15. McKenzie (1994, 108) writes, "A massive federal study of condominiums and cooperatives revealed that owners were encountering serious construction defects with alarming frequency." Cited is the Department of Housing and Urban Development 1975. McKenzie (1994, 130) further states, "Recent surveys suggest that as many as one-third of all CIDs have major defects in original construction." Cited is Barton and Silverman 1987, 9.

16. McKenzie 1994, 10–11, 202. The first incident is reported by McKenzie from his attending a meeting of the Bernardo Home Owners Corporation. The others are newspaper accounts; Goldstein 1991; United Press International 1987; McCullough 1991.

17. MacCallum 1971, 3–10.

18. McKenzie 1994, 132.

19. McKenzie 1994, 19, 162. For the study referred to, the author cites Barton and Silverman 1987, 13; and Barton and Silverman 1989.

20. For a revision of the popular image of company towns as exploitive of their residents, see Fishback 1992, chapters 8 and 9.

21. MacCallum 2000.

22. See McKenzie 1994 for an account of the historical development of CIDs.

23. McKenzie 1994, 52–55. The reference is to *Neponsit Property Owners' Association, Inc. v. Emigrant Industrial Savings Bank,* 278 N.Y. 248 (1938). For a list of cases following Neponsit, see Reichman 1976.

24. See David T. Beito's chapter on the private places of St. Louis in this volume.

25. Robert H. Nelson, for example, advocates legislation to extend CID governments to already established neighborhoods nationwide. See especially Nelson 1999, reprinted as chapt. 13 in this volume.

26. McKenzie 1994, 177.

27. Nisbet 1953. Nisbet acknowledged to the author in a letter of October 21, 1991, quoted here by permission of his widow, that, "yes, such organizations as you describe them assuredly fit the category of intermediate associations and perhaps also communities."

REFERENCES

Barton, S. E., and C. J. Silverman. 1987. *Common Interest Homeowners' Association Management Study.* Sacramento: Department of Real Estate.

————. 1989. The Political Life of Mandatory Homeowners' Associations. In *Residential Community Associations: Private Governments in the Intergovernmental Systems?* Washington, D.C. U.S. Advisory Commission on Intergovernmental Relations.

Bressi, T. W. 1994. Planning the American Dream. In *The New Urbanism: Toward an Architecture of Community,* ed. P. Katz. New York: McGraw Hill.

Department of Housing and Urban Development. 1975. *Condominium and Cooperative Study.* 3 vols. Washington D.C.: Department of Housing and Urban Development.

Federal Housing Administration. 1964. Planned-Unit Development with a Homes Association. Washington, D.C.: Urban Land Institute. Land Planning Bulletin No. 6.

Fishback, P. V. 1992. *Soft Coal, Hard Choices: The Economic Welfare of Bituminous Coal Miners, 1890–1930.* New York: Oxford University Press.

Foldvary, F. 1994. *Public Goods and Private Communities.* Aldershot, U.K.: Edward Elgar Publishing.

Goldstein, S. 1991. Don't Even Think About Pink Flamingos. *Philadelphia Inquirer,* October 27, 1.

Heath, S.. 1957. *Citadel, Market and Altar.* Baltimore: Science of Society Foundation.

MacCallum, S. H. 1970. *The Art of Community.* Menlo Park, Calif.: Institute for Humane Studies.

————. 1971. Jural Behavior in American Shopping Centers: Initial Views on the Proprietary Community. *Human Organization, Journal of the Society for Applied Anthropology* 30 (1): 3–10.

————. 1972. Associated Individualism: A Victorian Dream of Freedom. *Reason* 4 (1):17–24.

————. 1997. The Quickening of Social Evolution: Perspectives on Proprietary (Entrepreneurial) Communities. *The Independent Review* 2 (2): 287–302.

————. 2000. The Entrepreneurial Community in the Light of Advancing Business Practice and Technology. Paper presented at the seventieth annual Conference of the Southern Economic Association, November 10–12, 2000, Arlington, Virginia, Session SDAE VII, No. 145M: "Technological Advancement and The Changing Context of Public Policy." Available from the author.

McCall, K.. 1997. Homeowners Forced to Sign Away Rights to Associations. *Las Vegas Sun,* February 10.

McCullough, M. 1991. It's a Swing Set! There Goes the Neighborhood. *Philadelphia Inquirer,* October 9, 1.

McKenzie, E. 1994. *Privatopia: Homeowner Associations and the Rise of Residential Private Government.* New Haven: Yale University Press.

Nelson, R. H. 1999. Privatizing the Neighborhood: A Proposal to Replace Zoning with Private Collective Property Rights to Existing Neighborhoods. *George Mason Law Review* 7 (4):827–80.

Nisbet, R. A. 1953. *The Quest for Community.* London: Oxford University Press.

Osborn, F. J. 1946. *Green-Belt Cities: The British Contribution.* London: Faber and Faber Limited.

Peyser, T. 2000. Looking Back at Looking Backward. *Reason* (August–September): 34.

Purdom, C. B. 1949. *The Letchworth Achievement.* London: J. M. Dent and Sons.

Reichman, U. 1976. Residential Private Governments: An Introductory Survey. *University of Chicago Law Review* 43:253–306.

United Press International. 1987. Court Finds Wife Too Young for Retirement Condo. *San Diego Daily Transcript,* December 11.

Weissberg, R. 1997. Election Day: A Means of State Control. *Chronicles* 20(11):11–13.

4

Epilogue

Introduction to
Part 4
Epilogue

In the concluding chapter, Alexander Tabarrok provides an overview of *The Voluntary City* from the perspective of public economics and the theory of market failure. As long ago as 1969, Harold Demsetz suggested that market-failure theory was itself a failure because it denigrated real markets on the basis of a comparison with "ideal" markets that exist only in theory. Tabarrok's chapter draws on the other chapters of *The Voluntary City* to show that quite different conclusions flow from a comparative approach in which real institutions are compared with real institutions. It is "child's play," as Deepak Lal (1999) has observed, to find departures from neoclassical models of perfect competition and, thereupon, to jump to the conclusion that markets fail and government intervention is desirable. Better institutions are easy to design on the blackboard; it is considerably more difficult to produce them in practice.

In his conclusion, Tabarrok suggests that the term "market-failure theory" is loaded and for that reason potentially misleading. He writes that "'[m]arket challenge' is a better term than 'market failure.' Market-challenge theory can identify areas where empirical investigation is likely to be especially valuable and interesting. Empirical investigation may discover market failure, or it may discover practices and institutions that help markets to succeed in the face of challenges."

REFERENCES

Demsetz, H. 1969. Information and Efficiency: Another Viewpoint. *Journal of Law and Economics* 12 (April): 1–22.

Lal, D. 1999. *Unintended Consequences: The Impact of Factor Endowments on Long-Run Economic Performance.* Cambridge: MIT Press.

15

Market Challenges and Government Failure

Lessons from the Voluntary City

Alexander Tabarrok

The earlier chapters in this volume should come as something of a shock to readers familiar with the economic literature on public goods and externalities. This literature suggests rather strongly that private provision of public goods and goods associated with externalities is either impossible or at best highly inefficient compared to public production. Contrary to this literature, *The Voluntary City* illustrates that a gamut of "market-challenging" goods like roads, health insurance, unemployment insurance, police services, education, and law can and indeed have been provided privately. In a number of cases, such goods are provided privately today. What lessons can public-goods theory draw from these examples of privately provided public goods? And why in many cases did private provision give way to public provision? I attempt to offer some answers to these questions in the first and second parts of this chapter. I conclude with some comments on the city as the locus of civilization.

Public-Goods Theory and Practice

Many economists are theoretical empirics; they make empirical statements on the basis of theory. In his classic paper on externalities, James Meade (1952) argued that subsidies and taxes "must be imposed" on beekeepers and apple farmers because pollination, performed by the bees, is an unpaid positive externality to the apple farmer and the nectar from apple blossoms is an unpaid positive externality to the bee-keepers. It was left to Steven Cheung (1980) to examine the yellow pages to find that in farming communities both nectar and bee pollination are regularly bought and sold in markets. In his influential textbook, Paul Samuelson gave the lighthouse as a paradigmatic example of a good that must be provided by a government because "a businessman could not build it for a profit." Ronald Coase (1988b) replied by pointing to the long history of British lighthouses, which were built by businessmen looking to make a profit.

Like Coase's piece on lighthouses and Cheung's on the fable of the bees, many of the chapters in this book can be seen as refutations by existence. Are law and the police "obvious" examples of goods that only the government can supply, as Paul Samuelson says? Bruce L. Benson (chapter 6) points to the long history of the privately evolved and enforced law merchant and its continued use in international trade. And Stephen Davies (chapter 7) notes that until the 1850s police in Britain were privately provided. Are markets chaotic, haphazard, unruly, and thus inconsistent with urban planning? In reply, David T. Beito (chapter 3) points to the private places of St. Louis and Robert C. Arne (chapter 5) to Chicago's Central Manufacturing District (CMD). Beyond existence, the earlier chapters in *The Voluntary City* indicate some of the ways in which markets overcome many of the challenges that they are issued.

Large-Scale Development and Contracts as Methods of Internalization

Several chapters in *The Voluntary City* make a simple but striking point: private ownership can occur on a larger scale than is often conceived. In a large-scale commercial or residential development, externalities are internalized and public goods become private, excludable goods. Arne's chapter discusses in detail the United States' first industrial park, Chicago's Central Manufacturing District, which as early as 1915 included rail transport, docks, warehouses, sewers, and its own electric-power utility, police force, and ambulance service. Firms located in the CMD had access to CMD banks, financial consultants, and builders. Externalities involving pollution, fire prevention, and aesthetics were all internalized and controlled by the CMD.

The CMD had no difficulty understanding that profit maximization required that it produce goods, including collective-consumption goods, and services, including the control of externalities. A hotel, an apartment complex, a movie theater, or a shopping mall does exactly the same thing for its customers. A proprietary city is nothing more than a large hotel, as both Spencer Heath MacCallum (chapter 14) and Fred E. Foldvary (chapter 11) discuss.

The private provision of collective-consumption goods and the internalization of externalities does not require that the development be continually owned by a unified entity as is the case for the CMD, hotels, and apartment complexes. Since the value of future production of goods and services is capitalized into land value, a landowner or a developer has a strong incentive to design institutions such that collective-consumption goods continue to be provided even after ownership becomes decentralized.

Davies (chapter 2), for example, points out that in the years between 1740 and 1850 Britain experienced an astonishingly rapid increase in population and an even more rapid increase in urban population. Yet the towns of Britain accommodated the increase as "a tidal wave of brick and stone swept over fields, turning them into new urban areas." New homes were built in the millions; indeed, entire new cities rose from the fields, including "great architectural achievements of lasting value." Yet "[a]ll of this happened in a society with no apparatus of planning laws and regulatory bodies, no public building regulations, no zoning or land-use laws, no direct pubic action to supply housing or urban services."

The key to Britain's laissez-faire urbanization was "a sophisticated use of property rights." An individual builder had little incentive to install street lighting, sewage, or pavement for sidewalks or other easements since single customers would not pay for the entire cost of a sidewalk or sewage system and the transaction costs of negotiating for such things with a large number of neighbors were prohibitive. Yet, as a group, homeowners were willing to pay more for these amenities than their cost, which opened up a profit opportunity for landowners and developers. Rather than selling land-simple, landowners would sell plots in a development that came complete with streets, sewage systems, lighting, and so forth. Since customers were willing to pay more for houses with attached collective-consumption goods, builders were willing to pay more for lots in such developments. Thus landowners profited by predeveloping their land.

Externalities involving fire prevention and aesthetics were also efficiently internalized. Typically, builders were required to satisfy contractual terms as to the "type and quality of the materials to be used in the building . . . the thickness of walls, the nature and quality of roofing . . . the size and placement of windows . . . the height of buildings . . . the layout and appearance of the facades," and so forth. Covenants ran with the land, so landowners could contractually bind future homeowners. Homeowners were often forbidden, for example, from "keeping pigs, making soap, or keeping a house of ill repute." Covenants thus performed the same tasks that zoning does today but in a much more flexible, efficient, and nonpoliticized manner.[1]

Covenants existed in the context of the common law. Indeed, to be fully effective the common law had to evolve an understanding of their purpose and utility. Davies points out that it was not until some decades after their widespread use that the common law came to accept that neighbors could sue to have "type of use and nuisance" covenants enforced. Prior to that time covenants had been understood as pure contracts that created obligations between the seller and the buyer of the home only. Respect for the rights and obligations incurred by contract was probably highest in nineteenth-century British common law than ever before or since.[2] The example of Houston, which has no zoning laws, indicates, however, that covenants continue to be a viable alternative to zoning and other land-use controls (Siegan 1972).

The connection between the common law and covenants is one of general importance. Markets work well when property rights are well defined. Coase's lighthouses could not have been privately provided had not lighthouse owners had a property right in the services they produced (Coase 1988b). The choice between private and public provision may often be better understood as a choice between well-specified, tradable, and severable property rights and the amorphous, nontradable, collectively held "rights," which often represent government provision.

It can be difficult to optimally specify rights for goods involving externalities and publicness. But the gains from doing so can be large. Recent efforts to assign property rights to various aspects of the electromagnetic spectrum, for example, have resulted in efficiency gains in the billions of dollars (Hazlett 1998). As another example, consider the problem of transportation in urban areas. In many cities, public transportation systems are poorly maintained, infrequently used, and expensive (to the taxpayer if not always to the rider). Private systems, however, have also faced their share of problems. The main difficulty of private systems is the conflict between scheduled, fixed-route transport and jitney transport. Scheduled systems operating on fixed routes offer the consumer dependability. Jitneys—essentially shared-ride cabs traveling along quasi-fixed routes—provide flexibility, speed, and convenience. In an ideal setting, jitneys would complement fixed-route transport, but in practice jitneys impede fixed-route transport by swooping in just before scheduled service to grab up waiting customers. When such claim jumping becomes common, jitneys can drive scheduled transportation out of the market. But without scheduled service, claim jumping no longer works and the market for jitneys also declines. To solve this problem, Daniel Klein, Adrian Moore, and Binyam Reja (1997) propose an ingenious new property right, a "curb right" (also see Tabarrok forthcoming). The point to be made here is that externalities and publicness problems often disguise ill-defined property rights.

Prices and the Discovery Process

Once given the right to charge passing ships, lighthouse owners had few problems collecting duties because of the close location of lighthouses and ports at which almost all passing ships would want to dock (Coase 1988b). Song lyrics are an example of a nonexcludable good par excellence, but writers have been able to charge for their lyrics because rights to their ideas (copyrights) are enforced. Even the producer of fireworks might be able to devise a reasonable if imperfect system for charging viewers of fireworks if that producer had the legal right to fine non-paying viewers. (Buchanan 1967 points out that a television broadcaster has property rights to his or her broadcast despite the fact that the broadcast, like fireworks, is simply in the air.) The cost of enforcing private-property rights to the display of fireworks could exceed the cost of a coercive tax system, but this should not be assumed. The threat of audit and fine is enough to induce most people to pay their taxes; perhaps a similar system could induce most people to pay their fireworks fee "voluntarily." Disney World in Florida is physically large enough to internalize virtually all viewers of its fireworks and finds that consumer demand is high enough to produce a fireworks show every night. With even an imperfect system of firework property rights we might discover that the demand exists for many more and longer firework shows. Or perhaps the forced riders under today's system are so extensive that fewer fireworks shows are optimal. Without prices it is difficult to know which of these scenarios is accurate.

A true believer in the public-goods paradigm might respond that even if it were possible to charge fireworks viewers, it would not be desirable. Samuelson (1958, 335) said precisely this with respect to a more important good than fireworks—television broadcasts. "Being able to limit a public good's consumption does not make it a true-blue private good," he wrote. "For what, after all, are the true marginal costs of having one extra family tune in on the program? They are literally zero. . . . [Y]ou will [thus] realize that our well-known optimum principle that goods should be priced at their marginal costs would not be realized in the case of subscription broadcasting." Within the standard model, Samuelson's technical point is impeccable. In the standard model, however, the benevolent dictator who sets prices has full information about consumer demand. In the real world, prices fulfill more than an allocative function—prices also transmit information about consumer demand to entrepreneurs who, at positive prices, are eager to profit from serving that demand.

Jora Minasian (1964), for example, pointed out that pricing television broadcasts (pay TV) helped entrepreneurs to figure out what sort of programming consumers most valued. If movie-theater owners were forced to price at marginal cost (zero), how would they know what movies were most in demand? What incentives would exist to produce those movies? The welfare losses from failing to meet the technical conditions of optimality could easily be dwarfed by the welfare losses from failing to use prices to discover consumer demand.

In addition to discovery, prices also provide the means and motivation to serve consumer demand. The demand for conservation of the elephant is high, but public systems of protection have failed abysmally in serving that demand. Elephant herds in Zimbabwe, however, have been effectively protected by local tribes who were given property rights to the herds (Sugg and Kreuter 1994). The profits from farming ivory and selling limited hunting rights have provided both the incentive and the means to protect the elephants from poachers and to increase the size of the herds. The right to fish in lakes and streams is a privately owned, transferable property right in England and Scotland, and polluters can be sued to protect this right. Modern technology makes it possible to create property rights in pods of whales and schools of fish, and this is being done for fish in New Zealand and Iceland (De Alessi 2000). Unfortunately, politicians may often prefer amorphous, nontradable, collectively held "rights" because in effect these leave control of the resource in their hands.

The proprietary community discussed by Arne, Donald J. Boudreaux and Randall G. Holcombe (chapter 12), Beito, Foldvary, and MacCallum internalizes public goods and externalities, and the system as a whole uses prices and property rights to discover and serve consumer demand. Sea Ranch, for example, a California development of ten thousand residents, has its own privately owned roads, sewers, electricity, fire protection, security patrols, hiking trails, golf, tennis, swimming—even a private airstrip. Reston, Virginia, and Irvine, California, are similarly privately developed cities; many other examples are given in the chapters of this volume that deal with proprietary communities.

The proprietary-community model is closely related to the model of Charles Tiebout (1956).[3] The Tiebout model is often presented as an equilibrium statement: given a set of assumptions such as perfect mobility of labor, an equilibrium exists in which every individual lives in that community that produces precisely those public goods that maximize that individual's utility. It is easy to show, however, that the assumptions required are (a) extreme, relative to the real world; and (b) tendentious, in that other assumptions under which an equilibrium does not exist are equally plausible (see, e.g., Stiglitz 1977; Epple and Zelenitz 1981; Caplan 2001). The real lesson of the Tiebout model is dynamic. Tiebout identified a force, voting with one's feet, that would discipline local governments and provide information about which public goods and services are most valued by residents.[4]

The Tiebout insights are magnified when applied to proprietary communities. This is clearest in the case of fully proprietary communities such as hotels and apartment buildings and also online communities such as AOL, Prodigy, and MSN. Residents of these communities who leave for other communities signal to the owners their displeasure and make that signal effective by taking their money with them.[5] Owners of proprietary communities thus have strong incentives to bundle public and private goods at a price that pleases their customers.

The most valuable public goods are constantly changing, just as the most valuable private goods are constantly changing. The signal provided by prices and mobility is therefore of great importance. Many hotels and apartment buildings, for example, are upgrading their telephone and cable wiring so that they can offer their residents high-speed Internet connections. The same incentives apply to developers, who are also adding such infrastructure.[6] The case of developers is somewhat different, however, in that once the homes in these communities are sold they shift along the proprietary axis away from the hotel model and toward the model of ordinary government-run communities.[7] In his contribution to this volume, MacCallum argues that the hotel/apartment model should be extended to single-resident homes precisely so that the benefits of both profit maximization and Tiebout mobility are maintained.

Motivational Assumptions and the Free-Rider Problem

Daniel Klein's chapter on American turnpikes (chapter 14) makes two contributions to *The Voluntary City*. On the surface level it is a refutation by existence: private turnpike companies built thousands of miles of roads in early America, belying the arguments that government provision was necessary. Indeed, such roads were built because government failed to provide roads of sufficient quantity or quality. On a deeper level, Klein uses the history of turnpike companies to empirically challenge models that treat the "free-rider" problem as ubiquitous and insurmountable. Klein notes that toll regulation, as well as technological factors, made for-profit provision of turnpikes unprofitable. The indirect benefits of a road connecting a town to larger markets were large but mostly unexcludable. According to the standard model no turnpikes at all should have been built. Yet in the states Klein examines, hundreds of turnpikes built thousands of miles of road.

How was the free-rider problem overcome? Klein points to the importance of social pressure, public spiritedness, and social esteem. Turnpike organizers would gather together all the leading members of a town at a local inn and make their case for the benefits of a new road. Rousing speeches, boosterism, and calls for generosity would generally call forth donations for the public good. When the road was complete the leaders of the drive and the large contributors could take satisfaction in the public gratitude and esteem that their efforts earned.

Would such efforts work today in an age of (supposedly) greater anomie and disconnectedness from community? Klein is optimistic, pointing to the billions raised by the nonprofit sector through entirely voluntary means. The extreme self-interest assumption upon which the strong version of the free-rider hypothesis rests is also coming under closer scrutiny. Evolutionary psychologists argue that pure altruism is limited to kin. Humans, however, come into the world not only with a "propensity to truck, barter, and exchange," as Adam Smith said, but also with the corollary propensities "to learn how to cooperate, to discriminate the trustworthy from the treacherous, to commit themselves to be trustworthy, [and] to earn good reputations" (Ridley 1996, 249). Cooperation is therefore much more prevalent than simple economic models would predict.[8]

The "cooperation" of the evolutionary biologists (and also of the game theorists) is not the dreamy romantic conception in which we all just get along. Even when promoting cooperation, nature is red in tooth and claw. Our cooperative propensities are designed for individual advantage. It is thus a mistake to conclude that because humans are social animals they are collective animals. The lesson of evolutionary psychology is that *man is social only because he is individualistic.*[9] When humans must deal with one another voluntarily, they are forced to recognize that the other has interests not identical with their own and to use their cooperative propensities to arrive at mutually beneficial bargains. But our cooperative propensities are tools brought into play only when necessary. Remove the requirement of voluntariness, and no generalized instinct for cooperation takes over—all that remains is unconstrained self-interest.

Adam Smith laid out the argument for private property in the case of private goods. The contingent nature of our social propensities implies that private property and the other institutions of a liberal society that protect individual spheres of action—that is, individual rights—are also important in the production of goods requiring collective action. As Matt Ridley (1996) puts it, "we are not so nasty that we need to be tamed by intrusive government, nor so nice that too much government does not bring out the worst in us."

In their chapters on the friendly societies of Britain and Australia and the fraternal lodges of America, historians David G. Green (chapter 9) and Beito (chapter 8) also raise issues of social solidarity and moral crowding out. According to Green, the friendly societies of Great Britain were "self-governing mutual-benefit associations founded by manual workers to provide against hard times." When in need, members of a friendly society could draw upon sick pay, and in the event of a death the widows and orphans of members had rights to financial support. The friendly societies also provided medical care through society-owned HMO-type organizations. Amazingly, when the British government introduced compulsory social insurance in 1911, the friendly societies already covered at least nine million individuals. Americans did not join fraternal orders to the same extent as British workers joined friendly societies, perhaps because America was less urbanized than Britain. Nevertheless, in 1920 about 30 percent of all adults over the age of twenty belonged to a lodge. Members of a lodge were entitled to draw on sick pay, to expect help in finding a job, and to purchase life insurance.

Social solidarity was generated in the friendly and fraternal societies through a highly democratic governance structure and through ritual and teaching. Green tells us that teachings in the societies began with initiation and continued as members progressed "through a series of 'degrees' during which the society taught values such as hard work, liberty, tolerance toward others, and fraternalism toward fellow members." According to Beito, the societies were also "leading outlets for sociability and prestige."

It was critical to the operation of the societies that they be voluntary. Individuals self-selected into groups are more likely to support those groups wholeheartedly than those coerced into joining. Freedom of association also meant that members could discipline unruly members. According to Beito, the Boston Marine Society, for example, levied fines for not attending the funerals of deceased members and would expel members for drunkenness or gambling. Each of these requirements can be understood as generating those feelings of fraternity on which these societies were founded. Attending funerals would help to generate support for payments to widows and orphans. Expelling drunks and gamblers was necessary to maintain the solidarity that flows when aid is given to those who "through no fault of their own" have fallen on hard times.

The democratic structure, teachings, and rituals of the societies were more than window dressing; they were critical to their operation. The societies knew that charity can create dependency. But a man would not ask his brother for aid if self-help had not been exhausted. The *mutual* and *fraternal* nature of the societies had, therefore, a real purpose. In a quote cited by Beito, Mary Ann Clawson writes, "Fraternal association provided the ritualized means by which their members could define one another as brothers; biologically unrelated individuals thus used kinship to construct the solidarity necessary to accomplish a variety of tasks." Secure in the knowledge that a member would not ask for help were it not necessary, the societies were free to emphasize that when help was given it was done not out of charity but as mutual aid by right of membership. In this way, the difficult waters of dependency, shame, and conceit were navigated. In the mutual-aid societies, fraternity reinforced self-reliance instead of undercutting it as in the modern welfare state.

As government provision of social services increased, the fraternal and friendly societies were crowded out of the field of social services. Perhaps more importantly, government did not and could not provide an alternative to the moral education that had been provided by the fraternal and friendly societies. In America and Britain both, the replacement of mutual aid with government aid produced crime, family breakdown, and chronic unemployment (see, e.g., Murray 1984).

Law and Government as Privately Created Public Goods

Boudreaux and Holcombe explore a fascinating aspect of private communities, the private creation of political constitutions. As already noted, the community developer has an incentive to bundle public goods and externality control with the homes in such a way as to maximize the value of living in the community. The developer, however, cannot foresee every possible future circumstance—perhaps future homeowners will desire a community pool or high-speed Internet access. How are such decisions to be made? Under the hotel model, argued for by MacCallum (chapter 14) and discussed by Foldvary (chapter 11), management retains the right to make these decisions. In the case of a typical home development the developer leaves residents with a system for self-governance, in other words, a political constitution. Boudreaux and Holcombe's insight is that a system for self-governance is a public good just like a local park. Thus, developers have an incentive to leave homeowners with self-governance systems that maximally increase the value of living in the community.

Politics do not disappear in private communities, but Boudreaux and Holcombe's insight explains why politics in private communities are likely to be less wasteful and inequitable than in "public" communities—the insight is also an important contribution to political philosophy. Traditional contractarian political philosophy defines the ideal constitution as that constitution that would be agreed to by individuals behind a "veil of ignorance" (Rawls 1971; Buchanan and Tullock 1962). Although they do not phrase the issue in this way, Boudreaux and Holcombe implicitly offer an alternative definition: the ideal constitution is that constitution that would be created by a neutral and knowledgeable third party with strong incentives to maximize the constitution's value to future citizens. Importantly, the standard criticism of contractarian theory, that real constitutions are never made behind a veil of ignorance and always are and always will be a product of the powers of the day, has much less weight against the new-contractarian alternative. In a competitive market, the developer of a proprietary community does have strong incentives to design a constitution neutrally, knowledgeably, and with the goal of maximizing the constitution's value to future citizens. It is interesting to bear this in mind when one notes that proprietary communities are typically not run as majoritarian democracies. Unlike public communities, proprietary communities often rely on supermajority rule, property requirements, and deviations from the one person–one vote rule. Condominiums, for example, often assign votes in proportion to condominium value (Barzel and Sass 1990).

Public Goods Created by Neither Government nor Firm

It is obvious that communication is necessary for any community of individuals to survive and prosper. Does it follow that government should produce a language for the community residents? It is difficult to exclude someone from the benefits of language, and the use of language by A does not impede (indeed, it adds to) the use of language by B. Language, therefore, appears to satisfy the characteristics of a public good. Yet the idea of government producing language is ludicrous. For government to come into being, language must already exist.[10] Friedrich Hayek (1973, 72) makes the same point with respect to law. "Law," he writes, "is older than legislation." In all early civilizations, law was understood, like language, as something its citizens possessed rather than created. Similarly, the early "lawgivers," like Hammurabi and Solon, were understood to be codifying or recording preexisting law just as the writers of dictionaries would later codify and record, rather than invent, language. Legislation could not have existed unless a community was already governed by law.

Law for Hayek is the product of a spontaneous order, a process of evolution similar to the one that creates language. Law is a product of human creation but not of human design. Legislation, since designed, always has the possibility, even probability, of being designed to fulfill some narrow purpose of the legislator that conflicts with that of the legislated. Law, in contrast, tend to be purpose-independent, general, and abstract. Hayek (1973) sees law as the fountainhead of all civilization and thus writes, "[I]t is in the *ius gentium,* the law merchant, and the practices of the ports and fairs that we must chiefly seek the steps in the evolution of law which ultimately made an open society possible" (82).[11]

Even more than the common law, the law merchant (*lex mercatoria*), Benson's subject (chapter 6), is an example of the spontaneous evolution of law because the law merchant was "*voluntarily produced, voluntarily adjudicated, and voluntarily enforced*" (emphasis original). The law merchant had to possess those properties of purpose-independence, generality, and abstractness that Hayek lauds as the root of civilization because a voluntary system could not otherwise survive. And the law merchant had to be voluntary because it governed trade among merchants from widely different polities. Of course, the law merchant did not spring into being fully formed, but over time "those practices that proved to be the most efficient at facilitating commercial interaction supplanted those that were less efficient."

The evolution toward efficiency of the law merchant had two aspects. First, as the benefits of international trade grew, incentives were created to eliminate the obvious biases against alien merchants that existed in local customs. Second, and more important, was the evolution toward efficiency of the substantive rules governing contacts, debts, credits, future deliveries, agents, liability, and so forth, where the efficient rule was neither obvious nor constant through time. The proximate causes of evolution toward efficiency were that (a) arbitrators were themselves merchants and typically experts in the areas of commerce under dispute; and (b) arbitrators looked to contract and merchant intentions in deciding cases. The final cause: the voluntary nature of the system.

Often an evolutionary process is the only realistic method for discovering efficient rules. The facts the legal system must deal with are so numerous, complex, changing, and unpredictable that no single mind or organization could encompass them all, let alone calculate an optimal plan on that basis. A constructed legal system for international trade law is as likely to achieve optimality as a constructed life form is to achieve evolutionary fitness. To be sure, once they exist we may be able to identify efficient rules and understand why they evolved as they did. We may even be able to nudge rules and institutions in more efficient directions, just as word mavens attempt to resist the abuse of language. But for the system in toto there is no alternative to the evolutionary process. Science, language, and of course the economy itself are other examples in this genre (Hayek 1988; Mises 1990).

Complexity and lack of information also make the efficient production of more traditional public goods quite difficult. Conventional economics suggests, for example, that governments should finance bridge building because for optimum efficiency the services of a bridge must be priced at marginal cost—which is typically assumed to be zero. But in such a system how do we know whether the total value of the bridge exceeds that of the resources used to produce the bridge? Which of many possible bridge locations would maximize consumer surplus? Should the bridge be four lanes wide or only two? With pedestrian traffic or without? Entrepreneurs acting in markets have strong incentives to pursue the best answers to these questions. Similar incentives are lacking and often perverse in government provision. Thus, Coase (1988a) argues that proponents of marginal-cost pricing give insufficient "weight to the stimulus to correct forecasting which comes from having a subsequent market test of whether consumers are willing to pay the total costs of the product. Nor do they recognize the importance of the aid which the results of the market test give in enabling more accurate forecasts to be made in the future."

Bruce L. Benson's chapter on law is complemented by historian Stephen Davies's chapter (chapter 7) on the private provision of police in eighteenth- and nineteenth-century Britain. Davies's chapter is a useful reminder of the poverty of imagination. Most people are incredulous when told that London had no public police until 1829 and that the rest of Britain was governed by private police and prosecution until at least the late 1850s. Imagining a state of anarchy, they are thrown into confusion on finding that the first public police, Sir Robert Peel's "bobbies," were detested by most citizens, who viewed them as "an infringement on English social and political life."[12] The citizens had good reason to jeer the bobbies, as future events would demonstrate (see the discussion following). Moreover, the citizens knew they were already well served by private police and prosecution associations.

It is not surprising that the preindustrial system of crime control was private and informal; this is to be expected in any agricultural, village-based society. What is interesting is how the system evolved to meet the challenges of urbanization and mobility. Urbanization brought problems as criminals become more anonymous and mobile, but it also brought new tools for combating crime. Newspapers and rewards, for example, made it practical and profitable to pursue criminals over a wider geographical area. The most important innovation, however, was the prosecution association.

A private system of police and prosecution has an obvious problem. Apprehending and prosecuting a criminal would typically cost more than the value of any recovered goods. An individual victim, therefore, would have few incentives to pursue criminals, and knowing this the criminals would have few incentives to refrain from committing crimes. Alternatively stated, deterrence is a public good—the social benefits of punishing criminals exceed the private benefits. As early as the 1690s, however, a solution to this problem was hit upon. Individuals would form themselves into prosecution associations, collectively agreeing to share the costs of apprehension and prosecution.

Prosecution associations operated much like insurance companies. When a member was robbed the association would take on the costs of printing handbills, placing newspaper ads, offering rewards, hiring detectives and lawyers, and so forth. Crucially, one of the key goals of the prosecution association was to recover stolen property. The private good of property recovery was thus tied with the public good of deterrence.[13] Some prosecution associations also entered the field of insurance proper, offering compensation for nonrecovered stolen goods. It is interesting that contemporary insurance companies perform many of the same tasks as did prosecution associations. Especially in large cases they will offer rewards for stolen property, hire detectives, pay for lawyers, and so forth. The prosecution association is thus not as unfamiliar an organization as it initially appears.

A prosecution association further internalized the value of its deterrence efforts by advertising the names of its members. Merchants would also post signs indicating their membership in an association. This had the same effect and purpose as when merchants today commit to prosecuting all shoplifters, even when the value of the goods stolen is less than the cost of prosecution.

A common complaint against private crime-fighting efforts is that they impose a negative externality on others as criminals shift their attention to less-hardened targets. There is some truth to this complaint, but care must be taken in applying the argument. First, if virtually everyone target-hardens, then the negative externality created by additional target-hardening is negligible and efficiency is not compromised.[14] Second, from the criminal's point of view, private target-hardening has an income as well as a substitution effect. Assume, for example, that car thieves operate like taxi drivers. They travel the city looking for "customers." On lucky nights the thieves find a Porsche ripe for the taking, but on other nights only a Pinto is available. The few nights on which they find a Porsche make up for the many on which only Pintos are available. On average the marginal thief just covers opportunity costs. Now assume that every Porsche owner installs a sophisticated alarm system but that no Pinto owners do. The substitution effect pushes thieves away from Porches and toward Pintos, but car theft is now less profitable than it was formerly. Marginal thieves no longer cover their opportunity costs and therefore drop out of the market. Thus, it is quite possible that the probability of a Pinto being stolen falls when Porsche owners harden their targets.[15]

Although prosecution associations would rarely pay the full costs of prosecuting a criminal on behalf of a nonmember, they would often contribute toward apprehension by offering a reward. A prosecution association representing 30 percent of the homes in a neighborhood, for example, could rationally offer a reward for the apprehension of a criminal *before* that criminal assaulted the home of any member.

We know that prosecution associations were successful in lowering the crime rate where they operated. We do not know for certain whether prosecution associations on net raised or lowered the probability that a nonmember would be a victim of a crime. But the evidence is suggestive that on net prosecution associations reduced crime for members and nonmembers alike. Certainly as prosecution associations expanded in size and scope (joining with other associations) this was the direction of evolution. We also know that the general public was largely satisfied with the private system of police and did not demand the new public system, which had a purpose quite different from that of the private system (see the discussion later in this chapter).

Education

Most children in the world today are educated in government schools. This is puzzling since the economic arguments for government schooling are weak. Various externality and capital-market-imperfection arguments suggest that education would be underprovided in a free market. Yet when education was provided privately and without compulsion in Great Britain and the United States, almost all children, including poor children, received many years of schooling. Public schools largely displaced private schools and did not expand the market (see James Tooley's contribution to this volume [chapter 10] and West 1994). Moreover, if the goal is to *increase* the amount of schooling, the appropriate method is a subsidy, not government provision. Although a subsidy guarantees increased consumption of the subsidized good, government-provided schooling can actually cause less education to be purchased. Private schools in the United States, for example, operate on average twenty education days longer than public schools, and they do so with smaller student-to-teacher ratios, suggesting on both counts that in a free market parents might buy their children more education than they are now given in government schools.[16]

Government provision of education is also surprising given the data on the costs and outputs of private education. Studies of Catholic high schools, for which there are better data than other private schools, show consistently that compared to the public schools they put a greater emphasis on academics and that students achieve higher test scores and are more likely to attend college even after controlling for other factors such as family background.[17] In the United States, moreover, per-pupil expenditure at private schools is about half than at the public schools.[18] Thus, even if private and public schools taught students equally well, it would still be the case that private schools are substantially more efficient than public schools. Surveys reveal that parents are much more satisfied with private schools than public schools. This is true even when parents have their choice of public school and a fortiori when parents are forced to send their child to an assigned school.[19] Private schools are better than public schools on a number of margins not just in the contemporary United States but over a wide range of countries and time periods (Coulson 1999).

The private-education market in the United States and the markets for education around the world discussed by Tooley demonstrate that education could be provided privately. Why then is education not by and large provided in a free market? The answer is more likely to lie in politics than in economics. This issue will be discussed further later in the chapter.

The Rise, Fall, and Rise Again (?) of the Voluntary City

Many of the private institutions discussed in *The Voluntary City* were eventually replaced with more coercive, government-run programs. The "public-choice" literature explains in detail why we should not expect governments to act as social-welfare maximizers.[20] It does not follow that governments act as welfare minimizers, but it does follow that we should not be especially puzzled when worse institutions replace better institutions. Space precludes an examination of the precise role that special interests, ideology, economic efficiency, and chance events played in the evolution of each of the institutions discussed in *The Voluntary City*. We instead focus on two issues of special interest. First, we examine government failure as a cause of the birth, and now the rebirth, of the voluntary city. Second, we examine the somewhat peculiar cases of police and education. Private police and private education were not replaced with public alternatives because of market failure. Nor did the replacements have much to do with the sorts of issues typically discussed in the public-choice literature, although these were not entirely absent. Instead public police and education replaced private alternatives because the public sector produced values that the private sector could not. The open question, discussed later, is whether those values were and are appropriate to a liberal civilization.

It is worth noting, because it turns the standard story upside down, that many of the private institutions discussed in *The Voluntary City* arose in response to government failure! Beito (chapter 3) points out that entrepreneurs began building the private places of St. Louis when, due to political gridlock, city government failed to provide the infrastructure that St. Louis residents demanded. Klein (chapter 4) indicates that private roads were built because government failed to produce roads of sufficient quantity or quality. Benson (chapter 6) shows that the law merchant arose because local courts were slow, inefficient, and unfamiliar with merchant practices.

As city government in St. Louis improved, the private places began to decline in importance. Similarly, as the common-law courts adopted the methods and rulings of the merchant courts, the merchant courts and arbitration in general declined. In contemporary times both of these institutions have made a comeback as government failure has again grown. Beginning in the 1960s, public St. Louis began to collapse, infrastructure started to deteriorate, crime rates began to rise, and property values began to fall, making parts of St. Louis in the 1980s virtually unlivable. Under these circumstances, the private places enjoyed a renaissance. Municipal residential streets were privatized— deeded back to neighborhood associations that had the right to close the streets off to the public. Amid the chaos of St. Louis, the private places maintained islands of order (Newman 1980). In light of the advantages of the private places, Robert H. Nelson (chapter 13) argues for legal changes that will make privatizing neighborhoods easier and more efficient. Arbitration too returned in a major way as the public courts become slower, more inefficient, and unfamiliar with merchant practices. The growth in private policing, moreover, has been explosive (Benson 1998).

One should not conclude from this account that public and private institutions operate in an efficient, competitive equilibrium. Obviously, government taxes rather than sells, and this substantially reduces the crucible of customer satisfaction. It is typical, for example, that customers of private suppliers are also taxed for public supply even if public supply is not utilized. Parents who send their children to private schools must also pay property taxes for the support of public schools. Firms that use arbitration to settle disputes must also pay for the public courts from which they are escaping. Communities that hire security guards for the protection of person and property must also pay taxes for the support of public police. Governments can and also do regulate the private sector in order to raise the costs of their competitors. As Benson explains, for example, the common-law courts subverted the authority of the law merchant by making merchant law appealable in the public courts (thus also substantially changing the practice of merchant law).

What should be concluded from this is that despite large advantages, the government often fails. Markets will spontaneously arise to address government failure when such failure is extreme. But we should not wait for extreme failure before turning to markets. Eliminate the advantages of the public sector, and the voluntary city will soon supplant government provision.

Why the Public Sector Sometimes Remains

As Davies shows, in eighteenth- and nineteenth-century Britain the private police system effectively served the working class and the merchants who paid for it. The private system, however, did not serve the demands of the British elite. The elite were concerned with public order, political stability, and morality. The private system, in contrast, focused on violent crimes and crimes to property.[21] The government, in other words, could not call upon the private police to suppress a riot or to launch a moral crusade against, say, drunkenness or prostitution. The public police were created because the elites, a significant fraction of the voting population, wanted to control what they perceived as an unruly public. Indeed, soon after their creation the public police were used to suppress the Chartists. The Chartists were seen as a threat to political stability because they demanded universal manhood suffrage, abolition of the property qualification for membership in Parliament, and other democratic reform measures. The *Encyclopedia Britannica* entry on police summarizes the suppression as follows: "[P]itched battles with (and ultimate street victory over) the Chartists in Birmingham and London proved the ability of the police to deal with major disorders and street riots."[22] The public police served the interests of the ruling elite, and it was not surprising, therefore, that most citizens detested and jeered them. The public police were created not to control crime but to control people.

Notice that the shift from private police to public police changed the nature of the good produced. This is true in general—what is produced depends on how production is financed. The typical model of a public good contrasts public with private financing, all the while holding the nature of the good constant—such a procedure is illegitimate.

Police and, as discussed later, education are dramatic examples of this process, but it is equally true that a public road or lighthouse is likely to be of different size, location, and structure than a "similar" private road or lighthouse. Public charity (welfare) is not the same thing as private charity, to give another important example. The differences in public and private provision are not superficial but fundamental and systematic. A proper model of public and private collective-good provision must, therefore, make the nature of the good produced endogenous to the production financing.[23]

Recognizing that public provision changes the nature of the good produced may also help us to explain why public provision occurs despite manifest disadvantages. The example of police has been given already, and education is discussed following. The lighthouse is perhaps a more prosaic example. In the *Devil's Dictionary* Ambrose Bierce defined the lighthouse as a "tall building on the seashore in which the government maintains a lamp and the friend of a politician." The devil might further ask whether it was on behalf of the lamp or the friend that the lighthouse was publicly produced.

Around the world, education is provided for the most part in government-run schools. I argue that this is so not because public education improves on some output of private education or produces some output of private education at lower cost (the evidence on these questions is that the opposite is true) but rather because public education produces something that private education cannot—to wit, indoctrination. This aspect of public education was present from the establishment of the first modern public schools, those of sixteenth-century Germany. The German public schools were established with the great support and encouragement of Martin Luther. In his letter of 1524 to the German rulers, Luther wrote:

> Dear rulers . . . I maintain that the civil authorities are under obligation to compel the people to send their children to school. . . . If the government can compel such citizens as are fit for military service to bear spear and rifle, to mount ramparts, and perform other martial duties in time of war, how much more has it a right to compel the people to send their children to school, because in this case we are warring with the devil, whose object it is to secretly exhaust our cities and principalities of their strong men.[24]

As Rothbard (1999, 21) points out, Luther's reference to the devil was not metaphorical: "Reformers advocated compulsory education for all as a means of inculcating the entire population with their particular religious views, as an indispensable aid in effective 'war with the devil' and the devil's agents. For Luther, these agents constituted a numerous legion: not only Jews, Catholics, and infidels, but also all other Protestant sects."

Religion also played an important role in the creation of the American common school. During the 1840s and 1850s Catholic immigrants from Ireland and Germany swept into the United States, and the Protestant majority used the public schools to enforce their cultural and religious values (Ravitch 1974; Kaestle 1973; see also for summaries High and Ellig 1988; Coulson 1999; and Richman 1994). (At the time, the Protestant bible was widely taught in the public schools.) Even when religion per se was not involved, the inculcation of particular values was of paramount importance to the leaders of the common-school movement. Horace Mann, for example, promised:

> When [public schooling] shall be fully developed, when it shall be trained to wield its mighty energies for the protection of society against the giant vices which now invade and torment it;—against intemperance, avarice, war, slavery, bigotry, the woes of want and the wickedness of waste,—then there will not be a height to which the enemies of the [human] race can escape, which it will not scale, nor a Titan among them all, whom it will not slay.[25]

Mann's statement is remarkably similar to that of Luther. Mann's devil is secularized (the Titan that public education will slay is presumably metaphorical), but like Luther, Mann sees the public schools as a weapon to be marshaled against the enemies of the human race.

In the twentieth century, the state itself sought to indoctrinate children through its control of education. The examples of Communist Russia and China are merely the most extreme. Ingvar Carlsson, Swedish education minister and later prime minister, said that the "school is the spearhead of Socialism."[26] Using data from the late 1980s, Lott (1999; 1987) finds that states that extensively control the media through, for example, ownership of television stations (an obvious indoctrination device) also tend to invest a lot in public education (a less obvious indoctrination device).[27]

West (1975, 123) nicely summarizes the support for public education when he writes:

> The French Physiocrats wanted a national system of education because they could use it to propagate their new found knowledge of the "secrets" of the workings of the economy. . . . For the nine-

teenth century cleric, the "ignorance" which led to crime was primarily the ignorance of the teachings of his particular church. For the utilitarian the crucial issue was ignorance of the laws of the state or in other words the want of knowledge and effective warning of the pain that would inevitably follow from certain actions. For Malthus it was the ignorance of his population principle which mattered most. Public education for him was needed to suppress the "sophistries" of persons such as Condorcet. The latter happened to be the successful instigator of French state education, and undoubtedly intended it to instruct according to his conception of truth.

Each of these reformers understood that only *tax-financed, government-run* schools could serve their needs. Private schools are too diffuse and decentralized to be wielded as weapons. Moreover, private schools are run from the bottom up on behalf of the paying customers, the parents. A private school that tried to impose foreign views on its students would quickly find its plans for indoctrination frustrated as it lost customers to other, more responsive schools.

Conclusions

The theoretical empiric skips lightly from a mathematical model of a market in which optimality fails to a conclusion of "market failure" to a policy prescription for government intervention. Each step of the process is fraught with danger. Models cannot tell us how private actors will innovate to surmount challenges. Meade's model failed as a description of the apple/bee market because he assumed from the beginning that markets in externalities could not exist. This is not to say that it is possible to create a market for every externality. It is instead to point out that what makes such a market possible for bees and blossoms are facts about bees and blossoms that are unlikely to be known to an economist.

Neil Skaggs and J. Lon Carlson (1996, 543) write that where collective-consumption goods are involved, "the market has no choice but to fail." In truth, however, there are many such choices—from internalization to large-scale development, contractual and legal innovations, tie-in sales, creation of private substitutes, and provision through nonprofit firms and socially motivated organizations.[28] Upon empirical examination "market failure" often turns out to be better described as "imagination failure."

"Market challenge" is a better term than "market failure." Market-challenge theory can identify areas where empirical investigation is likely to be especially valuable and interesting. Empirical investigation may discover market failure, or it may discover practices and institutions that help markets to succeed in the face of challenges.

Even supposing that a market challenge is not met or is met poorly it does not follow that government action is a superior alternative. The public-choice school of political economy has reminded us that politicians and bureaucrats are as self-interested as entrepreneurs and that markets often channel self-interest into socially productive arenas better than do government institutions.

What Sort of Civilization Do we Want?

This volume is entitled *The Voluntary City,* but it could equally justly have been called *The Voluntary Civilization.* Cities are the birthplaces of most innovations in art, culture, and science, and they are the engines of economic growth (Jacobs 1969; Bairoch 1988). The city is thus the root of civilization. Indeed the etymology of the word "civilization" is found in the Latin word *civis,* meaning an inhabitant of a city. Crime, housing, transport, education, order, political governance—these are issues related to cities, but seen in a larger light they are also issues that every civilization must grapple with. Are civilizations best governed coercively from the top down or are they best governed by the institutions of private ordering—markets, contracts, property rights, and decentralized law?

Many of the chapters in *The Voluntary City* suggest that private ordering offers performance superior to the coercive institutions of government. In the case of housing, roads, city planning, and so forth, arguments of this sort may be enough to decide the issue. But, recalling Ambrose Bierce, if the lighthouse is maintained for the friend rather than for the lamp, it is no use complaining that the lamp is poorly lit and of little aid to passing ships. In these cases *The Voluntary City* raises questions of political constitutions and metarules of governance. In other cases, a question of values arises. If the purpose of public education is indoctrination then there is no use complaining that public education is expensive and all too often fails to teach the basic skills of reading, writing, and arithmetic. The same issues arise with respect to public police. The choice of public versus private becomes in these cases a choice of values. What sort of civilization do we want? Sparta or

Athens? A civilization in which a dominant majority imposes its view of the good? Or a civilization that is open to all equally? A civilization of indoctrination in common values or one of tolerance? The question cannot be answered here, but it can be said that if we are to achieve the voluntary civilization, we must begin with *The Voluntary City.*

NOTES

I would like to thank Tyler Cowen, Carl Close, and Dan Sutter for comments.

1. Zoning has not been especially effective at eliminating the crack houses that plague many inner-city American neighborhoods. Perhaps a covenant-based civil-law remedy would be more effective.

2. Compare Atiyah 1979 with Gilmore 1974, but note that the essays in Buckley 1999 see the death of contract as much exaggerated.

3. The relationship between the Tiebout model and proprietary communities was first discussed by Buchanan and Goetz 1972.

4. It is interesting that voting with one's feet is a much older method of disciplining governments than actual voting. One of the reasons why modern civilization arose in Europe was a highly decentralized political system—more than five hundred independent "governments" as late as the sixteenth century—meant that entrepreneurs and innovators could escape tyrannical power.

5. Individual users of hotels typically stay for only short periods of time, but as a group demanders of hotel services can be said to leave one hotel or chain like Holiday Inn and move to another like the Marriott, which is why these chains must compete.

6. The speed and efficiency with which hotels, apartments, and housing developments are adding high-speed bandwidth is usefully contrasted with the slow and often corrupt process that has characterized city installation of cable TV. On the latter see Hazlett 2000 and Hazlett and Spitzer 1997.

7. Of course, as indicated earlier, we can expect that these once-proprietary communities will have better procedures for producing new public goods or handling externalities.

8. Ostrom, Walker, and Gardner 1992 provides a nice experimental verification of the surprising ability of humans to cooperate even when individual "incentives" push in the opposite direction.

9. The social cooperation of humans is thus on an entirely different basis from that of the ants.

10. Clearly, governments can and do influence the development of languages by suppressing some languages and subsidizing others. The argument here is that despite the fact that language is a public good, government is not necessary for its creation.

11. *Ius gentium,* the law of nations or international law.

12. The quote is from the *Encyclopedia Britannica* 2000 entry on "Police." Available at <http://www.britannica.com> and accessed in March 2000.

13. Prosecution associations were also social associations, much like the friendly societies discussed by David G. Green (chapter 9). On the importance of tying private goods, including social activities, to public goods see Olson 1965.

14. In technical terms, what matters for efficiency is the size of the externality on the margin at the laissez-faire equilibrium. The marginal externality may be small even when the inframarginal externality is large. Education, for example, may generate positive externalities, but if the laissez-faire equilibrium has virtually everyone sending their child to school the marginal externality is negligible. An additional prosecution association might generate a negative externality when only 10 percent of the (local) population is covered by other associations. But if 80 percent of the population is covered already, the externality is likely to be negligible.

15. The model of crime I am proposing, where high-value and low-value crimes are complementary, is not true of all crimes. When police wear bullet-proof vests, for example, this is not likely to cause an "income effect" on murderers, but neither is it likely to create a substitution effect.

16. If the government provided each family with three pounds of sugar and most consumers wanted more, they could supplement on the private market. A program of freely provided government sugar cannot, therefore, cause less sugar to be consumed. (This ignores income effects, which may be important if government-provided sugar is costlier than sugar on the private market, as is true for education.) On a number of margins, however, such as hours in the day, student-to-teacher ratio, quality of learning materials, academic emphasis, etc., it is difficult to supplement public schooling, so both in theory and in practice public education can cause less schooling to be consumed.

Parents who purchase private education today are likely to be among those who *most* desire more education than the government provides, but they are unlikely to be the only such parents, let alone the only parents who would prefer private to government education. As an indication, note that the Children's Scholarship Fund, which offers vouchers for poor urban students in grades K through 8, received over a million applications for the forty-four thousand vouchers they had available. The family of the typical recipient must add about one thousand dollars to the voucher to pay for tuition. Thus poor parents are clearly willing to pay to have their children educated in non–government run schools. On the Children's Scholarship Fund, see Moe 1999.

17. See Coleman and Hoffer 1987; Bryk, Lee, and Holland 1993; and Evans and Schwab 1995.

18. See the Condition of Education 1996 / Issues in Focus: Public and Private Schools: How Do They Differ? From the National Center for Education Statistics. Available at <http://nces.ed.gov/pubs/ce/c97006.html>. See also the review in Coulson 1999. Lott 1987 finds a greater than 50 percent difference in costs even after controlling for the reduced wages of some nonprofit workers.

19. See the Condition of Education 1996 and Coulson 1999.

20. See, for example, Shleifer and Vishny 1998; Stigler 1988; Olson 1982; and Mitchell and Simmons 1994.

21. The private system focused on violent crimes and crimes to property because this was what people were willing to pay for. Members of the prosecution

associations were not willing to pay to suppress gambling, prostitution, or other victimless crimes, nor were they willing to pay for an attack on moral failings such as adultery or to suppress public demonstrations for suffrage and other political rights.

22. From *Encyclopedia Britannica* 2000 entry on "Police."

23. Instead of examining private and public production *ceteris paribus* (all else equal) the model must work *mutatis mutandis* (the necessary changes having being made).

24. Quoted in Rothbard 1999, 20.

25. Quoted in Coulson 1999, 80.

26. Quoted in Lott 1999.

27. Importantly, Lott 1999 finds little relationship between ownership of television stations and non-indoctrinating spending such as spending on health care.

28. On mechanisms used to overcome market challenges see, in addition to the chapters in this volume, the essays in Cowen 1988. Tabarrok 1998 contains an innovative contractual method that might be used to produce public goods. Glaeser and Shleifer 1998 explains how nonprofit firms can arise even when entrepreneurs are purely self-interested. Glaeser and Shleifer thus explain how nonprofit firms are an aspect of markets rather than being alternatives to markets as traditionally conceived.

REFERENCES

Atiyah, P. S. 1979. *The Rise and Fall of Freedom of Contract.* Oxford: Clarendon Press.

Bairoch, P. 1988. *Cities and Economic Development: From the Dawn of History to the Present.* Chicago: University of Chicago Press.

Barzel, Y., and T. R. Sass. 1990. The Allocation of Resources By Voting. *Quarterly Journal of Economics* 105 (August): 745–71.

Benson, B. 1998. *To Serve and Protect.* New York: New York University Press.

Bryk, A.S., V. E. Lee, and P. B. Holland. 1983. *Catholic Schools and the Common Good.* Cambridge: Harvard University Press.

Buchanan, J. M. 1967. Public Goods in Theory and Practice: A Note On the Minasian-Samuelson Discussion. *Journal of Law and Economics* 10:193–97.

Buchanan, J. M., and C. Goetz. 1972. Efficiency Limits of Fiscal Mobility: An Assessment of the Tiebout Model. *Journal of Public Economics* 1:25–43.

Buchanan, J. M., and G. Tullock. 1962. *The Calculus of Consent.* Ann Arbor: University of Michigan Press.

Buckley, F. H. 1999. *The Fall and Rise of Freedom of Contract.* Durham, N.C.: Duke University Press.

Caplan, B. 2001. Standing Tiebout on His Head: Tax Capitalization and the Monopoly Power of Local Governments. *Public Choice* 108 (1/2): 101–22.

Cheung, S. N. S. 1980. The Fable of the Bees: An Economic Investigation. In *The Theory of Market Failure,* ed. Tyler Cowen. Fairfax, Va.: George Mason University Press. First published in *Journal of Law and Economics* 16 (1973): 11–13.

Coase, R. H. 1988a. *The Firm, the Market, and the Law.* Chicago: University of Chicago Press.

———. 1988b. The Lighthouse in Economics. In *The Firm, the Market, and The Law.* Chicago: University of Chicago Press. First published in *Journal of Law and Economics* 17 (1974): 357–76.

———. 1988c. The Marginal Cost Controversy. In *The Firm, the Market, and The Law.* Chicago: University of Chicago Press. First published in *Economica* 13 (1946):169–82.

Coleman, J. and T. Hoffer. 1987. *Public and Private High Schools: The Impact of Communities.* New York: Basic Books.

Coulson, A. J. 1999. *Market Education.* New Brunswick, N.J.: Transaction.

Cowen, T. 1988. *The Theory of Market Failure: A Critical Examination.* Fairfax, Va.: George Mason University Press.

De Alessi, M. 2000. Fishing for Solutions: The State of the World's Fisheries. In *Earth Report 2000,* ed. R. Bailey. New York: McGraw-Hill.

Epple, D., and A. Zelenitz. 1981. The Implications of Competition among Jurisdictions: Does Tiebout Need Politics? *Journal of Political Economy* 89:1197–1217.

Evans, W. N., and R. M. Schwab. 1995. Finishing High School and Starting College: Do Catholic Schools Make a Difference? *Quarterly Journal of Economics* 110(4):941–74.

Gilmore, G. 1974. *The Death of Contract.* Columbus: Ohio State University Press.

Glaeser, E. L., and A. Shleifer. 1998. Not-For-Profit Entrepreneurs. N.p..

Hayek, F. A. 1973. *Law, Legislation and Liberty: Rules and Order.* Vol. 1. Chicago: University of Chicago Press.

———. 1988. *The Fatal Conceit: The Errors of Socialism.* Chicago: University of Chicago Press.

Hazlett, T. W. 1998. Assigning Property Rights to Spectrum Users: Why Did the FCC License Auctions Take 67 Years? *Journal of Law and Economics* 41 (2): 529–76.

———. 2000. Wiring Washington. *Reason* (February). Available at <www.reason .com/0002/co.th.selected.html>.

Hazlett, T. W., and M. Spitzer. 1997. *Public Policy Towards Cable Television: The Economics of Rate Controls.* Washington, D.C.: AEI Press.

High, J., and J. Ellig. 1988. The Private Supply of Education: Some Historical Evidence. In *The Theory of Market Failure: A Critical Examination,* ed. T. Cowan, 361–82. Fairfax, Va.: George Mason University Press.

Jacobs, J. 1969. *The Economy of Cities.* New York: Vintage.

Kaestle, C. F. 1973. *The Evolution of an Urban School System: New York City 1750–1850.* Cambridge: Harvard University Press.

Klein, D. B., A. T. Moore, and B. Reja. 1997. Curb Rights: Eliciting Competition and Entrepreneurship in Urban Transit. *Independent Review* 2 (1): 29–54.

Lott, J. R. 1987. Why Is Education Publicly Provided? A Critical Survey. *Cato Journal* 7 (2): 475–501.

————. 1999. Public Schooling, Indoctrination, and Totalitarianism. *Journal of Political Economy* 107 (6): S127–57.

Meade, J. E. 1952. External Economies and Diseconomies in a Competitive Situation. *Economic Journal* 52:54–67.

Minasian, J. R. 1964. Television Pricing and the Theory of Public Goods. *Journal of Law and Economics* 7:71–80.

Mises, L. von. 1990. *Economic Calculation in the Socialist Commonwealth.* Auburn, Ala.: Ludwig von Mises Institute.

Mitchell, W. C., and R. T. Simmons. 1994. *Beyond Politics: Markets, Welfare, and the Failure of Bureaucracy.* Boulder, Colo.: Westview Press.

Moe, T. M. 1999. The Public Revolution Private Money Might Bring. *Washington Post,* May 9, sec. B, p. 3.

Murray, C. 1984. *Losing Ground.* New York: Basic Books.

Newman, O. 1980. *Community of Interest.* Garden City, N.Y.: Anchor Press.

Olson, M. 1965. *The Logic of Collective Action.* Cambridge: Harvard University Press.

————. 1982. *The Rise and Decline of Nations.* New Haven: Yale University Press.

Ostrom, E., J. Walker, and R. Gardner. 1992. Covenants Without a Sword: Self Governance Is Possible. *American Political Science Review* 86:404–17.

Otteson, J. R. 2000. Freedom of Religion and Public Schooling. *Independent Review* 4 (4):601–13.

Ravitch, D. 1974. *The Great School Wars: New York City 1805–1873.* New York: Basic Books.

Rawls, J. 1971. *A Theory of Justice.* Cambridge: Harvard University Press.

Richman, S. 1994. *Separating School and State.* Fairfax, Va.: Future of Freedom Foundation.

Ridley, M. 1996. *The Origins of Virtue: Human Instincts and the Evolution of Cooperation.* New York: Penguin Books.

Rothbard, M. N. 1999. *Education: Free and Compulsory.* Auburn, Ala.: Ludwig von Mises Institute.

Samuelson, P. A. 1958. Aspects of Public Expenditure Theories. *Review of Economics and Statistics* 40:332–38.

————. 1964. Public Goods and Subscription TV: Correction of the Record. *Journal of Law and Economics* 7:81–83.

Shleifer, A., and R. W. Vishny. 1998. *The Grabbing Hand: Government Pathologies and Their Cures.* Cambridge: Harvard University Press.

Siegan, B. H. 1972. *Land Use Without Zoning.* Lexington, Mass.: Lexington Books.

Skaggs, N. T., and J. L. Carlson. 1996. *Microeconomics: Individual Choice and Its Consequences.* 2d ed. Cambridge: Blackwell Publishers.

Stigler, G. J., ed. 1988. *Chicago Studies in Political Economy.* Chicago: University of Chicago Press.

Stiglitz, J. E. 1977. The Theory of Local Public Goods. In *The Economics of Public Services,* ed. M. S. Feldstein and R. P. Inman. New York: Halsted Press.

Sugg, I., and U. P. Kreuter. 1994. *Elephants and Ivory: Lessons from the Trade Ban.* London: Insitute of Economic Affairs.

Tabarrok, A. 1998. The Private Provision of Public Goods Via Dominant Assurance Contracts. *Public Choice* 96:345–62.

———. Forthcoming. *Entrepreneurial Economics: Bright Ideas from the Dismal Science.* Oxford: Oxford University Press.

Tiebout, C. M. 1956. A Pure Theory of Local Expenditure. *Journal of Political Economy* 64(5):416–24.

West, E. G. 1975. *Education and the Industrial Revolution.* New York: Barnes and Noble.

———. 1994. *Education and the State.* 3d ed. Indianapolis: Liberty Press.

Contributors

The Editors

David T. Beito is Associate Professor at the University of Alabama. He received his Ph.D. in history at the University of Wisconsin in 1986. Professor Beito is the author of *Taxpayers in Revolt: Tax Resistance during the Great Depression* and *From Mutual Aid to the Welfare State: Fraternal Societies and Social Services, 1890–1967.* An urban and social historian, he has published in the *Journal of Interdisciplinary History,* the *Journal of Policy History,* the *Journal of Southern History,* and the *Journal of Urban History,* among other scholarly journals. He is currently writing a biography of Dr. T. R. M. Howard, a black civil rights pioneer, entrepreneur, and mutual-aid leader.

Peter Gordon is Professor in the School of Policy, Planning, and Development and in the Department of Economics at the University of Southern California. He received his Ph.D. from the University of Pennsylvania in 1971. Professor Gordon has published in most of the major urban-planning, urban-transportation, and urban-economics journals. He has consulted for local, state, and federal agencies; the World Bank; the United Nations; and many private groups. Professor Gordon is coeditor of the journal *Planning and Markets,* an all-electronic refereed journal (<www-pam.usc.edu/>).

Alexander Tabarrok is Vice President and Research Director for the Independent Institute. He received his Ph.D. in economics from George Mason University, and he has taught at the University of Virginia and Ball State University. Papers by Dr. Tabarrok have appeared in the *Journal of Law and Economics, Public Choice, Economic Inquiry,* the *Journal of Health Economics,* the *Journal of Theoretical Politics,* and many other journals. He is the editor of *Entrepreneurial Economics: Bright Ideas from the Dismal Science.*

Additional Contributors

Robert C. Arne is a Ph.D. candidate in history at the University of Chicago. He holds a master's degree from the University of Chicago and is preparing a thesis that probes the influence of Herbert Spencer upon modern professional society.

Bruce L. Benson is DeVoe Moore Distinguished Research Professor of Economics at Florida State University. He received his Ph.D. from Texas A&M University, and he has taught at Pennsylvania State University and Montana State University. Professor Benson has been an Earhart, F. Leroy Hill, and Salvatori Fellow. His research interests focus on law and economics, with emphasis on private alternatives to publicly provided law and legal services, the evolution of legal institutions, and the economics of crime. He has published over one hundred articles in scholarly journals, contributed more than thirty book chapters, and authored four books: *The Enterprise of Law; The Economic Anatomy of a Drug War: Criminal Justice in the Commons* (with D. Rasmussen); *American Antitrust Law in Theory and in Practice* (with Melvin L. Greenhut); and the Independent Institute book *To Serve and Protect: Privatization and Community in Criminal Justice.*

Donald J. Boudreaux is Professor of Economics at George Mason University. He received his Ph.D. in economics from Auburn University and his J.D. from the University of Virginia. Professor Boudreaux has taught at Clemson University and George Mason University, and his many scholarly articles have appeared in the *Southern Economic Journal,* the *Arizona Law Review, History of Political Economy,* the *Supreme Court Economic Review,* and *Constitutional Political Economy,* among many others.

Stephen Davies is Senior Lecturer in the Department of History at Manchester Metropolitan University. He received his Ph.D. from the University of St. Andrews in 1984 and has published a number of papers on the history of crime and policing in Western Europe. He is currently at work on two books—a history of nineteenth-century feminism and a history and analysis of the private provision of public goods in Britain from 1750 to 1850.

Fred E. Foldvary received his Ph.D. in economics from George Mason University. He has taught economics at the Latvian University of Agriculture; Virginia Tech; John F. Kennedy University (Walnut Creek, California); California State University at Hayward; the University of California at Berkeley Extension; and Santa Clara University. Professor Foldvary is the author of *The Soul of Liberty; Public Goods and Private Communities,* and the *Dictionary of Free Market Economics.* His areas of research include public finance, governance, ethical philosophy, technology, and land economics. He is currently coediting a book, *Technology and the Case for Free Enterprise.*

David G. Green is the Director of CIVITAS: The Institute for the Study of Civil Society. His many books include *Power and Party in an English City; Mutual Aid or Welfare State* (with L. Cromwell); *Working-Class Patients and the Medical Establishment; The New Right: The Counter Revolution in Political, Economic and Social Thought; Reinventing Civil Society;* and *Delay, Denial and Dilution: The Impact of NHS Rationing on Heart Disease and Cancer* (with L. Casper); among others.

Randall G. Holcombe is DeVoe Moore Professor of Economics at Florida State University. He received his Ph.D. in economics from Virginia Polytechnic Institute and taught at Texas A&M University and at Auburn University prior to coming to Florida State in 1988. Dr. Holcombe is also Chairman of the Research Advisory

Council of the James Madison Institute for Public Policy Studies, a Tallahassee-based think tank that specializes in issues facing state governments. He is the author of eight books, including *Public Finance and the Political Process; An Economic Analysis of Democracy,* and *The Economic Foundations of Government,* and more than one hundred articles and reviews published in academic and professional journals. His primary areas of research are public finance and the economic analysis of public-policy issues.

Paul Johnson is the author of more than 30 books, including the classic history of the twentieth century, *Modern Times, A History of the American People, The Birth of the Modern, A History of Christianity,* and *The Civilization of Ancient Egypt.* His most recent book is *The Renaissance: A Short History.*

Daniel Klein is Associate Professor of Economics at Santa Clara University. He received his Ph.D. from New York University in 1990. Professor Klein has published many scholarly papers in the *Journal of Economic History,* the *Journal of Transport Economics and Policy, Economics and Politics,* the *Law and Society Review,* and *Economic Inquiry,* among others. Professor Klein is the coauthor of *Curb Rights: A Foundation for Free Enterprise in Urban Transit* and the editor of *Reputation: Studies in the Voluntary Elicitation of Good Conduct* and *What Do Economists Contribute?*

Spencer Heath MacCallum is a social anthropologist who has published numerous papers on social anthropology and classical liberalism. He is the author of *The Art of Community* and the director of the Heather Foundation, which administers, among others, the intellectual estates of Spencer Heath and E. C. Riegel.

Robert H. Nelson is Professor of Environmental Policy at the School of Public Affairs, University of Maryland. He is an authority on land and natural resource management, with a particular emphasis on management of federally owned resources. His professional writings have appeared in many journals and books, including the *Journal of Economic Literature,* the *Journal of Political Economy,* the *Annual Review of Ecology and Systematics,* the *Journal of Policy Analysis and Management,* the *Natural Resources Journal,* and the *University of Colorado Law Review.* Professor Nelson is the author of four books: *Zoning and Property Rights; The Making of Federal Coal Policy; Reaching for Heaven on Earth: The Theological Meaning of Economics;* and *Public Lands and Private Rights: The Failure of Scientific Management.* Professor Nelson worked in the Office of Policy Analysis—the principal policy office serving the U.S. Secretary of the Interior—from 1975 to 1993. He has served as the senior economist of the congressionally chartered Commission on Fair Market Value Policy for Federal Coal Leasing (Linowes Commission) and as the senior research manager of the President's Commission on Privatization. He has been a visiting scholar at the Brookings Institution, visiting senior fellow at the Woods Hole Oceanographic Institution, and visiting scholar at the Political Economy Research Center.

James Tooley is Professor of Education Policy at the University of Newcastle, England, where he directs the Centre for Market Solutions in Education (<www.katallaxia.org>). He also directs the education program at the Institute of Economic Affairs in London. Professor Tooley has held research positions at the Universities of Oxford and Manchester and the National Foundation for Educational Research, as well as short-term teaching positions at Simon Fraser University (Canada) and University of the Western Cape (South Africa). He is the author of several books and monographs including *Reclaiming Education, The Global Education Industry; Education Without the State,* and *Disestablishing the School.* Much of his recent work on private education and privatization of education in developing countries has been on behalf of the International Finance Corporation, a division of the World Bank.

Index

439

Coase, Ronald, 322, 406, 418
Cobbett, William, 229
Coke, Lord Edward, 132
collective action: associations and federal-
    ism, 97n. 33; cities versus small towns,
    157; versus zoning, 323. *See also* group
    action and selective incentives
collective goods, 285; land value and, 407;
    market failure and incentive to contribute
    to the provision of, 282. *See also* goods;
    public goods
collective ownership, 307, 312; facilitation
    of neighborhood associations in existing
    neighborhoods and, 356; versus individ-
    ual ownership, 308; joint ownership
    between private and public entities and,
    323. *See also* corporations; homeowners'
    associations (HOAs); ownership; private
    ownership
colleges, x
Colombia, 246
Colquhoun, Patrick, 172
Columbia planned community, 299
commerce: early turnpikes, 82; shopping
    centers, 264, 267, 271, 334, 380; shopping
    malls, 103, 380, 390, 391, 396. *See also*
    business; trade
commercial arbitration: accelerating use of,
    139; decline of New York Chamber of
    Commerce services, 137–38; lawyers and,
    139, 140; private courts, 142–44; U.S.
    Civil War blockade and, 133–34. *See also*
    arbitration
commercial law, 146n. 6; codification of
    merchant court custom, 131; medieval
    Europe, 266; medieval Europe, develop-
    ment of, 128; New York Chamber of
    Commerce and, 135–36. *See also* law
common interest developments (CIDs), 256,
    396; civil society and, 8; construction
    defects and, 398n. 15; contracting and,
    387; exemption from constitutional
    review, 377; gated communities, 7, 342;
    growth-control laws and, 6–7; investment
    and site value, 392; lawsuits and, 390–91;
    market distortion and consumer demand
    for, 378; pioneers of, 394; versus privati-
    zation of government, 395; proprietary
    communities and, 375, 377, 379; statis-
    tics, 5, 371; voting and, 385–86. *See also*
    homeowners' associations (HOAs)

common law: arbitration versus litigation,
    140–41; covenants and, 408; English
    leases, 386
common-law courts: in Great Britain, 147n.
    37; reversal of hostility toward arbitra-
    tion in the U.S., 136
common-law system: arbitration clauses,
    134; international trade and, 132;
    Vynior's Case and, 132
communications: Chicago CMD, 108;
    crime investigation and newspapers,
    158–59, 163, 418; television, 410, 425
communities: Anglo-Saxon system in
    England, 261; consensual, 285; as
    corporations in medieval Europe, 260;
    hotels as, 262, 265–66, 332; housing
    quality in Great Britain and, 15; inten-
    tional, 283; leadership and, 381, 382;
    Letchworth (England), 275, 378, 381,
    397n. 12; political versus private, 257;
    provision of civic goods and, 284; volun-
    tary, 117; Welwyn (England), 275, 378,
    381, 397n. 12. *See also* entrepreneurial
    communities; private communities;
    towns
communities (U.S.), 389; aggressive
    enforcement of CC&Rs, 387; benefit-cost
    analysis and zoning, 347; California
    growth controls and housing prices, 346;
    Columbia (MD), 298–99; constitutions as
    contracts and, 333; democratic gover-
    nance and, 271; entrepreneurial opportu-
    nity and, 385; gated, 7, 342; hotel model
    and, 256–57, 411, 415; and management
    of, 381; Park West (VA), 295–97; private
    places as, 60–61; proprietary administra-
    tion of, 271, 273; religious congregations
    and, 85; Reston (VA), 297–99; Sawgrass
    Players Club (FL), 299–302; St. Louis
    neighborhoods, 344; town meetings and
    turnpike stock pledges, 88; voting and,
    386. *See also* contractual communities;
    industrial communities; neighborhood
    associations; neighborhoods; proprietary
    communities; residential communities
community, 8; association and, 337, 354;
    cities as territorial associations and,
    338; definition of, 266; turnpike
    company investment and, 92. *See also*
    society
Community Associations Institute (CAI),

corruption: British judicial system, 155; social institutions and, 151; St. Louis, 54–55

Council of Better Business Bureaus, 141

courts, the (England): common-law system versus international trade, 133; competing systems, 131–32; enforcement of covenants and, 31; merchant versus royal, 130–31; Statute of the Staple and, 131

courts, the (medieval Europe), 422; appeal and, 130, 131, 423; emergence of, 128; merchant compliance and, 129–30, 148n. 82; Statute of the Staple and, 131. *See also* merchant courts

courts, the (U.S.): California Supreme Court, 346; colonial arbitration, 135–36; common interest developments and, 394–95; homeowners associations and, 377; hostility to arbitration, 136; Los Angeles County Superior Court, 142; Missouri Supreme Court, 50, 67n. 11, 71nn. 58, 59; New York Supreme Court, 395; private, 142–44; state, 138, 139; St. Louis covenants and, 63; St. Louis pollution and, 58; St. Louis taxes and, 65; Supreme Court and voting, 333, 339; Supreme Court and zoning, 316, 320, 331, 348; zoning and, 347. *See also* public courts

covenants (Great Britain), 36; building clause, 28–29; collective-action problems, 34; development of, 33; enforcement of, 30–31, 35; kinds of, 29–30; as market institutions, 34, 35; public goods and, 34–35; replaced by national planning, 37; variation on policy, 32; versus zoning, 408. *See also* contracts

covenants (U.S.), 60; factors motivating the use of in housing developments, 331–32; Hammett Place indenture (St. Louis), 52; indentures versus free riders, 58–59; industrial parks and, 267–68; land developers and public goods, 291–92; leaseholds, 270; neighborhood associations, 310–11; Park West (VA), 295; Portland Place indenture (St. Louis), 52; Reston (VA), 297, 298; Sawgrass Players Club (FL), 300, 301, 302; subdivisions and weakness of, 373; Vandeventer Place indenture (St. Louis), 49–50, 51; zoning and, 62–63. *See also*

contracts

craft guilds, 185; Freemasonry, 186–87, 198nn. 14, 21

crime, 429n. 21; income and substitution effect, 419, 429n. 15; social institutions and, 151; target hardening versus theft, 419

crime (Great Britain): absence of court trials and, 154; versus the death penalty, 154; displacement from one neighborhood to another and, 170, 419; versus preventative policing, 173; versus rewards for information, 158, 162, 163–64, 176n. 38, 418, 419, 420; Tory versus Whig view of, 172–73; urbanization and, 155, 157, 158, 418. *See also* law enforcement (Great Britain); police (Great Britain); prosecution associations

crime (U.S.), 112; versus inner-city residents, 343; versus private places, 66; Tocqueville on America, 86

crime investigation, 152

crime investigation (Great Britain): absence of, eighteenth century, 153; advertising and, 158–60, 163, 168, 169; transfer of control from civil society to the state, 168

criminal justice, 124; private courts and, 144

criminal law, 174; Colquhoun and, 171; moral degeneracy and, 171–72. *See also* law

criminal prosecution (Great Britain): and high cost of, 153, 162; likelihood of conviction versus severity of judgment, 156. *See also* prosecution associations

culture, American bias against tenancy, 393–94. *See also* society

Davies, Stephen, 5, 124, 151–81, 406, 407, 408, 418, 423; on urban growth in Great Britain, 15

Davis, Joseph, 80, 86

debt, residential associations, 278

democracy, 354–55; voting and, 383

Democracy in America (Tocqueville), 85, 92

deregulation, 6. *See also* privatization

Devil's Dictionary (Bierce), 424

Dimsdale, Thomas, 165–66, 176n. 33

dispute resolution: environmental, private mediation, 143; neighborhoods, private mediation, 144–45; for profit, 141–42. *See also* arbitration; litigation

tied sales and, 57; trustees and, 49–50, 63, 64, 68n. 15; versus urban decay, 66; urban growth and, 15. *See also* St. Louis
private property. *See* property
private schools (England): biases of government inspectors, 231; versus public schools, 227; versus taxation, 226
private schools (India): commercial business principles and, 240; and government recognition of, 236, 241–42; versus government schools, 242; versus government schools, teacher accountability, 244–45, 247; pupils and fees, 237 table; student performance versus government schools, 246; teacher-pupil ratios, 238 table, 245; teachers and, 237 table, 238 table, 239, 240, 242; teachers and salaries, 238 table. *See also* statistics, schools
private schools (U.S.): attendance and, 235; Catholic, 420–21; curricula and, 233–34; versus public schools, 420–21, 429n. 16
private streets, 275; Chicago CMD, 106; decline of, 16; St. Louis, 47–48
privatization, xii; federal welfare and, 4; of inner cities, 342–45; of local government, 340, 395; neighborhood associations, 311; St. Louis neighborhoods, 344; suburbs and, 341
PROBE (Public Report on Basic Education in India), 243–46, 247, 249n. 12
production, 308. *See also* manufacturing
profit: city government and, 115–16; CMD and, 110, 407; corporate landlords in Great Britain and, 24; dispute resolution, 141–42; early turnpikes, absence of toll rate increases, 78; economic versus political entrepreneurship, 114–15; elephants and, 410; externalities and, 406; local governance and, 361n. 171; New England turnpikes, 79–80, 81, 94nn. 9, 13, 95n. 20; predeveloping of land and, 407; toll bridges versus turnpikes, 80; versus traditional government, 293. *See also* investment
Progress and Poverty (George), 259
Progressives, 316, 354, 355, 363n. 237
property: collective ownership of, 356; definition, 264; economic forces transforming ownership, 308; exemption of CIDs from government review and, 377; freedom of contract versus politics, 395; Parliament and, 423; predictability versus

voting and, 385–86; private goods and, 413; prosecution association protection of, 164; as socially divisive, 342. *See also* land; multiple-tenant income property (MTIP); ownership
property owners: constitutional rules and subdividing, 292; contractual government and voting, 303; neighborhood possession of property rights to neighborhood entry and, 324; residential associations, debt and voting, 278; restrictive covenants and subdivisions, 373; Sawgrass Players Club, assessments and residential development units, 301. *See also* landlords; landowners
property rights: Coasian principles and, 322–24; coercive redistribution of, via zoning, 319–20, 325; elephants and, 410; evolution of, 320–22, 357n. 5; versus growth control measures, 6; high-quality neighborhood environments and, 326; laissez-faire urbanization and, 407; markets and, 408; municipal sale of zoning and, 325, 327; social capital and, 7; urbanization and, 19–20
property taxes: neighborhood association secession from municipalities and, 351; RCAs and, 277
property value: decline of Vandeventer Place (St. Louis), 50; municipalities and voting, 339; Reston (VA), 297, 298. *See also* land value
proprietary cities, 407
proprietary communities, 396n. 3; CIDs and, 375, 377, 379; contracts and leases, 281; decay through monopoly or neglect, 263; design and, 272; the inner city and, 256; internalization of externalities, 410–11; online, 411; public goods and, 285; public services and, 262; as real-estate complexes, 269; society reform and, 275; voting and, 416; Walt Disney World, 264. *See also* residential improvement districts (RIDs); shopping centers
proprietary government, 261
prosecution associations, 5, 124, 429n. 13; Barnet association, 165–66, 176n. 33; disappearance of, 168; essential aims of, 160–61; focus of, 429n. 21; free-riders and, 163, 166, 176n. 46, 177n. 56; membership and subscriptions, 161–62; motives for joining, 166, 167; negative

INDEPENDENT STUDIES IN POLITICAL ECONOMY

For further information and a catalog of publications, please contact:
THE INDEPENDENT INSTITUTE
100 Swan Way, Oakland, California 94621-1428, U.S.A.
Telephone: 510-632-1366 • Facsimile: 510-568-6040
E-mail: info@independent.org • Website: http://www.independent.org